T0302356

International Innovation Networks and Knowledge Migration

Migration is conceived differently in Europe compared with countries like the US, Canada or Australia. *International Innovation Networks and Knowledge Migration* confronts traditional views on migration with modern theories of brain circulation and innovation networks, showing that migration leads to mutual benefits for both the home and host countries.

This new volume brings together several case studies and empirical in-depth analyses, constructed from the strong migration relationship between Turkey and Germany that has existed for more than 50 years. Bringing together over 20 international contributors, this book highlights that knowledge migration and cultural diversity can strongly stimulate entrepreneurial activities, competence acquisition and economic development of countries and regions. The authors highlight the considerable scope for improvement of European migration policies in order to be better prepared to successfully process structural changes stemming from an aging society in Europe, and an increasing international division of labour.

This volume is suitable for those who study industrial economics, international economics and European economics. It is also of interest to those who want to delve deeper into the Turkish–German migration nexus.

Andreas Pyka is Full Professor at the Chair for Innovation Economics, University of Hohenheim, Germany.

Yeşim Kuştepeli is Full Professor at the Department of Economics Faculty of Business, Chair of Economic Policy, Dokuz Eylül University, Turkey.

Dominik Hartmann is Marie Curie Postdoctoral Fellow at the Chair for Innovation Economics, University of Hohenheim, Germany.

Routledge/Lisbon Civic Forum Studies in Innovation
Series editors:
Horst Hanusch, *University of Augsburg, Germany*
Tibor Palánkai, *Corvinus University of Budapest, Hungary*
Ryszard Wilczynski, *Warsaw University of Finance and Management, Poland*
Andreas Pyka, *University of Hohenheim, Germany*
Carmen Ruiz Viñals, *Universitat Abat Oliba, Spain*

International Innovation Networks and Knowledge Migration

The German–Turkish nexus

Edited by Andreas Pyka, Yeşim Kuştepeli and Dominik Hartmann

Routledge
Taylor & Francis Group

LONDON AND NEW YORK

First published 2017
by Routledge
2 Park Square, Milton Park, Abingdon, Oxon OX14 4RN

and by Routledge
711 Third Avenue, New York, NY 10017

Routledge is an imprint of the Taylor & Francis Group, an informa business

© 2017 selection and editorial matter, Andreas Pyka, Yeşim Kuştepeli and
Dominik Hartmann; individual chapters, the contributors

The right of the editors to be identified as the authors of the editorial material,
and of the authors for their individual chapters, has been asserted in accordance
with sections 77 and 78 of the Copyright, Designs and Patents Act 1988.

All rights reserved. No part of this book may be reprinted or reproduced or
utilized in any form or by any electronic, mechanical, or other means, now
known or hereafter invented, including photocopying and recording, or in any
information storage or retrieval system, without permission in writing from the
publishers.

Trademark notice: Product or corporate names may be trademarks or registered
trademarks, and are used only for identification and explanation without intent
to infringe.

British Library Cataloguing in Publication Data
A catalogue record for this book is available from the British Library

Library of Congress Cataloging in Publication Data
Names: Pyka, Andreas, editor. | Kuştepeli, Yeşim, editor. | Hartmann,
Dominik, 1980- editor.
Title: International innovation networks and knowledge migration : the
German-Turkish nexus / edited by Andreas Pyka, Yeşim Kuştepeli and
Dominik Hartmann.
Description: Abingdon, Oxon ; New York, NY : Routledge, 2016.
Identifiers: LCCN 2016004980| ISBN 9781138914018 (hardback) | ISBN
9781315691077 (ebook)
Subjects: LCSH: Knowledge economy—Turkey. | Knowledge economy—Germany. |
Technology transfer—Turkey. | Technology transfer—Germany. | Diffusion
of innovations—Turkey. | Diffusion of innovations—Germany. |
Turkey—Emigration and immigration--Economic aspects. |
Germany—Emigration and immigration--Economic aspects.
Classification: LCC HC495.I55 I57 2016 | DDC 338.943/06—dc23
LC record available at https://lccn.loc.gov/2016004980

ISBN: 978-1-138-91401-8 (hbk)
ISBN: 978-1-315-69107-7 (ebk)

Typeset in Times New Roman
by Fish Books Ltd.

Contents

Figures

Tables

Contributors

Sedef Akgüngör received her bachelor degree in Agricultural Economics from Ege University (1984), her master's degree in Economics from Michigan State University (1991) and her PhD in Agricultural Economics from Michigan State University (1992). She has conducted research in agricultural economics, regional development, and clusters and published many papers nationally and internationally. Akgüngör has worked as a coordinator and researcher in Eurocores and ECRP programmes by European Science Foundation and bilateral international projects funded by TUBİTAK. She has also conducted the Turkish coordination of a European Union FP7 project. She is a member of İzmir Development Agency Clustering Committee. After working in Ege University and Işık University, since 2005 she has continued her academic studies in Dokuz Eylül University.

Ceyhan Aldemir received his bachelor degree from American University of Beirut, his master's and PhD degrees from Ege University Faculty of Business. He has taught both graduate and undergraduate courses in several universities, including Ege University (1973–1982, full time), Dokuz Eylul University (1982 to date), Koç University (adjunct), Celal Bayar University (adjunct), Adnan Menderes University (adjunct), Muğla University (adjunct), Rochester Institute of Technology, St John Fishers College, Rochester, NY, USA (visiting professor), Cornell University (visiting scholar), Troy State University, European Campus, (visiting professor), University of Maryland, European Campus (visiting professor), Saxion University, Deventer, Holland, (visiting professor), Artevelde Hogeschool, Ghent, Belgium, (visiting professor). He has conducted research in cross-cultural management, organizational behaviour, organization and management. In addition to national projects, Aldemir has also worked as researcher and coordinator in Eurocores and ECRP programmes by European Science Foundation. He has published papers in many national and international journals such as *Journal of Higher Education, International Journal of Manpower* and *International Journal of Emerging and Transition Economies*. He co-edited the book *İnsan Kaynakları Yönetimi* with Gönül Budak and Alpay Ataol in 2004.

Mehmet Aldonat Beyzatlar is an Assistant Professor in the Department of Economics in Faculty of Business at the Dokuz Eylül University of Izmir where he has been a faculty member since 2009. He completed his PhD and MSc in Economics at Dokuz Eylül University and his undergraduate studies in Industrial Engineering at Çankaya University. His research focuses on transportation economics and social network analysis, ranging from theory to empirics. He has collaborated with valuable researchers in several other disciplines of economics in projects such as "Inventing Europe: Technology and the Making of Europe, 1850 to the Present" and "Knowledge Transfer in Turkish–German Innovation Networks in the Context of European Integration Project".

Canan Balkır is Professor of Economics and Jean Monnet professor in European Economic Integration and has been the coordinator of Jean Monnet Centre of Excellence at Dokuz Eylul University. She received a research grant from the EC Commission in 1982, was a Fulbright scholar in USA, research fellow at the Institute of Development Studies, UK; British Council Scholar at the University of Exeter, UK. She received first prize from the Turkish Academy of Sciences in 2011 for her book on *International Economic Integration: Theory, Policy and Practice – EU and Others*. She is currently working on an edited book titled *The EU's Expanding Trade Policy: Challenges for the Customs Union with Turkey* with Ghent University. Her recent publications include co-editing *Europeanisation of Public Policy in Southern Europe* with T. Bolukbasi and E. Ertugal (Routledge, 2014, "Europeanization of Trade Policy: an Asymmetric Track" in *Europeanization of Turkish Public Policies* (2016), "Different Trajectories yet the Same Substance: Croatia and Turkey" (The Substance of Democracy Promotion, ed. M. Aknur, 2015) and "A Comparison of Residence, Social Security and Citizenship Strategies of Turkish Return Migrants and Dutch Retirement Migrants in Turkey" in *Waves of Diversity* (2015).

Tobias Buchmann is an expert in innovation network analysis. In his empirical work he has produced important new insights by applying novel methodological approaches such as stochastic actor based model for network analysis. His fields of interest cover innovation networks, complexity and firm strategies with an empirical focus. Tobias Buchmann is currently a PostDoc at the University of Hohenheim. He completed his doctoral thesis on "The Evolution of Innovation Networks" in 2014. He graduated with a master in European Studies in 2008 from the University of Bonn and a master in Economics (2007) from the University of Hohenheim. He further received a PhD from the University of Hohenheim (2014).

Çağrı Bulut is an associate professor of management and director of graduate school at Yasar University, Turkey. He has a degree in economics from Istanbul University, an MSc in strategy, and a PhD in business administration from GIT, Turkey. Prior joining to Yasar University, he served as postdoctoral economist to FAO of The United Nations, CountrySTAT Project. He has a wide range of publications on strategy and management of innovation and corporate entrepreneurship. He has given lectures in several European countries as visiting professor such as Italy, Germany, Portugal, Latvia and Slovenia. He has taken role in many projects, some funded from The Scientific and Technological Research Council of Turkey (TUBITAK) and ISI-FRAUNHOFER. He is serving as member of Entrepreneurship Education Commission at TUBITAK, board member of five faculties at Yasar University, and many other organizations supporting Entrepreneurship. He is a member of the review and editorial boards at prominent business journals. Moreover, Dr Bulut is the Ambassador of Academy of Management, Entrepreneurship Division to Turkey. He is coordinator of an Erasmus project and partner in several entrepreneurship and innovation studies.

Gönenç Dalgıç is a doctoral student of business administration and a lecturer in business engineering at Yasar University, Izmir, Turkey. She received a BS degree in international relations and an MS degree in management and organization from Dokuz Eylül University, Izmir, Turkey. She spent one semester as a guest researcher in the Business Start-Ups and Entrepreneurship Institute at University of Hohenheim, Stuttgart, Germany. Moreover, she is a member of two different project teams that conducts empirical research on innovation and corporate sustainability. Her research interests in business studies are in the areas of corporate sustainability, entrepreneurship and innovation.

Çağaçan Değer has received his PhD in economics from Middle East Technical University. His research focuses on applied general equilibrium modeling. He has published research and participated in projects on economic dimensions of social security, aging population and regional analysis through input-output models. He is currently an assistant professor at the Department of Economics, Ege University.

Özge Filiz Yağcıbaşı graduated from Dokuz Eylül University Department of Economics in 2009. She holds a master's degree in economics from Bilkent University, completed in 2012. Currently, she is pursuing her PhD in economics at Ege University where she is also a research assistant. Her past and current research has focused on dynamic stochastic general equilibrium models, monetary policy and economic growth.

Alexander Gerybadze studied economics and mathematics in Heidelberg and Business Administration in Stanford. After completing his doctorate in the field of evolutionary models of technical change, he worked at the VDI Technology Center (1981–1983) and was involved in implementing microelectronics support programmes. He was a partner of Arthur D. Little International and worked in the field of strategic management and technology and innovation management in different European countries as well as in North America (1983–1991). In 1991, he joined the faculty of St Gallen Business School and built up a new master curriculum and a research programme on management of technology. Since 1996 Alexander Gerybadze holds a chair of international management at the Department of Business Administration at Hohenheim University. His current research focuses on R&D strategies and international location decisions in multinational corporations, and how this affects the relationship between the national innovation strategy and investment strategies of transnational firms.

Mehmet Güçlü has received his PhD in economics from Ege University. He has received the title of associate professor in 2013. His research focuses on monetary economics, financial economics and macroeconomics. He has also participated in İzmir Regional Development Agency's "Culture Inventory and Culture Economy of İzmir" project. He is currently an associate professor at the Department of Economics, Ege University.

Yaprak Gülcan received her bachelor degree in economics from Kansas University (1992), her master's degree in economics from Dokuz Eylül University (1996) and her PhD in economics from Dokuz Eylül University (1999). She has conducted research in macroeconomics, international economics, and regional development, and published many papers nationally and internationally. Gülcan has worked as coordinator and researcher in Eurocores and ECRP programmes by European Science Foundation and bilateral international projects funded by TUBİTAK. Between 1998 and 1999, she has conducted research in Glasgow University in the context of British Chevening Scholarship. She continues her academic research at the Dokuz Eylül University Faculty of Business Department of Economics since 1999.

Sule Gündüz has received her BSc degree in economics at Middle East Technical University, Ankara–Turkey with honours. After graduation she worked in the banking sector for 12 years. She has graduated from the master programme in economics at the University of Dokuz Eylul, Izmir Turkey. She has completed her PhD course work PhD in Economics and is writing her PhD thesis at Dokuz Eylul University. She has been working as a full-time lecturer at Dokuz Eylul University since January 2015. She has been awarded a scholarship from the Scientific and Technological Research Council of Turkey from 2011 until 2014. She has been a visiting scholar of Hohenheim University to make research on innovation networks between Turkey and Germany in the renewable energy sector. As for the future research agenda, she would like to focus more on natural resources, innovation and energy related issues.

Horst Hanusch is professor emeritus of the University of Augsburg where he held the chair for public finance and innovation economics. He is the secretary general of the International Joseph Alois Schumpeter Society. His research interests focus on economic development and growth and in particular innovation driven transformation processes as well as comprehensive Neo-Schumpeterian economics (CNSE). CNSE extends the innovation and future-orientation of the industrial sector on the financial and public sectors highlighting the co-evolutionary processes in economic development.

Dominik Hartmann is an EU Marie Curie Postdoctoral Fellow at the University of Hohenheim and the MIT Media Lab. He holds a bachelor in business administration from the University of Augsburg, a master in international economics from the University Complutense de Madrid, and a PhD in innovation economics from the University of Hohenheim (2012). Moreover, he was granted with a Mercator-IPC fellowship at the Istanbul Policy Center – Sabanci University in 2012/2013 and with a EU Marie Curie International Outgoing Fellowship at the Massachusetts Institute of Technology (MIT) in 2014/2015. His research combines methods from network science, data visualization and development economics to reveal the relationships between international innovation networks, economic complexity and the evolution of income inequality.

Barbara Heller-Schuh graduated in history, German language and literature studies at the Karl Franzens University in Graz, Austria, and in knowledge management at the Danube University in Krems, Austria. Since 2002 she has worked as a scientist at the Innovation Systems Department of AIT Austrian Institute of Technology. Her main research interests cover research and innovation policy, innovation networks as well as higher education research. She has been involved in several research and consulting projects dealing with the exploration of collaborative R&D projects to analyse network structure and dynamics at different policy levels. More recently, she carried out studies analysing the governance and funding systems of universities. Furthermore, she is responsible for the maintenance of the EUPRO database, a comprehensive database containing cleaned and standardized information about all accessible projects and their participants of the EU-Framework Programmes.

Andreas Kuckertz is professor of entrepreneurship at the University of Hohenheim, Germany. Moreover, he is a member of the board of FGF e.V., the leading academic association for research in entrepreneurship, innovation, and small and medium sized enterprises in the German-speaking countries. His research on various aspects of entrepreneurship, strategy, and innovation has been published in journals such as *Journal of Business Venturing*, *Journal of Business Research*, *International Journal of Technology Management*, *Entrepreneurship and Regional Development* and *Strategic Entrepreneurship Journal*.

Neşe Kumral has received her PhD from Dokuz Eylul University. She became an associate professor in 1998 and a full professor in 2004. Her research focuses on regional economics and regional planning. She has published national and international works on the regional economics and policymaking dimensions of tourism, competitiveness, resilience, smart specialization, creativity and culture. She continues to conduct research at the Department of Economics of Ege University.

Yeşim Kuştepeli received her bachelor degree in economics from Middle East Technical University (1992), her master's degree in economics from Clemson University (1994) and her PhD in economics from Clemson University (1999). She has conducted research in macroeconomics, public economics, regional development, and innovation and published papers nationally and internationally. Kuştepeli has worked as researcher in Eurocores and ECRP programmes by European Science Foundation, in a European Union FP7 project and a bilateral international project funded by TUBİTAK. She has also conducted the Turkish coordination of a bilateral international project funded by TUBİTAK in the IntenC programme. She continues her academic research at the Dokuz Eylül University Faculty of Business Department of Economics since 2000.

Annekatrin Niebuhr is senior researcher at the Institute for Employment Research and professor of empirical labour economics and spatial econometrics at the University of Kiel, Germany. She studied economics at the University of Kiel and the University of Wales in Swansea and received her doctorate from the University of Kiel in 1998. From 1999 to 2004 she worked as a senior economist in the department of European Integration at the Hamburg Institute of International Economics. Her current research interests include the following topics: the determinants and effects of labour migration and the economic consequences of cultural diversity.

Irene Peschkov (née Prostolupow) graduated in economics (MSc) at the University of Hohenheim in Stuttgart in 2013. During her master thesis, she spent some time at the Austrian Institute of Technology in Vienna doing research on innovation networks. In her thesis she analysed Turkish–German Innovation networks in the European research landscape. Since June 2013 she is working as a Senior-Consultant in the automotive sector at the Xpuls business solutions GmbH.

Andreas Pyka graduated in Economics and Management at the University of Augsburg in 1998 and spent afterwards two years as a PostDoc in Grenoble, France participating in a European research project on innovation networks. Following the Post Doc he worked as an assistant professor at the chair of Prof. Dr Horst Hanusch at the University of Augsburg. His fields of research are Neo-Schumpeterian economics and evolutionary economics with a special emphasis on numerical techniques of analysing dynamic processes of qualitative change and structural development. From October 2006 to March 2009 he worked at the University of Bremen as professor in economic theory. Since April 2009 Andreas Pyka holds the chair for innovation economics at the University of Hohenheim, Stuttgart.

Sheida Rashidi-Kollmann completed her bachelor's degree in engineering in her hometown, Tehran, before she moved to Germany in 2005. Later on after spending two working years in Hungary in the field of knowledge management, she started the master programme "International Business and Economics" at the university of Hohenheim in Stuttgart in 2009. She chose innovation economics as the major specialization elective. Being a part of "migrated community in Germany" raised her interest even more towards the subject of migration and innovation on which she wrote her master thesis at the innovation economics chair supervised by Andreas Pyka.

Sylvie van Cour works as a business development manager for a medium-sized automotive supplier in Munich, Germany. Furthermore, she is a lecturer at the University of Esslingen. She received her PhD at the University of Hohenheim at the Chair of International Management and Innovation. Her research analyses the relevance of highly skilled and mobile people for economic development and multinational companies.

Kevin van Hove is a PhD student at Dokuz Eylül University's Graduate School of Social Sciences, Department of European Studies, working with Prof. Balkır. He is currently doing research for his dissertation on Turkish entrepreneurship and social progress in Ghent, Belgium. He was awarded a scholarship from Turkey. Received his bachelor degree in Social Works from Hogeschool Ghent with distinction, during which he did four months of fieldwork in southern India. He has a master degree in international politics with distinction from Ghent University. His master thesis concentrated on the relevance of the targets from the 1996 Peace Agreements for the state formation policy in post-Guatemala.

Eberhard von Einem is a guest professor at the Center for Metropolitan Studies of the Technical University of Berlin. Until his retirement, Dr von Einem has been professor for urban and regional economics at the University of Applied Technology and Economics, Berlin. Trained both as a city and regional planner and an economist at the Technical University of Berlin, the University of Freiburg and the University of California at Berkeley, he received his doctoral degree from the Technical University of Berlin in 1979. He is a co-founder of the Institute for Urban Research and Industrial Policy, Berlin and served as consultant to federal and state ministries as well as to major cities, the EU and the private sector for more than 15 years. He has been granted guest fellowships by the Joint Centre for Urban Studies of the MIT and Harvard University and by the Science Centre Berlin and has been teaching both at the University of Mannheim and the University of Kassel. His current research interests include: urban and regional economic development, industrial change, industry-services links, cross boarder migration, generation and absorption of knowledge, creative cities, regional labour markets, housing, real estate management, urban regeneration, and historic preservation. He has published several books and about 80 papers both in referenced journals and working paper series. In 1999 he received the German Industrial Research Prize. He also is a member of the German Academy for City and Regional Planning and the Regional Studies Association.

Florian Wackermann has received his PhD at the University of Augsburg in the field of economics of innovation. His research interest has been in Neo-Schumpeterian economics as well as public sector management. Furthermore, he has completed master programmes at Université de Rennes in France and at Wayne State University in the USA. Besides his academic work, Dr Wackermann has gained ample experience in the private sector. He was export manager of H. & E. Reinert Westfälische Privat-Fleischerei as well as Directeur Général of its French subsidiary being in charge of running the company in France as well as coordinating and expanding the export activities of the mother company in Europe and Asia. Currently, he is member of the executive board of Heinrich Nabholz Autoreifen focusing on business development. Besides, he holds a worldwide leadership position serving as Co-Chair of the Rotaract and Interact Committee for Rotary International.

Acknowledgements

Many people and institutions helped in the creation of this book. We thank the BMBF and TÜBITAK for their financial support of the collaborative project "Turkish–German Innovation Networks in the context of the European Union"; the BMBF within the project 01DL12031 and TÜBITAK within the project 110K524 in the IntenC Programme. Moreover, Dominik Hartmann thanks the Mercator Foundation and the Istanbul Policy Center for the financial support during his IPC Mercator fellowship in Istanbul. Dominik Hartmann and Andreas Pyka acknowledge support from the Marie Curie International Outgoing Fellowship No. 328828 within the 7th European Community Framework Programme. Moreover, we are grateful for the research assistance of numerous Master and PhD students and their contributions to the TGIN workshops at the University of Hohenheim, the Dokuz Eylül University in Izmir and the Jean Monnet Centre of Excellence at the DEU Weekend Schools in Cesme and Muğla, Turkey. We also want to thank Routledge, Fish Books Ltd and Bianca Janic (University of Hohenheim) for her great help with formatting and copy-editing the final articles.

1 Introduction

*Andreas Pyka, Yeşim Kuştepeli, Canan Balkır
and Dominik Hartmann*

Introduction

Rapidly changing conditions in the world economy force firms, regions and countries to innovate and diversify in order to maintain their competitive advantages (Pyka and Hanusch 2006; Hartmann 2014). While local or company internal research and development (R&D) activities are important, no single firm can keep pace with the current speed of technological development in isolation. For this reason accessing external knowledge and actively engaging in international innovation networks becomes crucial (Pyka and Scharnhorst 2010). Recently, several large developing and emerging countries like Turkey, Malaysia, Brazil, India or China have been able to diversify their economies and initiate a technological catch-up process. In this process, international investment, migrant diasporas and innovation networks have played an important role. At the same time, the European Union has emphasized the need to become the most dynamic knowledge based economy in the world to create more and better jobs. An important issue to achieve this goal is the mobility of knowledge, which emphasizes the role of cultural diversity and interactive learning. However, few studies so far have scrutinized the international innovation networks and knowledge migration between European Member states and EU Member candidates like the emerging economy of Turkey.

Recent approaches on innovation and economic growth highlight that people from different cultural backgrounds and knowledge bases can provide different perspectives and develop new solutions to existing problems, thereby spurring entrepreneurial and economic as well as engineering and marketing creativity (Florida 2002; Saxenian 2006; Page 2008). In a globalising world, intercultural boundary spanners, innovation networks and asset augmenting investments create new patterns of knowledge exchange in various ways and different economic realms. Saxenian (2002, 2005, 2006), in her analysis of the diversity of the workforce in the Silicon Valley and on commuting entrepreneurs spanning networks between different countries, argues that high-skill immigration benefits both the host and home country by the process of brain circulation. She suggests that highly skilled workers, far from replacing native workers, tend to start new businesses and generate new jobs and wealth by creating new social and professional networks to mobilize the information, know-how, skill and capital. With these networks, they are able to bridge both the host and home countries. In this way, international migration becomes a two-way process which can support a process of reciprocal innovation by making the transfer of human capital and technology possible. Instead of brain drain, the focus can move towards knowledge exchange and mutual learning as well as on economic gains, resulting from commuting entrepreneurs, knowledge migration and international innovation networks.

International boundary spanners and innovation networks also enhance mutual understanding and knowledge exchange between countries by resolving or even preventing misunderstandings that can occur due to varying values and attitudes. By doing this, they enable international cooperation and knowledge exchange. The long history of Turkish–German migration offers many opportunities to explore this. The grown Turkish–German relationships provide for a large potential to create knowledge and innovation driven dynamics, which can contribute strongly to the economic welfare in both countries. Moreover, an improved technological integration can also be an important step towards more social integration between Turkey and Germany and towards Turkey's EU integration process.

In this book, we merge the two literatures on innovation networks and knowledge migration and apply it to the Turkish–German case. We analyse the Turkish–German innovation networks in order to gain a better understanding of the mechanisms and dynamics behind and to discover potential risks and shortcomings which might hinder network development. This book provides practical and theoretical insights on:

- how the knowledge linkages between both sides are formed;
- which bottlenecks are important to be dissolved; and
- which strengths and best practices can be fostered.

Once we know the structural and dynamic features of the networks we are able to avoid negative features, overcome rigidities and enhance knowledge flows.

Certainly Turkey's innovation capabilities still lack behind European innovation leaders, such as Switzerland, Germany or the Scandinavian countries. However, in the last decades, Turkey has started to diversify its export portfolio into more advanced sectors, experienced a remigration of its skilled diaspora network and saw the rise of several new applied universities and research centres. Understanding the Turkish–German innovative networks also helps to explore the impact of Turkish immigrants on development of bilateral innovation activities between two countries in the context of the European economic integration.

The goal of the European Union to develop towards the leading knowledge-based economy is strongly supported by the emergence of innovation networks which connect core European regions with European periphery and catching-up regions characterized by strong dynamics. Given the aging problem in the EU and its impact on the future growth, the EU has to strengthen its human capital, so to decrease the productivity gap and pursue a growth strategy based on knowledge and innovation.

It must be noted that recently also a large amount of refugees, especially from Syria, have been migrating to Turkey, Germany and Europe. It is still too early to estimate the effect of the partially high-skilled, partially lowed skilled migrants on the economic linkages and knowledge exchange between Europe and the Middle East. However, while there are certainly major differences between the new movement of refugees and the historical grown migration relationships between Turkey and Germany, there are also some commonalities concerning the potentials and problems, in particular concerning policy designs which aim at a fast integration into labour markets, as well as opportunities for new economic linkages and knowledge exchange between German, Turkey, Syria, Europe and the Middle East. We are convinced that there are lessons to be learnt in this difficult and complex field from our analysis of migration and innovation.

In what follows, we briefly introduce to the history of knowledge exchange and migration between Turkey and Germany. Then we highlight the previous findings and role of immigration for innovation in Europe, before we present the structure of this book.

The history of Turkish–German knowledge exchange and migration

Turkey and Germany are two countries with various political, economic, social and cultural ties that have developed over the last centuries. The history of Turkish–German relations is noteworthy since it entails interesting cases of knowledge migration and cross-border learning.

While during the seventeenth to the middle of the twentieth century, emphasis was certainly put first on military and political ties, the exchange of knowledge could also be observed. One example is the establishment of the Germany Military Commission (GMC) in 1882, which helped the Ottoman army in fields such as the reorganization and the introduction of the modern military exercises. Since 1890, German academics and educators helped in increasing the effectiveness of the higher education system, establishing and/or developing academic organizations (such as departments and universities) and create manifold academic links between both countries. In the early twentieth century, multiple German schools and hospitals were built in Istanbul. Moreover, as early as 1913, around 1300 Ottomans, mainly students and foreign workers, lived in Berlin. Between 1941 and 1945, Turkey opened its door to many German emigrants fleeing from the Nazi regime. German Jewish scholars made remarkable contributions to Turkey's scientific and academic studies in these years. Their legacy includes the reformation of higher education, establishment of new faculties and institutions, and more importantly education of new Turkish scholars. Today, these emigrants still play an important role in the ongoing modernization of Turkey.

In 1949 Turkey became a member of the Council of Europe. Due to Germany's economic boom phase ("Wirtschaftswunder") and the related shortages on the labour supply side, as well as Turkey's need to export surplus labour force, Turkey and Germany signed the Labour Recruitment Agreement (number 505-83

SZV/3-92-42) in 1961. This agreement lead to large-scale emigration from Turkey to Germany and made Turks the largest group of the immigrants numbering 649,000 between 1961 and 1974, and reaching almost three million later in the 1980s (İçduygu 2012).

The first immigrants were employed almost exclusively in industry. In the 1970s many Turkish migrants began opening grocery stores or working in markets offering goods which were difficult to get in Germany and thereby complement the so far dominant industrial employment of Turkish migrants. This trend even accelerated in the 1990s and afterwards. In 2010 almost 80,000 private businesses were founded in different sectors by Turkish migrants in Germany. Today a large percentage of Germans with Turkish migration background access higher-skilled jobs with an academic education. Very recently a new trend is observable, namely that many of the high-skilled German citizens with a Turkish background re-migrate at least temporarily to Turkey. The labour market in Germany still is not fully prepared to allow for top careers in German industry with a Turkish name. Their good education and the demand for high-skilled labour in the centres of the Turkish economy, though, partially absorbs these Germans with a Turkish background.

Turkey continues to be a country of outmigration. However, with the above mentioned reversal of high-skilled migration from Germany to Turkey it has become a country of immigration. In 2000, the share of Germans in the foreign born population of Turkey amounted to 21.4 per cent (273,500), the majority of these being highly skilled second-generation migrants who returned to their parents' home country in order to benefit from employment opportunities in Turkey (Biffl 2011).

Naturally the large patterns of migration between Germany and Turkey has also significantly contributed to the knowledge exchange and economic ties between both countries. Today, multidimensional economic, social and technological relationships exist between Turkey and Germany. With respect to economic ties, Germany is Turkey's top goods export market according to 2011 data, amounting to US$11.7 billion, with clothing accessories, road vehicles, textile and fabrics being among the top export goods. On the other hand, Germany is Turkey's second largest supplier of goods in 2011, amounting to US$20.1 billion. Road vehicles, machinery and electrical machinery are the top import categories.

Moreover, in 2009, Germany and Turkey jointly celebrated 50 years of bilateral development cooperation. During this fifty-year period, more than €4.3 billion of funding has been provided to Turkey from Germany in the form of loans and grants under financial cooperation. Germany has also invested heavily in Turkey. Among the 29,000 international firms in Turkey, 4,800 are German firms. Although due to the economic crisis in 2008 the total German FDI (foreign direct investment) decreased from US$110.5 billion in 2010 to US$54.4 billion in 2011, the German FDI to Turkey increased from US$597 million to US$605 million during the same period, showing the commitment of German companies to invest in Turkey (Kustepeli *et al.* 2013).

Although the phenomenon of innovation networks in the Turkish–German relations can be considered to be in its early stages, there are multiple cases of successful knowledge migration and innovation networks which indicate the rich possibilities for economic integration and development of Turkish–German innovation networks. Turkey can benefit from Germany's comparative advantage in high-technology sectors and Germany could benefit from the youth and high education level of the Turkish labour force. These benefits are accessible through innovation networks where actors from both sides cooperate and exchange knowledge with goals of R&D and innovation. Innovation networks between the two countries can contribute to the increase of the mutual consideration and positive public perception of each other by showing:

- the German side that Turkey can be an the important source of knowledge and high economic potential,
- the Turkish side that German agents can offer possibilities for cooperation and mutual learning, leading to economic win-win situations and
- revealing the important contributions that Turkish citizens in Germany and German citizens in Turkey can have for innovation, jobs and growth in both countries.

The development of efficient Turkish–German innovation networks can also contribute to Turkey's EU accession process. It is noteworthy that Germany's stance on Turkey's accession to the EU has been very important from the beginning. Partially due to its need for workers during the German Wirtschaftswunder, Germany convinced other European countries to sign the "Ankara Agreement Establishing an Association Between The European Economic Community and Turkey" (Mayer 2008). However, the prolonged accession process has recently reduced the expectations of Turkish business community and policy-makers. Added with uncertainties of global challenges and the political uncertainty converged around the "open-endedness" of the membership process, the relationship with Europe has become more problematic. Because of this situation, it is now particularly important to promote commuting entrepreneurs and innovation networks in order to foster knowledge exchange and mutual understanding.

Immigration and innovation in the European Union

Migration plays an important role in the exchange of knowledge and thereby generating positive economic dynamics. In general, a more liberal immigration policy can support economic growth rates by improving the prerequisites of mutual knowledge generation and diffusion responsible for innovation. In this light, innovation is the outcome of interactions between heterogeneous agents that have sufficiently different knowledge in order to generate new combinations (Boschma and Martin 2010). The variety of knowledge to be creatively combined is positively correlated to the inflow of knowledge carried by migrants.

The European Union's 2020 growth strategy gives priority to growth and innovation, as well as to migration policies. In particular, the EU's Global Approach to Migration and Mobility through the Blue Card Directive provides the instrument to foster competitiveness through highly skilled migration into the EU. Among other factors, the economic dynamics and future competitiveness of the European Union is currently considered to be endangered by the aging of the European society. The impact of population shrinkage, coupled with the ageing of key European societies, implies not only problems for the pension, health and welfare systems across the EU but also for the creativity of the European economy. Migration, and in particular migration of high-skilled is considered as an effective strategy against these hazards.

Due to their different cultural backgrounds, it is likely that migrants and native workers have fairly diverse abilities and knowledge. This means that there might be skill complementarities between foreign workers and natives in addition to those which are to be expected among workers on the same qualification levels. The attempt to attract highly-skilled migrants relies on the observation that highly-skilled migrants can over-proportionally contribute to innovation and economic development not only in the host countries but also in their home countries (Venturini, Montobbio and Fassio 2012; McCraw 2012).

Maré, Fabling and Stillman (2011) suggest that the potential of immigration to alter the demographic and skill composition of the workforce in the destination country may be fostered by positive feedback effects: skilled migration increases the number of research workers and additionally immigrants provide different types of knowledge and thereby increase the knowledge variety. Accordingly, immigration is likely to increase the knowledge base quantitatively and qualitatively and thereby contribute intensely to innovation (ibid.).

There are also studies analysing the contribution of immigration to innovation which do not find evidence of a positive correlation. For instance, Peri (2011) shows that highly-skilled migrants do not affect innovation in Europe. However, Ozgen, Nijkamp and Poot (2011) found that it is the variety rather than the size of the foreign community that spurs patent applications in Europe. It can be argued that different sectors of the economy differ substantially in innovation rates and R&D intensity and, accordingly, the impact of immigration may also differ across different industries.

Structure of the book

The chapters in this book provide an in-depth picture of international innovation networks and knowledge migration. While focusing on Turkish–German innovation networks, it offers an overview of main theoretical approaches and new methods helping to explore the complex relations and knowledge exchange between catching-up economies and technological advanced countries within the context of the European economic integration process.

The following chapters are presented in three parts, analysing different facets of international innovation networks and knowledge migration:

• mapping the future orientation and innovativeness of economies, to get an understanding about the innovative capabilities of countries and regions;

- knowledge migration, diaspora networks and commuting entrepreneurs, to get a better understanding of how migration can contribute to the innovative performance of these regions; and
- international innovation networks and the Germany–Turkey nexus, which reveals the structure of the knowledge changes and innovation networks between Turkey and Germany.

Part I: Mapping the future orientation and innovativeness of economies

The first set of chapters deals with the innovation and productive capabilities of Turkey from a global perspective. Horst Hanusch, Andreas Pyka and Florian Wackermann analyse in Chapter 2 the patterns of future orientation in Central and Eastern Europe. For this purpose, they apply the comprehensive Neo-Schumpeterian economics (CNSE) approach. CNSE combines the idea of future orientation of innovation economics for all spheres of economic life, namely in the industry, finance and the public sector (also called the three pillars of CNSE). The CNSE approach is applied to an empirical study of eleven Central and Eastern European economies. The country patterns of the three pillars are identified in a cluster analysis. This gives a fine-grained picture of institutional and structural set-ups for the analysed countries and reveals the distinct profile of the future-orientation underlying the Turkish economy compared to other new European member states and accession candidates.

Dominik Hartmann analyses in Chapter 3 the economic diversification and innovation system of Turkey from a global comparative perspective, in which he argues that Turkey needs to put more political emphasis on innovation and economic diversification in order (i) to prevent a deep economic crisis once the construction boom comes to an end, (ii) to facilitate sustained economic and technological catch-up, and (iii) to open up the way for better mutual understanding and renewed cooperation with the EU. This chapter also shows the economic diversity performance of Turkey and explains why the European Union puts policy emphasis on knowledge and innovation. Moreover, it and outlines a set of innovation and diversification policies, highlighting economic win-win situations through international cooperation and innovation networks.

Chapter 4 by Akgüngör, Yaprak Gülcan and Yeşim Kuştepeli addresses international trade flows, variety and patent applications. This chapter analyses the impact of trade on innovativeness in Turkey's regions with specific emphasis on Turkish–German trade relationships in the context of international trade and economic diversification. The findings confirm the hypotheses that there is a positive relationship between (i) related variety and innovation, and (ii) trade and innovation. Exports enhance innovativeness at the regional level. The innovativeness is further enhanced when the exported goods are related in variety. Unrelated variety has a significant impact on innovations, but its impact is relatively smaller than the impact of related variety.

In Chapter 5 the authors Değer, Güçlü, Yağcıbaşı and Kumral state that culture is crucial, not only as part of our social structure, but also as part of our economic order. Due to lack of clarity as to what constitutes culture, measurement is difficult. In economics, this difficulty is overcome by relying on predefined sector classifications to distinguish culture industries. Adopting this approach, the authors investigate the extent of culture industries in Europe through three-star analysis, and reveal that culture industries have a weak presence in Europe. On a sectorial level, "book and journal publishing", "news agency activities" and "architectural activities" are strongest. Geographically, culture industries appear to be strongest in Central and Northern Europe and weakest in Eastern Europe. With a focused analysis on Turkey and Germany, the authors observe that Turkey lags considerably behind in cultural industries.

Part II: Knowledge migration, diaspora networks and commuting entrepreneurs

Part II contains chapters addressing the relationship between migration and innovation. It starts in Chapter 6 with a survey on the recent literature by Sheida Rashidi-Kollmann and Andreas Pyka. In a world characterized by competition on a global scale, structural change driven by innovation and aging societies in industrialized economies and the competition for the best talents on labour markets is becoming global and more intensive. Therefore it is not surprising that old-fashioned brain drain explanations for migration are no longer convincing. In the knowledge-based economies of the twenty-first century, the ideas of brain circulation and international (diaspora) innovation networks become prevalent. This chapter is a survey on the theoretical and empirical approaches which address the important relationship between migration and innovation.

Annekatrin Niebuhr provides in Chapter 7 a review on the recent evidence of the economic effects of migration and cultural diversity. The number of migrants worldwide has considerably grown during the last decades and gives rise to an increasing cultural diversity in the host societies. Scholars point to potential costs and benefits of immigration and an increasing cultural diversity. As the economic consequences of diversity have received much less attention compared to the labour market effects of migration, evidence on the issue is still incomplete and ambiguous. However, the majority of studies seems to be in support of beneficial, but moderate effects of cultural diversity.

In Chapter 8, Canan Balkır and Kevin van Hove analyse the phenomenon of German–Turkish entrepreneurs, their networking activities through business associations, and the growing importance given to migrant entrepreneurship in the European Union. Facing a high rate of unemployment, Turkish migrants have been pushed towards entrepreneurship, facing difficulties, stemming both from themselves and from the host community. Thus, self-employment is less of a voluntarily chosen occupation and more of a reactive survival mechanism. The business organisations they have established became to be valued more in the political process as an important leverage for successful integration. Although it has been cited in many studies that migrants have the potential to provide different types of knowledge and hence are likely to contribute to innovation, the identification of the role of German–Turkish entrepreneurs in innovation networks is in its infancy and requires further study.

Dalgıç, Kuckertz and Bulut reveal in Chapter 9 the role of social capital, knowledge and innovation propensity in transnational entrepreneurial behaviour of Turkish–German entrepreneurs. Their focus is on Turkish–German entrepreneurs (i.e. entrepreneurs who operate from Germany, but have their cultural roots in Turkey). Their analysis sheds light on the phenomenon of transnational (or cross-border) entrepreneurship as both the individual entrepreneur and their firms are at least to some degree transnational by origin. The authors are interested in factors affecting the tendency of those Turkish–German entrepreneurs to internationalize their entrepreneurial efforts and suggest that this behaviour is driven by a firm's innovation propensity, opportunity recognition, knowledge and social capital. Their sample of 86 Turkish–German entrepreneurs and their firms supports these arguments.

Sylvie van Cour, Alexander Gerybadze and Andreas Pyka study in Chapter 10 the Turkish Diaspora Networks in Germany. They analyse the diaspora networks of the highly skilled Turkish and identifies specific characteristics of Turkish diaspora networks. The authors concentrate on the functionality and impact of diaspora networks and migration on the generation of innovation and discuss the nation-specific findings.

In Chapter 11, Eberhard von Einem studies the knowledge transfer to Istanbul, and asks a relevant question: is the Turkish industry benefitting from re-migration? He argues that cross-national knowledge transfer cannot fully be explained by transmitting codified knowledge (e.g. via publications and the internet), but involves also personal exchange of tacit knowledge (e.g. through teaching, reading, training, conferences and/or cooperation in networks). Re-migration contributes to this process; in fact, trans-national migration seems to be one of the most important cross-national knowledge pipelines. Experts moving across regional or national boarders carry their skills and knowledge with them, thus helping receiving countries to improve their human capital. This chapter illustrates that a transfer-process of both technical skills and practical hands-on knowledge can be observed through re-migration of the 2 million Turks that have been returning from Germany and other EU countries back to Turkey.

Part III: International innovation networks: The Germany–Turkey nexus

Following the broadly designed studies of the two sections above, the third set of chapters offers a deeper visualization and analysis of the structures of concrete innovation networks between Turkey and Germany.

Dominik Hartmann and Tobias Buchmann start in Chapter 12 with a study on comparative technological advantages and patent networks of Turkey. They use EPO patent data to reveal the evolution of the technological strengths and weaknesses of Turkey in comparison with Germany and the average values of 28 European economies in 35 technology fields between 1981 and 2010. While Turkey is significantly lagging behind in the absolute number of patents, their results show that Turkey has started to diversify its patent portfolio and is developing comparative technological advantages in several technology fields. By applying network analysis, they illustrate, though, that this diversification of the Turkey's patent portfolio is strongly dependent on large firms from the US and Germany. Their findings suggest that Turkey can significantly gain from the cooperation with international partners in the future, however, Turkey needs to put further emphasis on building up endogenous capabilities to generate, modify, appropriate and protect new technologies.

In Chapter 13, Irene Peschkov, Andreas Pyka and Barbara Heller-Schuh study the Turkish–German innovation networks in the European research landscape. For this purpose they examine the structure of research networks of the European Framework Programmes (FP) that are established by joint participation of organizations in research projects, in particular German research organizations with Turkish participants in FP5 to FP7 in the knowledge-intensive technology fields of ICT, biotechnology and nanoscience. A better understanding of these networks allows for improving the design of research policies at national levels as well as at the EU level. The empirical examination of network properties reveals that the diverse networks show a range of similarities in the three technology fields in each FP such as small-world properties. Moreover, the findings show that German actors play a specific role in most of the examined research networks with Turkish participation.

Yaprak Gülcan and Ceyhan Aldemir provide in Chapter 14 an analysis of the historical roots and context of Turkish–German academic and scientific innovative networks. They show that scientific and commercial networking and trust are indispensable ingredients in building up healthy, cost-free network relations. Since 1890, German and Turkish researchers have exchanged knowledge in many scientific areas. In the Turkish higher education system an important role and a strong effect of German actors is to be observed. As a result of a long and effective collaboration between Germany and Turkey and in addition to a high-level transfer of knowledge and ongoing economic integration, there exists an academic multi-actor innovation network. The network relations between Turkish and German institutions in the academic sector are strong and persistent, producing many academic projects, papers and patents.

In Chapter 15, Sule Gündüz, Mehmet Beyzatlar and Yeşim Kuştepeli present a case study on Turkish German innovation networks in the renewable energy sector, in which they measure and visualize the network relations between twelve renewable energy firms. By mapping the structure of the network, the position of the actors in the sector and their interconnections to each other can be observed. The results reveals that the knowledge flows between the agents are rather limited. Due to harsh competition in this sector, the firms do not or only rarely interact, thus the spread of knowledge and networks is sparse. Without doubt, further technological upgrading and success of this sector requires much more emphasis on local and international innovation networks, raising the knowledge flows and productivity of the sector.

Summary of the results

Our knowledge of the effects of migration on innovation is still in its infancy, in particular with respect to the knowledge migration between European member states and accession candidates. The first insights, however, reveal that successful integration of high-skilled migrants can increase the variety of knowledge and promote innovation. The direction of the potentials is bi-directional (i.e. receiving and sending countries can explore and exploit opportunities). Migration is no longer a once-and-for-all decision, but migrants move on in their careers and very often move back to their countries of origin to found new firms and support knowledge transfer from the receiving country.

The case studies in this book show that Turkey can gain from technological knowledge of a complex European economy, while Germany can also gain access to new perspectives and markets through the back-and forward migration of Turkish–German citizens and the expanding scientific and business relations. Moreover, it must be highlighted that this book concentrates on the economic and technological relationship and potential economic gains between Turkey and Germany rather than discussing the cultural, political and religious differences. Instead of focusing on cultural differences and integration problems that might go along with migration, we highlight the win–win situations that can result from cultural diversity and international knowledge exchange.

With this book we follow the aim to provide a new perspective on international innovation networks and knowledge migration in the context of the European integration process.

References

Biffl, G. (2011) Turkey and Europe: the role of migration and trade in economic development. Paper presented at the Conference on Migration and Development: Comparing Mexico–US and Turkey–Europe, University of California – Davis, 1–2 May.

Boschma, R. and Martin, R. (2010) The aims and scope of evolutionary economic geography. In R. Boschma and R. Martin (eds), *The Handbook of Evolutionary Economic Geography*, 3–39. Cheltenham: Edward Elgar Publishing.

Florida, R. L. (2002) *The Rise of the Creative Class, and How it's Transforming Work, Leisure, Community and Everyday Life*. New York: Basic Books.

Hartmann, D. (2014) *Economic Complexity and Human Development: How Economic Diversification and Social Networks Affect Human Agency and Welfare*. New York: Routledge.

İçduygu, A. (2012) 50 years after the labour recruitment agreement with Germany: the consequences of emigration for Turkey. *Perceptions* 2: 11–14.

Kustepeli, Y., Balkır, C., Akgungor, S., Gulcan , Y., Beyzatlar, M. A. and Gunduz, S. (2013) Turkish–German economic relations via foreign direct investment and patents. *Journal of Entrepreneurship and Innovation Management* 1(2): 23–50.

Maré, D. C., Fabling, R. and Stillman, S. (2011) *Immigration and Innovation*. Discussion paper, April. Bonn: IZA.

Mayer, M. M. (2008) Germany's preferences on the Ankara agreement: ministerial actors between Cold War security concerns. Paper presented at Turkish European Ambitions and the Wirtschaftswunder, Fourth Pan-European Conference on EU Politics of the ECPR, University of Latvia, Riga, 25–27 September.

McCraw, T. K. (2012) Innovative immigrants. *The New York Times* (1 November), www.nytimes.com/2012/11/02/opinion/immigrants-as-entrepreneurs.html?page wanted=all.

Ozgen, C., Nijkamp, P. and Poot, J. (2011) *Immigration and Innovation in European Regions*. Discussion paper no. 5676. Bonn: IZA.

Page, S. E. (2008) *The Difference: How the Power of Diversity Creates Better Groups, Firms, Schools, and Societies*. Princeton, NJ: Princeton University Press.

Peri G. (2011) *The Impact of Immigration on Native Poverty through Labor Market Competition*. NBER working paper 17570, November. Cambridge, MA: National Bureau of Economic Research.

Pyka, A. and Hanusch, H. (eds) (2006) *Applied Evolutionary Economics and the Knowledge-Based Economy*. Cheltenham: Edward Elgar.

Pyka, A. and Scharnhorst, A. (eds) (2010) *Innovation Networks: New Approaches in Modelling and Analysing*. Berlin: Springer.

Saxenian, A. (2002) Brain circulation: how high-skill immigration makes everyone better off. *The Brookings Review* 20(1): 28–31.

Saxenian, A. (2005) From brain drain to brain circulation: transnational communities and regional upgrading in India and China. *Studies in Comparative International Development* 40(2): 35–61.

Saxenian, A. (2006) *The New Argonauts: Regional Advantage in a Global Economy*. Cambridge, MA: Harvard University Press.

Venturini, A., Montobbio, F. and Fassio, C. (2012) *Are Migrants Spurring Innovation?* Migration Policy Centre Report. San Domenico di Fiesole: Robert Schuman Centre for Advanced Studies.

Part I

Measuring the future orientation and innovativeness of economies

2 Patterns of future orientation in Central and Eastern Europe

*Horst Hanusch, Andreas Pyka and
Florian Wackermann*

Introduction

In the so-called "fifth enlargement" of 2004 and 2007, Malta, Cyprus, Estonia, Latvia, Lithuania, Poland, the Czech Republic, Slovakia, Slovenia, Hungary, Romania and Bulgaria joined the European Union. In particular, the former communist economies had to undergo severe structural transformations after the fall of the iron curtain and still when they entered the European Union showed marked differences with respect to the western part. Obviously, these differences also frame their strategies to react to the challenges of the current worldwide financial and economic crisis. It is time to ask the question how the new member countries perform in the restructuring of their economies and in their refurbishment with the crisis. *The Economist* (20–26 March 2010, p. 29) reported that "The idea of a single 'ex-communist region' called Eastern Europe does not bear scrutiny." In fact the economies of the new member countries show severe structural dissimilarities, which are to be considered in the evaluation of the performance as well as in the design of policy strategies to manage the transformation processes.

In March 2010, the EU Commission renewed the Lisbon Agenda with the so-called Europe 2020 growth strategy. There it is outlined: "Europe is recognised the world over for its high quality of life, underpinned by a unique social model. The strategy should ensure that these benefits are sustained and even further enhanced, while employment, productivity and social cohesion are optimised." Like the Lisbon Goal, this goal is challenging and extraordinarily difficult to be accomplished in particular in the current economic crisis. From the point of view of economics, the following major issues have to be addressed:

1   The decisive economic elements and forces responsible for the achievement of the agenda must be identified.
2   An adequate economic approach should be developed which explicitly includes these elements.
3   For the application of this theoretical approach on the empirical realm the right methodological concept must be found.
4   The fourth major issue is to apply this operationalisation to Europe. A severe

difficulty here stems from the fact that Europe is not a unity composed of homogeneous components but a collection of heterogeneous countries. Accordingly, the method chosen should focus on detecting patterns of similarities and dissimilarities among the countries under investigation.

5   This discovery of patterns is a necessary step for a further analysis which focuses on the manifestation of success in the sense of the Lisbon Agenda and compares patterns of similarity with patterns of performance.

These five points also structure the content of our paper. In the first section we derive the economic substrate of the Lisbon Agenda and Europe 2020. It can be shown that the Lisbon Agenda as well as the Europe 2020 is mainly based on innovation and the resulting future orientation. We then elaborate comprehensive Neo-Schumpeterian economics (CNSE) as an adequate theoretical framework suitable for the enforcement of the Lisbon agenda. In order to apply CNSE, we develop an indicator based three-pillar model in the following section, composed of an industry, a financial and a public sector part. This three-pillar concept is applied to 11 Central and Eastern European countries, encompassing the ten new member states of the EU on the continent (thus excluding Cyprus and Malta) as well as Croatia, which was not yet a member of the European Union in the period examined. A study which tried to find clusters for 14 older EU-members (EU-15 excluding Luxemburg) has been conducted in 2006.

We then focus on dissimilarities and similarities of the various economies and their pillars. This analysis allows for the detection of whether there is variety in the composition of the three pillars for the different countries or whether one finds a convergent structure of groups of countries. This allows us to get a first hint on the convergence and divergence of structures in geographic areas in Europe. The study is done by a cluster analysis. Our paper ends with some conclusions and the agenda for future research.

The economic substrate of the Lisbon Agenda

One of the most frequently cited statements of the famous Lisbon Agenda claims that *Europe should become the most competitive and dynamic knowledge-based economic region in the world*. What does this mean in economic terms?

Today, economists widely agree that technological progress is the central determinant of growth and dynamics in modern economies. These dynamics are propelled by innovative activities in all parts and spheres of the economy and the society as the main driving force of change and development. Behind innovation understood as a process of unpredictable and discontinuous crowding out of established and appearance of new products, production technologies and organizational solutions, we most importantly find knowledge generation and diffusion processes. As a consequence, looking at the competitiveness of firms, regions, countries or even a union of countries, it is no longer price-competition which plays the central role, but the competition for innovation which really counts (Saviotti and Pyka 2008). Under this angle, the dynamics which are relevant and have to be observed include not only quantitative features of economic growth but also qualitative features of economic development and structural change. Obviously, dynamic processes understood and analysed in this vein are fed by multiple sources which also mutually influence each other in a co-evolutionary way. These sources encompass actors like entrepreneurs, firms and households as well as financial actors as banks, venture capitalists and private equity firms. Public actors and institutions like governments, universities, schools, research institutes, patent offices and regulatory authorities also play a role.

Keeping in mind this comprehensive innovation-oriented view of the Lisbon Agenda, which economic approach might be suited for its enforcement?

Comprehensive Neo-Schumpeterian economics

The Lisbon Agenda and its successor, Europe 2020, formulate a strategy for keeping and even improving the competitiveness of the European Union. Therefore, its overall goal must be seen in securing the welfare for European citizens. Without doubt, economics is the science which focuses on economic welfare and the ability to increase it. This can be stated as a goal for all schools in economics, among the most important being the Neoclassical school, the Neo-Keynesian approach and Neo-Schumpeterian economics. But the angle of analysis differs sharply among these various approaches. Boiling down the Neoclassical approach to its essentials, it can be characterized by rational individuals acting on markets where the price mechanism is responsible for an efficient allocation of resources within a set of given constraints. Neo-Keynesian economics, briefly characterized, turns out to be a demand-oriented macro approach based primarily on short term processes occurring in non-perfect markets. Accordingly, the knowledge-driven and the ensuing innovation-driven processes characterizing long run development are by far not central to both of these approaches.

One of the decisive differences of Neo-Schumpeterian economics with respect to other approaches in economics can be found in its emphasis on different levels of economic analysis and their particular interrelatedness. Due to the dominance of the Neoclassical school in the twentieth century, the approach of a micro foundation of macroeconomics has wide appeal. The aggregation from micro to macro becomes possible because of the idea of representative households and firms. Although this approach may seem convincing due to its analytical stringency, its mechanistic design may lead to difficulties when it comes to the analysis of dynamic phenomena endogenously caused by the economic system.

Neo-Schumpeterian economics, by contrast, seeks to get a grip on these dynamic phenomena of economic reality. In order to do this, important meso-level aspects between the micro and the macro level of economic analysis are considered (e.g. Dopfer, Foster and Potts 2004). It is the meso-level of an economic system in which the decisive structural and qualitative changes take place and can be observed.

To understand the processes driving the development at the meso-level, Neo-Schumpeterian economics puts a strong emphasis on knowledge, innovation and entrepreneurship at the micro-level. Innovation is identified as the major force propelling economic dynamics. In this emphasis on innovation, the major difference in the Neo-Schumpeterian approach with respect to alternative economic approaches can be identified. Generally, one may say that novelty (i.e., innovation) is the core principle underlying the Neo-Schumpeterian approach. Innovation competition takes the place of price competition as the coordination mechanism of interest. Of course, prices are also of significance, but concerning the driving forces of economic development, they are by far not central. Whereas prices are basic concerning the adjustment to limiting conditions, innovations are responsible for overcoming previous limiting conditions and – as in economic reality, everything except human creativity has an end – setting new ones.

The focus on novelties is thus the most important distinctive mark of Neo-Schumpeterian economics. By its very nature, innovation, and in particular technological innovation, is the most visible form of novelty. Therefore, it is not very surprising that Neo-Schumpeterian economics today is most appealing in studies of innovation and learning behaviour at the micro-level of an economy, in studies of innovation-driven industry dynamics at the meso-level, and in studies of innovation-determined growth and international competitiveness at the macro-level of the economy (e.g. Hanusch and Pyka 2007c).

To summarize, in Neo-Schumpeterian economics the central actors under investigation are entrepreneurs and entrepreneurial firms, the most important process under investigation is innovation and the underlying knowledge creation and diffusion processes. Here, in sharp contrast to Neoclassical Economics, the notion of innovation focuses on the removal and overcoming of limiting constraints and the setting of new ones.

However, Neo-Schumpeterian economics, in its present shape, restricts itself to the dynamics of the industry side only. Even with this shortcoming, Neo-Schumpeterian economics seems to be the most adequate approach in tackling the enforcement of the Lisbon Agenda. Nevertheless, to fulfil its extreme challenges, namely to successfully hold ground in global innovation-oriented competition with the aim to enforce a development which makes Europe the *most dynamic knowledge-based economic region in the world*, the Neo-Schumpeterian approach has to be put on a broader conceptual basis.

For this purpose, we suggest comprehensive Neo-Schumpeterian economics (CNSE) as elaborated in Hanusch and Pyka (2007a). CNSE has to offer a consistent theory which encompasses all realms relevant to an improved understanding of economic processes involving change and development. This becomes even more pressing in cases in which the different realms are in close relation, mutually influencing each other, which is very likely the case for economic development. In other words, a comprehensive understanding of economic development must inevitably consider the *co-evolutionary* processes between the different economic domains.

Consequently, we argue that it is high time for Neo-Schumpeterian economics to devote considerable attention to the role of the financial and public sector with respect to economic development. In particular, we introduce the comprehensive

Neo-Schumpeterian approach as a theory composed of three pillars: one for the real side of an economy, one for the monetary side of an economy, and one for the public sector. Economic development then takes place in a co-evolutionary manner, pushed, hindered and also even eliminated within these three pillars (Figure 2.1).

In order to understand the crucial co-evolutionary relationship, one must explore the bracket encompassing all three pillars, namely their orientation towards the future which introduces uncertainty into the analysis. The relationships between the three pillars drive or hinder the development of the whole economic system in a non-deterministic way. Consider, for example, the case of the financial sector, exaggerating the developments taking place in the real sector and leading to dangerous bubble effects which might cause a breakdown of the whole economy. Or think of the case in which the public sector cannot cope with the overall economic development, and areas such as infrastructure and education become the bottlenecks of system development.

A comprehensive Neo-Schumpeterian economic theory focusing on innovation driven qualitative development should offer theoretical concepts to analyse the various issues of all three pillars: industry dynamics, financial markets, and the public sector. Innovation and, as a consequence thereof, uncertainty, are ubiquitous phenomena characteristic of each of these pillars and are also intrinsically interrelated. An improved understanding of the development processes can only be expected if the co-evolutionary dimensions of the three pillars are taken

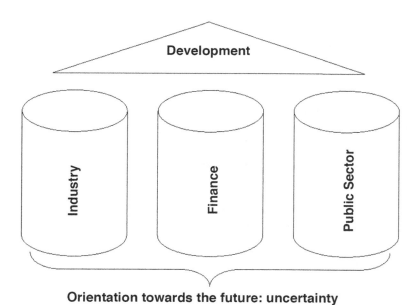

Figure 2.1 The three pillars of comprehensive Neo-Schumpeterian economics.

into account. This is illustrated within the concept of a Neo-Schumpeterian corridor shown in Figure 2.2.

In a CNSE perspective, there exists only a narrow corridor for a prolific development of socio-economic systems. Profound Neo-Schumpeterian development takes place in a narrow corridor between the extremes of uncontrolled growth and exploding bubbles, on the one hand, and stationarity (i.e., zero growth and stagnancy) on the other hand. Economic policy in the sense of CNSE strives to keep the system in an upside potential including both overheating protection (i.e. on the macro-level bubble explosions and on the micro-level insane explosive growth) and downside-protection, that is on the macro-level stagnation and on the micro-level bankruptcy.

To summarize, the essence of CNSE is captured by the following definition: CNSE deals with dynamic processes causing qualitative transformation of economies driven by the introduction of novelties in their various and multifaceted forms and the related co-evolutionary processes. These processes are not merely restricted to industry but also include the financial and public sphere of an economy and thereby encompass all spheres of economic and societal issues.

The indicator-based three-pillar approach

It is a central aim of this empirical study to gain new findings as regards the structural characteristics and the functioning as well as the competitiveness of economies in 11 countries which have just recently joined the EU (or will join in the near future, as in the case of Croatia) from a Neo-Schumpeterian angle.

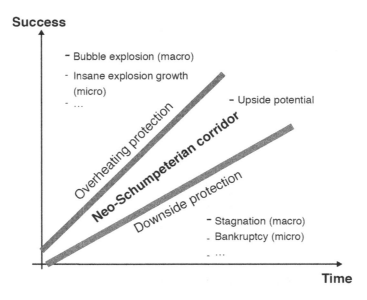

Figure 2.2 The Neo-Schumpeterian corridor.

Data

To achieve this objective, our analysis is grounded on a comprehensive set of indicators (Hanusch and Pyka 2007b). In total, more than seventy variables have been collected, reflecting many different activities in the various EU economies which are related to innovation. In dependence of data availability, the indicator sets comprise different years, namely from 2001 to 2006.

Above all, the set of variables reflects structural specifics, yet the data are also comprised of several indicators for the functioning of the economies, including inputs in the innovation process such as R&D related indicators as well as variables on the knowledge base and the institutional structure. To summarize, the data we draw upon must reflect all types of activities for the three pillars introduced above, immediately entailing the future-oriented characteristics.

The utilized indicators originate from various sources, the most important one being Eurostat, the statistical office of the European Union. The central additional data sources are the World Bank, UNESCO and the European Private Equity and Venture Capital Association (EVCA). From these databases, patent statistics, R&D expenditure data as well as several indicators of national education systems and of qualification structures of national workforces have been extracted.

The indicators for the three pillars

The crucial feature of the *industrial pillar* in a CNSE conception is its orientation towards the future. In order to comprise this dimension structurally as well as from a process perspective, we divided the pillar in three independent dimensions. In a first step, we considered the knowledge base in the country in order to associate them in educationally comparable groups. Second, we considered the openness of the economy through an analysis of the export of high technology. The third step encompasses the integration of the innovativeness and the efforts undertaken in R&D. Altogether, the three categories can enable us to draw a picture of the structural relatedness between the different countries with respect to their real sector.

Concerning the *financial pillar* we focus once again on the future orientation, which therefore must be expressed in the selection of indicators. We concentrated on the availability of venture capital as a variable which can both reflect the willingness and the ability to finance innovation in a country. Furthermore, it includes the perspectives which the financial markets attribute to the development in the respective economy.

The future orientation of the *public pillar* is centred around the institutions and the economic structure in the different countries. The indicators are linked to the public life in general and range from the use of e-government services to the public budget deficit. It also includes aspects relating to the workforce as well as the energy intensity in each country. Taken together, these indicators can offer a comprehensive picture of the structure and the institutional setup of the public role in each of the economies.[1]

Pattern detection: similarities and dissimilarities

By using the conceptual framework of our CNSA, the specific targets of the study are to detect and then to analyse cross-national (dis-)similarities in the structure and composition with respect to the future orientation and innovativeness of the economies.[2]

To meet these objectives, cluster analysis techniques are applied to the data (e.g. see Jobson 1992). The general rationale behind this analytical tool is to test a sample for the degree of structural commonalities between the units of analysis. Its outcome is a categorisation of the analysed units so that the coherence of each group (or cluster) as well as the heterogeneity across different clusters is maximized. To determine the coherence of a certain cluster and to calculate the existing diversity of different clusters, distance values between the units of analysis need to be determined on the basis of the characteristics of each entity. From the various methods to calculate distances between the entities, the squared Euclidean distance measure is applied, because it is a frequently applied distance measure of metric data. Furthermore, it more strongly accounts for differences between entities than the linear Euclidean distance does.

Hence, the distance between two countries i and j can be calculated as follows:

$$d(i,j) = \sum_{k=1}^{m} (a_{ik} - a_{jk})^2 \qquad (2.1)$$

Here, represents the parameter value of characteristic $k = 1, \ldots, m$ for country $i = 1, \ldots, n$.

Thus, the entire quantitative data matrix is

$$A = (a_{ik})_{mxn}.$$

The determination of distances between entities is a crucial but at the same time preliminary step in the entire cluster analysis. It needs to be completed by the application of a classification algorithm. Depending on the quality of the underlying data and on the research target, various classification procedures exist.

The data are characterized by a relatively small number of units of analysis (i.e., eleven countries in total) and at the same time by a relatively large number of variables (more than seventy variables in total) as well as by a cardinal data level.

Given these specifics of the underlying data and the country sample, a hierarchical, two-step cluster method (which rests upon the average-linkage principle of cluster membership) is applied to the sample.

The determination of the inter-cluster diversity between two classes K and L, $v(K, L)$, can thus be described formally as follows:

$$v(K,L) = \frac{1}{|K| \cdot |L|} \sum_{\substack{i \in K \\ j \in L}} d(i,j) \qquad (2.2)$$

with both distinctive classes K and L (i.e. $K \neq L$) belonging to the entire classification K.

Since it is not intended to impose a given, pre-determined classification of countries ex ante, an agglomerative classification method is utilized. This method starts with single-country clusters and entails a step-wise concentration of countries according to their degree of structural similarities. Given that it is intended to attach all countries in the sample to a certain cluster and that cases in which a certain country belongs to several clusters shall be ruled out, the selected clustering method yields an exhaustive as well as a disjunctive classification. A classification is exhaustive if

$$\bigcup_{K \in K} K = N,$$

with N being the total amount of analysed objects. A disjunctive partition meets the condition that , so that

$$K, L \in K, K \neq L, \text{ so that } \quad K \cap L = \phi .$$

The clustering method is applied to each pillar of the countries under study.

In order to determine the optimal number of clusters, the so-called elbow criterion (see Hanusch and Pyka 2006b) is applied. The elbow criterion is a commonly employed measure in cluster analysis that guarantees intra-cluster homogeneity and at the same time inter-cluster heterogeneity. Countries grouped within one cluster show strong similarities concerning the future orientation of the different pillars, whereas countries allocated to different clusters are structurally heterogeneous in this respect.

Empirical results

The following sections deal with the description of detected clusters and the analysis of their composition. We will discuss each pillar and the overall implications on the comparability and similarity between the analysed countries.

Clusters in future orientation of Central and Eastern European countries

Before we look at the individual pillars and their respective cluster separation, it is worth looking at the global analysis where all variables and indicators are taken into account. This will give us an idea of the overall distribution of the countries in the different clusters and will help in the interpretation of the pillar-related

	Bg	Cz	Ee	Lv	Lt	Hu	Pl	Ro	Si	Sk	Hr	Tr
global analysis	2	1	1	1	1	1	3	2	5	1	4	6

Figure 2.3 Country clusters of the global analysis.

Note: country codes are as follows: Bg, Bulgaria; Cz, Czech Republic; Ee, Estonia; Lv, Latvia; Lt, Lithuania; Hu, Hungary; Pl, Poland; Ro, Romania; Si, Slovenia; Sk, Slovakia; Hr, Croatia.

clusters. Figure 2.3 maps the countries to the various clusters, which are expressed by numbers and shades of grey.

The most striking result of this global analysis is that there is one large cluster comprised of the Baltic countries Estonia, Latvia and Lithuania as well as the medium-sized central European countries Czech Republic, Hungary and Slovakia. This hints towards a structural similarity in the future orientation in these countries during the analysed time period. The table can also be read in such a way that the countries in cluster 1 are similar enough to be grouped into one cluster and too dissimilar to be compared with the other economies in our sample. This result does, however, not mean that the different countries are characterized by the same quantitative values, rather only the structural composition is similar. Furthermore, we find that the two newest accession states, Bulgaria and Romania, make up their own cluster. Consequently, they are considerably different from all the other countries under observation and they share some similarities. The four countries which are left all form individual clusters implying that they are too different from the other economies to be compared with them. This applies to the largest country in terms of population, Poland, to Croatia, which was not yet a member of the European Union at the time of data collection, to Turkey, the only state which has not yet joined the European Union, as well as to Slovenia, which became the first of the new member states to adopt the euro as their currency in 2007.

In the first cluster, we find countries which experienced a growth rate between 1 and 10 per cent in 2007. Consequently, the global analysis does not yet tell us where the most promising starting point or termed negatively the most pressing bottlenecks are to be expected. Therefore, it is important to break the dimensions even further up and look at the different components in order to be able to better differentiate the distinct influences which may help explaining the different developments.

Results in the individual pillars

As explained above, we have analysed the real sector by looking at the three different dimensions of "knowledge base", "openness" and "innovative efforts". The first thing we notice is that there is considerable variation in the clusters which were formed according to those three domains. Only Estonia + Croatia and Latvia + Slovakia form pairs of countries which belong to the same cluster (1-1-1 in the first case and 1-2-1 in the second) in each of the three dimensions.

This means that those pairs can be considered to have a fairly similar industrial structure. All other countries are comparatively individual in the set-up of their real sector. Nevertheless, in each dimension, we have a largest cluster which is made up of seven countries which are relatively close in their structure.

When looking at the knowledge base in Central and Eastern Europe, we find that the main cluster has grown compared to the global analysis because Poland and Croatia have joined it and only Lithuania has left this cluster. It now contains seven countries; Bulgaria and Romania form a cluster on their own again. In this analysis, we find three single-country clusters which are made up of Lithuania and Slovenia and again Turkey.

With respect to the openness of the countries, the picture changes considerably. We are only left with three clusters and there is no imminent geographical or historical link between the countries within a cluster. The first cluster has shrunk to three economies and is only comprised of the Czech Republic, Estonia, and Croatia. The second cluster now counts eight countries. Bulgaria and Romania are now joined by Poland, Slovenia and Slovakia, as well as by the two Baltic States Latvia and Lithuania, and Turkey. It is interesting to note that while Estonia and Latvia shared the same cluster when looking at the knowledge base (Figure 2.4a), it is Latvia and Lithuania in the case of openness. Apparently, similarities and dissimilarities in the Baltic States are not as clear cut as one might expect. Hungary makes up a cluster of its own, which shows that it is different from all the other countries in the sample in this category. This difference can be traced back to Hungary's historically determined close connection with the Austrian economy.

Our third category in the industrial pillar leads to a separation into five groups again where we find four single-country clusters and have one large cluster made up of seven countries. For the first time, Bulgaria and Romania do not show a similar setup in their innovative efforts, where Bulgaria belongs to the large cluster together with the – once again reunited – three Baltic states, Hungary, Slovakia and Croatia. Romania is too different from all other countries and,

	Bg	Cz	Ee	Lv	Lt	Hu	Pl	Ro	Si	Sk	Hr	Tr
Global analysis	2	1	1	1	1	1	3	2	5	1	4	6
(a) knowledge	2	1	1	1	3	1	1	2	4	1	1	5
(a) openness	2	1	1	2	2	3	2	2	2	2	1	2
(a) innovative efforts	1	3	1	1	1	1	5	2	4	1	1	2
(b) financial markets	1	3	4	4	4	2	5	3	4	4	4	4
(c) public sector	2	1	1	1	1	1	1	2	1	1	3	4

Figure 2.4 Country clusters of the (a) industrial pillar, (b) financial pillar and (c) public pillar.

Note: country codes are as follows: Bg, Bulgaria; Cz, Czech Republic; Ee, Estonia; Lv, Latvia; Lt, Lithuania; Hu, Hungary; Pl, Poland; Ro, Romania; Si, Slovenia; Sk, Slovakia; Hr, Croatia.

consequently, forms together with the accession country Turkey its own cluster. The same is true for the Czech Republic, Poland and Slovenia. While Poland and Slovenia already belonged to single-country clusters in the above analyses, it is the first time for Romania and the Czech Republic to be significantly different from all other countries.

Even though we once again find a large cluster made up of six countries (Figure 2.4b), the future-orientation in the financial market differs most strongly from the result of the global analysis. For the first time, Bulgaria constitutes a cluster on its own and Romania finds itself in a cluster together with only the Czech Republic. Hungary which has been struck so hard by the current economic crisis is forming a cluster on its own, just like Poland. The seven-country cluster is made up of the three Baltic states Estonia, Latvia and Lithuania – even though we found Latvia in considerably larger distress during the financial crisis than the other two countries –, the two countries which by now have introduced the Euro, Slovenia and Slovakia, as well as Croatia and Turkey as the only two countries which have not been a member of the EU in the time interval of this study.

The pattern of clusters in public pillars shows to be strongly politically determined (Figure 2.4c). We find a large cluster made up of those eight countries in our study which joined the European Union in 2004: the Czech Republic, Estonia, Latvia, Lithuania, Hungary, Poland, Slovenia and Slovakia. This implies that their institutional setup is somewhat harmonized and comparable.

Obviously different enough to this first group, the clustering algorithm identifies Bulgaria and Romania in one public pillar group. Not surprisingly, these two countries joined the EU together in 2007. Finally, the only candidate country, Croatia, is put in a single-country cluster. In a different single country cluster we find Turkey whose public sector not surprisingly shows structural similarities to no other country in our sample. There is no causality check in our data, so we cannot imply if the perspective of membership to the European Union has led to a harmonization in the public structure or if the similarity has allowed those countries to fulfil the accession criteria at similar moments. Nevertheless, the correspondence of the clusters to the different accession dates is striking.

Conclusions

Innovativeness and orientation towards the future are central elements of the Lisbon Agenda and the Europe 2020 strategy. CNSE offers an appropriate theoretical approach for the enforcement of the Lisbon Agenda. Our cluster analysis demonstrates that from an empirical point of view, CNSE can be operationalized without major difficulties. It is central to maintain future orientation as a common feature of both the Lisbon Agenda and our three-pillar approach. This target can be achieved by relying on a comprehensive set of indicators reflecting different activities related to innovation.

Of course, due to its composition of very heterogeneous member countries, Europe will not come up with a simple pattern of pillar compositions. Does this mean that each country needs a specific policy design to achieve the Lisbon strategy? From the results of this analysis, we suggest that this is not the case. Countries can be attributed to clusters according to their similarities and differences. These groups of countries with similar pillar compositions can then be analysed according to their performances in such areas as patenting, growth, and employment in order to identify bottlenecks as well as catalysers of economic development. This procedure has the advantage that only comparable countries are used for comparisons in the sense of benchmarks concerning their future orientation and innovativeness. This avoids a major problem of all international comparisons, namely neglecting the complex interdependencies and complementarities stemming from two sources: First, countries composed of very different pillars (e.g., the Slovenian vs. the Croatian public pillar) are not used for comparisons and for deviating policy conclusions. Second, within groups of countries with similar structures of pillars, one can analyse the joint functioning of the industrial, the public and the financial pillars. Besides the design of the three pillars, one can thus demonstrate that an important dimension of economic development is constituted by the co-evolutionary relations between the three pillars.

Our methodology of pattern detection allows for a fine-grained analysis of the composition of the main institutional and structural components of an economy (the three pillars: industry, finance and public sector) in the various countries with a particular orientation towards the future. This cluster analysis has provided strong evidence for a pronounced heterogeneity in the structural composition of the eleven observed countries. Only Slovakia and Latvia are found to be in the same cluster for the global analysis as well as all subsectors which we analysed. Interestingly, both countries have experienced rather successful economic growth rates before the crisis and their future orientation might serve as a benchmark for other economies in their clusters. Furthermore, we cannot detect a clear geographic pattern in the overall analysis. The Baltic States do show some homogeneity in certain subgroups, as do the Black Sea abutters Bulgaria and Romania. Nevertheless, there is no clear and persistent geographical structure visible comparable to the situation for Western European countries. Turkey, who since many years has been waiting to become a member of the European Union shows in many categories remarkable differences and is allocated to single country clusters. From this observation follows that the tasks ahead of Turkey are still enormous, if it wishes to resemble the future orientation of the three pillars towards Europe.

Future research should concern within-the-cluster analyses in order to show rankings in the specific groups and point to bottlenecks or benchmark situations. With the help of linear programming tools such a ranking can be performed which will allow to evaluate the relative strength of single economies in their clusters concerning their future orientation. A dynamic analysis could further help to detect the changes in these patterns in time. In particular the current financial and economic crisis very likely will change the current pattern due to different defence strategies. Looking at the shifts produced and the country structures which have proven to be better suited to cope with the crisis might be an insightful goal for future research.

The empirical analysis of the capabilities of the EU countries in achieving the goals of the Lisbon Agenda presented here allows for the design of a sound, well balanced and differentiated policy. This policy design, on the one hand, avoids being too general in the sense of neglecting the heterogeneity of countries in the European Union. On the other hand, it considerably reduces the complexity which stems from this heterogeneity by grouping countries with similar pillar compositions. This allows for a well-adapted design of policy measures according to the specificities of the various country groups identified in Europe and differing according to their innovativeness and future-orientation (i.e. their capabilities to achieve the goal of the Lisbon Agenda). The development of policy designs following CNSE is certainly on the agenda for future research.

Appendix   Indicators used in the analysis

Knowledge base

- Students' enrolment at the ISCED levels 5–6 in science, mathematics, and computing, engineering, manufacturing, and construction in per cent of all students, 2003–2004
- Female students' enrolment at the ISCED levels 5–6 in science, mathematics, and computing, engineering, manufacturing, and construction in per cent of all female students, 2003–2004
- Male students' enrolment at the ISCED levels 5–6 in science, mathematics, and computing engineering, manufacturing, and construction in per cent of all male students, 2003–2004
- Graduates (ISCED 5–6) in science and technology in per cent of all fields, 2003–2004
- Female graduates (ISCED 5–6) in mathematics, science and technology in per cent of female graduates in all fields, 2003–2004
- Male graduates (ISCED 5–6) in mathematics, science and technology in per cent of male graduates in all fields, 2003–2004
- Graduates (ISCED 5–6) in science and technology in 1000s, 2003–2004
- Graduates (ISCED 5–6) in mathematics, science and technology per 1000 of population aged 20–29, 2003–2004
- Female graduates (ISCED 5–6) in mathematics, science and technology per 1000 of female population aged 20–29, 2003–2004
- Life-long learning (adult participation in education and training) – percentage of the population aged 25–64 participating in education and training over the four weeks prior to the survey, 2002–2005
- Life-long learning (adult participation in education and training) – females – percentage of the female population aged 25–64 participating in education and training over the four weeks prior to the survey, 2002–2005
- Life-long learning (adult participation in education and training) – males – percentage of the male population aged 25–64 participating in education and training over the four weeks prior to the survey, 2002–2005

- Youth education attainment level – percentage of the population aged 20 to 24 having completed at least upper secondary education, 2002–2005
- Youth education attainment level – females – percentage of the female population aged 20 to 24 having completed at least upper secondary education, 2003–2005
- Youth education attainment level – males – percentage of the male population aged 20 to 24 having completed at least upper secondary education, 2003–2005

Openness

- High-tech exports: exports of high technology products as a share of total exports, 2002–2004

Innovative efforts

- Gross domestic expenditure on R&D (GERD) – percentage of GDP, 2002–2004
- GERD by source of funds – industry – percentage of GERD financed by industry, 2002–2004
- GERD by source of funds – government – percentage of GERD financed by government, 2002–2004
- GERD by source of funds – abroad – percentage of GERD financed by abroad, 2002–2004
- Patent applications to the European Patent Office (EPO) – number of applications per million inhabitants, 2002–2003
- Patents granted by the United States Patent and Trademark Office (USPTO) – number of patents per million inhabitants, 2000–2003
- Percentage of GERD financed by industry in % of GERD, 2002
- Percentage of GERD performed by the Government Sector in % of GERD, 2002
- Percentage of GERD performed by the higher education sector in % of GERD, 2002
- Personnel in R&D in full-time equivalents (FTE), 2003
- Personnel in R&D in head count (HC), 2003
- Personnel in R&D in the business enterprise sector in FTE, 2003
- Personnel in R&D in the government and private non-profit sector in FTE, 2003
- Personnel in R&D in the higher education sector in FTE, 2003
- Number of researchers in FTE, 2003
- Number of researchers per million inhabitants in FTE, 2003
- Number of researchers in HC, 2003
- Number of researchers per million inhabitants in HC, 2003
- Number of researchers in the business enterprise sector in FTE, 2003
- Number of researchers in the government and private non-profit sector in FTE, 2003

- Number of researchers in the higher education sector in FTE, 2003
- Technical personnel in FTE, 2003
- Technical personnel per million inhabitants in FTE, 2003
- Technical personnel in HC, 2003
- Technical personnel per million inhabitants in HC, 2003
- Other R&D personnel in FTE, 2003
- Other R&D personnel in HC, 2003

Financial sector

- Total amount of venture capital invested in €1000, 2004–2005
- Venture capital as a percentage of GDP, 2004–2005

Public sector

- Inequality of income distribution – ratio of total income received by the 20% of the population with the highest income to that received by the 20% of the population with the lowest income, 2003
- At-risk-of-poverty rate before social transfers – total – share of persons with an equivalized disposable income, before social transfers, below the risk-of-poverty threshold, 2003
- Early school-leavers – percentage of the population aged 18–24 with at most lower secondary education and not in further education or training, 2003–2005
- Early school-leavers – females – percentage of the female population aged 18–24 with at most lower secondary education and not in further education or training, 2002–2004
- Early school-leavers – males – percentage of the male population aged 18–24 with at most lower secondary education and not in further education or training, 2003–2006
- Comparative price levels – comparative price levels of final consumption by private households including indirect taxes (EU-25=100), 2002–2005
- Market integration – trade integration of goods – average value of imports and exports of goods divided by GDP, multiplied by 100, 2005
- Market integration – trade integration of services – average value of imports and exports of services divided by GDP, multiplied by 100, 2005
- Employment rate – total – employed persons aged 15–64 as a share of the total population of the same age group, 2002–2005
- Employment rate – females – employed women aged 15–64 as a share of the total female population of the same age group, 2002–2005
- Level of internet access – households – percentage of households who have Internet access at home, 2004–2005
- ICT expenditure – IT – expenditure on information technology as a percentage of GDP, 2003–2004
- ICT expenditure – telecommunications – expenditure on telecommunications technology as a percentage of GDP, 2003–2005

- E-government usage by individuals – total – percentage of individuals aged 16–74 using the Internet for interaction with public authorities, 2004–2006
- E-government usage by individuals – females – percentage of individuals aged 16–74 using the Internet for interaction with public authorities, 2004–2006
- E-government usage by individuals – males – percentage of individuals aged 16–74 using the Internet for interaction with public authorities, 2004–2006
- E-government usage by enterprises – percentage of enterprises which use the Internet for interaction with public authorities, 2004–2006
- Broadband penetration rate – number of broadband lines subscribed in percentage of the population, 2004–2006
- Total greenhouse gas emissions – index of greenhouse gas emissions and targets in CO_2 equivalents (actual base year = 100), 2001–2004
- Energy intensity of the economy – gross inland consumption of energy divided by GDP (index, 1995=100) Kgoe (kilogram of oil equivalent) per 1000 euro, 2001–2004
- Share of electricity from renewables to gross electricity generation: ratio between the electricity produced from renewable energy and the gross national electricity consumption, 2001–2004
- GDP per capita in PPS – GDP per capita in purchasing power standards (PPS), (EU-25=100), 2003–2006
- Real GDP growth rate – growth rate of GDP volume – percentage change on previous year, 2003–2006
- Labour productivity per person employed – GDP in PPS per person employed relative to EU-25 (EU-25=100), 2004–2006
- Employment growth – total – annual percentage change in total employed population, 2002–2005
- Employment growth – females – annual percentage change in female employed population, 2003–2005
- Employment growth – males – annual percentage change in male employed population, 2003–2005
- Public balance – net borrowing/lending of consolidated general government sector as a percentage of GDP, 2002–2005
- General government debt – general government consolidated gross debt as a percentage of GDP, 2002–2005

Notes

1 A complete listing of all utilized data sources can be found in the Appendix to this chapter.
2 A similar approach has been applied in Balzat and Pyka (2006) in an analysis of national innovation systems.

References

Balzat, M. and Pyka, A. (2006) Mapping national innovation systems in the OECD area. *International Journal of Technology and Globalisation* 2(1/2): 158–176.

Dopfer, K., Foster, J. and Potts, J. (2004) Micro-meso-macro. *Journal of Evolutionary Economics* 14: 263–279.

Hanusch, H. and Pyka, A. (2006) Comprehensive Neo-Schumpeterian economics and the Lisbon-Agenda: detecting patterns of varying future-orientation in Europe. *Galileu Revista de Economia e Direito* XI(1): 17–40.

Hanusch, H. and Pyka, A. (2007a) The principles of Neo-Schumpeterian economics. *Cambridge Journal of Economics* 31: 275–289.

Hanusch, H. and Pyka, A. (2007b) The troika of economic growth and development: applying a comprehensive Neo-Schumpeterian approach to OECD countries. *Galileu Revista de Economia e Direito* XII: 17–40.

Hanusch, H. and Pyka, A. (eds) (2007c) *The Elgar Companion to Neo-Schumpeterian Economics*. Cheltenham: Edward Elgar Publishers.

Jobson, J. D. (1992) *Applied Multivariate Data Analysis, Volume II: Categorical and Multivariate Methods*. Berlin: Springer.

Saviotti, P. P. and Pyka, A. (2008) Product variety, competition and economic growth. *Journal of Evolutionary Economics* 18(3): 323–347.

3 The economic diversification and innovation system of Turkey from a global comparative perspective

Dominik Hartmann

Introduction

Recent empirical research in economics has shown that economic diversification is a key determinant for economic growth, inequality reduction and human development (Hidalgo *et al.* 2007; Hidalgo and Hausmann 2009; Frenken *et al.* 2007; Rodrik 2004; Hartmann 2014; Hartmann *et al.* 2015). Economic diversification in turn is determined by the capacity of countries to create, absorb, diffuse and implement knowledge and technology (Freeman 1987; Lundvall 1992; Saviotti and Pyka 2004; Saviotti and Frenken 2008). Consequently, governments and companies should aim to promote innovation systems that allow them to create new products, processes and service and stay competitive in the global markets (Schumpeter 1912; Lundvall 1992; Hartmann 2014). In order to creating new jobs and staying competitive, the European growth strategy aims at making Europe the most dynamic knowledge-based economy in the world (Hartmann 2007; European Commission 2010). While recently the political focus has shifted to short-term solutions of urgent problems like the European financial and political crisis, or more recently the refugee crisis, the need to establish prolific innovation systems and creating knowledge-based jobs continues to be a key challenge. This is not only the case for European Union's member states like Spain, France or Germany, but even more so for accession candidates like Turkey or countries in the Balkans.

This policy-oriented chapter combines empirical data on the innovation performance and complexity of countries with recent approaches from innovation economics in order to discuss the reasons why Turkey should to put more political emphasis on innovation and economic diversification. The main reasons for the case of Turkey are:

- to prevent a deep economic crisis, once the construction boom comes to a halt;
- to facilitate sustained economic and technological catch-up; and
- to open up the way for better mutual understanding and renewed cooperation with the EU.

Turkey has made significant improvements in its technological and productive capabilities in the last decade. Indeed, in 2013 Turkey had a higher level of export diversity than countries such as Greece, Russia and Brazil. Increasingly companies, politicians and academia have put emphasis on innovation and diversification into value added sectors. However, the data shows that there is still a long way to go for Turkey to bridge the gap with the central European member states or reaching also the rapid technological upgrading rates of countries such as Bulgaria or China. For this reason, there is a need for Turkey to put more emphasis on R&D and general education as well as a need to put explicit focus on (i) internal and external knowledge transfers, and (ii) diversification into related sectors which could become a cornerstone of a sustained economic development strategy. After a decade of stability and significant growth, Turkey now has an historic opportunity for technological and economic catch-up. To make this happen, a more widespread awareness of the importance of diversity and innovation is necessary and concerted action between companies, government and academia from different regions and political perspectives should be promoted. Otherwise, its economic success story may result in a deep crisis.

The remainder of this chapter is structured as follows. I first show the economic diversity performance of Turkey in a global comparison. I then explain the reason for the need to focus on economic diversification. After illustrating the relatively weak (though improving) innovation performance of Turkey in comparison with other EU countries, I explain the reasons why the EU puts policy emphasis on knowledge and innovation, and why this is relevant for Turkey. Next I outline a set of innovation and diversification policies. Finally I give concluding remarks and suggests that emphasis on innovation could revitalize the Turkish–EU accession negotiations, by putting the focus on economic win-win situations through international cooperation and innovation networks.

The value of economic diversification

Many empirical and theoretical studies in economics testify to the indispensability of economic diversification for sustained economic growth (Saviotti and Pyka 2004; Saviotti and Frenken 2008; Hidalgo and Hausmann 2009; Hausmann *et al.* 2014). The seminal work of Imbs and Wacziarg (2003) illustrates that countries tend to diversify their economy for most of their development path and only at very high income levels start to specialize. This specialization, though, involves very complex and sophisticated products, often requiring a great variety of inputs and organizational skills.

Economic diversification has a variety of positive effects, such as economic growth, systemic stability and a more even distribution of political power (Hartmann 2014). All these effects are in particular important for emerging countries like Turkey. Many innovation and development economists agree that economic diversification is both a key driver and outcome of economic development (Saviotti 1996). In his seminal works, Joseph Schumpeter (1912, 1939) illustrated that long-run economic development is driven by creative destruction processes, in which the introduction of novelties (new products, processes, inputs, organization and marketing methods) lead to the rise of new sectors and the decline or reshaping of other sectors. Prominent examples are steam engines, railroads, electricity, automobiles or recently information and communication technologies. All of these technologies led to significant changes in the production system and triggered entirely new possibilities for investment, economic growth and job creation (Freeman 1982).

Certainly some sectors become obsolete during this creative destruction process (e.g. stagecoaches for post deliveries), however, in many cases, traditional technologies reorganize and lose their relative share of the market but do not become obsolete. For instance, printed newspapers or books have lost shares due to the Internet and electronic devices, however, they have not become completely obsolete. It can be noted that from the beginning of the Industrial Revolution to the present day, the number of products has massively expanded. The most competitive economies are capable of producing and exporting a huge variety of products and thus also provide their people with a wide variety of occupational choices. Indeed, Adam Smith's concept of the division of labour does not necessarily mean the specialization of countries in just a few products, but rather leads to an enormous number of different occupations and inputs which are necessary to produce these products. Furthermore, several economists such as Jacobs (1969) or Weitzman (1998) have shown how economic development is closely connected to the recombination of ideas and knowledge. Jacobs (1969), in particular illustrates how the access to a diversity of ideas within cities allows for creativity and the rise of new goods and services.

Economic diversification is also needed is in order to prevent major economic crises on the demand side (Pasinetti 1981, 1983). If the growth of an economy is merely driven by the growth in efficiency of the existing sectors, then over time less and less workers are necessary. This decrease is caused first by better routines and increased efficiency in workers, and second by machines that replace workers. This can lead to unemployment, problems on the demand side and social instability. Hence the introduction of new products and sectors is necessary to overcome systemic crises, create jobs and increase demand (Saviotti 1996; Saviotti and Pyka 2004). A more diversified economy is also more capable in dealing with economic shocks or the decline of particular sectors; thus it contributes to economic stability and makes an economy more capable of dealing with uncertainty. This is particularly relevant for Turkey. If Turkey does not manage to significantly increase its economic diversification, it might run into a deep economic crisis when the construction and housing boom levels out. This is precisely the problem in the current economic crises of countries, such as Portugal or Spain. Once the housing bubble in these countries has burst, workers, especially the low skilled, were unable to find work in other sectors, because they did not exist. The disruption in demand by both unemployment as well as the steep cuts in the income of house owners further reduces demand, entering into a vicious circle, which could only be overcome by the rise of new sectors.

Finally, economic diversification tends to favour democracy building and social welfare, by distributing economic and political power among more agents and requiring the establishment of more democratic institutions (Hartmann 2014; Hartmann *et al.* 2015). Economies with a varied set of different sectors tend to become more democratic, as different economic groups gain in economic, political and creative power. In order to produce a varied set of goods and service in a globally competitive way, it is necessary to have a great variety of specialized and inter-connecting skills in different sectors, such as infrastructure, universities, laboratories, suppliers, design, machinery, chemistry, ICT and marketing. To some degree this can be internalized within huge industrial conglomerates or companies. However, the last decades have shown that in order to become com-petitive, many activities need to be outsourced and be produced by more flexible small and medium enterprises. Sometimes these SMEs and their workers themselves become powerful economic agents. Examples of this can be seen with the automobile supplier Bosch, which became itself a powerful agent, or the thousands of millionaires created by the success of the IT services company Infosys in India, which made many of its employees and shareholders wealthy as well.

This dynamic occurred many times during different periods of the Industrial Revolution that saw profound economic, social and political transformation, with the rise of new economic agents, favouring a more democratic system. Innovation and diversification seldom can be accomplished by planning alone, but requires drawing upon the creativity of the people and innovation systems in which all agents from public and private institution can learn from each other. For this reason, good education systems are needed to be able to provide both the general and specialized skills to make economic diversity viable. A well-educated population then favours more democratic systems. In contrast, countries that are very dependent on a few resource-exploiting economic sectors tend to establish and reproduce very hierarchic power structures that are based rather on economic rent-seeking than on interactive learning and knowledge.

The examples of some oil-rich countries (such as Russia, Nigeria and several Arab countries) show that resource richness together with a lack of economic incentives to diversify – for instance owing to monopoly powers and close relations between political and economic elites – leads to top-down structures with comparatively low levels of innovation. The rich have no incentive to change the system, the poor and low educated are not able to and the small fraction of the middle class searches for social stability and is driven into oppor-tunistic rent-seeking and risk minimizing behaviour. This leads to a vicious circle, with low levels of opportunity based innovation, and economic stagnancy. Some might mention China as a country with a high rate of technological upgrading and innovation, but with a hierarchic political system. However, it should not be forgotten that China still has serious problems with poverty and inequality. The average per capita income in China is US$7,476, having both some very rich and many poor Chinese citizens (UNDP 2011). For the next development step, a better distribution of wealth, higher levels of individual freedom and a more egalitarian and democratic organization will be necessary in order to establish a knowledge-based economy and achieve more widespread welfare. Having a more democratic society, with educated and empowered people, facilitates creative skills and interactive learning and thus a more innovative and diversified economy.

The economic diversification of Turkey in a global comparison

A significant advance in the measurement of economic diversity and productive development was made by a group of researchers around Ricardo Hausmann and Cesar Hidalgo at the Harvard Center of International Development and the MIT Media Lab. They show with the help of large export data sets and network analysis techniques that the position in the global product space and sectoral diversification are key explanatory factors for the economic growth of countries over time (Klinger and Hausmann 2006; Hidalgo *et al.* 2007). In the so-called Economic Complexity Index in 2008, Turkey ranked 43rd out of 128 countries (Hidalgo and Hausmann 2009; Hausmann *et al.* 2014). This indicator measures both the number and quality of sectors in which the country exports. In this way, the measures take into account differences in country size and product quality by using thresholds of revealed comparative advantage instead of absolute export values (Hidalgo and Hausmann 2009; Hausmann *et al.* 2014). Measuring the variety and quality of the products a country exports seems to be indeed a good proxy indicator for the productive capabilities of countries. It infers the productive capabilities of countries by measuring whether the country merely exports standardized agricultural products or whether it is capable of producing and exporting a varied set of complex products such as machinery or chemical products. In 2013, Japan, Switzerland and Germany showed the highest economic complexity scores (see Table 3.1). Their technological knowledge, education and institutions and other factors allow these countries to achieve competitive advantages in many sectors and sell large quantities of varied products to the global market. Turkey's position is at number 40 in the economic complexity ranking, significantly behind central European countries and other large developing countries such as China (22nd) or Mexico (23rd). However, it is noteworthy that Turkey places in front of other large emerging economies like Brazil (56th) and India (50th), and also in front of other European member and potential candidate states such as Greece (48th), Macedonia (61) or Albania (75th). Moreover, its level of economic complexity is close to the ones of Portugal (37th) and Bulgaria (39th).

Furthermore, over the last decades Turkey has significantly increased its export portfolio in terms of both quantity and quality. Figure 3.1 (acquired from MIT's Observatory of Complexity) shows the steep increase in the overall level of exports from US$2 billion in 1977 to US$34 billion in 2002 to US$152 billion in 2013. Apart from further augmenting its exports of textiles, it has also significantly increased in mining, chemical and health related products, construction materials and equipment and machinery and metal products. This positive export diversification has helped Turkey to move up in the economic complexity ranking from 54th in 1977 to 51st in 2002 and to 40th in 2013.

Table 3.1 Position of Turkey in the economic complexity ranking 2013.

Rank	Country (EU accession)	Complexity value
EU member states, Japan and USA		
1	Japan (N/A)	2.29217
2	Switzerland (N/A)	2.15827
3	Germany (1952)	1.95057
5	United Kingdom (1973)	1.58
11	France (1952)	1.49
13	United States (N/A)	1.47
25	Croatia (acceding)	0.99
26	Romania (2007)	0.93
32	Spain (1986)	0.93
37	Portugal (1986)	0.69
39	Bulgaria (2007)	0.58
48	Greece (1981)	0.19
EU (potential) accession candidates		
40	**Turkey**	**0.466553**
41	Bosnia and Herzegovina	0.414588
61	Macedonia	−0.0212555
75	Albania	−0.342037
Other large developing countries		
22	China	0.964874
23	Mexico	0.950146
38	Russia	0.547873
50	India	0.261756
56	Brazil	0.152432
72	Indonesia	−0.249507
92	Iran	−0.738944

Source: data from atlas.media.mit.edu

A further positive prediction made by the Atlas of Economic Complexity (Hausmann *et al.* 2014) is that Turkey could achieve a considerable average economic growth rate (of approximately 2.83% per year between 2009 and 2020) by closing its holes in the product space. This means that Turkey is already producing several intermediate products and is building up systemic production capabilities that are necessary diversify into more complex products. However, the overall distance to the most diversified economies such as Germany and Japan is still huge. Moreover, according to the predictions of Hausmann *et al.* (2014), Turkey does not reach the expected economic growth rates of some EU member states such as Bulgaria (3.30%) and Romania (3.39%), or developing countries such as India (4.26%) or China (4.32%).

Now the question arises how Turkey can further promote its economic diversification. One key task is to upgrade the technological and innovation

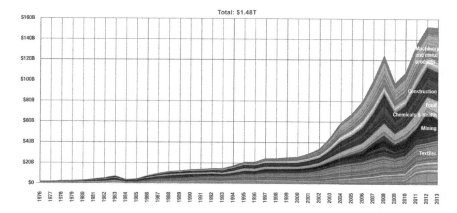

Figure 3.1 Evolution of Turkish exports from 1976 to 2013.

Source: The Observatory of Economic Complexity (http://atlas.media.mit.edu, accessed 15 November 2015)

capabilities of companies, scientists and regions. However, to establish innovation and diversification as key goals, another fundamental question must be addressed first: why should the Turkish decision makers, policy makers, and opinion leaders promote economic diversification?

Turkey's innovation capabilities in comparison with EU and emerging market countries

Economic diversification is closely connected with countries' innovation capabilities. Without the introduction of novelties into the production system, diversification is very difficult to obtain. For this reason, if a country wants to attain diversified and competitive economies, it needs to establish innovation systems, in which the network of its public and private institutions, companies, universities and civil society manage to generate, implement and diffuse new technologies and knowledge (Freeman 1987). Indeed, across the world, companies and governments increasingly put innovation and technology at the core of their economic development strategy. The promotion of technology and innovation forms the key rationale in common between the growth strategies of the European Union since 2000 and also fast growing economies such as China and India. Before turning to the political focus of the EU (as it regards to innovation), it is useful to first look at the empirical data on Turkey's innovation capabilities in a global comparison.

Many company managers, researchers and the government in Turkey are increasingly becoming aware of the urgent need to upgrade technological capabilities and to diversify in order to maintain the growth dynamics. For instance, the goal of the Turkish government's National Science, Technology and

Innovation Strategy 2011–2016 is "to contribute to new knowledge and develop innovative technologies to improve the quality of life by transforming the former into products, processes, and services for the benefit of the country and humanity" (Tübitak 2010). Some progress has been made, for instance in creating internationally competitive universities, technology parks and research centres. As the EU Innovation Union Competitiveness Report 2011 states:

> The growth of the Turkish research and innovation system is evidenced in all the main indicators. Turkey improved at a higher rate than the other countries with comparable industrial structure and knowledge capacity, in particular in human resources for research and innovation.
>
> (Cited in Kara 2012)

However, actual knowledge and innovation performance is still weak, as seen in the huge distance between Turkey and technology leaders like Germany. For instance, whereas 2,672 applications for European Patent Office (EPO) patents at the EPO between 1978 and 2010 came from Turkey, 1.5 million applications came from Germany. A technological gap, which appears even more aggravated when we take into account the fact that a significant number of these few Turkish patent applications (only 0.03% of EPO patents) are often driven by foreign companies, such as Ford, Bosch or Daimler. The number of Turkey's patents has been growing exponentially in recent years; however, the explosion in patents is a phenomenon all across the world, and Turkey still faces a long but necessary journey in order to come close to the technological capabilities of the most competitive economies. Furthermore, other EU member countries in close geographically proximity like Bulgaria and Romania have shown significantly higher absolute performances as well as growth rates. Turkey ranks 69th out of 145 countries in World Bank's 2012 Knowledge Economy Index (see Table 3.2).

This index consists of indicators pertaining to the economic incentive regimes, innovation achievements, education and ICT (further detailed information is available at http://web.worldbank.org). Figure 3.2 allows for the comparison of both the absolute and relative progress of Turkey between 1995 and 2012 in comparison with other European and Central Asian countries. On the horizontal axis is the performance in the knowledge economy index in 1995 and on the vertical axis the performance in 2012 is illustrated. We can see that Turkey falls significantly behind other European countries in this index and could not show the same improvements in this period as found in Bulgaria, Romania, Spain or Germany. This shows that Turkey has a long way to go in its transition towards a knowledge-based economy, deriving its income from high-value added activities based in knowledge and technology.

In addition, Turkey has one of the lowest places in the ranking on the EU's Innovation Union Scoreboard (Pro Inno Europe 2012; see Table 3.3). This composite indicator considers a more comprehensive variety of indicators on different dimensions of innovation inputs and outputs of European and some comparative countries. The innovation summary index consists of innovation

Table 3.2 Performance in World Bank's Knowledge Economy Index 2012.

Rank	Country	Knowledge Economy Index	Economic Incentive Regime	Innovation	Education	ICT
EU member states, Japan and USA						
1	Sweden	9.43	9.58	9.74	8.92	9.49
2	Finland	9.33	9.65	9.66	8.77	9.22
8	Germany	8.9	9.1	9.11	8.2	9.17
12	United States	8.77	8.41	9.46	8.7	8.51
14	United Kingdom	8.76	9.2	9.12	7.27	9.45
21	Spain	8.35	8.63	8.23	8.82	7.73
22	Japan	8.28	7.55	9.08	8.43	8.07
24	France	8.21	7.76	8.66	8.26	8.16
30	Italy	7.89	7.76	8.01	7.58	8.21
34	Portugal	7.61	8.42	7.62	6.99	7.41
36	Greece	7.51	6.8	7.83	8.96	6.43
39	Croatia	7.29	7.35	7.66	6.15	8
44	Romania	6.82	7.39	6.14	7.55	6.19
45	Bulgaria	6.8	7.35	6.94	6.25	6.66
EU (potential) accession candidates						
49	Serbia	6.02	4.23	6.47	5.98	7.39
57	Macedonia (FYR)	5.65	5.73	4.99	5.15	6.74
69	**Turkey**	**5.16**	6.19	5.83	4.11	4.5
70	Bosnia and Herzegovina	5.12	5.55	4.38	5.77	4.77
82	Albania	4.53	4.69	3.37	4.81	5.26
Other large developing countries						
55	Russian Federation	5.78	2.23	6.93	6.79	7.16
60	Brazil	5.58	4.17	6.31	5.61	6.24
72	Mexico	5.07	4.88	5.59	5.16	4.65
84	China	4.37	3.79	5.99	3.93	3.79
94	Iran, Islamic Rep.	3.91	0.73	5.02	4.61	5.28
108	Indonesia	3.11	3.47	3.24	3.2	2.52
110	India	3.06	3.57	4.5	2.26	1.9

Source: World Bank's Knowledge Assessment Methodology 2012 (http://info.worldbank.org/etools/ kam2/KAM_page5.asp, retrieved on 16 February 2013)

enablers (such as human resources, open research systems and finance), firm activities (such as firm investments, linkages and entrepreneurship or IPCs held by companies) as well as output (such as economic effects in sales or the number of companies innovating).

Thus, this indicator also shows a significant gap between Turkey and other European countries in its technological and innovative capabilities. This leads to questions about innovation and policy. Why is innovation so important and why should policy makers and firm managers promote innovation?

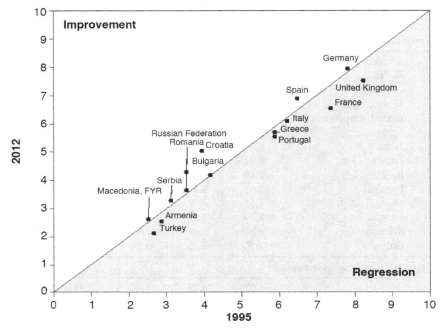

Figure 3.2 Comparative performance of Turkey in the Knowledge Economy Index.

Source: World Bank's Knowledge Assessment Methodology 2012 (http://info.worldbank.org/
etools/kam2/KAM_page5.asp, accessed 16 February 2013)

Lack of innovation in the Turkey–EU debate

It is worth noting that innovation and technology is not a key topic in the political debate on Turkey–EU relations. It seems that rather weak focus has been put on this core economic strategy of the European Union. This is understandable given the other more urgent daily problems and the increasing (though still small) percentage of Turkish scholars working on innovation. However, more emphasis on innovation and upgrading into a knowledge-based economy seems crucial to understanding the EU goals and promoting the EU–Turkey accession negotiations. While the EU holds discussions with Turkey about border management, human rights and the chapters of negotiations, the central European member states officials have been discussing among themselves in the last decades about economic competitiveness, innovation and job creation. Refocusing the discussion on these common economic interests of both the EU and Turkey may also help to reinforce the EU–Turkey negotiations. Of course, putting innovation higher on the agenda needs time, as these topics for instance have not been core

Table 3.3 Performance in the Innovation Union Scoreboard indicators.

Rank 2011	Country	2007	2011	Change 2007–2011	Human resources	Research systems	Finance and support	Firm investments	Linkages and entrepreneurship	Intellectual assets	Innovators	Economic effects
Innovation leaders												
1	Switzerland	0.78	0.83	0.07	0.85	1.00	0.59	0.79	0.61	0.95	1.00	0.85
2	Sweden	0.75	0.75	0.01	0.89	0.82	0.90	0.69	0.79	0.80	0.56	0.62
3	Germany	0.66	0.70	0.06	0.61	0.55	0.58	0.64	0.63	0.79	0.99	0.74
Innovation followers												
6	United Kingdom	0.62	0.62	0.00	0.73	0.79	0.70	0.45	0.84	0.47	0.31	0.61
7	Netherlands	0.57	0.60	0.05	0.64	0.87	0.70	0.31	0.59	0.68	0.37	0.57
8	Austria	0.58	0.60	0.03	0.59	0.65	0.51	0.51	0.63	0.77	0.61	0.47
10	France	0.51	0.56	0.10	0.68	0.66	0.64	0.40	0.51	0.49	0.47	0.57
11	**EU average**	**0.52**	**0.54**	**0.04**	**0.56**	**0.53**	**0.58**	**0.44**	**0.49**	**0.55**	**0.51**	**0.59**
Moderate innovators												
16	Italy	0.41	0.44	0.07	0.43	0.43	0.35	0.29	0.39	0.52	0.56	0.48
17	Portugal	0.34	0.44	0.29	0.45	0.48	0.52	0.32	0.46	0.35	0.72	0.37
19	Spain	0.40	0.41	0.02	0.44	0.54	0.47	0.26	0.25	0.41	0.33	0.47
21	Greece	0.33	0.34	0.04	0.48	0.33	0.19	0.22	0.46	0.14	0.67	0.35
23	Croatia	0.26	0.31	0.19	0.53	0.18	0.28	0.29	0.40	0.09	0.40	0.37
Modest innovators												
26	Romania	0.23	0.26	0.16	0.40	0.15	0.24	0.41	0.10	0.07	0.17	0.49
29	Bulgaria	0.17	0.24	0.38	0.46	0.19	0.16	0.31	0.09	0.20	0.11	0.31
25	Serbia	0.25	0.28	0.12	0.39	0.35	0.67	0.23	0.21	0.02	0.09	0.38
28	Macedonia (FYR)	0.23	0.25	0.12	0.33	0.11	0.00	0.24	0.18	0.02	0.48	0.39
31	**Turkey**	**0.18**	**0.21**	**0.18**	**0.07**	**0.21**	**0.39**	**0.08**	**0.22**	**0.10**	**0.56**	**0.27**

Source: data from PRO INNO Europe (2012)

topics in Turkey's university research and education on the European Union and International Relations. However, the business and policy making world is increasingly aware of the crucial role of innovation for economic development. Turkey has, for instance, taken the chairmanship of EUREKA, an EU research and innovation initiative which subsidies applied research for European companies engaging in research projects with two or more European partners.

Innovation and diversification policies

Without a significant upgrade in its innovation capabilities, the recent growth of Turkey is at risk of eventually ending. In this scenario, Turkey runs the risk of entering the same housing bubble burst and economic crisis that Spain did. To sustain Turkey's growth and diversify into higher value added sectors, there is an urgent need to make innovation a top priority in economic and social policy making. This entails placing a strong emphasis on knowledge, innovation networks and diversity of ideas. Accordingly, the Turkish government, companies and society need to find together a proper mix of internal and external capability upgrading and an appropriate industrial diversification strategy. This economic growth strategy must stress the indispensability of diversification into both related and unrelated sectors across the Turkish regions (Gülcan *et al.* 2010). A requisite for this is the promotion of qualitative entrepreneurship and finding a proper coordination of tasks between the regional and national governments (Rodrik 2004; Frenken *et al.* 2007; Lin and Monga 2011). The following sections outline a set of policy tasks that are recommended.

Emphasis on education and applied R&D

In order to raise the quality and quantity of R&D, the government needs to introduce incentives and subsidies. Beyond the establishment of critical infrastructures (such as laboratories) the government need to promote an institutional environment that allows freedom and demands creativity, while at the same time enabling young early career researchers, for instance, to reap the fruits of their efforts. There is also a need for the government to provide incentives for companies to promote training, applied R&D and learning by doing as key factors needed for innovation (Arrow 1962). For this reason, emphasis should be put on the establishment of technical training facilities and deliberate learning and innovation processes in companies should be enabled. Whereas R&D and technical training are crucial to achieving innovation, establishing a decent level of education is even more important to raise the interactive knowledge generation of the society and the productivity of the economy. An average duration of schooling years in Turkey of merely 6.5 years (UNDP 2011) is simply too low for it to be a leading economy. In 2003, Turkey made a school curriculum reform aiming to promote the quality of education, but still the implementation must be improved and further reforms must be made. Naturally, this is a slow and difficult process, as it requires the establishment of an appropriate infrastructures, the education of the teachers and appropriate tools to fully apply a new curriculum, promoting creativity and critical thinking, in the classroom. A well-performing innovation system requires a creative, well-educated and proactive labour force. This is not only necessary for production but it is also indispensable for having pro-active consumers. The innovativeness of an economy does not only depend on the technology by governments and companies, but it also flourishes with the critique and advice from the consumers. Modern technologies and changes increasingly result from the feedback and interactive learning between producers with well-educated and informed consumers. For this reason, it is beneficial to actively promote the rights, influences, wages and skills of consumers. In addition, a more widespread and better education system also introduces more meritocratic structures into an innovation system, by allowing more people to enter into the competition for good positions and qualitative entrepreneurship. Unequal access to higher education hampers the competition for good results and positions. Accordingly, more people should have the basic educational skills, such as functional literacy, critical and analytic thinking in order to being able to compete, cooperate and being creative. It is worth noting that a better and more widespread education also allows more people to cooperate in R&D projects and qualitative ventures, by being able to understand more complex details. Increasing access to and quality of education, as well as R&D, generates considerable costs. Yet undertaking these burdens are indispensable for Turkey's transformation into a leading economy.

Embedded autonomy of the state and cooperation between science, government and businesses

While competition can introduce important dynamics for knowledge creation and innovation into an economy, equal cooperation is a driving force for prolific innovation systems. Since, virtually no company is capable of maintaining an overview and mastery of all the relevant technologies and information in the modern world, deliberate focus should be put on R&D collaboration between academics, companies and government agencies, between different regions and different sectors. In fact, several initiatives to promote technology parks, such as the technology development zones law have been made (e.g. Tübitak 2011); however, the interaction between the government, academia and companies must still be improved significantly, to understand the needs and demands of each other as well as to create and diffuse new technologies through interactive learning and problem-solving activities. This involves a more science-based political decision process along with concerted action by the different implied economic agents to achieve critical masses and competitiveness in new sectors. Promoting an embedded autonomy of the state can be a crucial driver for the future-orientation of an economy (Evans 1995; Rodrik 2004). While free market forces can certainly be a powerful mechanism for the promotion of innovation and productivity, achieving the initial critical masses to make the emergence of new sectors viable often requires the initial help of future-oriented states. For instance, the initial investment in the necessary infrastructure, such as basic research facilities and laboratories, is often too expensive for single firms. For this reason, governments – in close cooperation with researchers and the business sector – need to identify into which sectors the economy is able to and should diversify. One question that a country's set of agents must answer is to what degree they aim at upgrading existing sectors and diversifying into related sectors (i.e. for instance moving from food processing to global food design brands) and to what degree the government should enable the emergence of entirely new activities and sectors (i.e. unrelated variety, which is for instance moving into in bio- or nanotechnology). To answer these questions the government needs to work both in close cooperation with existing companies and research facilities in order to have enough understanding about the endogenous capabilities of its country. However, the government, companies and universities also need the necessary autonomy in order to overcome the influence of both too much corporate or government interference, and to stop investing into unsuccessful activities (Rodrik 2004).

Empower regional policy makers and the collaboration between the national and regional governments

Finding a proper mix of promoting related and unrelated economic variety growth goes together with an appropriate coordination of tasks and concerted action of national or regional governments in promoting innovation and sectoral strategies. Considering the huge economic inequality and diversity within Turkey, there are good reasons for Turkey to empower the regions and their capacities to engage in diversification policies, making use of their respective skill sets. This is especially important for promoting related variety growth. Often regional policy makers and companies know best what works in their regions, where bottlenecks are and where there are opportunities (Boschma 2004). But of course they also require support and new information from outside. As such, the national government should help and promote interactive learning between different regions. It is worth noting that many EU countries have a multi-layered government structure with policies on the EU, the national and regional levels. Strong regional governments are important drivers of new ideas, competition, cooperation and diversity.

Pushing related variety growth and cross-linkages

Typically companies, regions or countries cannot jump easily into radically new technologies or industries (Hidalgo *et al.* 2007). Thus, the emphasis on understanding and making use of the opportunity for related variety growth are key for employment generation and cumulative technological upgrading (Frenken *et al.* 2007). As mentioned above, related variety growth refers to the introduction of new products, processes and sectors that are similar to the previously existing sectors and or require a similar knowledge base (ibid.). Examples may be the introduction of pears where there are apples or the upgrading of these products into jams or juice, or introducing a variety of new types of electronic appliances and car parts. This is especially important for the immediate generation of income and increasing the sophistication of a sector. This requires the constant improvement of products and processes and the deliberate promotion of testing new similar products. It also requires the establishment of specialized research institutions, the deliberate promotion of spin-off companies as well as empowering the regional government. Importantly, related variety growth can also create bridges between formerly disconnected sectors. For this reason, bridging technologies, such as (industrial) design or metrologies or logistics technologies, should be promoted. It is of note that sometimes governmental policy papers present internationally fashionable sectors such as ICT or Nanotechnology as their key technology goals; however the crucial importance of general purpose and bridging technologies in upgrading the existing sectors and making new ones viable is often neglected. Cross-cutting technologies, such as design or measurement technologies, are necessary to link different industries and to reach systemic competitiveness.

Enabling unrelated variety growth

The national and regional governments should also create a seedbed for the emergence of entirely new sectors. Naturally, radical innovation can hardly be planned, as we cannot precisely foresee what will be radically new and commercially successful technologies in the future, or otherwise they wouldn't be radically new. However, governments, civil society and companies can increase the probability of innovation by facilitating creativity, diversity and cooperation. Interactive learning and creativity can be promoted by more horizontal power structures, empowerment and freedom of expression, as well as both widespread and elite education. Furthermore, a large number of technologies and sectors may not yet exist in a country, but that country may nonetheless have all the important ingredients needed to master them. Accordingly, Lin and Monga (2011) suggest that national governments should produce what other countries with similar resources endowments, but significantly higher incomes, produce and focus on what could be learnt from them (ibid.). Furthermore, there are of course new sectors such as ICT, renewable energies or biotechnology in which Turkey should not let itself be left behind and which can trigger further waves of innovation. Most regional governments alone however, do not have the means to fund the necessary investments in infrastructure and frontier basic and applied research facilities needed to let unrelated variety growth happen.

Promote outward-oriented research and development policies

A point that has often been missed by previous import-substitution approaches (meant to fostering the development of the national industrial structure) are the positive effects of outward-oriented investment and innovation strategies. Inward-oriented development is often not sufficient and would deprive companies of an enormous source of knowledge inputs and partners from whom to learn from. By promoting the building of R&D facilities by Turkish companies abroad or encouraging contact between Turkish scientists and entrepreneurs, new knowledge and international innovation networks can be created. Ann-Lee Saxenian (2006) has shown, for instance, that many of the Indian entrepreneurs in Silicon Valley build up and link also to companies in India, and not only in the United States. It is through these means that these so-called commuting entrepreneurs trigger knowledge transfers between more central and peripheral regions, promote business relations and promote economic win-win situations. Indeed, Turkey has a huge diaspora abroad, yet the possibility of members of the diaspora becoming innovators and bridge builders is still underexploited. Beneficial economic win-win situations can result from knowledge migration, transnational entrepreneurs and innovation networks between Turkey and Germany. Indeed, leading global companies increasingly engage not only in asset exploiting activities, based on lower wages and resources in other countries, but also deliberately engage in asset expanding activities, profiting from the creativity and knowledge in other countries (Cantwell *et al.* 2004). Thus, while the promotion of local knowledge generation is important, also outward-oriented strategies, investing in R&D facilities can be very beneficial for the domestic knowledge upgrading and innovation.

Trigger entrepreneurship and self-discovery processes

A key task for the promotion of economic development in less developed regions is the promotion of self-discovery processes (Hausmann and Rodrik 2003). Often it is not so much the lack of R&D itself, but rather risk-minimizing behaviour and lack of knowledge about existing technologies that hamper diversification in less developed regions. Many entrepreneurs and companies merely engage in very similar activities to the companies around them in order to minimize the risk of failure. Simply founding another textile, trade or low-technology agricultural company though may not be enough to sustainably upgrade the regions and promote diversification into more value-added sectors. For instance, a micro-entrepreneur establishing yet another small retailer may indeed help him and his family out of acute poverty. However, at the same time, many economic agents entering into these activities may further lower the already low benefits margins and thereby not allow the micro-entrepreneurs really upgrading into value-added small and medium companies. Accordingly, institutional mechanisms must be developed in such a way to allow trial and error processes for creative companies that aim to enter into new sectors. The Turkish government should promote people and companies in the eastern and central Anatolian regions to find out which nationally and globally existing technologies work in these places and can be produced competitively. This requires deliberately pushing knowledge transfers and experimentation with products in less developed regions and providing the population with social security in case an innovative venture fails.

Conclusion: a historical chance for Turkey's long-run economic development and EU integration

As we have discussed above, there are multiple reasons why countries in general and Turkey in particular needs to promote innovation and economic diversification. No doubt that establishing a competitive innovation system and promoting economic diversification requires considerable financial and political efforts. However, after a decade of high average growth rates Turkey has a historical opportunity for economic catch-up and also further integration as a more equal partner with the EU. Focusing on innovation policies is crucial to achieving this goal. Innovation and diversification policies are important for economic growth and job creation; but they also open up further possibilities for integration with the European Union and the global economy. The reasons why this is the case are manifold. First, because more emphasis on economic diversification brings the debate on Turkey's integration into the EU more in line with the EU Lisbon Agenda and Europe 2020 growth strategy, and promotes discussion on a more equal level. Whereas the EU makes innovation, efficiency and economic growth the priority of the political agenda for its member countries, in the debate with Turkey it focuses on border management, the Middle East and human rights. By deliberately putting innovation and diversification on the top of the agenda of meetings with EU representatives and heads of states, Turkey may draw the attention away from stagnating positions and instead opening up new possibilities for mutual understanding.

Second, focusing on innovation also implies the need to be open for diversity and cooperation, thus it promotes freedom and democracy, some of the key political and social goals of the European Union. Third, innovation also implies enabling both competition and cooperation between different agents and regions of an economy. Accordingly it favours an institutional architecture that engages in multilayered policy-making on the regional, national and international level. Last but not least, focusing on innovation and diversification deliberately promotes transnational entrepreneurship and international cooperation.

In sum, Turkey has made significant advances with respect their innovation performance and economic growth. However, to prevent a systemic crisis and make the next step towards a knowledge-based economy, it needs to deliberately promote interactive learning, innovation, and economic diversification.

Acknowledgements

The author would like to express his gratitude for financial and technical support from the Istanbul Policy Center (IPC)–Mercator Initiative within his fellowship at Mercator–IPC, as well as the BMBF for their financial support within the TUR 10/65 project on Turkish German innovation networks. Moreover he acknowledges support from the Marie Curie International Outgoing Fellowship No. 328828 within the 7th European Community Framework Programme. Any errors are the sole responsibility of the author.

References

Arrow, K. J. (1962) The economic implications of learning by doing. *The Review of Economic Studies* 29(3): 155–173.

Audretsch, D. B. and Thurik, A. R. (2000) Capitalism and democracy in the 21st century: from the managed to the entrepreneurial economy. *Journal of Evolutionary Economics* 10: 17–3.

Boschma, R. (2004) Some reflections on regional innovation policy. Paper prepared for the Expert Group meeting on "Constructing Regional Advantage", Brussels, 7 December 7.

Cantwell, J., Dunning, J. and Janne, O. (2004) Towards a technology-seeking explanation of US direct investment in the United Kingdom. *Journal of International Management* 10: 5–20.

European Commission (2010) *Europe 2020: A Strategy for Smart, Sustainable and Inclusive Growth*. Communication from the Commission. Brussels: European Commission Publications Office.

Evans, P. (1995) *Embedded Autonomy: States and Industrial Transformation*. Princeton, NJ: Princeton University Press.

Freeman, C. (1982) Innovation and long cycles of economic development. International Seminar on Innovation and Development in the Industrial Sector, University of Campinas, 25–27 August.

Freeman, C. (1987) *Technology Policy and Economic Performance: Lessons from Japan*. London: Frances Pinter Publishers.

Frenken K., Van Oort F. and Verburg T. (2007) Related variety, unrelated variety and regional economic growth. *Regional Studies* 41: 685–697.

Gu, S. and Lundvall, B.-Å. (2006) *China's Innovation System and the Move toward Harmonious Growth and Endogenous Innovation*. Working paper. Copenhagen: DRUID. Available at www3.druid.dk/wp/20060007.

Gülcan, Y., Kustepeli, Y. and Akgüngör, S. (2010) The effect of variety on regional economic growth in turkey: a panel data analysis. Presentation at AAG 2010, Washington, DC, 14 April.

Hartmann, D. (2007) Understanding the Lisbon Strategy and policies from a Neo-Schumpeterian point of view. *Revista Universitaria Europea* 7: 15–40.

Hartmann, D. (2014) *Economic Complexity and Human Development: How Economic Diversification and Social Networks Affect Human Agency and Welfare*. New York: Routledge.

Hartmann, D., Guevara, M., Jara-Figueroa, C. and Hidalgo C. (2015) Linking economic complexity, institutions and income inequality. arXiv 1505.07907. Available at http://arxiv.org/pdf/1505.07907.pdf.

Hausmann, R. and Rodrik, D. (2003) Economic development as self-discovery. *Journal of Development Economics* 72(2): 603–633 (doi:10.1016/S0304-3878(03)00124-X).

Hausmann, R., Hidalgo, C. A., Bustos, S., Coscia, M., Simoes, A. and Yildirim, M. A. (2014) *The Atlas of Economic Complexity: Mapping Paths to Prosperity*. Cambridge, MA: MIT Press.

Hidalgo, C. and Hausmann, R. (2009) The building blocks of economic complexity. *PNAS* 106(6): 10570–10575.

Hidalgo, C., Klinger, B., Barabasi, L. and Hausmann, R. (2007) The product space conditions the development of nations. *Science* 317: 482–487.

Imbs, J. and Wacziarg, R. (2003) Stages of diversification. *American Economic Review* 93(1): 63–86.

Jacobs, J. (1969) *The Economy of Cities*. New York: Random House.

Kara, O. (2012) An emerging innovation hub at the crossroads of Europe and Asia. *EUREKA News* 96 (Autumn/Winter). Available at www.eurekanetwork.org/sites/default/files/publications/eureka-news-96.pdf.

Klinger, B. and Hausmann, R. (2006) *Structural Transformation and Patterns of Comparative Advantages*. CID Working paper no. 128. Cambridge, MA: Harvard Center for International Development.

Lin, J. and Monga, C. (2011) Growth identification and facilitation: the role of the state in the dynamics of structural change. *Development Policy Review* 29(3): 264–290.

Lundvall, B.-Å. (1992) *National Systems of Innovation: Towards a Theory of Innovation and Interactive Learning*. London: Frances Pinter Publishers.

Marx, K. (1867) *Das Kapital: Kritik der politischen Ökonomie. Buch I: Der Produktionsprocess des Kapitals*. Hamburg: Verlag Otto Meissner.

Pasinetti, L. L. (1981) *Structural Change and Economic Growth*. Cambridge: Cambridge University Press.

Pasinetti, L. L. (1983) *Structural Economic Dynamics*. Cambridge: Cambridge University Press.

Pro Inno Europe (2010) *European Innovation Scoreboard 2009*. Brussels: European Union.

Pro Inno Europe (2012) *Innovation Union Scoreboard*. Brussels: European Commission.

Rodrik, D. (2004) *Industrial Policy for the 21st Century*. Cambridge, MA: John F. Kennedy School of Government, Harvard University. Available at www.hks.harvard.edu/fs/drodrik/Research%20papers/UNIDOSep.pdf.

Saviotti, P. P. (1996) *Technological Evolution, Variety and the Economy*. Cheltenham: Edward Elgar.

Saviotti, P. P. and Frenken, K. (2008) Export variety and the economic performance of countries. *Journal of Evolutionary Economics* 18(2): 201–218.

Saviotti, P. P. and Pyka, A. (2004) Economic development by the creation of new sectors. *Journal of Evolutionary Economics* 14(1): 1–35.

Saxenian, A. L. (2006) *The New Argonauts: Regional Advantage in a Global Economy*. Cambridge, MA: Harvard University Press.

Schumpeter, J. A. (1912) *Theorie der wirtschaftlichen Entwicklung*. Berlin: Duncker and Humblodt.

Schumpeter, J. A. (1939) *Business Cycles: A Theoretical, Historical and Statistical Analysis* (2 volumes). New York: McGraw-Hill.

Tübitak (2010) *The National Science, Technology and Innovation Strategy (2011–2016)*. December. Ankara: Scientific and Technological Research Council of Turkey.

Tübitak (2011) *Science, Technology and Innovation in Turkey 2010*. Ankara: Scientific and Technological Research Council of Turkey.

UNDP (2011) *Sustainability and Equity: A Better Future for All*. Human Development Report 2011. New York: United Nations Development Programme.

Weitzman, M. L. (1998) Recombinant growth. *Quarterly Journal of Economics* 113: 331–360.

World Economic Forum (2012) *Global Competitiveness Report 2012–2013*. Geneva: World Economic Forum.

4 International trade flows, variety and patent applications

Evidence from Turkey–Germany external trade

Sedef Akgüngör, Yaprak Gülcan and Yeşim Kuştepeli

Introduction

Innovation is a central process in driving economic growth through short-term productivity gains and long-term employment growth and innovative economic activities. In addition to the organizational characteristics of the firms, the environment within which the firms operate is a significant variable in achieving competitiveness. Competitiveness at the regional scale is explained by the presence of clusters of firms, spill-overs and geographic concentration of linked industries, available knowledge and technology (Saltelli, Annoni and Tarantola 2011). There is a positive correlation between regional innovation and regional competitiveness where policy and decision makers recognize the importance of innovation in designing policies to enhance the economic strength and resilience of cities, regions and nations (Seppänen 2008). Innovation process draws on knowledge that is often sourced locally (Almeida and Kogut 1999; Stuart and Sorenson 2003; Brechi and Lissoni 2009) and with strong path dependencies (Boschma and Iammarino 2009; Essletzbichler and Rigby 2007).

Among the factors that explain innovativeness at the regional level, the literature points out the importance of globalization and increase in external trade (Fernandes and Paunov 2010). A reduction in international trade costs and resulting increase in external trade can have significant impacts on the firms' decision to invest in research and development. Other benefits of external trade on innovation is that trade relationships can facilitate knowledge sharing, stronger and denser network ties which creates increased opportunities for developing new products and processes (Atkeson and Burstein 2010). Marquez-Ramos and Martinez-Zarzoso (2009) emphasize the significance of positive relationship between technological innovations and exports. International trade theory highlights the importance of technological innovations in explaining international competitiveness as well (Fagerberg 1995). Economic development is a dynamic process that derives from industry and trace (Schumpeter 1943). New products, new ideas play significant roles in international trade and increased international trade induces skill-based technological change (Acemoğlu 2003). There is empirical evidence on the positive effect of international trade on knowledge flows and exchange of knowledge (Sjöholm 1996).

While external trade can explain regional innovativeness, it is likely that there is a concurrent impact on innovations on external trade as well. Regions where export volume is high, may be more likely to innovate; and innovative regions may be more likely to export. This brings the issue of a simultaneous relationship between exports and innovativeness. The significance of this interaction is important to know in understanding the relationship between exports and patent applications. If exports from a region have a significant impact on patent applications in the region, then it should be true that more patent applications in a region will enhance the region's export performance.

In explaining regional innovations, there is a different stream of literature that points out the importance of variety and change in the technological content of exports. Diversity promotes ideas and innovations. Nourishing effects of diversity on regional growth are more likely to exist when the number of related industries is high enough to enhance the effectiveness of knowledge spillovers (Frenken *et al.* 2007). The literature on agglomeration economies state that growth and diversity go parallel in regions since diversity triggers new ideas, induces knowledge spillovers, and provides valuable resources that are required for innovation to take place (Glaeser *et al.* 1992). Over the past decade, considerable number of academics examined the effect of related variety on regional growth using different variables. The studies found positive interaction between relatedness and growth in many case studies, such as Italy, the Netherlands and Spain (Frenken *et al.* 2007; Saviotti and Frenken 2008; Boschma and Iammarino 2009; Lazzeretti *et al.* 2010; Boschma *et al.* 2012; Akgüngör, Kuştepeli and Gülcan 2013). All studies confirm that relatedness across industries plays a role in regional growth.

The example of Turkey and Germany presents an interesting case study here. Turkey and Germany are two nations with political, military, economic, social, cultural and historical ties along the years. The relationship between Turkey and Germany has gained momentum within the framework of "Contract Labour Migration" that was signed by Turkey and Germany in 1961. Such intensive multi-faceted relations continue today with strong international trade ties as well as Turkish immigrants currently living in Germany. It is therefore evident that there are dense political, economic and cultural relations between Turkey and Germany and long-term trading relationship influences innovation.

The aim of this chapter is to analyse impact of trade on innovativeness in Turkey's regions with specific emphasis on Turkey–Germany trade relationships. This chapter investigates the innovation networks between Turkey and Germany in the context of international trade and economic diversification. Specifically, the research questions that are posed are:

1 Do Turkey's exports to Germany explain innovations at the regional level in Turkey?
2 Does variety in the regions' export composition explain regional innovations?

Both questions are concerned with understanding how regional innovations (and networks) can be improved and increased. If the export volume as well as relatedness across exported goods has a positive impact of a region's innovations, then the policies towards increasing regional innovativeness should be geared towards both promoting exports to Germany as well as making sure that export composition consists of diverse set of goods (variety).

The remainder of the chapter begins with a brief overview of Turkey and Germany trade relationship, after which we provide a theoretical framework and hypotheses. We present our data and an outline of our model, before summarizing the empirical results and reporting our conclusions.

Brief overview of the external trade of Turkey with Germany

Germany is Turkey's largest trading partner among all its trade partners. The share of the value of exports to Germany among Turkey's total export volume was 9.6 per cent in 2014; 9.0 per cent in 2013; 9.6 per cent in 2012; 10.3 per cent in 2011 and 10.1 per cent in 2010. The share of value of imports from Germany is also within the range of 9-10 per cent where Germany ranks as the second largest market in Turkey's imports after Russia. The item that has the highest share in exports to Germany is textile and wearing apparels. The item with highest share in imports from Germany is motor vehicles, followed by chemicals (Turkish Statistics Institute 2015).While Germany has a significant place among all trade partners of Turkey, patent applications of German origin also have a considerably large share within total patent applications in Turkey as well (Figure 4.1). The distribution of patent applications in Turkey across different nations reveals that between 2001 and 2013, the average share of patents of Turkish origin was 26 per cent, while the average share of patents of German origin was 18 per cent followed by US (17%) and France (6%). Except for 2001 and 2002, Germany had the largest share in foreign county patent applications to Turkish Patent Institute (TPE) ranging between 14 per cent and 21 per cent in total applications with mostly production of pharmaceuticals followed by manufacture of chemicals and manufacture of special machinery.

Germany, with more than 5800 firms, is the biggest foreign investor in Turkey. Foreign investment of German origin is mostly in trade and trade brokerage followed by services and construction. With regards to foreign firms in manufacturing industry, the largest number is machinery, chemicals and food (Republic of Turkey, Ministry of Economy 2015).

Trade relations and interactions between Turkey and Germany are likely to continue over the years. Figure 4.2 presents an overview of the composition of export markets of Turkey and change over the years. Although the share of Germany in Turkey's total trade has declined over the years due variety of Turkish export market, historically Germany still continues to have a unique place in Turkey's external trade relations. Figure 4.3 presents the change in Turkey's total value of exports and imports as well as exports and imports to Germany. It can be seen that trade ties with Germany have stayed stable and even

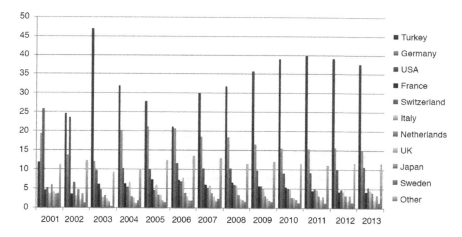

Figure 4.1 Number of patent applications in Turkey and the nationality of the applicants.

increased over the years. In addition, patent and utility model applications as a measure of innovations move together with external trade.

In summary, it is deemed to be important to explore how Turkey–Germany trade relationship contributes to innovation (patent and utility model applications) in Turkey. The findings will provide evidence of whether external trade relationship and particularly exports to Germany has an impact on enhancing regions' innovativeness. This interaction is crucial to know to gear new policies towards developing exports to Germany and at the same time increase potential for further innovations.

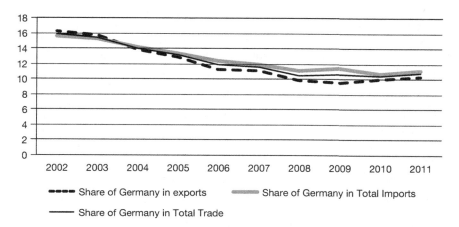

Figure 4.2 Share of Germany in Turkey's total external trade.

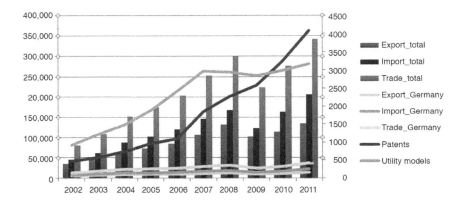

Figure 4.3 Turkey's external trade and innovations (2001–2012 average). Vertical axes show external trade expressed in thousands of euros (left) and number of patent applications (right).

Theoretical framework

The theory puts forward the idea that international trade is not only trade of goods and services but it consists of movement of ideas and innovations. The benefits of international trade on countries' welfare has been a topic of interest since Adam Smith and David Ricardo who have argued that countries benefit from specializing on goods and services in which they have competitive advantage. The theory of international trade and economic growth has been further enhanced with the works of Krugman (1980, 1991) where he contends that countries benefit from trade because the producers benefit from economies of scale and consumers benefit from wider product variety in the market. Neither theory looked specifically on the benefits of trade on exchanging ideas and innovations. Spulber (2010) presents a model where he argues that without international trade in technology, a country's human capital is equal to population multiplied by base productivity. When international trade occurs, human capital increases by the amount of technology.

The model developed by Spulber (2010) shows that innovation and international trade together play an important role in domestic markets where technology trade increases product variety, national income and total gains from trade. Different scholars present the similar idea that technological innovations and international trade go parallel in regions and countries (Egger and Keuschnigg 2011; Damijan and Kostevc 2010).

The literature on innovation and technological change has long emphasized the crucial importance of trade for learning as a process for technological accumulation (Fagerberg 1988). Trade has a positive impact on innovation and growth when comparative advantages lie in sectors in which the region has its greatest potential for learning or when imports in its comparatively disadvantaged sectors provide a competitive stimulus toward more rapid learning. The effects of trade show that the interaction between technology and trade turn into parallel directions as technological competence has a positive impact on regional competitiveness, while international trade boosts the generation and transfer of innovations, giving rise to cumulative causation mechanisms (Dosi and Soete 1988; Fagerberg 1995; Boschma and Iammarino 2009).

Following the theoretical discussions identified above, the chapter asserts that international trade influences regional innovativeness. This leads to Hypothesis 1 in the context of Turkey's export relationship with Germany:

> **Hypothesis 1:** Turkey's exports to Germany has a significant impact on regional innovativeness.

The second hypothesis follows the literature on variety, related variety and unrelated variety that are used to illustrate the interrelations among actors, activities and objects required to describe an economic system. Over the past decade, considerable number of academics examined the effect of related variety on regional growth by using different variables where related variety and unrelated variety are both significant in explaining regional innovations (Castaldi, Frenken and Los 2013). Related variety enhances innovations as related technologies are more easily recombined into new technologies. Unrelated variety enhances technological breakthroughs since radical innovations stem from previously unrelated technologies opening up whole new functionalities and applications. Variety is used to describe and observe changes in the composition of the sectors that make up the economic system (Saviotti and Frenken 2008; Krüger 2008; Silva and Teixeira 2008). Here, the effect of export variety on innovations are tested through Hypothesis 2:

> **Hypothesis 2:** Related variety and unrelated variety in exports has an impact on regional innovativeness.

Data and model

This study takes the definition of innovation as new products and models. Although this is a narrow definition of innovation, availability of secondary data obligates to use the number of patent and utility model applications as a measure of region's innovativeness. Indeed, many authors have used patent and utility models as a proxy for innovations (Soete and Wyatt 1983; Griliches 1990; Eaton and Kortum 1996, 1999; Kortum 1997; Jones 2002; Hagedoorn and Cloodt 2003). Thus, innovation is measured by patent and utility models data, which are obtained from Turkish Patent Institute (TPE) for the period 2002–2011 at the NUTS3 level for 81 provinces of Turkey.

To empirically examine the effect of related and/or unrelated variety of exports on innovation, we use entropy measures. The main advantage of the entropy measure, and the reason for its use in the context of diversification is that entropy can be decomposed at each sectors' digit level. We use export data of Turkey at the four-digit level. The export data is obtained from the Turkish Statistical Institute (TUIK) database and covers the NUTS3 level as the spatial unit of analysis for all 81 provinces for the period 2002–2011. Equations 4.1, 4.2 and 4.3 demonstrate the calculation of entropy measures. Here, P_g is the two-digit share of sectors and p_i is four-digit share, where i is an element of s_g where s_g is the two-digit sector.

$$P_g = \Sigma_{i \in S_g} p_i \tag{4.1}$$

The entropy at the two-digit level, or unrelated variety (*UV*), is given by:

$$UV = \Sigma_{g=1}^{G} P_g \log_2 \left(\frac{1}{P_g}\right) \tag{4.2}$$

Related variety (*RV*), as the weighted sum of entropy within each two-digit sector, is given by:

$$RV = \Sigma_{g=1}^{G} P_g H_g \tag{4.3}$$

where

$$H_g = \Sigma_{i \in S_g} \frac{p_i}{P_g} \log_2 \left(\frac{1}{p_i/P_g}\right) \tag{4.4}$$

Entropy measure implies that four-digit entropy is equal to the sum of two-digit entropy as unrelated variety and the weighted sum of four-digit entropy within each two-digit class as related variety. Related variety is considered to be the indicator for Jacobs's externalities because it measures the variety within each of two-digit classes. The concept of related variety goes beyond the traditional dichotomy of localization economies and Jacobs's externalities (Boschma and Iammarino 2009). Therefore, it is expected that the economies arising from variety are especially strong between subsectors, as knowledge spills over primarily between firms selling related products. By contrast, unrelated variety measures the extent to which a region has a diverse set of different types of activities. Unrelated variety is expected to be an effective tool for regional resilience and a tool to create employment during times of economic crisis (Jacquemin and Berry 1979; Attaran 1986).

The dependent variable of the econometric model is the number of patent and utility models (*P*) in the region. Independent variables are related variety (*RV*), unrelated variety (*UV*) and exports (*EX*) as specified in Equations 4.5 and 4.6.

The econometric model further puts forward that the number of patents determines international trade and more innovative regions are more likely to export. The econometric model therefore accounts for the simultaneous relationship between exports and number of patents as specified below:

$$P_t = b_0 + b_1 RV_t + b_2 UV_t + b_3 EX_t + \varepsilon_t \tag{4.5}$$

$$EX_t = a_0 + a_1 P_t + \gamma_t \tag{4.6}$$

Following the hypotheses outlined above, the econometric model should lead that the coefficient estimators associated with the RV_t, UV_t and EX_t variables will have positive and significant values.

Empirical results

The preliminary investigation of the variables demonstrates that regions are more innovative (as measured by of patent and utility applications) when the value of external trade is high. Figure 4.4 shows the graph of patent and utility model applications on Turkey's NUTS3 regions and corresponding values of exports and imports. The figures are average values of patent and utility applications and external trade volume for the period of 2002–2011.

Figures 4.5 and 4.6 demonstrate the average values of related variety and unrelated variety of Turkey's NUTS3 regions and corresponding patent and utility model applications. The graphs show that there is a positive relationship between patent and utility model applications and variety (both related and unrelated).[1]

In order to derive a quantitative result to explore further the relationship between patent and utility model applications and exports and variety measures, we estimate the econometric model outlined above. The first step of the empirical estimation is to test whether the time series part of the panel data is stationary. To test whether the data is stationary, we use panel unit root tests (Levin, Lin and Chu 2002; Im, Pesaran and Shin 2003; Fisher-type tests using ADF and PP tests). The results demonstrate that there is no need to correct the data to make it stationary.[2]

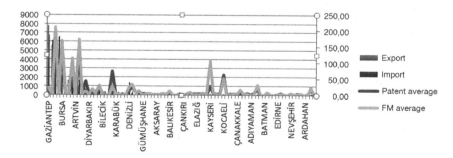

Figure 4.4 External trade and patent and utility model applications (2002–2011 average; Turkey's NUTS3 regions). Vertical axes show number of patent and utility model applications (left) and external trade value in thousands of euros (right).

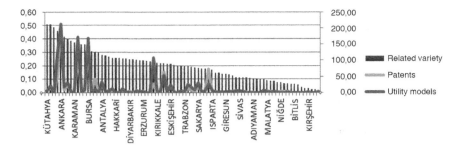

Figure 4.5 Related variety and patent and utility model applications (2002–2011 average; Turkey's NUTS3 regions). Vertical axes show related variety (left) and number of applications (right).

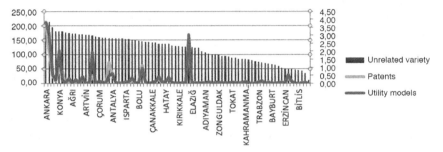

Figure 4.6 Unrelated variety and patent and utility model applications (2002–2011 average; Turkey's NUTS3 regions). Vertical axes show related variety (left) and number of applications (right).

The second step of the empirical estimation is to understand whether there is a simultaneous relationship between the export variable and patent variable. The usual procedure to understand whether the two variables have a simultaneous relationship is to conduct a Hausman test. The value of the Hausman test is 9.154. This value is greater than the critical value at the 5 per cent significance level, implying that there is a need to correct for simultaneity of the model.

To account for simultaneity between the *EX* and *P* variables, we use an instrument for the *EX* variable. The instrument is closely correlated with the *EX* variable but should not correlate with the error term in the equation.

The equation with an instrument for the *EX* variable is demonstrated in Equation 4.7.

$$P_t = b_0 + b_1 RV_t + b_2 UV_t + b_3 \widehat{EX}_t + \varepsilon_t \tag{4.7}$$

where $\widehat{EX}_t = f(P_t, RV_t, UV_t, TG_t)$.

Table 4.1 represents the effects of trade, related variety and unrelated variety on patent and utility model applications of 81 provinces of Turkey. Model 1 includes total international trade volume, related variety and unrelated variety as independent variables. Model 2 includes trade volume with Germany, related variety and unrelated variety as independent variables.

According to Table 4.1, both trade variable and variety variables have positive and significant impact on patent and utility model applications in the region. A 1 per cent increase in total exports increases the patent and utility model applications by 0.6 per cent. The elasticity estimate for the impact of export to Germany on patent and utility model applications is 0.4, meaning that overall impact of exports on innovations is higher that the impact of exports to Germany.

The estimate of the coefficient on related variety is significant at the 1 per cent level. We also note that the elasticity of related variety on patent and utility model applications is 0.238 when the model is estimated by using Turkey's total exports as the export variable. The elasticity estimate increases to 0.352 when we include exports to Germany in place of total exports. The difference between the two elasticity estimates shows that the impact of related variety on patent and utility model applications increases when the model accounts for variations in exports to Germany instead of overall exports.

The coefficient estimate of unrelated variety is also positive. However, the significance of the estimated coefficient of unrelated variety is weaker than that of related variety. The coefficient estimate of *UV* is significant only at the 5 per cent level for Model 1 and 10 per cent for Model 2.

Conclusion

This study analysed the impact of trade on innovativeness in Turkey's regions with specific emphasis on Turkey–Germany trade relationships in the context of international trade and economic diversification. The findings confirm the

Table 4.1 Two-stage least squares panel regression results. Dependent variable is *P*.

	Model 1	*Model 2*
Constant	-9.541^{***} (-14.913)	-4.257^{***} (-9.396)
RV	0.238^{***} (4.035)	0.351^{***} (5.658)
UV	0.236^{**} (2.016)	0.227^{*} (1.839)
TINT	0.620^{***} (19.776)	
TG		0.415^{***} (16.476)
R^2	0.425	0.368
DW	1.251	1.103
F-stat	154.737^{***}	121.802^{***}

Note: ***, ** and * denotes the rejection of H_0 at 1%, 5% and 10% levels of significance, respectively. *P*: patent and utility model; *RV*: related variety; *UV*: unrelated variety; *TINT*: total international trade; *TG*: total international trade with Germany. All variables are in natural logarithms.

hypotheses that there is a positive relationship between (i) related variety and innovation, and (ii) trade and innovation. Exports enhance innovativeness at the regional level. The innovativeness is further enhanced when the exported goods are related in variety. Unrelated variety has a significant impact on innovations, but its impact is relatively smaller than the impact of related variety on innovations.

The results have significant policy implications, particularly in evaluating the likely impacts of providing incentives to exporters. Export ties and related variety in exported goods have a significant potential of influencing the regions' innovativeness through increased R&D, increased network ties, and increased sharing of knowledge and thus more innovations. As this study demonstrates, the case of Germany and Turkey presents a strong example for the process.

The patent and utility applications by the German firms and individuals have substantial share in total applications. In fact, Germany ranks as second as applicants to Turkish Patent Institute after firms and individuals of Turkish nationality. Between 2000 and 2013, among the total of 106,733 patent and utility model applications, 58,833 applications are made by foreign candidates where an average of 17 per cent are German, followed by Turkish applicants (25% of total applicants). Within the total of 58,833 foreign applications, 13,330 are in "Manufacture of pharmaceuticals, medicinal chemicals and botanical products" followed by "chemical products" with 4,911 applicants and machinery (4,251 applicants). Here, the pharmaceutical industry has a significant importance for Turkey in the coming years where there is much attention and investment towards improving the pharmaceutical research and development capacity. The sector has a potential to create high value added products and has a capacity to create critical masses for creating innovative products. The significance of the pharmaceutical industry is highly acclaimed in Turkey's long-term development goals where the aim is to make Turkey one of the top economies in health products and services (AIFD 2013). One recent example is the BioIzmir project, which aims to make Izmir an intersection point with the health industry and an innovation centre for the pharmaceutical industry.[3]

The results of the study provide systematic evidence for making even stronger ties with German firms and for increasing the potential for exports. Another meaningful result is that the export composition (related variety) is significant in creating new opportunities for regional innovation.

Further research will likely to provide more understanding of the strength and density of network ties between the Turkish and German firms, particularly for the pharmaceutical industry. More research is needed to comprehend how networks facilitate interactions, knowledge sharing and more innovations.

Notes

1 Note that in producing graphs between patent and utility models and trade, related variety and unrelated variety, we had to exclude Istanbul due to Istanbul's unproportionally higher level of patent and utility model applications which makes variation in the rest of the NUTS3 regions unnoticeable.

2   The results are available on request.
3   See www.investinizmir.com/en/haberler/s/243.

References

Acemoğlu, D. (2003) Labor- and capital-augmenting technical change. *Journal of the European Economic Association*, 1(1): 1–37.

AIFD (2013) Turkey's Pharmaceutical Sector: Vision 2023 Report. Istanbul: PWC. Available at www.aifd.org.tr/PDF/2023_Rapor/2023_strat_en.pdf.

Akgüngör, S., Kuştepeli, Y. and Gülcan, Y. (2013) An overview of industry clusters and the impact of related variety on regional performance in Turkey. *European Review of Industrial Economics and Policy*, No: 5

Almeida, P. and Kogut, B. (1999) Localization of knowledge and the mobility of engineers in regional networks. *Management Science* 45(7): 905–917.

Atkeson, A. and Burstein, A. (2007) *Innovation, Firm Dynamics, and International Trade*. Working paper no. 13326. Cambridge, MA: National Bureau of Economic Research.

Attaran, M. (1986) Industrial diversity and economic performance in US areas. *The Annals of Regional Science* 20(2): 44–54.

Boschma, R. A. (2005) Proximity and innovation: a critical assessment. *Regional Studies* 39: 61–74.

Boschma, R. A. and Iammarino, S. (2009) Related variety, trade linkages, and regional growth in Italy. *Economic Geography* 85(3): 289–311.

Boschma, R. A., Minondo, A. and Navarro, M. (2012) Related variety and regional growth in Spain. *Papers in Regional Science* 91(2): 241–256.

Breschi, S. and Lissoni, F. (2009) Mobility of inventors and networks of collaboration: An anatomy of localised knowledge flows. *Journal of Economic Geography* 9(4): 439–468.

Castaldi, C., Frenken, K. and Los, B. (2013) *Related Variety, Unrelated Variety and Technological Breakthroughs: An Analysis of U.S. State-Level Patenting*. Working papers 13-03. Eindhoven: Eindhoven Center for Innovation Studies.

Damijan, J. P. and Kostevc, Č. (2010) *Learning From Trade Through Innovation: Causal Link Between Imports, Exports and Innovation in Spanish Microdata*. Discussion paper 264/2010. Leuven: Licos.

Dosi, G. and Soete, L. (1988) *Technical Change and International Trade*. Open Access publication (urn:nbn:nl:ui:27-6339). Maastricht: Maastricht University.

Eaton, J. and Kortum, S. (1996) Trade in ideas: patenting and productivity in the OECD. *Journal of International Economics* 40(3/4): 251–278.

Eaton, J. and Kortum, S. (1999) International technology diffusion: theory and measurement. *International Economic Review* 40(3): 537–570.

Egger, P. and Keuschnigg, C. (2011) *Innovation, Trade and Finance*. CEPR discussion paper 8467. Washiongton, DC: Center for Economic and Policy Research.

Essletzbichler, J. and Rigby, D. L. (2007) Exploring evolutionary economic geographies. *Journal of Economic Geography* 7: 549–571.

Fagerberg, J. (1988) International competitiveness. *Economic Journal* 98: 355–374.

Fagerberg, J. (1995) User-producer interaction, learning and comparative advantage. *Cambridge Journal of Economics* 19: 243–256.

Fernandes, A. and Paunov, C. (2010) *Does Trade Stimulate Innovation? Evidence from Firm-Product Data*. OECD Development Centre working paper 286. Paris: OECD Publishing.

Frenken, K., Van Oort, F. and Verbung, T. (2007) Related variety, unrelated variety and regional economic growth. *Regional Studies* 41(5): 685–697.

Glaeser, E. L., Kallal, H. D., Schinkmann, J. A. and Shleifer, A. (1992) Growth in cities. *Journal of Political Economy* 100: 1126–1152.

Griliches, Z. (1990) Patent statistics as economic indicators: a survey. *Journal of Economic Literature* 28(4): 1661–1707.

Hagedoorn, J. and Cloodt, M. (2003) Measuring innovative performance: is there an advantage in using multiple indicators? *Research Policy* 32: 1365–1379.

Im, K. S., Pesaran, M. H. and Shin, Y. (2003)Testing for unit roots in heterogeneous panels. *Journal of Econometrics* 115: 53–74.

Jacquemin, A. P. and Berry, C. H. (1979) Entropy measure of diversification and corporate growth. *Journal of Industrial Economics* 27(4): 359–369.

Jones, C. (2002) Sources of US economic growth in a world of ideas. *American Economic Review*, 92(1): 220–239.

Kortum, S. (1997) Research, patenting, and technological change. *Econometrica* 65(6): 1389–1419.

Krüger, J. (2008) The sources of aggregate productivity growth: US manufacturing industries, 1958–1996. *Bulletin of Economic Research* 60(4): 405–427.

Krugman, P. (1980) Scale economies, product differentiation, and the pattern of trade. *The American Economic Review* 70 (5): 950–959.

Krugman, P. (1991) Increasing returns and economic geography. *Journal of Political Economy* 99(3): 483–499.

Lazzeretti, L., Capone, F. and Cinti, T. (2010) The regional development platform and related variety: some evidence from art and food in Tuscany. *European Planning Studies* 18(1): 27-45.

Levin, A., Lin, C.-F. and Chu, C.-S. J. (2002) Unit root tests in panel data: asymptotic and finite-sample properties. *Journal of Econometrics* 108: 1–24.

Marquez-Ramos, L. and Martinez-Zarzoso, I. (2009) *The Effect of Technological Innovation on International Trade. A Nonlinear Approach*. Economics discussion paper 2009-24. Kiel: Kiel Institute for the World Economy.

Republic of Turkey, Ministry of Economy (2014) *Uluslararasi Doğrudan Yatirimlar 2013 Yili Raporu*. Ankara: Republic of Turkey, Ministry of Economy. Available at www.ekonomi.gov.tr/portal/content/conn/UCM/uuid/dDocName:EK-211016.

Romer, P. M. (1990) Endogenous technological change. *Journal of Political Economy* 98: 71–102.

Saltelli, A., Annoni, P. and Tarantola, S. (2011) Innovation and competitiveness indicators. Paper prepared for JRC EU Commission, Budapest. Available at http://ec.europa.eu/dgs/jrc/downloads/events/201104-budapest/20110405_budapest_saltelli.pdf.

Saviotti, P. P. and Frenken, K. (2008) Export variety and the economic performance of countries. *Journal of Evolutionary Economics* 18: 201–218.

Schumpeter, J. (1943) *Capitalism, Socialism and Democracy*. New York: Harper.

Seppänen, S. (2008) Regional innovation systems and regional competitiveness: analysis of competitiveness indexes. Paper presented at DRUID-DIME Academy Winter 2008 PhD Conference on Geography, Innovation and Industrial Dynamics, Aalborg, Denmark, 17–19January.

Silva, E. G. and Teixeira, A. C. (2008) Surveying structural change: seminal contributions and a bibliometric account. *Structural Change and Economic Dynamics* 19(4): 273–300.

Sjöholm, F. (1996) International transfer of knowledge: the role of international trade and geographic proximity. *Review of World Economics (Weltwirtschaftliches Archiv)* 132(1): 97–115.

Soete, L. and Wyatt, S. (1983) The use of foreign patenting as an internationally comparable science and technology output indicator. *Scientometrics* 5: 31–54.

Spulber, D. F. (2010) The quality of innovation and the extent of the market. *Journal of International Economics* 80: 260–270.

Stuart, T. and Sorenso, O. (2003) The geography of opportunity: spatial heterogeneity in founding rates and the performance of biotechnology firms. *Research Policy* 32: 229–253.

Turkish Statistics Institute (2015) *What Figures Say*. Ankara: Turkish Statistics Institute.

5 Culture economy in Europe

Analysis of selected countries

Çağaçan Değer, Mehmet Güçlü,
Özge Filiz Yağcıbaşı and Neşe Kumral

Introduction

Culture is an important aspect of human existence. Defined as the arts and other manifestations of human intellectual achievement regarded collectively, culture inevitably has an economic dimension. A most obvious example is the sale of art objects. But there is more to culture and economics. Works collected by Towse (2003) emphasize different dimension of economics and culture such as financing culture and art, welfare impact of cultural production, implications of intellectual property rights and culture as an economic institution.

This study focuses on culture as an economic cluster. Clusters as we know them now have gained theoretical foothold through the seminal work of Porter (1990). Porter (1998) defines clusters as "critical masses – in one place – of unusual competitive success in particular fields". Clusters typically contain a network of actors that contain, but are not limited to, firms, universities, government and institutes. Competitiveness through a cluster extends beyond simple cost cutting practices and includes competition through improved efficiency and innovation. Spatial proximity implied by clusters enables transfer of tacit knowledge, which provides considerable competitive edge. Such dynamics simply become more powerful through time. Some evident examples of successful clusters include the Silicon Valley (software industry), Southern Germany (automobile industry) and Northern Italy (fashion industry). Inspired by such examples, many countries have initiated support programmes to create innovative clusters of their own.

A leap of thought is to question whether culture has a similar disposition. And such an approach requires culture to be defined as an industry. The appearance of the term "cultural industries" dates back to the Horkheimer and Adorno (1944) titled *Philosophische Fragmente* where economization of art is criticized; a task that requires definition of culture as an economic entity. Lack of a concrete definition of culture economy, or culture industries, has echoed through time. Thus a number of definitions exist. Garnham (1983) uses the term cultural industries to represent modes of production and organizations of corporations that result in the production and distribution of cultural goods and services as marketable commodities. UNESCO-UIS (2009) emphasizes that the goods produced by a culture industry must embody or convey cultural expressions, no matter what the commercial value they have. Despite the differences of opinion regarding an exact definition, there is a consensus that cultural industries have impact on economic aggregates such as national income, employment, trade balance, etc.

The difficulties relating to the definition of cultural economies have had considerable adverse impact on quantitative analysis. Even if an agreement on exact classification of cultural industries could be possible, there are considerable data disadvantages as well. The problem lies in which sectors to include. Once these sectors have been identified, data availability becomes the next major problem. Existence of these concerns at a national level makes an international comparison of culture industries a very difficult task. One must dig up a database that enables consistent representation of culture industries. Given such difficulties, international comparisons are virtually non-existent.

The aim of this study is to present an international comparison of culture industries in Europe, with a special focus on Germany and Turkey. Due to data limitations, the considered country sample is a subset of EU countries. To maximize the number of countries in the sample, year 2009 is chosen for analysis. When addressing the stated aim, this work makes two main contributions: First, a relatively detailed sectoral picture is considered by focusing on four-digit NACE Rev 2 data. Turkey is then considered, for the first time, in terms of culture industries in an international setting. We next present a literature review on cluster analysis of culture economy sectors, followed by our three-star analysis. After comparing Turkey and Germany in terms of a number of variables, we summarize our findings and conclusions.

Literature review

Emergence of culture in economics can be dated back to 1960s. Initial studies were mainly about the role of state and the efficient use of public resources (such as subsidies and expenditures) on cultural activities (Farchy and Sagot-Duvauroux 1994; Heilbrun and Gray 2001). Earlier, cultural activities were considered to contribute to the society only in an intellectual sense and their economic contributions were ignored for decades. After the consecutive financial crisis experienced in the following two decades, the need to allocate scarce resources for the most efficient sectors urged policy makers to measure the economic contribution of cultural industries. By the end of the 1990s, many studies had shown that cultural industries have a high positive impact on crucial economic aggregates such as gross domestic product, gross value added and employment (Lash and Urry 1994; Bernard and Jensen 1999; Pine and Gilmore 1999). Furthermore, studies indicated that cultural industries propose a great potential for creating a spillover effect, attracting qualified labour and investment to sub-national regions, and trigger creativity and innovation for overall economy (UNESCO-UIS 2009).

Evaluation of culture from a development perspective begins with the Report of the World Commission on Culture and Development (UNESCO 1996). This was followed by reports and research from various other institutions such as Council of Europe (1997), UNESCO (1998, 2000), UNESCO-UIS (2005) and

World Bank (2003). A common characteristic of these texts is the emphasis on importance of culture and the implied need for policies required to stimulate cultural industries. However, the data analysis required to for policy formulation proved to be a most formidable task, primarily due to lack of data. Even though many institutions provide data, and conduct analysis through their own data, the overabundance of variety in definition of cultural industries makes comparable numerical analysis virtually impossible.

The issue is further complicated by the confusion between the concepts of *creative industries* and *culture industries*. In 1997 the British government introduced the term creative industries as a substitute for cultural sector (Eisenberg *et al.* 2006). This substitution met with resistance. In the concentric circles model adopted by the European Union, Throsby (2001) included both industrial and non-industrial sectors in the cultural sector. On the spot consumption of art, such as fairs and concerts, were classified to be non-industrial. Mass production and export possibilities helped define the industrial sectors, such as books and films. In relation to the creative sector, culture was defined to be a creative input necessary for the production of non-cultural goods (European Commission 2006). From a European planning perspective, this places cultural industries within creative industries as a subset.

Despite the lack of data and conceptual ambiguity, many studies have attempted to examine cultural and creative industries at different geographical scales ranging from city to subnational regions and all the way to national level. Due to the lack of data for developing countries and subnational economic units such as cities and regions, existing studies focus on national level analysis of culture industries for developed countries. For example, Söndermann *et al.* (2009) provides a comprehensive overview of culture and creative economies in Germany. With details on sub-sectors, impacts of creative and cultural industries on growth, employment and export are examined through descriptive statistics and policy recommendations for further improvement of these sectors are presented. Similar studies are available for USA (Heilbrun 1996; Beyers 2006), Sweden (Power 2002), southeast England (Pratt 2004), Vienna (Holzl 2005) and London (O'Brien and Feist 1997).

Efforts for mapping creative industries begin with Creative Industries Mapping Study by the UK Department of Culture, Media and Sport (DCMS). Cunningham and Higgs (2008) recently updated this study and alleged three iterations of creative industries mapping to date. Mommaas (2004) investigates five cultural clustering projects in Netherlands and conclude that even in the short run such clusters seem to be good opportunities. However, possibility of divergence of interest exists in the long run and such processes may undermine mutual trust in a cluster. Mommaas (2004) argues for the need of deeper research to understand underlying complex dynamics in a cluster.

Lazzeretti *et al.* (2009) is the first paper to empirically examine the reasons for creative industries to cluster. Spain and Italy were compared and results indicated different patterns of clustering. But in both countries, high density of human capital and creative class is observed. Markusen *et al.* (2008) set two metrics (industry and occupation), and compared the size and character of the creative economy with these metrics for the Boston Metro Area and the US. Results suggested higher employment estimates for cultural industries, which verifies the importance of cultural activities in regional economy. Due to the lack of proper spatial data, Domenech *et al.* (2011) uses firm level data from sixteen European countries in order to determine clusters of creative industries by geo-statistical modelling and prepares a detailed cluster map for cultural industries.

Like any other economic activity, cultural and creative industries can be assumed to have a tendency to cluster in order to profit from each other's existence. This can be easily verified with observations on well-known examples such as Hollywood and the Silicon Valley. However, to the best of our knowledge, studies about the relation between clusters and cultural and creative industries are limited. This appears to be a fertile ground for research on casting culture industries into the economic clustering approach.

Analysis

Even though data for many economies at sector detail is becoming more and more accessible, it is difficult to obtain detailed data on culture industries for a number of countries. A comprehensive source is EUROSTAT's Annual Detailed Enterprise Statistics for Services. Still, data availability considerably restricts the sample, forcing this study to omit countries like France and England. The examined country sample includes a number of EU countries (Austria, Bulgaria, Cyprus, Finland, Germany, Hungary, Italy, Latvia, Lithuania, Norway, Poland, Portugal, Romania, Slovenia, Sweden) and Turkey for 2009. The list of NACE Rev 2 industries are listed in Table 5.1. The analysis is performed in two stages. First, a comparative picture of the culture economy in the sample countries is presented. Then, clustering of the culture economy in various countries is examined through three-star analysis.

Employment profile of culture industries

The countries considered in the sample have employed more than 137 million people in 2009; of this sum, about 1.12 million were employed in the culture industries. In other words, the culture economy accounts for 0.82 per cent of total employment (Table 5.2). The countries with the highest shares of culture economy employment in total employment are Sweden (1.33%), Norway (1.25%) and Finland (1.19%). The countries with the lowest shares of culture economy employment in total employment are Turkey (0.37%), Romania (0.46%) and Poland (0.63%). Figure 5.1 implies that culture industries account for a considerably small portion of employment.

Table 5.3 presents the shares of employment by culture economy industries (sectors) in total culture economy employment for each country in the sample. The table shows that the highest level of employment is by sector "architectural activities". Total employment by this sector in year 2009 was about 332,000, which corresponds to about 30 per cent of employment in total culture economy

Table 5.1 Sectors covered as culture industries.

NACE Rev.2	Description
47.43	Retail sale of audio and video equipment in specialized stores *
47.61	Retail sale of books in specialized stores *
47.63	Retail sale of music and video recordings in specialized stores *
58.11	Book publishing *
58.13	Publishing of newspapers *
58.14	Publishing of journals and periodicals *
58.21	Publishing of computer games
59.11	Motion picture, video and television programme production activities *
59.12	Motion picture, video and television programme post-production activities *
59.13	Motion picture, video and television programme distribution activities *
59.14	Motion picture, projection activities *
59.20	Sound recording and music publishing activities *
60.10	Radio broadcasting
60.20	Television programming and broadcasting activities
63.91	News agency activities *
71.11	Architectural activities *
74.10	Specialized design activities
74.20	Photographic activities
77.22	Renting of video tapes and disks *
85.52	Cultural education
90.01	Performing arts
90.02	Support activities to performing arts
90.03	Artistic creation
90.04	Operation of arts facilities
91.01	Library and archives activities
91.02	Museum activities
91.03	Operation of historical sites and buildings and similar visitor attractions

Note: * These sectors are included in the analysis. Other sectors have been omitted due to lack of data.

employment. Also with high shares of employment are "publishing of newspapers" (16%) and "retail sale of audio and video equipment in specialized stores" (10%). By themselves, these three sectors account for more employment than the employment due to all other sectors considered in the analysis.

Figure 5.2 shows the number of workers per establishment in culture economy. In year 2009, the average number of workers per establishment in the culture economy sectors is 7.6. Culture industry of Germany has twice the employment generation ability; number of workers per establishment is 15.9. Six of the considered countries (Germany, Cyprus, Latvia, Lithuania, Austria and Finland) are able to generate employment above the EU-16 average. Turkey and Norway are very close to but below the average. The industry with the highest number of workers per establishment is "publishing of newspapers". This branch of economic activity employs 31.2 workers per establishment. The highest employment generation of this industry is in Germany, 105.3 workers per establishment in newspaper publishing industry.

Table 5.2 Employment, 2009.

Country	Culture economy employment (number of people)	Total employment (number of people)
Bulgaria	22,094	3,253,600
Germany	432,755	38,471,100
Italy	179,975	23,025,000
Cyprus	4,279	382,900
Latvia	9,268	908,500
Lithuania	12,112	1,317,400
Hungary	32,190	3,781,800
Austria	44,588	4,077,500
Poland	99,599	15,868,000
Portugal	35,492	4,968,600
Romania	42,332	9,243,500
Slovenia	8,659	980,700
Finland	29,213	2,457,300
Sweden	59,928	4,499,300
Norway	31,137	2,499,500
Turkey	78,306	21,270,700
Total	1,121,927	137,005,400

Source: Eurostat (http://epp.eurostat.ec.europa.eu).

Three-star analysis

While reviewing the history of cluster mapping practices, Ketel *et al.* (2012: 7) claim that they have devised the three-star method in 2005, while attempting to transfer a US model for clusters to Europe; which, in turn, led to an analysis of 10 new EU members in terms of economic clusters (Ketel and Sölvell 2006).

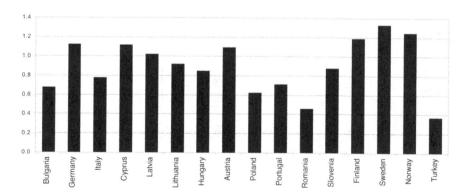

Figure 5.1 Share of culture economy employment in total employment (%).
Source: Eurostat (http://epp.eurostat.ec.europa.eu).

Table 5.3 Employment of culture industries by country, 2009 (no. people).

Country	J5811	J5813	J5814	J5821	J5911	J5912	J5913	J5914	J5920	J6391	M7111	N7722	G4743	G4761	G4763
Bulgaria	1,282	3,117	1,644	11	1,175	422	239	247	447	811	5,717	89	4,972	1,690	231
Germany	23,467	96,167	40,879	1,282	22,965	3,107	3,117	23,543	6,273	3,818	106,958	8,288	54,325	36,135	2,431
Italy	10,903	10,558	15,608	98	23,640	2,133	1,768	6,299	1,860	2,421	79,252	5,287	5,473	12,370	2,305
Southern Cyprus	50	746	336	135	159	0	16	134	44	172	1,493	272	130	546	46
Latvia	798	1,219	2,087	6	321	44	46	203	96	214	2,863	122	478	690	81
Lithuania	1,358	2,263	1,783	14	353	17	70	235	156	94	4,237	127	595	759	51
Hungary	3,745	3,058	4,201	18	4,110	534	856	306	738	2,419	7,086	434	1,088	3,391	206
Austria	1,945	3,853	3,090	67	3,019	153	260	2,004	956	834	14,412	761	7,540	5,425	269
Poland	16,320	7,217	8,000	255	7,653	585	930	1,806	3,523	2,231	33,214	2,548	5,634	9,375	308
Portugal	2,526	3,645	3,668	35	3,347	362	474	1,451	1,239	473	14,444	438	1,024	1,949	417
Romania	4,326	6,918	3,390	713	5,837	163	304	601	746	656	13,738	160	1,217	3,303	260
Slovenia	1,073	1,490	685	:	709	56	62	108	179	157	2,834	75	611	612	8
Finland	2,017	8,112	5,176	:	2,367	296	162	582	795	388	4,542	738	2,488	1,400	150
Sweden	4,201	14,738	6,713	1,697	6,406	480	1,025	1,356	1,961	1,274	7,112	1,078	8,690	2,822	375
Norway	1,969	9,235	3,362	245	1,948	266	220	1,315	469	434	5,376	604	1,049	3,747	898
Turkey	3,975	7,497	1,182	:	3,170	601	345	2,946	1,073	4,838	28,728	375	13,324	6,331	3,921
Total	79,955	179,833	101,804	4,576	87,179	9,219	9,894	43,136	20,555	21,234	332,006	21,396	108,638	90,545	11,957

Source: Eurostat (http://epp.eurostat.cc.europa.eu).

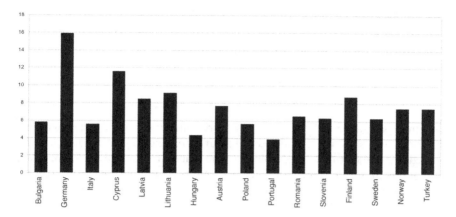

Figure 5.2 Employment per establishment (people).
Source: Eurostat (http://epp.eurostat.ec.europa.eu).

Exemplified by ECO (2014), the three-star method relies on measures of *size*, *dominance* and *specialization*. These are measured through employment data. Three-star analysis may be based on number of firms or establishments as well. However, such an approach may be misleading, for a region with few very large firms would be dominated by regions with many, very small firms. Hence employment data, rather than number of establishments, is preferred for three-star analysis.

Size is measured through employment concentration. For any industry, *i*, *size* is the ratio of employment in a country divided by employment in industry *i* for the whole sample countries. Let employment in industry *i* for any country be e_i and let employment in industry *i* for all sample countries be E_i. Then, *size* is calculated as:

$$\text{size} = \frac{e_i}{E_i} \tag{5.1}$$

Dominance is a measure of how concentrated an industry is within a given country. It is measured through the share of the considered industry's employment in the country's employment. Letting employment in industry *i* for any country be e_i and total employment in the country as e_t, *dominance* is calculated as:

$$\text{dominance} = \frac{e_i}{e_t} \tag{5.2}$$

Specialization introduces a comparison of a country to the whole sample of countries through employment concentration. On the one hand, specialization relates employment by industry *i* in a country to the country's whole employment. On the other hand, employment by industry *i* in the whole sample is related to the aggregate employment in the whole sample. Specialization measures concentration by comparing these two ratios. Specifically; let e_i be employment in industry i for any country, total employment in the country be e_t, employment in industry i for all sample countries be E_i, and total employment in the whole sample be E_t. Then, specialization is measured as:

$$\text{specialization} = \frac{e_i/e_t}{E_i/E_t} \tag{5.3}$$

The three-star analysis evaluates these three measures against predetermined threshold levels. If the calculated value of *size*, *dominance* or *specialization* exceeds the predetermined threshold, stars are granted (up to a maximum of three).

A problem at this stage is the determination of the threshold values for the stated measures. For *specialization*, unity is a natural threshold. If specialization is greater than 1, then the industry is more heavily concentrated in a country compared to the whole sample. Regarding dominance criteria, it is assumed that each country in the sample (16 countries) and each considered sector (14 sectors) have equal weight; thus the threshold criteria used for dominance is calculated as $1/(14 \times 16)$. Finally, for size, threshold is the ratios of culture employment in the whole sample divided by the total employment of all the sample countries.

The results of three-star analysis are presented in Table 5.4. This table can be examined in terms of countries and sectors; specifically, one may question which countries and which sectors have the highest total number of stars. Also, one may combine these questions to ask which sectors have the highest stars in which countries. This last question is addressed through maps of Europe that has colour codes related to the number of stars for each country. These maps are presented in the Appendix to this chapter.

Table 5.4 shows that no country has a three-star rating, because no country gets a star for dominance. This is a reflection of small employment shares of culture sectors in the considered sample. Thus, the lack of three star rating is taken to imply that culture industries do not have a strong presence in the considered sample. Culture industries can be regarded to be in a state of infancy. However, if countries such as France and England could be included in the sample, it is most likely that those countries could display adequate dominance to have three-star ratings.

Regarding the first question above to examine the results; consider which countries have the highest total star rankings. Norway, Germany and Sweden have 26, 25 and 24 stars respectively. They are followed by Finland and Austria, each with 24 stars. The lowest numbers stars are displayed by Cyprus, Latvia, Lithuania and Slovenia; each has only nine stars. Turkey has 16 stars; this is below the average of the considered group of countries. The main conclusion is that culture industries are stronger in middle and northern Europe, weakest in Eastern Europe. Turkey has a below average concentration of culture industries.

In terms of sectors, "Publishing of journals and periodicals" and "book publishing" industries both have 24 stars. "News agency activities" and "architectural activities" have 23 stars each. These are followed by "sound recording and music

Table 5.4 Results of three-star analysis by country and sector.

	Architectural activities	Book publishing	Motion picture projection activities	Motion picture, video and television programme distribution activities	Motion picture, video and television programme post-production activities	Motion picture, video and television programme production activities	News agency activities	Publishing of journals and periodicals	Publishing of newspapers	Renting of video tapes and disks	Retail sale of audio and video equipment in specialized stores	Retail sale of books in specialized stores	Retail sale of music and video recordings in specialized stores	Sound recording and music publishing activities
Austria	**	*	**	*	*	**	**	**	*	**	**	**	*	**
Bulgaria	*	*		**	**	*	**	*	*		**	*	*	*
Southern Cyprus	*		*				*	*	*			*	*	
Finland	*	**	**	*	**	**	**	**	*	**	**	*	*	**
Germany	**	**	**	**	**	*	**	**	**	**	**	**	*	**
Hungary	*	**		**	**	**	*	**	**	*	*	**	*	**
Italy	**	*	*	**	**	**	*	*	*	**	*	*	*	*
Latvia	**	**		*			**	*	*			*	*	
Lithuania	**	**	**					**	**			*		
Norway	*	**	**	**	**	**	**	**	**	**	*	**	**	**
Poland	*	**	*	*	*	*	*	*	**	**	*	*	*	**
Portugal	**	*	*	**	**	**	*	**	*	*	**	*	*	**
Romania	*	*	*	*		*	*	*	*		*	*	*	*
Slovenia	**	**		**	**	**		**	**	**	**			**
Sweden	*	**	*	*	*	*	**	**	**	**	**	*	*	**
Turkey	*		*	*	*	*	**	*	*	*	*	*	**	*

Source: author' calculations.

publishing activities" with 22 stars and "motion picture, video and television programme production activities" with 21 stars. Book and journal publishing related
activities appear to be strongest in the considered sample of countries. Lowest
star rankings are concentrated in motion picture and retail sale related activities.

"Architectural activities" are focused in central Europe, Italy and Portugal.
Latvia and Lithuania also display a relatively strong presence in this culture
industry. Such strength is reflected in the policies of relevant institutions. For
example, State Culture Capital Foundation of Latvia identifies, on its website,
architecture and design as branches to be supported. National Culture Policy Guidelines of Latvia's Ministry of Culture recognizes a need to support architecture.

"Book publishing" is stronger in central, northern and Eastern Europe.
Southern Europe and Turkey are observed to be lagging behind in "book publishing" industry. "Motion picture projection activities" are concentrated in Austria,
Germany and Norway. Zero star ratings are displayed by five countries. This
sector has the lowest number of stars, only 14, in the whole sample.

"Motion picture, video and television programme distribution activities" are
stronger in central and northern Europe, Italy and Portugal. Bulgaria and Hungary
also have a strong presence in this industry. The same group shows a strong presence in "motion picture, video and television programme post-production
activities" and as well. In this sector, Germany is replaced by Austria and Bulgaria
is replaced by Romania.

"News agency activities" are concentrated in northern Europe, Austria,
Hungary, Bulgaria and Turkey. "Publishing of journals and periodicals" is an
activity that is stronger in Portugal, Latvia and Lithuania in addition to central and
northern Europe, whereas "publishing of newspapers" is concentrated in Finland,
Germany Lithuania, Norway and Sweden. "Renting of video tapes and disks"
centres in northern Europe, central Europe and Italy; this industry appears to have
no significance in eastern countries of Europe.

"Retail sale of audio and video equipment in specialized stores" is an activity
that is not wide spread in Europe; only Germany, Austria, Finland and Bulgaria
have two stars in this industry. Similar observation holds for "retail sale of books
in specialized stores", with two stars for only Austria, Germany, Hungary and
Norway. "Retail sale of music and video recordings in specialized stores"
industry is even less represent, only Italy and Norway have two stars. These
observations are actually a repetition of a previous observation regarding culture
industries in Europe: retail sale related activities are not strong in Europe, as
implied by the low number of stars awarded to these industries in the conducted
analysis. Lastly, sound recording activities are heavily represented in Portugal, in
addition to central and northern Europe.

Turkey's relative status is observed to be below the average of the sample
countries. Turkey has two stars in only "retail sale of music and video recordings
in specialized stores" and "news agency activities". The importance of "retail sale
of music and video recordings in specialized stores" may be attributed to the
recent increase in the number of retail chains that focus on music and video discs,
periodicals and books.

Turkey and Germany: a comparison

Using the data from EUROSTAT, it is possible to present a comparative picture of Turkey and Germany in terms of culture industries. Table 5.5 presents a comparison in terms of number of establishments and number of persons employed. First two columns compare number of enterprises and number of persons employed. Data in these two columns is presented as value for Turkey, reported as percentage of Germany. Last four columns report number of persons employed per enterprise and wage adjusted labour productivity.

Table 5.5 reveals that both number of enterprises and number of persons employed are higher in Germany. Few exceptions exist. "Retail sale of music and video recordings in specialized stores" sector accounts for both more enterprises and higher number of persons employed in Turkey than in Germany. This situation may be explained by a higher use of on-line marketing in Germany, thus a lower need for retail sale establishments in Germany. "News agency activities" accounts for more employed persons in Turkey compared to Germany.

In general, German enterprises employ more people compared to Turkish enterprises. "News agency activities" is a notable exception: An enterprise in Turkey employs about 30 people on average whereas a German enterprise a little less than eight persons on average.

Table 5.5 also presents a comparison in terms of wage adjusted labour productivity. This measure of productivity can be viewed as labour productivity divided by average personnel cost. More technically, it is value added divided by personnel costs, adjusted by the share of paid employees in the total number of persons employed. Hence it can exceed 100 per cent if personnel costs are a minor part of created value added. When this measure of labour productivity is used to compare Germany and Turkey, the comparative picture appears to be less clear. A sector by sector count shows that labour productivity value as shown in the last column of Table 5.5 is higher for Turkey in the case of 8 sectors out of the 13 for which data is available. Turkey displays higher labour productivity especially in sectors related to motion picture related activities. There is also a tendency to have higher labour productivity values in Turkey for publishing sectors.

Table 5.6 presents an overview of Germany versus Turkey in terms of a number of monetary variables. These variables are wages and salaries, value added at factor cost, turnover per person employed, investment per person employed and production value. "Publishing of computer games" and "renting of video tapes and disks" sectors cannot be included in this comparison due to lack of data for Turkey. Compared to Germany, wages and salaries in Turkey are very low. The only case it reaches above 10 per cent is for the "news agency activities" sector. For "news agency activities", wages and salaries in Turkey are about 80 per cent. This is in accordance with the well-established opinion that labour is a lot cheaper in developing countries such as Turkey compared to developed countries such as Germany.

The value added created by culture industry sectors is also very low in Turkey compared to Germany. Only in case of "news agency activities" sector, Turkey

Table 5.5 Comparison of Turkey and Germany: employment and establishments.

	Number of enterprises (TR/GER, %)	Number of persons employed (TR/GER, %)	Average number of persons employed per enterprise		Wage adjusted labour productivity (%)	
			Germany	Turkey	Germany	Turkey
Architectural activities	31.91	26.86	3.3	2.8	146.9	169.8
Book publishing	36.23	16.94	12.6	5.9	183.7	210.7
Motion picture, projection activities	39.55	12.51	33.3	10.5	187.9	209.7
Motion picture, video and television programme distribution activities	13.37	11.07	8.3	6.9	370.4	431.4
Motion picture, video and television programme post-production activities	12.96	19.34	3.6	5.4	123.1	168.5
Motion picture, video and television programme production activities	16.46	13.80	5.4	4.5	144.3	252.6
News agency activities	31.91	126.72	7.8	30.8	106.8	196.7
Publishing of computer games	0.93	0.08	6	NA	268.4	NA
Publishing of journals and periodicals	10.79	2.89	23.2	6.2	164.2	145.5
Publishing of newspapers	47.54	7.80	105.3	17.3	156.1	150.6
Renting of video tapes and disks	16.34	4.52	7.4	2	194.0	NA
Retail sale of audio and video equipment in specialized stores	61.97	24.53	9	3.5	180.0	118.5
Retail sale of books in specialized stores	45.90	17.52	7.6	2.9	134.4	112.1
Retail sale of music and video recordings in specialized stores	333.88	161.29	3.1	1.5	105.4	29.5
Sound recording and music publishing activities	13.17	17.11	3.3	4.3	167.9	126
Total (if applicable)	37.51	18.09				

Note: Data are for year 2009. NA: data not available.
Source: authors' compilation from EUROSTAT's Annual Detailed Enterprise Statistics for Services.

creates more value added than Germany. This is reflected in terms of production value as well, as seen in the last column of Table 5.6. Production value of "news agency activities" sector in Turkey is nearly twice of that in Germany.

It can be observed from Table 5.6 that turnover per person employed of culture industry in Turkey is lower than Germany as well, with "news agency activities" sector being the only exception. Based on the definition of turnover in business statistics corresponding to the total value of market sales, value of sales per employed in Turkey are for most sectors less than the value of sales in

Table 5.6 Turkey and Germany: factor cost, investment and production (TR/GER, %).

	Wages and salaries	Value added at factor cost	Turnover per person employed	Investment per person employed	Production value
Architectural activities	5.34	6.47	46.13	40.00	13.07
Book publishing	3.18	3.76	28.59	173.68	5.67
Motion picture, projection activities	7.50	8.75	102.58	55.17	15.81
Motion picture, video and television programme distribution activities	6.18	6.67	101.25	60.00	16.25
Motion picture, video and television program post-production activities	4.61	4.87	69.77	65.85	14.75
Motion picture, video and television programme production activities	3.50	5.71	102.92	191.30	17.12
News agency activities	81.18	124.40	123.34	93.75	172.68
Publishing of computer games	NA	NA	NA	NA	NA
Publishing of journals and periodicals	0.65	0.62	32.74	49.06	1.04
Publishing of newspapers	3.57	3.37	75.36	372.22	6.08
Renting of video tapes and disks	NA	NA	NA	NA	NA
Retail sale of audio and video equipment in specialized stores	5.67	4.38	36.80	25.00	6.39
Retail sale of books in specialized stores	5.26	5.08	63.77	110.00	7.59
Retail sale of music and video recordings in specialized stores	9.84	10.96	8.79	500.00	15.48
Sound recording and music publishing activities	2.51	1.53	25.31	60.61	5.75

Note: Data are for year 2009. NA: data not available.
Source: Authors' compilation from EUROSTAT's Annual Detailed Enterprise Statistics for Services.

Germany. In other words, sales per person employed is less in Turkey compared to Germany.

Production value reported in the last column of Table 5.6 is the actual value of production based on sales, changes in stocks and resales of goods and services. The production value in Turkey is smaller than sales value in Germany as well, with the exception of "news agency activities". This is consistent with relatively low value added in Turkey and low wage and salaries in Turkey. The implication for Turkey is that, with lower employment and lower wages and salaries, Turkey creates less in terms of value added, production value and turnover per person employed. Despite a minor advantage in labour productivity, Turkey falls well behind Germany in terms of the aggregates presented in Table 5.6.

Regarding investment per person employed, Turkey is ahead of Germany in "book publishing", "publishing of newspapers", "motion picture, video and television programme production activities", "retail sale of books in specialized stores" and "retail sale of music and video recordings in specialized stores". These figures reflect that some Turkish enterprises in culture industry desire to grow by investing in capital. However this does not appear to be widely spread to all culture industry sectors.

Conclusion

As an economy matures, services sector gains importance and economic planning perspective is required to go beyond the commonly emphasized manufacturing sectors focused plans. Previously unexplored dimensions of economic activity, such as culture industries, gain importance through such transformations.

This study focuses on culture economy and culture industries. Such a task is difficult because there is considerable ambiguity regarding culture economy. The task is further complicated by lack of data. Despite these difficulties, this study presents an international comparison of culture industries for a sample of EU countries. The analysis relies on descriptive comparisons supported by a three-star analysis. A focus on Turkey versus Germany is also provided. In order to maximize country coverage, year 2009 is selected.

As a result of the conducted three-star analysis, it is observed that none of the countries have a three star rating. This is because culture industries do not receive a star for dominance in any of the countries. This may be taken as an indicator that, in terms of employment, culture industries account for a very small share in sample countries.

Norway, Germany and Sweden have the highest number of stars in aggregate; 26, 25 and 24 respectively. Finland and Austria both have 24 stars. Southern Cyprus, Latvia, Lithuania and Slovenia have only nine stars. Turkey is below the average with 16 stars. Culture industries are relatively stronger in middle and northern Europe and weaker in eastern Europe.

When considered in terms of sectoral detail; "book and journal publishing" has 24 stars. "News agency activities" and "architectural activities" have 23 stars each. "Sound recording and music publishing activities" have 22 stars, "motion picture, video and television programme production activities" have 21 stars. Lowest number of stars are concentrated in activities related to retail sale of music and motion pictures.

"Architectural activities" are concentrated in central Europe, Italy and Portugal. Latvia and Lithuania also have a strong presence in these sectors. This is probably a reflection of institutionalized support policies. "Book publishing" is strongest in central, northern and Eastern Europe. Southern Europe and Turkey are lagging behind the rest of the sample. Motion picture related activities are concentrated in Austria, Germany and Norway. "Retail sale of audio and video equipment in specialized stores" is not a strong activity in Europe. This sector has two stars in only Germany, Austria, Finland and Bulgaria. Similar statement holds for book sales as well; the sector has two stars in only Austria, Germany and Norway. Finally, "retail sale of music and video recordings in specialized stores" is identified to be a very weak sector; it has two stars in only Italy and Norway. Retail sale as part of culture industries is not a very strong activity in Europe.

Turkey lags behind the other countries in the sample. Turkey has two stars in only "retail sale of music and video recordings in specialized stores" and "news agency activities" and cannot display a strong presence in other sectors.

A comparison of Turkey and Germany shows that both number of enterprises and number of persons employed are dominantly higher for culture economies in Germany. Turkey appears to display higher labour productivity in most of the culture industry sectors considered in this study. Wages and salaries, created value added, turnover per person employed, investment per person employed and production figures for culture industry sectors in Turkey are extremely low compared to Germany. Only notable exception is "news agency activities" sector, which creates more production value, higher value added and more turnover in Turkey compared to Germany. Turkey's culture industry also displays low value added, production value and turnover compared to Germany. Relatively low investment tendencies of culture industries in Turkey, compared to Germany, imply that these sectors will display relatively slow growth in the medium to long run.

These results must be considered with two notes of caution. First, due to lack of compatible data, countries like France and England, deemed to be strong bases of culture industries, are left out of the analysis. Second, also due to lack of data, a number of sectors that are conceptually culture industries, such as "performing arts", could not be included in the analysis. Even though the presented analysis implies culture industries to be weak for not only Turkey but all sample countries, inclusion of the omitted industries and countries may show the culture industries to be more prominent and more focused on western Europe. Need for further study is obvious, and the field will prove to be most fruitful once a culture industry definition settles in the literature and internationally comparative data becomes available.

Appendix Three-star maps of sample countries

The legend for each map relates the number of stars to a shade of grey.

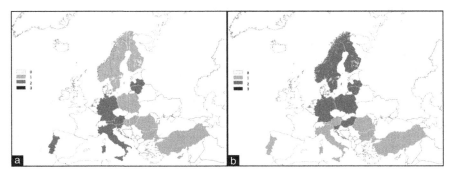

Figure 5A.1 (a) Architectural activities and (b) book publishing.
Source: based on Authors' calculations.

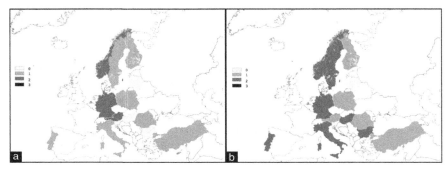

Figure 5A.2 (a) Motion picture projection activities, and (b) motion picture, video and television programme distribution activities.
Source: based on Authors' calculations.

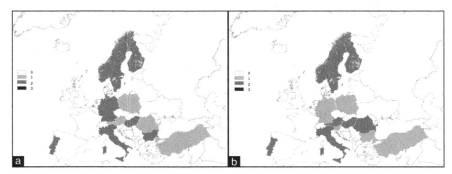

Figure 5A.3 (a) Motion picture, video and television programme post-production activities, and (b) motion picture, video and television programme production activities.
Source: based on Authors' calculations.

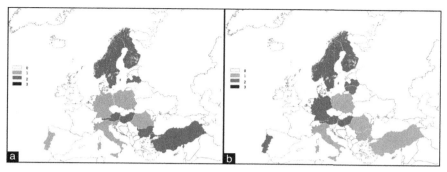

Figure 5A.4 (a) News agency activities, and (b) publishing of journals and periodicals.
Source: based on Authors' calculations.

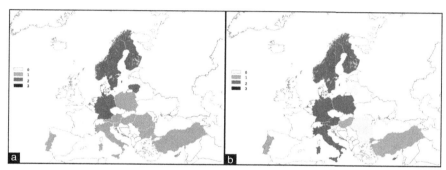

Figure 5A.5 (a) Publishing of newspapers, and (b) renting of video tapes and disks.
Source: based on Authors' calculations.

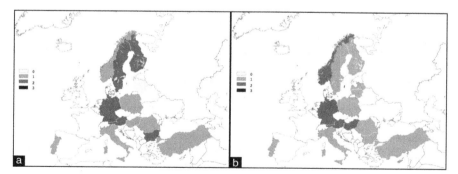

Figure 5A.6 (a) Retail sale of audio and video equipment in specialized stores and (b) retail sale of books in specialized stores.
Source: based on Authors' calculations.

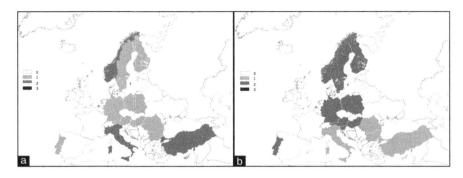

Figure 5A.7 (a) Retail sale of music and video recordings in specialized stores and (b) sound recording and music publishing activities.

Source: based on Authors' calculations.

References

Bernard, A. B. and Jensen, J. B. (1999) *Exporting and Productivity*. Working paper 7135. Cambridge, MA: National Bureau of Economic Research.

Beyers, W. B. (2006) Cultural and recreational industries in the United States. *The Service Industries Journal* 28(3): 375–391.

Council of Europe (1997) *In from the Margins: A Contribution to the Debate on Culture and Development in Europe*. Strasbourg: Council of Europe Publishing.

Cunningham, S. D. and Higgs, P. L. (2008) Creative industries mapping: where have we come from and where are we going? *Creative Industries Journal* 1(1): 7–30.

Domenech, R. B., Lazzeretti, L., Oliver, J. L. H. and Ruiz, B. T. (2011) *Creative Clusters in Europe: A Microdata Approach*. Conference paper ersa11p471. Louvain-la-Neuve: European Regional Science Association.

ECO (2014) European cluster observatory: methodology and indicators. Available at http://tinyurl.com/pwzm44y (accessed 10 September 2014).

Eisenberg, C., Gerlach, R. and Handke, C. (2006) Cultural industries: the British experience in international perspective. Available at http://tinyurl.com/omhbtyu (accessed 8 December 2014).

European Commission (2006) The Economy of Culture in Europe. Study prepared by KEA, European Affairs for the European Commission, Directorate-General for Education and Culture, Brussels. Available at http://tinyurl.com/ktctmca (accessed 4 December 2014).

Farchy, J. and Sagot-Duvauroux, D. (1994) *Economie des politiques culturelles*. Paris: Presses Universitaires de France.

Garnham, N. (1983) Toward a theory of cultural materialism. *Journal of Communication* 33: 314–329.

Heilbrun, J. (1996) Growth, accesability and the distribution of arts activity in the United States: 1980 to 1990. *Journal of Cultural Economics* 20(40): 283–296.

Heilbrun, J. and Gray, C. M. (2001) *The Economics of Art and Culture*. Cambridge: Cambridge University Press.

Holzl W. (2005) *Entrepreneurship, Entry and Exit in Creative Industries: An Explanatory Survey*. Working paper no. 1. Vienna: Vienna Science and Technology Fund.

Horkheimer, M. and Adorno, T. W. (1944) *Philosophische Fragmente*. New York: Social Studies Association.

Ketel, C., Lindqvist, G. and Sölvell, Ö. (2012) *Strengthening Clusters and Competitiveness in Europe: The Role of Cluster Organisations*. The Cluster Observatory Report. Stockholm: Stockholm School of Economics.

Ketel, C. and Sölvell, Ö. (2006) Clusters in the EU-10 new member countries. Available at http://tinyurl.com/lgn7z9c (accessed 10 September 2014).

Lash, S. and Urry, J. (1994) *Economies of Signs and Space*. London: Sage Publications.

Lazzeretti, L., Boix, R. and Capone, F. (2009) Why do creative industries cluster? An analysis of the determinants of clustering of creative industries. Paper presented at DRUID Society Summer Conference, Copenhagen, Denmark, 19 June.

Markusen, A., Wassall, G. H., DeNatale, D. and Cohen, R. (2008) Defining the cultural economy: industry and occupational approaches. *Economic Development Quarterly* 22(1): 24–45.

Mommaas, H. (2004) Cultural clusters and the post-industrial city: towards the remapping of urban cultural policy. *Urban Studies* 41(3): 507–532.

O'Brien, J. and Feist, A. (1997) *Employment in the Arts and Cultural Industries: An Analysis of the Labour Force Survey and Other Sources*. London: Arts Council of England.

Pine, B. J. II and Gilmore, J. H. (1999) *The Experience Economy*. Boston, MA: Harvard Business School Press.

Porter, M. E. (1990) *Competitive Advantage of Nations*. New York: The Free Press.

Porter, M. E. (1998) Clusters and the new economics of competition. *Harvard Business Review* (November). Available at https://hbr.org/1998/11/clusters-and-the-new-economics-of-competition.

Power, D. (2002) Cultural industries in Sweden: an assessment of their place in the Swedish economy. *Economic Geography* 78(2): 103–127.

Pratt, A. (2004) Mapping the cultural industries: regionalization; the example of South East England. In D. Power and A. Scott (eds), *Cultural Industries and the Production of Culture*, 19–36. New York: Routledge.

Söndermann, M., Backes, C. and Brunink, O. A. D. (2009) *Kultur- und Kreativwirtschaft: Ermittlung der gemeinsamen charakteristischen Definitionselemente der heterogenen Teilbereiche der Kulturwirtschaft zur Bestimmung ihrer Perspektiven aus volkswirtschaftlicher Sicht*. Cologne: Bundesministerium für Wirtschaft und Technologie.

Throsby, D. (2001) *Economics and Culture*. Cambridge: Cambridge University Press.

Towse, R. (2003) *A Handbook of Cultural Economics*. Northampton, MA: Edward Elgar.

UNESCO (1996) Our Creative Diversity: Report of the World Commission on Culture and Development. Paris: UNESCO.

UNESCO (1998) *World Culture Report: Culture, Creativity and Markets*. Paris: UNESCO.

UNESCO (2000) *World Culture Report: Cultural Diversity, Conflict and Pluralism*. Paris: UNESCO.

UNESCO-UIS (2005) *International Flows of Selected Goods and Services, 1994–2003*. Montreal: UNESCO Institute for Statistics.

UNESCO-UIS (2009) *Measuring the Economic Contribution of Cultural Industries: A Review and Assessment of Current Methodological Approaches*. Montreal: UNESCO Institute for Statistics.

World Bank (2003) *Urban Development Needs Creativity: How Creative Industries Affect Urban Areas*. November. Washington, DC: Development Outreach.

Part II

Knowledge migration, diaspora networks and commuting entrepreneurs

6 Migration and innovation

A survey

Sheida Rashidi-Kollmann and Andreas Pyka

Introduction

The patterns of migration processes are complex. A first, to some extent simple explanation for this complex picture is that countries use different methods of collecting data on migration flows. A further increase in the complexity of migration processes stems from the fact that the composition of migrants is subject to considerable change over time. In the globalized economy, high-skilled migration has intensified competition among countries to attract the best talents. Recent trends in international migration confirm that in developed countries more and more migrants arrive with tertiary education. International students and migrant entrepreneurs have become of outmost importance as a source of high-skilled migrants. The statistics of international students worldwide shows a strong increase for the last three decades. Moreover, migrant entrepreneurs employ on average at least 2.4 per cent of the total employed population in OECD countries. A considerable number of high-skilled individuals also arrive as envoys of multinational companies.

Traditionally high-skilled migration is mainly considered as a loss to the emigration countries and analysed under the heading *brain drain*. In this perspective, emigration of high-skilled leads to reduced economic growth for sending countries (most often synonymous for less developed countries). The implementation of policies to retract the *lost brains* (*repatriation policies*) adds a further research area to the migration literature. Return of high-skilled migrants is supposed to compensate the outflows for sending countries because the original home countries can potentially benefit from the skills and experience that migrants have gained abroad. However, impressing economic growth rates of economies like China, India or Taiwan and the role of the support from their emigrants for this economic success, is indicating that emigration of high-skilled labour, even without a return option, might be beneficial for sending countries.

Today, many studies of migration processes apply network analysis to disentangle the complexity of international migration flows. With the discovery of the meaning of skilled labour networks a shift from the *brain drain view* in skilled migration to a *brain circulation view* can be noticed. The emergence of *diaspora networks* comprising well-educated migrants improves access to capital, information and contacts for its members in the home and host countries. Different terms such as intellectual diaspora networks, scientific diaspora, knowledge networks abroad and diaspora knowledge networks are found in the literature to describe the same phenomenon. These networks reveal that knowledge migration is a phenomenon beyond the migration of people only. Diaspora networks support the diffusion of knowledge and are an important component for economic growth in knowledge-based economies.

Entrepreneurship and innovation, driven by knowledge accumulation and generation, are key drivers of economic development and growth. In these learning processes external knowledge plays an important role. External knowledge becomes available through spillovers and knowledge transfers among heterogeneous economic agents. Migration is a rich source to enhance the diversity among economic agents and their individual knowledge bases. The interaction between skilled workers with heterogeneous knowledge creates knowledge spillovers and spurs idea creation. Cultural diversity may open up rich sources of innovation and creativity because it extends variety in abilities and knowledge. Networks formed by immigrants, particularly transnational networks make communication and information exchange easier and support the exploration and exploitation of the opportunities offered by cultural diversity. This process of mutual learning and cross-fertilization is embedded in institutional structures which locally differ strongly.

In this paper we survey the theoretical and empirical literature on the relationship between innovation and migration. We begin with a descriptive view of figures describing the development of migration flows and their structuring over the past decades. We then survey the theoretical literature explaining migration of high skilled starting from traditional neoclassical approaches embedding migration into an equilibrium framework and ending with Neo-Schumpeterian approaches which reflect on the knowledge which travels back and forth with the migrants as well as the possibilities to improve the innovation potentials by cross-fertilization of different knowledge and cultural backgrounds. We survey the rare empirical studies of this phenomenon and collect evidence for a confirmation of the brain circulation and innovation network view related to Neo-Schumpeterian economics, and finally we present our conclusions.

A descriptive view on high-skilled migration

International migration and the measurement problem

Migration has existed throughout history, in different forms and influenced by wars, natural catastrophes, business cycles and political issues. The United Nations estimate that around 214 million people in the world live abroad (UNDESA 2009). This is about 0.3 per cent of the world population. Generally people migrate because of humanitarian reasons, family-related reasons or working reasons. Based on their migration intentions, migrants are classified in different categories (Castles 2000): refugees, asylum seekers, irregular migrants, forced migrants, labour migrants as well as high-skilled and business migrants.

Comparing international data on total immigrant population suffers from the different national views concerning who is an "immigrant". This makes research in this field so difficult. For example, some European countries, Japan and Korea refer to foreign residents; according to their definition, immigrants are viewed as persons with a foreign nationality. Other countries, basically the settlement countries such as the USA, Canada, New Zealand and Australia refer to foreign-born population by which they mean the first generation of migrants who have immigrated to the country of residence. Because the acquisition of the nationality by immigrants is likewise easier there, statistics on persons of foreign nationality are rare. The simplification of naturalization in several countries together with the increasing figures of migrants makes estimates based on the two different concepts less comparable. With an increasing share of immigrants and an increasing share among them acquiring the citizenship of the host country and become nationals the scale of population of foreign citizenship tends to remain stable or to grow only slowly, while the population of foreign-born continues to increase strongly (Dumont and Lemaître 2005: 116).

Pronounced asymmetries in data collection are a further distortion of comparisons of immigration flows. The taxonomies of the various countries with respect to different immigrant categories differ: Some countries for instance include asylum seekers in their immigrant population, some others not. Also the duration of the stay to be counted as an immigrant differs from country to country. Concerning *emigration*, the picture is even more complex. Several countries do not collect such information at all. Therefore, collecting data in order to compare countries with respect to the net migration flow is far from easy.

Trends in international migration

The time period between 1956 and 2004 covered in Figure 6.1 displays the trend of the net immigration to the OECD countries as a percentage of the countries' populations. The net international migration for OECD countries in 1956 was 10 per cent in the total population of OECD countries. In 2004 it was above 30 per cent and in 2002 this percentage peaked with almost 40 per cent. Most of the peaks in this time series can be traced back to specific historical events, for example the 1962 peak marks the end of the Algerian war and return of many French citizens from Algeria.

One of the important developments in international migration after World War II has been the emergence of *guest workers*: Western European countries such as Germany, Switzerland, Belgium and France recruited workers form less economically developed countries in their process of economic recovery. The peak in this development was reached in 1971. Among these countries Germany is mostly associated with guest workers (Keeley 2009: 25–26).

According to the OECD (2001), most recent trends in international migration are characterized by an upward trend which additionally exhibits the following characteristics:

- despite the greater inflow of asylum seekers the predominance of family linked migration can be observed
- growing employment-related immigration;
- development of new forms of immigration such as transfer of staff within multinational companies, the temporary movements of skilled workers to provide services, higher mobility of students; and
- also retired persons choosing to live abroad.

Furthermore, foreign populations are increasing and diversifying but remain concentrated around urban areas.

Concerning labour market oriented migration, since 1990 three major developments have opened up new possibilities in OECD countries: Southern European countries become immigration targets in the 1990s, the eastern enlargement of the European Union in 2004 and in 2007 and the US policy revision with respect to illegal immigrants who had entered the States in the 1980s.

Comparing net migration flows between North America and Europe it becomes obvious that although European countries are not traditional immigration countries, still net immigration to Europe is higher (Figure 6.2). The decline in 2009 is due to the financial crisis that affected GDP growth in most countries. Nevertheless European countries are faced with a rising labour demand. To some extent this is due to the demographic aging problem Europe is facing. And much of the new labour demand in Europe can be satisfied with

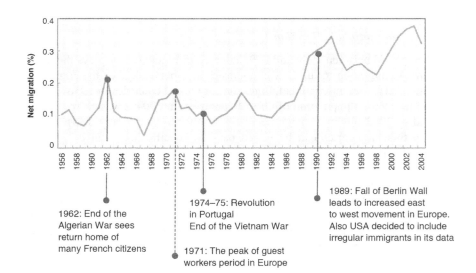

Figure 6.1 Net migration as percentage of total population in OECD countries, 1956–2004.

Source: adapted from Keeley (2009: 28).

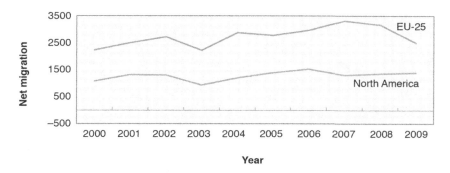

Figure 6.2 Inflow of foreign population into EU-25 and North America (thousands).
Source: adapted from the data provided in OECD (2011a: 341, appendix I).

Eastern European migrants because with the Eastern Enlargement Western European opened their labour markets towards the East (Stalker 2002).

Highly skilled immigration

For distinguishing between high-skilled migration and low-skilled migration, a definition of high-skilled migrants is necessary. So far, the concept of "high-skilled migrant" is not precisely defined. The terms and respective understanding of skilled and high-skilled persons is inconsistent across nations. Basically one finds a number of sub-categories which vary across countries. High-skilled specialists, independent executives and senior managers, specialized technicians, researchers, physicians, business people, key workers (i.e. staff with special skills) and sub-contract workers are all identified as high-skilled individuals. A straightforward method for gathering data is to define high-skilled as synonymous with tertiary education. Recent trends in international migration confirm that more and more migrants with tertiary education arrive in developed countries. A comparison between European and North-American countries confirms that North-America receives more highly educated immigrants. By 2002 among arriving immigrants in the United States 30 per cent have been adults with a tertiary education, while only 25 per cent of the new arrivals are high-skilled in Europe (Figure 6.3).

Figure 6.4 shows for the year 2001 the immigrant and emigrant high-skilled population in OECD countries and the high-skilled net migration. With the exception of some Central and Eastern European countries, Mexico, Ireland, Korea and Finland, net migration is positive for the OECD countries. This implies that most OECD countries benefit from the international mobility of high-skilled persons. For the United States the number of high-skilled net migration is strongly positive (+7.7 million), Canada and Australia are ranked second and third. The figure illustrates partially the brain exchange within OECD countries.

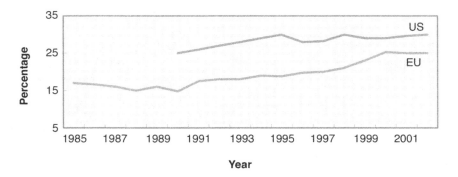

Figure 6.3 Percentage of new immigrant adults aged 15–64 with tertiary education.
Source: IOM (2008: 54).

In Table 6.1 Reiner (2010) compares (using data from 2008) the share of high-skilled migrants in North America and four large EU countries. This comparison shows that the European countries are characterized by a higher emigration rate of high-skilled (UK ranks highest with 16.7% followed by Germany with 8.8% whereas the value for the US is 0.5% and for Canada 4.9%). Additionally, the migration balances for *star scientists* for the six countries are displayed. According to ISI Highly Cited,[1] star scientists are defined as researchers that have been most highly cited in the period 1981–1999. Also this indicator expresses the advantageous position of the US. Accordingly, Reiner (2010: 499) summarizes:

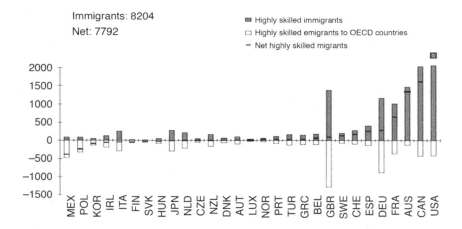

Figure 6.4 Immigrant and emigrant population 15+ with tertiary education in OECD countries (thousands).
Source: Dumont and Lemaître (2005: 126).

Table 6.1 High-skilled migration in North America and the big four EU countries.

Country	Share of foreign population with tertiary education	People with tertiary education, living abroad (%)	Migration balances for star scientists
Canada	38.0	4.9	0.0
USA	26.1	0.5	+23.4
UK	34.8	16.7	−3.6
France	18.1	3.9	+0.5
Germany	14.9	8.8	−1.7
Italy	12.2	7.0	−1.6

Source: Reiner (2010: 450).

"All and all, compared to USA and Canada, Europe seems to have a weak position in the competition for global talent."
After this descriptive overview of high-skilled migration, it is useful to see from which sources the high-skilled immigrants come and what their motivations are.

International students

International students' inflows represent an important source of high-skilled immigrants. In 2009 there have been 3.7 million international students enrolled worldwide, this is more than three times larger compared to the 1.1 million in 1990 (OECD 2011b). In the past three decades this number has been increasing drastically starting from 0.8 million in 1975. Not only the number of international students enrolled at universities and research institutes is increasing but also many of the international students after graduation intent to search for a job and stay in the host countries either temporarily - to gain first experience - or even for a longer time. For example in 2008–2009 around 17 per cent of international students in Austria and around 33 per cent of international students in Canada and 26 per cent in Germany changed their status from students and stayed in their host countries (OECD 2011b: 67). Beside this, several universities are offering double degrees, student exchange programs and overseas research opportunities for PhD students. In 2008 among 3.3 million international students worldwide, 2.3 million were enrolled at the universities in OECD countries. Most international students (almost 70%) come from outside the OECD area (OECD 2011a: 65) and among them the Chinese and the Indian fractions are strongest.

Migrant entrepreneurship

Migrant entrepreneurs contribute to the economy of the host country by creating new businesses. Every year, migrant entrepreneurs employ on average 2.4 per cent of the total number of employees in OECD countries. In the United States between 1995 and 2005, 25.3 per cent of technology- and engineering- based firms had at least one key founder who was foreign-born. 52.4 per cent of Silicon Valley start-ups had one or more immigrants as a key founder (Wadhwa *et al.* 2007). In Germany, in 2007 and in 2008 migrant entrepreneurs employed more than 750,000 persons. In Canada Chinese entrepreneurs employed 650,000 workers, the majority of which were not Chinese (OECD 2011a: 157). Therefore, migrant entrepreneurs, not only contribute to economic performance and growth, but also to entrepreneurship and innovation.

Intra-company transfers

A new form of high-skilled migration is intra-company transfers. As companies become multinational, the number of employees which move for a limited period to another country within the company increases. In several countries a considerable number of high-skilled individuals arrive as *transferees*. Several countries have adapted their policies to facilitate the movement of staff within firms. The number of intra-corporate transfers depends on the number and size of multinational enterprises in a country and their willingness or ability to recruit workers locally or to temporarily transfer their own employees. Intra-company transfers account for a small fraction of migration, although they may be a significant fraction of high-skilled labour movement (OECD 2011a: 56). Multinational firms make use of this flexibility in moving their specialists in response to their needs in different locations without having to be dependent on the existent regional competencies in the areas in which they are doing business. According to OECD data (ibid.: 57) in 2009 a total of 124 thousands intra-company transferees were observed within OECD countries. This figure excludes the figures within Europe which is counted as a single area.

Innovation and migration in economic theory: a survey

In the early literature on *migration* the topics of *brain drain* where discussed in a human capital framework. Scott (1970: 273) summarizes the central argument: "The human capital approach automatically leads economists to compare brain drain to capital movements and form questions about preventing it." The earliest theoretical works can be found in international trade theory, exploring whether and in what sense brain drain is a problem. Authors like Harry Johnson (1965) and later Grubel and Scott (1966) studied the positive and negative effects of moving scientists and professionals with respect to their country of origin. On the one hand, it is argued that countries faced with emigration of their high-skilled labour force might reduce their funding of higher education (Regets 2001: 245). On the other hand, observing the success of emigrants raises the incentives of natives for higher education, an effect in particular to be observed in developing countries.

Since the early 1980s *brain gain* and *reverse brain drain* issues have attracted increasing attention. A possible negative impact of immigration for the host country, which has been discussed, is the *crowding out* on the labour market of the native labour by immigrants. For example, Borjas (1999) argues that foreign students may crowd out native students from the best graduate schools. Regets (2001) is emphasizing a consistency problem in many of these political debates: If crowding-out effects are relevant and immigrants strengthen labour supply in the host countries, wages of high-skilled occupations decrease; from this follows lower incentives of the locals to invest in their human capital. At the same time, however, it is argued, that low-skilled immigration substitutes low-skilled natives and reduces wages at the lower wage levels. This will lead to stronger inequalities in income distribution. If both arguments are accepted, then the consequence is that high-skilled immigration reduces income inequality whereas low-skilled migrants increase the incentive for natives to invest in human capital. This effect is empirically not proven, but studies for the United States so far show that a higher proportion of foreign-born employees goes hand in hand with higher salaries (ibid.: 251).

In this discussion De Haas (2010) argues that the ambivalent view on migration is to be seen as part of a more general paradigm shift in social and development theory. Concerning the optimistic view, migration is viewed as a form of optimal allocation of production factors (ibid.), in particular in a strict neoclassical view. From late 1960s the pessimistic view on migration is connected with debates on *brain drain* effects. In this pessimistic perspective, migration increases inequalities (ibid.). The empirical evidence, however, challenges both, pessimistic and optimistic views and asks for a new approach. Pluralist views on migration and development interactions such as the *new economics of labour migration* (NELM) with its transnational perspective on migration and development offer such a new approach. In NELM the impacts of migration in a *knowledge-based economy* are emphasized. The strengthening of knowledge flows and collaboration between heterogeneous agents facilitated by immigrants together with the linkages they create with universities and training centres allow expecting a strong return on their human capital with the persons becoming economically active.

In cases the emigration of high-skilled workers and students were considered a "loss" in the productive capacity to the sending country - at least temporarily – the emigration countries have implemented special policies such as *restrictive*, *incentive* and *compensatory* policies in order to counteract the potential *brain drain* (Brown 2000). However, the effectiveness of these strategies remains dubious because the increasing trend in high-skilled migration was not affected. *Restrictive* policies, designed to make emigration more difficult, are effective only temporarily, if at all. *Incentive* policies are not a real option in developing countries: they can offer neither salaries nor infrastructures which are internationally competitive. *Compensatory* taxation (to be paid by the receiving country or the migrant) in order to compensate the loss to the sending country are also impossible: the loss cannot be measured in monetary terms.

Stark (2003) and Stark *et al.* (1997) evaluate the human capital formation in an economy with migration and without migration. They theoretically show that a carefully designed migration policy can be welfare-enhancing for the sending country. Related to human capital formation influenced by migration, Beine *et al.* (2001) discuss two contradictory impacts of high-skilled migration; a *brain effect* and a *drain effect*. Since in a poor country the return to human capital is low and therefore can lead to limited incentives to pursue education, allowing migration from this country increases the educated fraction of its population and given that only a proportion of educated finally emigrate, the average level of education increases. This impact of high-skilled migration constitutes the brain effect and is potentially positive if it dominates the drain effect. The size of the drain effect is determined by the number of educated persons that leave the country. Depending on the sizes of both effects, *beneficial brain drain* might exist. Beine *et al.* (2001: 288) further show evidence for their theory at the empirical level: "Beneficial Brain Drain is more than a theory, mainly because migration prospects seem to play a significant role in education decisions."

Regets (2001) additionally argues that the incentives for human capital invest-ment increase because *brain drain* leads to an increased scarcity of high-skilled workers in the sending country and raises the domestic returns to skills. A further positive effect stems from the improvement in the organization of labour markets for high-skilled workers in the sending country. In particular, in cases of a lack of demand for high-skilled workers, emigration acts as a *stabilizer* reducing the risk of investment in human capital.

For the authors emphasizing the positive aspects of high-skilled emigration effects on the sending country (Stark *et al.* 1997; Beine *et al.* 2001; Mountford 1997) an optimal level of migration exists where the negative brain drain effects are compensated for. A further argument often found in the literature has to be mentioned in this survey as well: The effect of remittances of emigrants to the sending countries. Skilled migrants earn more and therefore, other things being equal, are likely to remit more. Some authors argue that the negative effects of the brain drain are somewhat offset by inward remittances from migrants (Faini 2007: 179).

A more recent approach to the migration of high-skilled is the *brain gain through return migration* or even *brain circulation*. This approach applies a dynamic network perspective to consider the effects of economic connections of migrants within the host country and to his/her country of origin. This perspective highlights that emigration of high-skilled is not only a loss for the sending country. The migrants entertain linkages to their countries of origin which are used to transfer knowledge and to initiate economic activities. Also after a return of the migrants, established relations connect the origin and the host countries with important economic implications for both countries. Social ties between skilled workers facilitate the transfer of knowledge and the return of experienced high-skilled migrants well connected in international business may more than compensate for the brain drain of new outflows. Therefore, sending countries potentially benefit from the skills and social ties accumulated abroad by their emigrants.

In the literature different reasons for return migration are discussed: failure, conservatism, retirement and innovation (Wickramasekara 2003: 11). Return migration is analysed within different theoretical approaches (Cassarino 2004). The NELM views return migration as a normal step after the migrants met their targets. Attachment to homeland and households eventually brings the emigrants back home after their goals are met. The returnee has acquired skills and experiences which he/she brings into the economy of the country of origin. In terms of social network theory the returnees are viewed as owners of tangible and intangible resources.

Cassarino (2004: 265) states: "Just like the transnational approach to return migration, social network theory views returnees as migrants who maintain strong linkages with their former places of settlement in other countries." In the transnationalism theory, the returnees are seen as actors that mobilize resources stemming from general attributes such as religion and ethnicity, and social network theory emphasizes that actors mobilize resources available at the level of social and economic cross border networks. In both transnationalism and social network theory return is not seen as the end of the migration process but it is instead a stage of it.

According to the two theories, the sending countries eventually can benefit from brain gain by return of their emigrants. Gains may flow back to the developing country via returnees with enhanced skills, personal connections, and ideas for innovation (Saxenian 2005). The return option was implemented in the 1970s (until the 1990s) in so-called repatriation policies which should encourage high-skilled emigrants to return home. However, developing countries are usually not in the situation to offer the same incentives to their high-skilled migrants as they have access to in developed countries. Thus only a few newly industrialized countries such as China, India, South Korea, Hong Kong and Taiwan were successful in the implementation of these strategies (Brown 2002).

The standard labour market model of immigration assumes that migration is a mere reaction to the current economic conditions; nevertheless immigration evidently reacts to the countries' long-run prospects for economic growth and development. These long run impacts depend on how immigrants affect the economic growth rate. The early models of economic growth view growth as a result of an increase of the production factors, labour and capital, or improvement of technology leading to greater productivity. In evolutionary economics, instead, the key driver of economic evolution is entrepreneurship and innovation (Boschma and Martin 2010: 136). Creating variation and fostering the diffusion of varieties are the two important roles played by entrepreneurs. In evolutionary economics economic actors are heterogeneous implying that individuals as economic agents are endowed with different knowledge, skills, attributes and preferences.

Similarly, environments are heterogeneous, implying that they are endowed with different knowledge, institutions, resources as well as demand for products. Hence the entrepreneurial process depends on and is a result of the interaction between agents and their environment. External knowledge sources play a major role in the Schumpeterian view. External knowledge can become available through involuntary spillovers or intended knowledge transfers and collaborations. In her survey on empirical studies on location and innovation, Feldmann (1999) finds two major traditions: (i) the concept of geographically mediated spillovers which adds a geographic dimension to the determinants of innovation; and (ii) the determinants of differences in economic growth rates of different regions. In the first tradition authors try to quantify the impact of knowledge spillovers on innovation by referring to geography and based their estimations on production functions. Authors of the second tradition consider for example agglomeration economics which foster innovation, and with it regional economic growth. In addition to this diversity argument, networks and national institutions play important roles in the economic development, in particular in knowledge based economies.

The role of diversity

Boschma and Martin (2010: 142) stress a further perspective on migration and innovation by addressing the additional possibilities of cross-fertilization due to the migrants' knowledge: "Innovation is a product of interaction between actors that have sufficiently different knowledge, in order to make Schumpeterian new combinations." The combination of diverse knowledge plays an important role in the exploration of the knowledge landscape. Diversity is to be conceived as a broad concept which goes beyond diversity in production factors and resources, diversity in products but encompasses also diversity in technology and knowledge bases, behaviours and cultures. In other words, the concept of diversity stresses that economic agents are heterogeneous in all dimensions. The different types of diversities are not independent but mutually influence each other in a complementary way. Ozgen *et al.* (2010: 9) describe diversity in the economy with a multilayer concept, in which ethnic, linguistic, religious and personal perceptions of belongings interact with the effects of diversity on innovation. Migration increases the diversity in ethnic identities.

Constant *et al.* (2006: 5) define ethnic identity as the balance of the commitments with a host country and the country of origin. Keely (2003) focusses on the interaction between high-skilled migrants and the local labour force which enhances the knowledge spillover pool and supports the creation of new ideas. These interactions are not random but specific patterns are to be observed in the form of clusters and networks. The networks serve as channels of knowledge transfer which besides the exchange of knowledge contribute to mutual learning and new knowledge creation. The architecture of these networks depends on national institutions and therefore differ between countries which results in varying contributions to innovation.

Additionally, there is a trade-off between the positive and negative impacts of cultural diversity. The negative impacts stem from language and cultural barriers between native workers and high-skilled migrants which increase transaction costs. A higher diversity, hence, does not necessarily imply improved innovation performance. Too much cultural diversity in a region might frustrate mutual understanding, cause social stress situations or distortion of local identities. To illustrate this relationship between diversity and economic performance, De Graaff and Nijkamp (2010) introduce an inverted U-shape relation which allows for the derivation of an optimal level of diversity. Niebuhr (2009) considers the positive effects to outweigh the negative effects. This is caused by the strong complementary effects of the immigrants:

> Due to their different cultural backgrounds, it is likely that migrants and native workers have fairly diverse abilities and knowledge. Thus, there might be skill complementarities between foreign and native workers in addition to those among workers of the same qualification levels.
>
> (Niebuhr 2009: 564)

Cultural diversity therefore supports innovation and creativity because it strengthens variety in abilities and knowledge (Alesina and La Ferrara 2005; Niebuhr 2009). A similar argument can be found in Saxenian (2005) and Kerr (2008) who see an amplification of the knowledge spillover pool due to the increasing internationalization of its sources. In this process *ethnic entrepreneurs* are of crucial importance.

The role of networks

The participation in innovation networks is a source of competitive advantage for firms, regions and countries, in particular in knowledge intensive industries. The performance of innovation networks is strongly related with knowledge mobility in the network. Network structures link the diverse knowledge of agents and serve as channels for the exchange of knowledge. Pyka and Küppers outline:

> Innovation networks have three major characteristics: they are like co-ordination devices that enable and support the inter-firm learning by accelerating the diffusion of new knowledge. Second, the development of complementarities becomes possible within networks and finally innovation networks constitute an organizational setting that opens the possibility of exploration of synergies by combination of different technological competencies.
>
> (Pyka and Küppers 2002: 6)

Networks with immigrants, particularly transnational networks allow for communication and information exchange which without the network linkages would be difficult. This improves the availability of information on skills, technology and capital as well as on potential collaborators. It also facilitates the timely responses that are essential in a highly competitive environment (Saxenian 2005: 38).

Return migration is considered as knowledge transfer in a network where the country of origin benefits from skills which are gained by its emigrants in the resident countries. As the left side of Figure 6.5 displays, the linkage which exists in the case of return migration can be directed from the country of residence towards the country of origin only. In this case not the full potential of the network connection is exploited.

However, the linkages between country of residence and country of origin can also be bi-directional. Groups of high-skilled expatriates keeping connections with their homelands are called *diaspora networks* displayed on the right side of Figure 6.5. High-skilled immigration sometimes creates large, well-educated diaspora networks, which considerably improve access to capital, information and valuable contacts for firms in the countries of origin (Kuznetsov 2006). In the literature the notions of *intellectual diaspora networks* (Brown 2002), *scientific diaspora* (Barré *et al.* 2003), *technological and scientific diasporas* (Turner *et al.* 2003), *knowledge networks abroad* (Kuznetsov 2006) and *diaspora knowledge networks* (Meyer and Wattiaux 2006) are also used to describe the bi-directional knowledge flows in innovation networks of migrants between the countries of residence and the countries of origin. Diaspora networks therefore offer an alternative view which goes beyond the brain drain discussion. Indeed, the network approach to brain drain (Brown 2002) has massively changed the evaluation of high-skilled mobility. Instead of the traditional brain drain outflow, a *brain drain skill circulation* moves into the forefront which displaces the potential loss of human resources with a remote but accessible asset of expanded networks (Meyer 2001). Migration is no longer considered as a one-way path but as a dynamic process of networking and creation of linkages (Mahroum and Guchteneire 2006: 27). Meyer (2007) adds that the diaspora option allows for countries of origin to access not only the human capital acquired by their expatriates in the residence country, but also the access to social, cultural, intellectual and institutional capital. The diaspora networks do not have to be formally established but often are informal which is sufficient for the exchange of knowledge (Pyka 1997). Immigrants' networks, formal or informal, are developing structures which enhance the flow of knowledge, in particular tacit knowledge, and support the

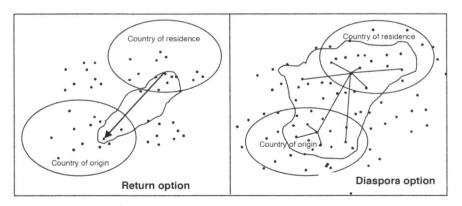

Figure 6.5 Return and diaspora option.
Source: Meyer (2007: 7).

development of new ideas and knowledge. It turned out that the networks constituted by skilled migrants are different compared to networks of low or unskilled migrants (Vertovec 2002) where knowledge exchange is less important. Diaspora networks for the exchange of knowledge follow similar principles to those which are observed in innovation networks in general. Direct communication between heterogeneous agents is important for the transfer of tacit knowledge.

Agrawal *et al.* (2006) develop and test a model of knowledge spillovers that depends on the social ties between inventors. They find that social ties which facilitate knowledge transfer continue to exist even after the network members are geographically separated. A further study by Agrawal and Oettl (2008) analyses the patterns of knowledge flows which occur when inventors move. In this study countries enjoy a competitive advantage if they are able to make use of the cross border knowledge flows (*national learning-by immigration*). Also the firms might benefit from the knowledge flows from the inventor's new country (*firm learning from diaspora*).

A particular role in these networks is played by transnational entrepreneurs (i.e. entrepreneurs who start a business drawing on resources from different countries). According to Drori *et al.* (2009), transnational entrepreneurs use their networks to explore profit opportunities in both countries and are engaged in both countries to promote their activities. With the exploitation of cross-border knowledge flows and prolific frameworks supporting transnational entrepreneurship, we refer already to the broad institutional set up which characterizes countries in the organization of their innovation processes, namely *national innovation systems*.

The role of national innovation systems

The concept of the national innovation system (NIS) (Freeman 1987; Lundvall 1992; Edquist 1997; Nelson 1993) captures the interactions between different institutions and organizations that create and adopt innovations in a country. In a NIS large parts of the knowledge base is tacit and originates from the routines of leaning-by-doing and learning-by-interacting among firms. Chris Freeman (1987) highlights the role of innovation networks - comprising private and public actors in an institutional embedding – in initiating, importing, modifying and diffusing new technologies. A NIS strongly shapes the patterns of information and knowledge flows among individuals, institutions and firms and accordingly of high-skilled migrants and transnational entrepreneurs. NIS differ strongly among different countries and due to the increasing internationalization of economic activities which embeds a NIS in the global innovation system (Tomlinson 2001: 32–33). NIS are also relevant for the possibilities to access international knowledge transfers. The globalizing innovation system is sketched in Figure 6.6 which includes firms and institutions at the national level as well as institutions and organizations at the global level which all interact in the development of the different national knowledge bases.

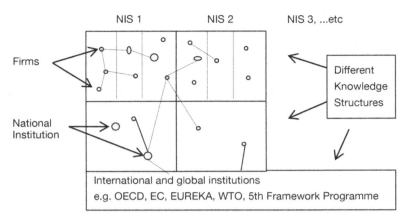

Figure 6.6 The globalizing system of innovation.
Source: Tomlinson (2001: 32).

Besides interactions of actors in the different NIS also the movement of agents in the globalizing innovation systems is essential for the national innovation performance. How immigration of high skilled economic agents affects the countries of origin and the countries of residence depends on the designs of NISs. But not only on a national level the impact of high-skilled migration differs, but also on a regional and metropolitan level the impact varies considerably. For example, Lee and Nathan (2010) show that high performing cities attract more high-skilled immigrants and therefore create a culturally diverse workforce which again supports their innovation performance.

Empirical studies on innovation and migration – a survey

Empirical research on the relationship between high-skilled migration and innovation is rare and predominantly focussed on North America and some other traditional immigration countries. The United States are a striking example of how immigrant scientists have contributed to national innovation performance. Hunt and Gauthier-Loiselle (2009) list the outstanding successes of high-skilled immigration to the US: 26 per cent of US based Nobel Prize winners in the 1990s are immigrants, 25 per cent of founders of public venture-backed US companies in the years 1990–2005 are immigrants and 25 per cent of new high-tech companies with more than one million dollars in sales in 2006 were founded by immigrants. Further, more than 50 per cent of the engineers and scientists employed in Silicon Valley are immigrants. This high innovation performance of the immigrants is related to their participation in national and regional innovation networks combined with their bounder spanning diaspora networks; for example, Saxenian *et al.* (2002) found that Taiwanese and Indian engineers have built networks in Silicon Valley which connect them with their homeland technology community and which are used for intense knowledge and information traffic.

The main topics investigated in the empirical literature are the crowd-out and/or crowd-in effects, scale-effects, entrepreneurship and the role of diversity. As a measure for innovation, mainly patent per capita data are used. Kerr and Lincoln (2008) investigate the influence of fluctuations of H-1B visas[2] and their influence on the rate of patenting by ethnic Indian and Chinese in the United States. The authors find that there is a significant correlation between the fluctuations of H-1B visa recipients and the rate of patenting. They also conclude that "total invention increases with higher admission levels primarily through the direct contributions of immigrant inventors" (ibid.: 30).

Related to the effects of students' mobility, Stuen *et al.* (2010) studied the contribution of foreign science and engineering students to the creation of new knowledge in science and technology in the US. Their study panel data of 2,300 science and engineering departments at 100 large American universities from 1973 to 1998. Their results indicate that foreign doctoral students significantly and positively influence publications and citations produced by US academic departments. Moreover, increased diversity seems to be the primary mechanism by which the foreign students improve research outcomes. By adding foreigners to the team, diversity within the teams is increased. Team members would bring in complementary skills. "Diversity of the student body can generate positive spillovers from the exchange and mixing of ideas, training and methods if students from different regions bring complementary and heterogeneous skills" (ibid.: 5).

Zucker and Darby (2007) study the geographic movements of star scientists which are ranked high in science and technology and find a relationship between star scientists' movements and their innovative activities in receiving countries. Star scientists are likely to cluster in regions endowed with high-tech firms. In their study they follow the careers of 5401 star scientists between 1981 and 2004. Zucker and Darby found that the physical presence of star scientists is a catalyst for economic improvements. It is not only the immediate contribution of immigrants to research activities but also the spillover effect from the foreign star scientists on natives that boosts innovation in the host country.

Hunt and Gauthier-Loiselle (2009: 20) conclude that "a college graduate immigrant contributes at least twice as much to patenting than his or her native counterpart". To assess the impact of immigration on innovation Hunt and Gauthier-Loiselle study individual patenting behaviour as well as state-level determinants of patenting. They measure the impact of high-skilled immigrants (ibid.: 5) on the US patent per capita between 1940 and 2000. If immigrants contribute in innovation activities and consequently increase patenting, then they should also have a positive impact on output per capita. Hunt and Gauthier-Loiselle empirically tested this for US data on the individual and the country level. On the individual level, the authors define three categories of high-skilled migrants; college graduates, holders of a post-college degree and those working as scientists and engineers. They show that immigrants were granted patents twice more compared to natives. 1.9 per cent of immigrants were granted patents compared to 0.9 per cent of natives. Patent per capita for immigrants was 0.057 compared to 0.028 for natives. Then using this data they estimated the direct effect of immigration on patenting, while ignoring the spillover or crowd-out effect. A one per cent increase in population made up of immigrants with college degree would increase patent per capita by 6 per cent. Due to positive spillovers, the benefit to patenting per capita could be as high as 9–15 per cent. They also found that immigrants who are scientists and engineers or who have post-college education boost patents per capita more than immigrant college graduates (ibid.: 5). In a study with a similar methodology, Chellaraj *et al.* (2005) test the contribution of foreign born graduates to US innovation and technological change. They use US time-series data to show that a rise in foreign students increases patent applications more than an increase in skilled immigration does.

Partridge and Furtan (2008) investigate the link between innovation and immigration in Canada and find that high-skilled immigrants with language proficiency in English or French have a significant impact on the innovation flow at the provincial level in Canada. Innovation outcome is measured with patents. They found that a 10 per cent increase of high-skilled immigrants led to 7.2 per cent increase in the overall number of patents in the province (ibid.: 128).

Regarding brain circulation and commuting entrepreneurial networks the work of Saxenian *et al.* (2002) study the role of US educated immigrants who span their activities across borders and create economic opportunities. They explore the scope and organization of the local and transnational networks that are built by immigrants, particularly by the first generation of Indian, Chinese and Taiwanese immigrants in Silicon Valley. In their survey, three issues are addressed: (i) The involvement of Silicon Valley's foreign-born professionals in the region's entrepreneurial economy, (ii) the nature of professional connections that first-generation immigrants are building to their native countries, and (iii) the extent to which immigrants are becoming transnational entrepreneurs and establishing business operations in their native countries. Their conclusions imply an extensive evidence of brain circulation between California and fast growing regions in India and China.

Ozgen *et al.* (2010) empirically investigate the link between migration and innovation in Europe. According to Ozgen *et al.*, immigration may enhance innovation through five channels: (i) a population size effect, (ii) a population density effect, (iii) a migrant share effect, (iv) a skill composition effect and (v) a migrant diversity effect. The first three mechanisms result from the fact that due to immigration, local demand rises. Additionally, since migrants are mostly attracted to the larger urban areas where job opportunities are best, they contribute to urban population growth, and thus strengthen the forces of agglomeration which encourages more innovation. The fourth mechanism, the skill composition effect refers to the way through which immigrants change the human capital stock of the host regions, because immigrants bring in new knowledge. According to Borjas (1999), immigrants are not a randomly selected sample of the population. There is a self-selection process in which the skilled workers who migrate may also be more entrepreneurial and less risk averse and considerably young (Ozgen *et al.* 2010: 3). Their mobility generates spillover benefits to the host countries and enhances the innovation activities there. Finally, the fifth mechanism stems from the larger cultural diversity in the host economy.

Ozgen *et al.* (2010) empirically study the effects of immigration on the innovativeness of the regions in Europe based on data from 12 countries (Austria, Belgium, Denmark, France, west Germany, Ireland, Italy, Netherlands, Portugal, Spain, Sweden and UK). They construct panel data of 170 regions across 12 countries in Europe (NUTS2).[3] Innovation outcomes are approximated by the number of patent applications per million inhabitants. Their results suggest that:

- Population size is insignificant.
- Population density is significant but has a negative sign.
- The share of immigrants is statistically insignificant and not necessarily associated with innovation.
- The average skill level of migrants is positively correlated with patent application. An increase in the average skill level of migrants[4] has a positive and statistically significant effect on patent applications.
- Cultural diversity in the regional population is significant which means that there are positive externalities in culturally more heterogeneous regions.

They find that an increase in the diversity index by 0.1 per cent increases patent applications per million inhabitants by about 0.16 per cent. Ozgen *et al.* conclude that in European regions with culturally diverse settings, higher competitiveness and availability of knowledge spillovers add to innovativeness. Their study also shows that there is a critical level of cultural diversity and that innovation is positively affected only if cultural diversity is above.

Niebuhr (2009) investigates empirically the relationship between cultural diversity and innovation in Germany. She used employment data instead of population data and differentiates between three levels of education: no formal vocational qualification, completed apprenticeship, university degree as well as 213 nationalities. By considering the cultural diversity of the labour force at different qualification levels, Niebuhr seeks to verify whether or not education is a significant influencing factor (i.e. taking into account that it might be only cultural diversity of highly qualified workers which affects the process of innovation). Her results confirm that German regions with a higher diversity in their workforce are characterized by higher levels of innovation activities.

A further study by Fabling *et al.* (2011) tests for New Zealand whether firms located in areas with relatively more immigrants are also more innovative. They find a positive relationship between innovation outcomes and workforce characteristics such as the proportion of migrants, the proportion of people new to the area, the proportion of migrants with high-skills and the employment density. However, this positive relationship is not evident for all innovation outcomes. Moreover, they did not find these relationships for neighbourhood areas. The missing direct link between innovation and local workforce characteristics implies that the spillovers from immigration to innovation are in their results not as strong as on previous studies (ibid.: 20). However, the results of Fabling *et al.* reflect the distinctive features of New Zealand's immigration patterns and innovation system. According to Fabling *et al.* (ibid.) it could be related to New

Zealand's relatively small size and low population density that the scope of spillovers and dense networks is limited.

Hansen and Niedomysl (2009) focus on the migration of creative persons in Sweden and address three issues:

- creative class members move more often compared to other migrant groups;
- creative persons are more selective in choosing their destination and consider the salutatory culture critical for their decision; and
- creative persons have different reasons to immigrate.

Using two different datasets, the authors identify the creative class which allows for comparison between them and other groups. Their empirical work illustrates that migration rates of the creative class are only marginally higher compared to other groups. Moreover, most migration activities for the creative class take place just after finishing university and that the creative class also moves for jobs rather than place.

Neil Lee and Max Nathan (2010), explore the impact of diversity on innovation in the population of London. London is known as one of the most diverse cities in the world, where 300 languages are spoken by schoolchildren (Gordon *et al.* 2009), and 31 ethnic minority groups and 38 per cent of the working-age population were born abroad (Spence 2008). Like Niebuhr (2009) the authors check if culturally diverse firms in London are more innovative and what forms of diversity are associated with what form of innovation. In order to measure cultural diversity they focus on two specific aspects of diversity, country of birth and ethnic group. They construct three diversity measures: (i) the London Annual Business Survey (LABS) coverage of workforce and ownership characteristics, (ii) country of birth, and (iii) ethnicity. In order to measure innovation they develop four broader innovation measures related to product and process innovation: exploring new products, modifications of existing product ranges and new equipment and new working methods. Their results illustrate that London's diversity is an economic asset. They find that diversity and innovative activity are much stronger associated for process innovation than product innovation. The role of "ethnic entrepreneurs" is of particular importance in knowledge-intensive firms in innovative product differentiation and in process innovation.

De Grip *et al.* (2009) analyse the determinants of labour migration after graduation as well as five years after graduation in 12 European countries. They analyse the country choice of the graduate migrants. They find that not only wage gains are determining migration decisions, but also differences in labour market opportunities, past migration experience. Additionally they show that international student exchanges are strong predictors for future migration. Surprisingly, their results show that job characteristics like skills utilization in the job and involvement in innovation do not affect migration decisions. Regarding the country choice, only countries like the US, Canada and Australia appear to attract migrants due their larger R&D intensity. Graduates with better grades are more likely to migrate to these countries.

Miguélez and Moreno (2010) analyse the contribution made by collaborative networks and the labour and geographical mobility of inventors to the process of knowledge creation and regional innovation performance. For this purpose, a knowledge production function framework at the regional level is applied which considers inventors' networks and their labour mobility as independent variables. They use patent data to identify individual inventors, and create a new dataset of individuals with information on personal address(es), their patenting histories, the owners of their patents (be it a firm, a university or other public institution, or the inventors themselves), and the co-authors in their patents. They find strong support for the positive relationship between regional labour market mobility and regional innovation intensity. The influence of networks is also fairly important, but the strength of these ties (measured with the network density) was found to have a negative influence on innovation. However, patenting activities do not explain the mobility pattern of individuals nor their cooperative relationships.

Table 6.2 summarizes the still rare, however, diverse results of empirical studies of the relationship between migration and innovation.

Conclusion

Knowledge-based economies are characterized by new patterns of competition on an international and global scale. Growing high-skilled mobility has raised the competition among countries in winning the best talents. High-skilled migration shows a positive and increasing trend since the beginning of 1990s. Traditional settlement countries, in particular the United States, benefit from immigrant populations. Their national policies are able to attract high-skilled immigrants. Studies confirm that non-US citizens contribute extensively to economic development of the US economy. For example, empirical studies concerning the registered international patents by immigrants or the contribution of transnational networks between immigrants and their homelands confirm this observation. Compared to North American countries, Europe shows higher inflows of international migrants. However, most immigrants arriving in Europe do not hold high skills in terms of education. Also, so far not enough studies of the European situation exist which allow for a better understanding of the contribution of immigrants to European economic development.

The present paper addresses the question of high-skilled migration effects. The traditional approach to high-skilled migration deals mainly with the loss to the emigration countries, namely the issue of *brain drain*. In this perspective, emigration of high-skilled results in reduced economic growth for sending countries. However, other approaches are becoming more popular which are likely to be closer to the reality of knowledge-based economies of the twenty-first century. For example, return migration of high-skilled emigrants compensates the outflows for sending countries. Although from a neo-classical economics point of view, return migration is the outcome of failed migration, the situation looks different from the angle of social network and transnationalism theory. Here, return migration gains an important role in transferring the local specific

Table 6.2 Empirical evidence on migration and innovation.

Study	Subject of research	Result
Brown (2002)	Diaspora networks.	Identification of 43 diaspora networks of highly skilled immigrants from developing countries worldwide.
Saxenian *et al.* (2002)	Focus on the development of Silicon Valley's regional economy and the roles of immigrant capital and labour in this process.	Immigrants have become a significant driving force in the creation of new businesses and intellectual property in the US and their contributions increased over the past decade.
Zucker and Darby (2007)	Relationship between star scientists' movements and their direct (also indirect) contribution to the receiving countries economic development. The authors follow the careers of 5401 star scientists between 1981 and 2004.	Physical presence of star scientists rather than the embodied knowledge in their work is a catalyst for economic improvements. Here is where the labour mobility of discovering scientists becomes very important in technology transfer – not only the direct contribution of immigrants in research activities matters, but also the spill-over effect from immigrants on natives boosts innovation in the host country.
Kerr and Lincoln (2008)	Impact of high-skilled immigrants on US technology formation. Fluctuations of H-1B visas on rate of Indian and Chinese patenting in the United States.	Fluctuations in H-1B admissions levels significantly influence the rate of Indian and Chinese patenting in cities and firms dependent upon the program relative to their peers. Weak crowding-in effects or no effects at all for native patenting. Total invention increases with higher admission levels primarily through the direct contributions of immigrant inventors.
Partridge and Furtan (2008)	Relationship between highly skilled immigrants with proficiency in language and patent flow in the province in Canada.	10% increase of highly skilled immigrants led to 7.2% increase in patent flow in the province.
Hunt and Gauthier-Loiselle (2009)	Impact of highly skilled immigration on the US patent per capita between 1940 and 2000.	College graduate immigrants contribute at least twice as much to patenting as their native counterparts.

Table 6.2 Continued.

Study	Subject of research	Result
Stuen *et al.* (2010)	Contribution of foreign science and engineering students publications and citations produced by US academic departments.	Foreign doctoral students significantly and positively influence publications and citations produced by US academic departments. Moreover, increased diversity seems to be the primary mechanism by which the foreigner students improve research outcomes.
Niebuhr (2009)	Relationship between cultural diversity in R&D employment in German regions and innovation.	German regions with diversity of workforce in terms of background have higher level of innovation activities.
Ozgen *et al.* (2010)	Relationship between innovation outcomes and workforce characteristics in 12 EU countries.	In those regions of Europe with a culturally diverse setting, higher competitiveness and availability of knowledge spill-overs add to innovativeness. Only beyond a critical level of cultural diversity of the migrant community, the innovation level is associated with the cultural diversity.
Fabling *et al.* (2011)	Tested if the firms located in areas with a relatively higher proportion of immigrants are more innovative than the others in New Zealand.	No direct link between innovation and local workforce characteristics in New Zeeland.
Hansen and Niedomysl (2009)	Evidence from Sweden, migration of creative class.	The migration rates of the creative class are only marginally higher than for other groups. Most migration activities for the creative class take place just after finishing university and that the creative class people move for jobs rather than place.
De Grip *et al.* (2009)	Determinants of labour migration after graduation as well as five years after graduation in 12 European countries.	Countries such as the USA, Canada and Australia appear to attract migrants due their larger R&D intensity. Graduates with higher grades are more likely to migrate to these countries.
Miguélez and Moreno (2010)	The importance of the labour mobility of inventors, as well as the scale, extent and density of their collaborative research networks, for regional innovation outcomes.	Positive correlation between intraregional labour mobility and regional innovation. Strength of network ties (measured as the network density) was found to have a negative influence on innovation.

knowledge across borders. That is why origin countries potentially benefit from the skills that migrants have gained in the foreign countries. In recent studies the role of diaspora networks appears significant. Recognizing networks formed by immigrants, especially transnational networks in which they keep their ties to their homelands, triggers a shift from *brain drain* to a *brain gain* or *brain circulation*. Transnational networks provide access to the knowledge and cultural specific know-how available at distant places, due to advances in communication and transportation technologies as well as changes in the competition pattern among countries. In this sense, both sending and receiving countries benefit from the mobility of high-skilled labour.

Neo-Schumpeterian economics in an evolutionary economics flavour stress the importance of knowledge and innovation for economic development and therefore are the adequate approaches for the analysis of the relation between innovation and migration. In the knowledge based economy the main driver behind economic development is innovation, the more innovation, the more dynamic the economy will be. Heterogeneity in economic agents and interactions between them is the source of idea creation. The mobility of labour contributes to diffusion of tacit knowledge. Cultural diversity is the result of international migration; this constitutes the basis for knowledge spillovers. The diversity brought by immigrants into the workforce overall has complementary effects to the native labour force. Diversity is, however, accompanied by costs due to language barriers and cultural barriers. The transfer of knowledge occurs in the networks and clusters which migrants form. Network structures link the diverse knowledge of the agents and facilitate the exchange of knowledge. That is why it is essential to explore the networks and their roles. Finally, it is the design of the National System of Innovation which creates the prerequisites for innovation activities. The extent to which immigrants contribute to innovation depends on the interaction between them and institutions embedded in the National Innovation System. Most results confirm that innovation is enhanced by the presence of high-skilled migrants.

Notes

1   ISI Highly Cited is a database of "highly cited researchers", scientific researchers whose publications are most often cited in academic journals, published by the Institute for Scientific Information.

2   H-1B visa is a programme that allows the American employer to seek short-term help from skilled foreigners in "specialty occupations". Science, engineering and computer-related occupations make up to 60 per cent of successful visa application. Between 2000 and 2005, 40 per cent of H-1B recipients were form India and 10 per cent came from China (Kerr and Lincoln 2008: 12). The visa is issued for three years with allowance for a single three-year renewal.

3   The Nomenclature of Units for Territorial Statistics (NUTS) is a geocode standard for referencing the subdivisions of European countries for statistical purposes. The NUTS 1 level refers roughly to states or large regions, NUTS 2 to provinces, and NUTS 3 to counties.

4   Proxied by migration from source countries from which emigrants are on average higher skilled.

References

Agrawal, A. and Oettl, A. (2008) International labor mobility and knowledge flow externalities. *Journal of International Business Studies* 39: 1242–1260.

Agrawal, A., Cockburn, I. and McHale, J. (2006) Gone but not forgotten: labor flows, knowledge spillovers and enduring social capital. *Journal of Economic Geography* 6: 571–591.

Alesina, A. and La Ferrara, E. (2005) *Ethnic Diversity and Economic Performance.* Cambridge, MA: National Bureau of Economic Research.

Barré, R., Hernandez, V., Meyer, J.-B. and Vinck, D. (eds) (2003) *Scientific Diasporas.* Paris: IRD.

Beine, M., Docquier, F. and Rapoport, H. (2001) Brain drain and economic growth: theory and evidence. *Journal of Development Economics* 64(1): 275–289.

Borjas, G. J. (1999) The economic analysis of immigration. In O. Ashenfelter and D. Card (eds), *Handbook of Labor Economics*, 1697–1760. Amsterdam: North Holland.

Boschma, R. and Frenken, K. (2011) The emerging empirics of evolutionary economic geography. *Journal of Economic Geography* 11: 295–307.

Boschma, R. A. and Martin, R. (2010) *The Handbook of Evolutionary Economic Geography.* Cheltenham: Edward Elgar.

Brown, M. (2000) Using the intellectual diaspora to reverse the brain drain: some useful examples. Paper presented at UNECA Regional Conference on Brain Drain and Capacity Building in Africa, 22–24 February, Addis Ababa, Ethiopia. Available at http://repository.uneca.org/handle/10855/21489.

Brown, M. (2002) Intellectual diaspora networks: their viability as a response to highly skilled migration. *Autrepart* 22: 167–178.

Cassarino, J.-P. (2004) Theorising return migration: the conceptual approach to return migrants, revisited. *International Journal on Multicultural Societies* 6(2): 253–279.

Castles, S. (2000) International migration at the beginning of the twenty-first century: global trends and issues. *International Social Science Journal* 165: 269–281.

Chellaraj, G., Maskus, K. E and Mattoo, A. (2008) The contribution of skilled immigration and international graduate students to US innovation. *Review of International Economics* 16(3): 444–462.

Constant, A., Shachmurove, Y. and Zimmermann, K. F. (2006) *The Role of Turkish Immigrants in Entrepreneurial Activities in Germany.* Working paper no. 05-029. Philadelphia, PA: PIER.

De Graaff, T. and Nijkamp, P. (2010) Socio-economic impacts of migrant clustering on Dutch neighbourhoods: in search of optimal migrant diversity. *Socio-Economic Planning Sciences* 44: 231–239.

De Grip, A., Fouarge, D. and Sauermann, J. (2009) *What Affects International Migration of European Science and Engineering Graduates?* IZA discussion paper no. 4268. Bonn: Institute for the Study of Labor. Available at http://ssrn.com/abstract=1434602.

De Haas, H. (2010) Migration and development: a theoretical perspective. *IMR* 44(1): 227–264.

Drori, I., Honig, B. and Wright, M. (2009) Transnational entrepreneurship: an emergent field of study. *Entrepreneurship Theory and Practice* 33: 1001–1022.

Dumont, J.-C. and Lemaître, G. (2005) *Counting Immigrants and Expatriates in OECD Countries: A New Perspective.* Paris: OECD.

Edquist, C. (1997) *Systems of Innovation: Technologies, Institutions, and Organizations.* London: Frances Pinter.

Fabling, R., Stillman, S. and Maré, D. C. (2011) *Immigration and innovation.* Wellington, NZ: Motu Economic and Public Policy Research.

Faini, R. (2007) Remittances and the brain drain: do more skilled migrants remit more? *The World Bank Economic Review* 21(2): 177–191.

Feldman, M. P. (1999) The new economics of innovation, spillovers and agglomeration: a review of empirical studies. *Economics of Innovation and New Technology* 8: 5–25.

Freeman, C. (1987) *Technology and Economic Performance: Lessons from Japan.* London: Frances Pinter.

Gordon, I., Tarvers, T. and Whitehead, C. (2009) London's Place in the UK Economy. London: City of London.

Grubel, H. G. and Scott, A. (1966) The international flow of human capital. *American Economic Review* 56(1/2): 268–274.

Hansen, H. K. and Niedomysl, T. (2009) Migration of the creative class: evidence from Sweden. *Journal of Economic Geography* 9: 191–206.

Hunt, J. and Gauthier-Loiselle, M. (2009) *How Much Does Immigration Boost Innovation?* IZA discussion paper no. 3921. Bonn: Institute for the Study of Labor.

IOM (2008) *World Migration 2008: Managing Labour Mobility in the Evolving Global Economy.* Geneva: International Organization for Migration.

Johnson, H. G. (1965) The economics of the "brain drain": the Canadian case. *Minerva* 3(3): 299.

Keeley, B. (2009) *International Migration: The Human Face of Globalisation.* Paris: OECD.

Keely, L. C. (2003) Exchanging good ideas. *Journal of Economic Theory* 111(2): 192–213.

Kerr, W. R. and Lincoln, W. F. (2008) *The Supply Side of Innovation: H-1B Visa Reforms and US Ethnic Invention.* HBS working paper 09-005. Boston, MA: Harvard Business School.

Kuznetsov, E. (2006) *Diaspora Networks and the International Migration of Skills: How Countries Can Draw on Their Talent Abroad.* Washington, DC: World Bank.

Lee, N. and Nathan, M. (2010) Knowledge workers, cultural diversity and innovation: evidence from London. *International Journal of Knowledge-Based Development* 1(1/2): 53–78.

Lundvall, B.-Å. (ed.) (1992) *National Innovation Systems: Towards a Theory of Innovation and Interactive Learning.* London: Frances Pinter.

Mahroum, S. and Guchteneire, P. de (2006) Transnational knowledge through diaspora networks. *International Journal on Multicultural Societies* 8(1): 1–3.

Meyer, J. P. (2007) *Building Sustainability: The New Frontier of Diaspora Knowledge Networks.* Bielefeld: Center on Migration, Citizenship and Development.

Meyer, J. P. and Wattiaux, J. P. (2006) Diaspora knowledge networks: vanishing doubts, increasing evidence. *International Journal on Multicultural Societies* 8(1): 4–24.

Meyer, J.-B. (2001) Network approach versus brain drain: lessons from the diaspora. *International Migration* 39: 91–108.

Miguélez, E. and Moreno, R. (2010) *Research Networks and Inventors' Mobility as Drivers of Innovation: Evidence from Europe.* Barcelona: AQR-IREA, Universitat de Barcelona.

Mountford, A. (1997) Can a brain drain be good for growth in the source economy? *Journal of Development Economics* 53(2): 287–303.

Nelson, R. (ed.) (1993) *National Innovation Systems: A Comparative Analysis*. Oxford: Oxford University Press.

Niebuhr, A. (2009) *Migration and Innovation: Does Cultural Diversity Matter for Regional R&D Activity?* HWWI research paper 3-1. Hamburg: Hamburg Institute of International Economics.

OECD (2001) *Trends in International Migration*. SOPEMI 2001. Paris: OECD.

OECD (2011a) *Trends in International Migration*. SOPEMI 2011. Paris: OECD.

OECD (2011b) *Education at a Glance: OECD Indicators 2011*. Paris: OECD.

Ozgen, C., Nijkamp, P. and Poot, J. (2010) Immigration and innovation in European regions. Draft paper, Migrant Diversity and Regional Disparity in Europe (MIDIREDIE) project. Amsterdam: Department of Spatial Economics, VU University.

Partridge, J. and Furtan, H. (2008) Increasing Canada's international competitiveness: is there a link between skilled immigrants and innovation? Paper presented at the American Agricultural Economics Assoc Annual Meeting, Orlando, FL, 27–29 July.

Pyka, A. (1997) Informal Networking. *Telenovation* 17(4): 207–220.

Pyka, A. and Küppers, G. (2002) *Innovation Networks: Theory and Practice*. Cheltenham: Edward Elgar.

Regets, M. C. (2001) Research and policy issues in high-skilled international migration: a perspective with data from the United States. In OECD (ed.), *Innovative People: Mobility of Skilled Personnel in National Innovation Systems*, ch. 17. Paris: OECD.

Reiner, C. (2010) Brain competition policy as a new paradigm of regional policy: a European perspective. *Papers in Regional Science* 89: 449–461

Saxenian, A. (2002) Transnational communities and the evolution of global production networks: the cases of Taiwan, China and India. *Industry and Innovation* 9: 183–202.

Saxenian, A. (2005) From brain drain to brain circulation: transnational communities and regional upgrading in India and China. *Studies in Comparative International Development* 40(2) (summer): 35–61.

Saxenian, A., Motoyama, Y. and Quan, X. (2002) *Local and Global Networks of Immigrant Professionals in Silicon Valley*. San Francisco, CA: Public Policy Institute of California.

Scott, A. (1970) The brain drain: is a human-capital approach justified? In W. L. Hansen (ed.), *Education, Income, and Human Capital*, 241–294. New York: National Bureau of Economic Research.

Spence, L. (2008) *ONS Ethnic Population Estimates: Mid-2006*. GD Briefing 2008-5.

Stalker, P. (2002) Migration trends and migration policy in Europe. *International Migration* 40(5): 151–179.

Stark, O. (2003) Rethinking the brain drain. *World Development* 32(1): 15–22.

Stark, O., Helmenstein, C. and Prskawetz, A. (1997) Brain gain with a brain drain. *Economics Letters* 55: 227–234.

Stuen, E. T., Mobarak, A. M. and, Maskus, K. E. (2010) *Foreign PhD Students and Knowledge Creation at US Universities: Evidence from Enrollment Fluctuations*. Working paper. Boulder, CO: University of Colorado.

Tomlinson, M. (2001) Employment growth, social capability and human mobility. In OECD (ed.), *Innovative People: Mobility of Skilled Personnel in National Innovation Systems*, ch. 3. Paris: OECD.

Turner, W., Henry, C. and Gueye, M. (2003) Diasporas, development and ICTs. In R. Barré, V. Hernandez, J.-B. Meyer and D. Vinck (eds), *Scientific Diasporas*. Paris: IRD.

UNDESA (2009) *Trends in International Migrant Stock: The 2008 Revision.* POP/DB/MIG/Stock/Rev.2008. New York: United Nations Department of Economic and Social Affairs, Population Division.

Vertovec, S. (2002) *Transnational Networks and Skilled Labor Migration.* Oxford: Transnational Communities Programme, University of Oxford.

Wadhwa, V., Saxenian, A., Rissing, B. and Gereffi, G. (2007) America's new immigrant entrepreneurs: part I. Duke Science, Technology and Innovation Paper no. 23. Available at http://ssrn.com/abstract=990152 (accessed 10 December 2011).

Wickramasekara, P. (2003) *Policy Responses to Skilled Migration: Retention, Return and Circulation, Perspectives on Labour Migration* (5th edn). Geneva: International Labour Office.

Zucker, L. and Darby, M. (2007) *Star Scientists, Innovation and Regional and National Immigration.* Working paper no. 13547. Cambridge, MA: National Bureau of Economic Research.

7 Economic effects of migration and cultural diversity

A review of recent evidence

Annekatrin Niebuhr

Introduction

Despite the recent economic and financial crisis, global migration continues to rise. The estimated stock of international migrants amounts to more 230 million in 2013 according to figures of the United Nations (2013). Since the early 1990 the number of migrants worldwide increased by around 50 per cent. At present migrants represent about 3 per cent of total global population. Immigration becomes more important, especially in the ageing European economies that will experience a pronounced decline of the labour force due to demographic change. Moreover, Ozgen (2013) notes that migration is increasing in absolute scale but also in complexity in many parts of the world. As the composition of the migrant population is often very different from that of the country of destination immigration is usually accompanied by an increasing cultural diversity of the host society (Nijkamp 2012).

Immigration and the growing cultural diversity of the population may have far-reaching economic implications. However, the understanding of the effects of international labour mobility is still rather limited as emphasized by Zimmermann (2005) although the consequences of migration are an issue of research for a long time. And the public and scientific debate on the topic is rather controversial. A key question in this context refers to the economic costs and benefits for the receiving economies. Research on the economic consequences of migration has up to now focused on labour market effects and, more precisely, on the question whether immigrants depress wages and increase unemployment of native workers. Concerns about a possibly adverse impact of immigration on the labour market outcomes of the resident workforce are a main reason behind calls for more tight immigration policies in many highly developed countries.

Economic theory provides some guidance on how immigration might impact on the host economy. But the implications of theoretical models are not clear-cut. A considerable number of empirical studies deals with labour market effects of immigration. However, empirical evidence is also far from unambiguous. While some investigations point to a significant negative impact of immigration on labour market outcomes of native workers (e.g. Borjas 2003; Borjas and Katz 2007), the findings of other studies suggest that the influence is negligible (e.g.

Card 2005; Ottaviano and Peri 2012). Dustmann *et al.* (2008) summarize that although the evidence is rather mixed, it is certain that the consequences are not evenly distributed across residents in the host countries.

Whereas the literature on labour market effects of immigration is voluminous, research on economic consequences of cultural diversity is still manageable though the number of corresponding studies is rapidly increasing in recent years. Economic theory suggests that diversity could give rise to beneficial effects due to skill complementarities among workers from distinct cultural backgrounds. Alesina *et al.* (2013) argue that people that differ by country of birth likely possess distinct productive skills because they have been educated in different school systems and were exposed to different experiences and cultures. However, scholars also point to potential costs of cultural diversity due to higher transaction costs. As the economic consequences of cultural diversity have received much less attention compared to the labour market effects of migration, evidence on the issue is still incomplete and ambiguous. However, the majority of studies seems to be in support of positive, but moderate effects of cultural diversity.

In this chapter I survey the recent theoretical and empirical literature on the relationship between migration, cultural diversity and economic performance. We focus on the economic effects in the country of destination. Migration is a pheno-menon that is quite diverse in terms of motives (e.g. work, education, forced migration, retirement) and migration likely has important consequences in the host country irrespective of the motive. However, in the following we only consider the mobility of workers and its impact on the host economy. Moreover, there are a number of dimensions by which immigration may affect the economy of the host country, such as the labour market performance of natives, the housing market, the supply of public services, as well as growth and innovation. In this review we focus on labour market outcomes, growth and innovation.

The chapter is organized as follows. Below we provide a brief overview of the theoretical arguments regarding economic effects of migration and diversity. Different definitions of cultural diversity and measurement issues are discussed in the next section. We then present some descriptive evidence on cultural diversity with a focus on the German labour market. After reviewing the empirical literature on the impact of migration and cultural diversity on economic perform-ance, the final section provides some conclusions.

Theoretical arguments

Economic theory provides some guidance on how immigration might impact on the economy of the host country. But the implications of theoretical models are not clear-cut. Traditional neoclassical approaches assume homogeneous labour and flexible labour markets. Labour market conditions are important determin-ants of migration in these models. Workers will move from low wage/high unemployment countries to economies that offer more favourable labour market conditions. In the country of destination immigration will increase labour supply. With homogeneous labour this change in labour supply likely results in significant adverse effects on the labour market outcomes of native workers because migrants and natives are assumed to be perfect substitutes.

However, theoretically the suspected adverse impact of immigration on natives' earnings or unemployment only emerges in a simple setting with homogeneous labour. If we introduce heterogeneous labour (with respect to skills and experience), the impact of immigration depends – amongst others – on the relation between native and immigrant labour, i.e. on the question whether the different groups of workers are substitutes or complement each other. Substitutes of foreign workers likely experience a deterioration of their labour market outcomes while complements should benefit from increasing productivity. A major concern in this context refers to the issue whether low-skilled immigrants are substitutes for low-skilled natives.

Dustmann *et al.* (2008) conclude that the ways how immigration impacts on labour market outcomes depends crucially on the skill structure of immigrants and natives. Moreover, assumptions about the elasticity of capital supply are of utmost importance. If the capital stock adjusts swiftly to changes in labour supply, then there will be no significant effects of migration on the labour market of the host country as long as immigrants perfectly resemble natives in terms of skills and experience. The additional labour supply will be absorbed simply by economic growth. However, if we allow for differences in the skill composition of native and foreign workers the change in labour supply results in adjustments of wage and/or employment. Native workers might benefit or experience adverse effects depending on their skill level and the skill composition of the migrants. Whether the average labour market effect of immigration is beneficial or detrimental again depends on the elasticity of capital supply.[1]

The theoretical arguments discussed so far assume that natives and migrants within a particular skill group and with similar experience are perfect substitutes, i.e. they are interchangeable. More recently, some studies relax this assumption and suggest that foreign workers and natives might be only imperfect substitutes even within the same skill and experience group (see Manacorda *et al.* 2012; Ottaviano and Peri 2012). Skills and knowledge of natives and foreign workers with similar formal qualification and same experience might significantly differ due to their distinct cultural background. Alesina *et al.* (2013) argue that people that differ by country of birth likely possess distinct productive skills because they have been educated in different school systems and were exposed to different experiences and cultures. This overall complementarity of foreign and native workers gives rise to beneficial effects of immigration on labour market outcomes of most groups of natives. Only the lowest skilled workers might suffer from small adverse effects (Dustmann *et al.* 2008). Thus, in order to determine the economic effects of immigration it is of utmost importance to find out whether foreign and native workers are (imperfect) substitutes or complements.

However, focussing on labour market effects alone implies a rather narrow perspective on the consequences of immigration and cultural diversity as differences in skills and knowledge of workers from distinct cultural background might impact on various dimensions of economic performance. Alesina and La

Ferrara (2005) describe different mechanisms through which cultural diversity might influence the economy of the host country. Diversity might have a direct impact on economic outcomes via differences in preferences or by influencing individual strategies. Moreover, diversity might have an influence on the production process.[2] In this review we focus on the latter approach.

Ottaviano and Peri (2006) develop a model of multicultural production where different cultural groups provide diverse services. Skills of foreign workers complement those of natives and cultural diversity of the labour force has a positive impact on regional productivity. However, there are also adverse effects of diversity on productivity because heterogeneity might hamper the exchange between different cultural groups. Lazear (2000) also considers costs of diversity arising from barriers to communication caused by different languages and cultures.[3] Communication among team members might also decline because persons tend to be attracted to similar individuals. Interaction should therefore decrease as groups become more heterogeneous (DiTomaso *et al.* 2007; Stock 2004). Moreover, Basset-Jones (2005) and Parrotta *et al.* (2014) argue that diversity may cause misunderstanding, conflicts and uncooperative behaviour.

We might also expect important effects of migration and cultural diversity on innovation. Ozgen (2013) argues that primarily more entrepreneurial and inno-vative people with strong incentives move due to the selective nature of migration processes. Indeed, benefits of cultural diversity might be of particular importance in research and development (R&D), whereas costs of diversity likely outweigh the beneficial effects in more standardized forms of production. Fujita and Weber (2004) emphasize that the creation of new knowledge relies heavily on the talents and skills of employees coming from a wide range of cultural backgrounds. The nature of innovation processes calls for interaction of differently skilled workers and a pooling of various ideas and abilities. Furthermore, Cohen and Levinthal (1990) argue that the absorptive capacity, i.e. the ability to detect, incorporate and use external information, probably increases with a more diverse knowledge base and worker heterogeneity. Diversity guarantees the consideration of a large set of problems and potential solutions thereby giving rise to more rapid and flexible problem solving (Alesina and La Ferrara 2005; Keely 2003). However, communi-cation costs of cultural diversity might be important for innovation as well since R&D activity involves intensive interaction among workers.

In sum, theory offers no clear-cut implications for the economic effects of immigration and cultural diversity in the host countries. Eventually the various and conflicting theoretical arguments leave the task of determining the impact of international mobility of workers on economic performance to empirical research.

Definition and measurement of cultural diversity

Measurement issues seem to be a minor problem in studies that investigate the economic effects of immigration. Corresponding analyses usually apply information on immigration stocks or flows to examine the consequences of immigration. In contrast, cultural diversity is neither easy to define nor is there consensus in the literature on how to measure it. Harrison and Sin (2006) provide a useful starting point in this context. They define the diversity of a group as "the collective amount of differences among members within a social unit". This definition gives rise to a relational concept of diversity and therefore requires a comparison of individuals or groups. Diversity is also a multi-dimensional concept because individuals may differ from each other in various characteristics such as age, gender, ethnicity, religion or income.

Depending on the variable of interest and the scale of measurement different forms of diversity are relevant. A typology by Harrison and Klein (2007) involves three distinct types of diversity: separation, variety and disparity.[4] Separation refers to the extent of differences amongst group members. Thus measurement requires metric variables such as age. In contrast, disparity refers to a concept of inequality (i.e. the extent to which group members differ with respect to a ratio-scaled variable such as income). The type of diversity discussed in the theoretical models above is best conceived as variety. Variety captures the distribution of group members with respect to characteristic values of a qualitative categorical variable, such country of birth or nationality. Corresponding measures of diversity indicate the extent to which individuals are evenly spread across different possible values of this variable. Minimum variety corresponds with a situation where all individuals belong to the same category, while the maximum is achieved when group members are equally spread across all possible categories.

Turning to the measurement of cultural diversity operationalization has to focus on important and quantifiable dimensions of the broad concept of cultural diversity. The concept involves mainly ethno-linguistic differences which include individual features, attitudes, shared rules and values. It refers to aspects such as ethnicity, language, religion, race and place of birth. However, the choice of a specific diversity measures depends on the research question and data availability. Empirical analyses use different information in order to measure cultural diversity within distinct units of observation. Most studies rely on population figures, labour force or employment data and determine the cultural background of individuals with the country of birth. Alesina *et al.* (2013) argue in favour of this kind of information as early age years are supposed to form an individual's values, perspectives and skills and corresponding differences likely last a lifetime. Moreover, variety that is caused by different education systems and societies is expected to create skill complementarities.[5]

Some analyses apply language or nationality instead of the birthplace information. Applying nationality has advantages and drawbacks. It implies that naturalized citizens are not registered as migrants in the diversity measure. However, using country of origin as a definition of the foreign workforce implies that we do not consider people with a migration background born in host country, unless we have information on the country of birth of the parents. Another caveat concerns the determination of foreign-born status that ignores the age of immigration. An individual that migrates at the age of 2 will be classified as foreign-born, but the person will socialize in the host society and is educated in the school system of the host country. Alesina *et al.* (2013) argue that this necessarily limits the extent of available foreign skills.[6]

An important drawback of all measures is that they are unable to distinguish between first- and second-generation migrants. First-generation immigrants arguably form a more diverse group than second- and third-generation immigrants because the latter grew up in the same country and attend the same school system. Alesina *et al.* (2013) note, however, that diversity measures still capture important differences between individuals because these are often intergenerationally transmitted.

The most frequently applied diversity measure is the so-called index of fractionalization which is identical with the inverse Herfindahl index:

$$F_{it} = 1 - \sum_{n=1}^{N} s_{nit}^2, \quad 0 \le F_{it} \le \left(1 - \frac{1}{N}\right) \tag{7.1}$$

with s_{nit} indicating the share of population with country of birth (language, nationality) n in observational unit i in year t. Observational units can be, for instance, work groups, organizations or regions. The index measures the probability that two individuals drawn randomly from the entire population have two different countries of birth. The range of the fractionalization index depends on the total number of categories N. When all individuals belong to the same category, the probability that two randomly selected individuals belong to different groups is 0, whereas the probability will be 1 if all individuals belong to different groups.

Ottaviano and Peri (2006) note that this indicator accounts for both richness of the distribution, i.e. number of different categories, and evenness of the distribution across groups. Cultural diversity will increase if the number of groups (countries of birth) rises or if the population shares of different groups converge. Alesina *et al.* (2013) state that a certain moderate level of diversity may come from a relatively small but very diverse pool of immigrants, or from a relatively homogenous but large fraction of immigrants in the population.

A disadvantage of the index of fractionalization is that it assigns disproportionately high weights to the largest groups. Therefore the measure is largely driven by the percentage of the dominant population group (i.e. the natives). As a result the index is highly correlated with the population share of the natives (foreigners). Consequently, some authors calculate the index for the group of foreign-born (i.e. they exclude the natives and consider the diversity among the immigrants; see e.g. Audretsch *et al.* 2010). In order to account for the relative frequency of the foreign-born some scholars consider the share of immigrants in addition to the inverse Herfindahl index applied to the foreign-born population (e.g. Ozgen *et al.* 2013).[7]

The Theil index, an entropy measure, does not suffer from this measurement problem. The corresponding diversity measure is given by:

$$T_{it} = -\sum_{n=1}^{N} s_{nit} \ln(s_{nit}), \quad 0 \le T_{it} \le \ln(N) \tag{7.2}$$

Cultural diversity is defined as sum of the products of the shares and log shares of each group. The maximum of the Theil index is $\ln(N)$, indicating that population is evenly distributed across N different categories (i.e. $s_{nit} = 1/N$ for all n). If there is just one group, the index takes the minimum value $\ln(1) = 0$. By taking logs the index assigns stronger weights to the tails of the distribution, i.e. to small groups. If the distribution of population across categories is characterized by one dominant group, the Theil index is more adequate measure of cultural diversity as it reflects both the share *and* the variety of the foreign-born population.[8]

Descriptive evidence on employment of foreign workers and cultural diversity

In this section we provide some descriptive evidence on cultural diversity at the regional and the firm level in Germany. Immigrants tend to choose large agglomerations as region of residence. This is reflected by the spatial pattern of employment of foreign workers.[9] Figure 7.1 shows the regional disparities in the percentage of foreign workers in total employment. There are first of all significant differences between East and West Germany. The relative frequency of foreign workers is lower than in West Germany in almost all East German regions, the only exceptions being Berlin and Dresden. Moreover, highly agglomerated regions such as the Ruhr area, Frankfurt and Munich achieve higher employment shares of migrants than urbanized and rural regions. Furthermore, there are also important differences between the northern and the southern part of West Germany. In particular, the federal state Baden-Württemberg shows above average employment of foreign workers. This region experienced high immigration from Mediterranean countries in the 1950s and 1960s.

Cultural diversity as measured by the inverse Herfindahl index and employment of foreign workers at different levels of educational attainment show similar patterns. Table 7.1 summarizes information on employment of foreign workers and cultural diversity differentiated by region type and qualification level of workers. The share of foreign employees in Germany amounts to 7 per cent in 2010. However, there is a significant variation across skill levels. Only 3.6 per cent of medium-skilled workers (completed apprenticeship training) have a foreign nationality. The percentage of immigrants is highest among the low-skilled employees (no formal vocational qualification) with a share of almost 14 per cent. High-skilled labour and employment in R&D show below average shares of migrants with less than 6 per cent.

The maximum and minimum values for the functional regions indicate that the employment share of foreign workers is marked by a considerable spread of more than 13 percentage points. We detect the largest range for low skilled labour. Highly agglomerated regions show the highest employment share of foreign workers. This applies to all skill levels and R&D employment. Altogether the figures point to a positive correlation between population density of the region and immigrant employment since we detect the lowest percentage of foreign labour in rural regions.

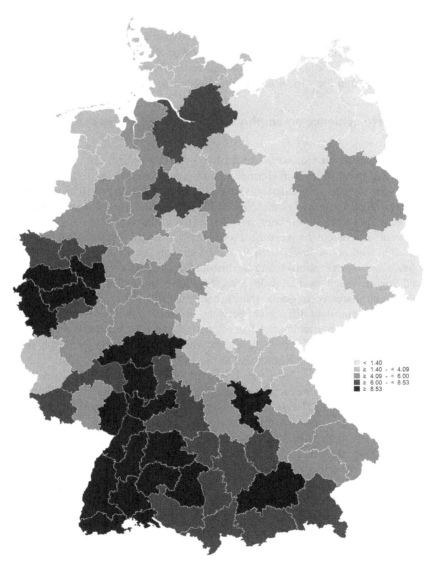

Figure 7.1 Share of foreign workers in total employment in Germany in per cent, 2010.
Source: Employment statistic of the Federals Employment Agency, own calculations.

Table 7.1 Employment of foreign workers and cultural diversity by region type and level of educational attainment, 2010.

	All skill groups	High skilled	Skilled	Low skilled	R&D employment
Share of foreign workers (%)					
Germany	7.0	5.4	3.6	13.9	5.7
Maximum across 91 regions	14.1	9.1	9.0	28.9	11.8
Minimum across 91 regions	0.6	1.6	0.2	0.5	0.3
Agglomerated regions	9.0	6.1	4.8	17.3	6.6
Urbanized regions	5.1	4.2	2.6	11.0	4.3
Rural regions	3.4	3.7	1.8	6.8	3.2
Diversity among foreign workers (inverse Herfindahl index)					
Germany	0.83	0.87	0.82	0.77	0.88
Maximum across 91 regions	0.86	0.88	0.86	0.85	0.90
Minimum across 91 regions	0.57	0.32	0.45	0.48	0.00
Agglomerated regions	0.82	0.87	0.82	0.76	0.88
Urbanized regions	0.82	0.86	0.81	0.77	0.88
Rural regions	0.83	0.80	0.82	0.79	0.86

Source: Employment statistic of the Federal Employment Agency, own calculations.

In the lower panel of Table 7.1 we present evidence on cultural diversity among the foreign workers (i.e. the natives are excluded from the calculation of the diversity measure). The mean immigrant share of 7 per cent corresponds with a value of the overall diversity measure (inverse Herfindahl index) of 0.83. Differences across region types are less pronounced for cultural diversity compared with the share of foreigners. Agglomerated regions achieve highest levels of cultural diversity for high-skilled workers. However, disparities across region types are rather small for the medium-skill level and, surprisingly, for R&D employment. Rural areas are marked by a relatively high diversity of the low-skilled workforce. Moreover, there are distinct differences between skill levels. The diversity of foreign labour is highest for the university graduates and workers employed in R&D. Altogether there seems to be a negative correlation between cultural diversity among migrant workers and their level of educational attainment.

There are also important differences in the employment of migrants across firm size categories (see Table 7.2). In 2010, about 19 per cent of all establishments in Germany employed foreign workers. The share of firms with at least one foreign worker shows a strong positive correlation with firm size. Whereas only 12.7 per cent of establishments with less than 10 employees engage migrant workers, 95 per cent of the large firms in Germany employ foreign labour. The share of foreign workers does not show a corresponding correlation with firm size. In fact we determine the same share of foreign workers for very small (< 10 employees) and very large firms (> 250 employees). The surprising results for the

Table 7.2 Employment of foreign workers and cultural diversity by firm size, 2010.

	All firms	<10 empl.	10–49 empl.	50–99 empl.	100–249 empl.	> 250 empl.
Share of firms with foreign workers	19.2%	12.7%	39.4%	69.9%	84.0%	95.0%
Share foreign workers	7.3%	7.5%	5.9%	6.6%	7.2%	7.5%
No. of nationalites	1.4	1.1	1.8	3.6	5.9	12.9
No. of cultural clusters	1.3	1.1	1.7	2.9	4.2	6.7
Cultural diversity among foreign workers	0.18	0.06	0.24	0.42	0.53	0.64
Observations	1,961,305	1,602,055	280,754	42,080	25,152	11,264

Source: IAB Establishment Panel, own calculations.

small firms might be driven by small and probably foreign owned firms where natives are likely the minority group. However, both the number of nationalities and of cultural clusters[10] clearly increases with firm size. This result is confirmed by the findings for the cultural diversity among the foreign workers that is rising as the number of employees in the establishment increases.

Empirical evidence on economic effects of migration and cultural diversity

With respect to the influence of migration on economic performance it is important to differentiate between effects in the sending and the host countries. Moreover, we have to distinguish between short-run and long-run effects.[11] In this review of the empirical literature, we only consider the impact on the host economy. Empirical evidence on both short-run effects on wages and (un)employment as well as medium- and long-run effects such as the impact on growth and innovation is discussed.[12]

The overwhelming majority of previous empirical studies deals with the labour market effects of international migration and, more precisely, with the question whether immigrants depress wages and increase unemployment of native workers. In contrast, the long-run effects of labour migration have not received that much attention in the migration literature up to now (see e.g. Hunt and Gauthier-Loiselle 2010). Moreover, empirical evidence is far from unambiguous. Although the significance of labour migration is rapidly increasing, especially in highly developed economies, the issue is still controversial and the understanding of the consequences of international labour mobility is rather limited (Zimmermann 2005).

A considerable number of studies investigate the consequences of immigration on the labour market outcomes of workers in the host countries. Most investigations provide evidence for the US, some studies analyse different European labour markets. A comprehensive survey of this extensive strand of literature is beyond the scope of the present chapter. Dustmann and Glitz (2005) and Longhi *et al.* (2008) provide recent and comprehensive surveys of the corresponding studies. Altogether, empirical evidence on the labour market effects of immigration is far from unambiguous. Borjas (2013) concludes that the literature seems to be full of contradictory results. While some analyses indicate a substantial negative impact of immigration on wages of the resident workforce (e.g. Borjas 2003; Borjas and Katz 2007), the findings of other studies suggest that the impact is negligible (e.g. Card 2005; Ottaviano and Peri 2012). Dustmann *et al.* (2008) summarize that although the evidence is rather mixed, it is certain that the consequences are not evenly distributed across residents in the host countries.

A possible explanation for the insignificant or small effects of immigration on labour market outcomes of natives might be that workers within the same skill and experience groups are imperfect substitutes because their cultural background differs as argued by Ottaviano and Peri (2012), for example. The relationship between cultural diversity caused by immigration and economic performance in the host countries is explored in a rapidly increasing number of studies. The effects of cultural diversity are investigated at different levels of aggregation (i.e. for different units of observation). The majority of analyses so far examine the diversity work teams. However, there is a growing number of studies which consider cultural diversity at the firm level, in industries or regions. Moreover, the impact of diversity on various outcome variables are such as sales, innovation, growth, productivity, employment, well-being and entrepreneurial activity is analysed. Methodologies applied in this field of research include case studies, experimental settings and regression analyses.

Whereas the impact of cultural diversity on economic performance is a fairly recent research topic in economics, there is an extensive human resource management literature that considers the consequences of work-team composition (especially of the top management). Hoogendoorn and van Praag (2012) investigate the effect of cultural diversity on the performance of business teams. Their results suggest that more diverse teams perform better in terms of business outcomes such as sales and profits. The authors interpret their findings as supporting the theoretical argument that heterogeneous teams possess a more diverse pool of relevant knowledge. In contrast, a meta-analysis by Bell *et al.* (2011) concludes that ethnic diversity negatively impacts on team performance. Altogether, evidence on the consequences of cultural diversity on the performance of work teams is rather inconclusive. Alesina *et al.* (2013) conclude that this ambiguity of findings is in line with the double-edged sword character of diversity since some studies detect beneficial effects on team performance while other investigations point to important transaction costs and declining team cohesion.

Only very recently researchers started to consider the heterogeneity of workers with respect to their cultural background on a more aggregate level and investigate the impact of diversity on firm performance or on the economic development of regions. Some current studies use firm-level data to analyse the relationship between diversity of the firm's staff and firm productivity. Parrotta *et al.* (2012) investigate the effects of diversity in terms of education, age and ethnicity on firm productivity based on a Danish matched employee–employer dataset. Their results suggest that cultural diversity adversely affects productivity. Thus costs of diversity seem to outweigh benefits. However, there is some indication of effect heterogeneity: positive effects of cultural diversity seem to be more pronounced for white-collar workers and R&D intensive sectors.

Trax *et al.* (2015) analyse the impact of cultural diversity on firm productivity in Germany. While the relative frequency of foreigners does not influence firm level productivity according to their results, the diversity of foreign workers tends to exert a strong positive effect on firm performance. Thus, it is not the relative weight of foreign workers but rather the composition of the migrant workforce, i.e. the number of different ethnic groups and the evenness of distribution across groups that matters for productivity. Moreover, their findings suggest that diversity of the regional labour force matters as well for firm productivity. However, firm level diversity seems to more important than cultural diversity at the regional level. The regression results also point to an important variation in the size of the effects. According to their estimates high-tech firms benefit more than low-tech firms and large firms achieve stronger positive effects than small establishments. The exporting behaviour of the firms also seems to positively influence the size of the diversity effect and the impact in manufacturing is more pronounced than in the service sector. Finally, Boeheim *et al.* (2012) report a positive effect of birthplace diversity of co-workers on the productivity of workers in Austria. Their findings confirm the evidence on effect heterogeneity reported for Danish and German firms as they detect above average productivity increases for white-collar workers and workers with short tenure.

There are also a few studies that investigate the relationship between cultural diversity and innovation at the firm level.[13] Ozgen *et al.* (2013) consider the impact of cultural diversity on innovation for a cross-section of Dutch firms. They report robust evidence that firms characterized by a relatively high share of foreign-born workers are less innovative. In contrast, a more diverse workforce in terms of cultural background tends to increase the likelihood of introducing an innovation. Moreover, the diversity effect is stronger in sectors that employ a relatively high share of skilled immigrants. Parrotta *et al.* (2014) and Østergaard *et al.* (2011) consider worker heterogeneity with respect to demographic charac-teristics and skills using Danish firm level data. Their results point to a significant influence of diversity on firm's likelihood of introducing a new product or service. The effects depend, however, on the specific dimension of heterogeneity. Findings of Niebuhr and Peters (2012) indicate that the number of cultural clusters among skilled workers increases the probability of innovation in German firms, whereas the employment share of foreigners has no significant effect on innovation activity. However, the relative frequency of migrants matters if the R&D employees are considered.[14]

Finally, some papers explore the significance of cultural diversity on economic performance of regions.[15] Suedekum *et al.* (2014), Audretsch *et al.* (2010) and Ottaviano and Peri (2005, 2006) report beneficial effects of cultural diversity on regional employment, entrepreneurial activity and productivity in the US and

Germany. The findings by Peri (2012) point to important positive effects of cultural diversity released by immigration on the productivity of US states. There are also investigations dealing with the link between innovation and worker diversity at an aggregate level. Niebuhr (2010) examines the relationship between cultural diversity of R&D workers and patent intensity for a cross-section of German regions. She detects a positive association between diversity and innovation that is in line with significant complementarities among of workers from diverse cultural backgrounds. This is confirmed by corresponding evidence in Ozgen *et al.* (2012). They identify a beneficial impact of ethnic diversity on the number of patent applications for European regions. In contrast, Maré *et al.* (2014) provide only weak evidence on an important impact of regional workforce composition on firm's innovation outcomes in New Zealand.

Conclusions

The literature on the effects of immigration on economic performance is voluminous. However, the majority of studies focus on labour market outcomes of native workers and their findings are far from clear-cut. Long-run effects on growth and innovation have received much less attention compared to labour market performance. This also applies to the economic effects of an increasing cultural diversity of the host economies. Although the number of corresponding studies is rapidly increasing in recent years, empirical evidence on this issue is still incomplete and ambiguous. In particular studies operating on the firm and the regional level are predominantly in support of positive effects of diversity. The benefits of diversity seem to largely outweigh transaction costs caused by heterogeneity of the workforce. But some results indicate that there might be also significant adverse consequences of diversity. Positive net effects of workforce diversity are detected primarily for high-skilled workers, in specific industries and distinct types of firms. Thus, the empirical literature points to a considerable heterogeneity of effects. Altogether we should not overrate the size of the effects. The majority of studies point to a fairly moderate impact of cultural diversity on economic performance.

The findings on the economic consequences of immigration and cultural diversity have important implications for different policies in the host countries such the regulation on migration, the set-up of the educational system and labour market institutions. The literature also provides valuable information for the human resource management of firms and their recruitment strategies. Diversity management in firms should promote the interaction and cooperation between employees with distinct cultural backgrounds taking into account the specific values and needs of foreign workers. Policies and management approaches should aim at realizing the beneficial effects of diversity, simultaneously minimizing costs resulting from communication barriers and possible conflicts. Access to education, especially the attainment of language skills, and labour market integration of migrants in the host economies are presumably of utmost importance in this context. However, comprehensive evidence on the role of policies and institutions as mediating factors of diversity effects is virtually non-existent.

This suggests that regarding the economic consequences of cultural diversity there are some open issues left for future research. Although several studies point to a robust correlation between cultural diversity and economic performance there is almost no evidence on the specific mechanisms at work up to now. Moreover, there are almost no analyses that try to disentangle positive and negative effects of diversity. So far the focus of research was on net effects. Furthermore, there are likely important mediating factors such as institutions that govern the relationship between cultural diversity and economic outcomes. The implementation of performance enhancing effects of diversity may require a specific set of rules, or regulatory framework. Ottaviano and Peri (2006), for instance, emphasize the role of a core of shared norms (integration) that might constitute a prerequisite for realizing the potential benefits of diversity. However, corresponding empirical evidence is scarce. Data availability is probably an important issue in this context because investigating the role of institutions calls for cross-country comparisons   that are severely hampered by lack of harmonized international datasets on cultural diversity.

Notes

1   Besides changes in factor prices, employment and capital supply there are other possible mechanisms by which the host country economy may adjust to immigration. For instance, the economy might fully absorb the additional labour supply through structural change (i.e. an increasing output share of industries that use the skills of foreign workers more intensively in their production process). Moreover, technological change might act as an alternative adjustment channel. The basic idea is that industries select a production technology that is more intensive in the use of the skills of migrants. See Dustmann *et al.* (2008) for a comprehensive discussion.
2   The significance of diversity for productivity, innovation, and growth has already been considered in numerous studies where diversity refers to the heterogeneity of firms and industries, diversity of people or varieties of inputs. Jacobs (1969) and Glaeser *et al.* (1992) investigate the beneficial effects of a diverse urban environment on innovation and growth. Romer (1990) highlights the significance of a variety of intermediate inputs for productivity in his seminal endogenous growth model.
3   Alesina and La Ferrara (2005) point out that adverse effects of diversity might also rest on the inability to agree on common public goods and policies.
4   See Dawson (2011) for a comprehensive discussion of the issue.
5   We refrain from a detailed discussion of cultural distance in this context. However, we might well assume that some groups, for instance Asian and Europeans, differ more from each other with respect to individual features, attitudes and shared rules than others such as different European citizens.
6   The most adequate classification might also differ from country to country. For example for the US diversity with respect to race is possibly an important issue, but this is less significant in the European context.
7   Note that both aspects are important. A high share of immigrants does not necessarily imply a high cultural diversity if all foreign-born belong to the same cultural group.

Moreover, high diversity among the immigrants does not indicate a high overall level of cultural diversity if the population share of immigrants is small. Alesina *et al.* (2013) propose a new diversity index that allows to differentiate between size and variety effects of immigration in order to account for the two aspects.

8   See Dohse and Gold (2013) for an in-depth discussion. The authors note that the Theil index accounts for non-linearities as a groups' contribution to diversity decreases with its size.

9   Whereas most studies on the effects of cultural diversity are based on population data, we use employment data instead. The advantage of our measure is a closer link to the production process. Moreover, nationality determines the cultural background of employees in the present analysis because information on the country of birth is not available in German statistics. As regional units of observation we choose functional regions which consist of several counties that are linked by intense commuting. They should therefore serve as a good approximation of regional labour markets.

10   In order to investigate the distribution of employment across cultural clusters we aggregate nationalities to 12 categories. The corresponding classification was developed in the GLOBE (Global Leadership and Organizational Behavior Effectiveness) project. The classification bases on information on common language, geography, religion, historical accounts and empirical studies (see Gupta *et al.* 2002).

11   Nijkamp and Poot (2012) note that the distinction between short- and long-run consequences of migration is not always clear cut because short-run effects may result in permanent changes due to path dependency.

12   We refrain from detailed presentation of different methodologies applied to determine the effects of migration and of identification problems such as unobserved heterogeneity and reverse causality related to different approaches.

13   There is another strand of literature that considers the impact of skilled immigration on innovation. However, these studies do not investigate the composition of the foreign workforce. Evidence is primarily available for the US (see e.g. Chellaraj *et al.* 2008; Hunt and Gauthier-Loiselle 2010).

14   Ozgen *et al.* (2014) compare diversity effects on innovation in Dutch and German firms. The authors conclude that cultural diversity of employees can make a positive, but modest and context-dependent, contribution to innovation.

15   Kemeny (2014) provides a review of the literature on economic effects of cultural diversity with a specific focus on economic development in cities. We do not consider studies that investigate the significance of ethnic and linguistic fractionalization on cross-country differences in growth. See Alesina and La Ferrara (2005) for a survey of the corresponding literature.

References

Alesina, A. and La Ferrara, E. (2005) Ethnic diversity and economic performance. *Journal of Economic Literature* 43: 762–800.

Alesina, A., Harnoss J. and Rapoport, H. (2013) Birthplace diversity and economic prosperity. Working paper no. 18699. Cambridge, MA: National Bureau of Economic Research.

Audretsch, D., Dohse, D. and Niebuhr, A. (2010) Cultural diversity and entrepreneurship: a regional analysis for Germany. *Annals of Regional Science* 45: 55–85.

Basset-Jones, N. (2005) The paradox of diversity management, creativity and innovation. *Creativity and Innovation Management* 14: 169–175.

Bell, S. T., Villado, A.J., Lukasik, M. A., Belau, L. and Briggs, A. L. (2011) Getting specific about demographic diversity variable and team performance relationships: a meta-analysis. *Journal of Management* 37: 709–743.

Boeheim, R., Horvath, G. and Mayr, K. (2012) Birthplace diversity of the workforce and productivity spill-overs in firms. WIFO working paper no. 438. Vienna: Österreichisches Institut für Wirtschaftsforschung.

Borjas, G. (2003) The labor demand curve is downward sloping: reexamining the impact of immigration on the labor market. *Quarterly Journal of Economics* 118: 1335–1374.

Borjas, G. (2013) The analytics of the wage effect of immigration. *IZA Journal of Migration* 2: 1–25.

Borjas, G. and Katz, L. (2007) The evolution of the Mexican-born workforce in the United States. In G. Borjas (ed.), *Mexican Immigration to the United States*, 13–56. Cambridge, MA: National Bureau of Economic Research.

Card, D. (2005) Is the new immigration really so bad? *Economic Journal* 115: F300–F323.

Chellaraj, G., Maskus, K. E. and Mattoo, A. (2008) The contribution of skilled immigration and international graduate students to US innovation. *Review of International Economics* 16: 444–462.

Cohen, W. M. and Levinthal, D. A. (1990) Absorptive capacity: a new perspective on learning and innovation. *Administrative Science Quarterly* 35: 128–152.

Dawson, J. (2011) Measurement of work group diversity. PhD thesis, Aston University, Birmingham.

DiTomaso, N., Post, C. and Parks-Yancy, R. (2007) Workforce diversity and inequality: power, status, and numbers. *Annual Review of Sociology* 33: 473–501.

Dohse, D. and Gold, R. (2013) *Measuring Cultural Diversity at a Regional Level*. Working paper no. 10. Vienna: WWWforEurope. Available at www.foreurope.eu/fileadmin/documents/pdf/Workingpapers/WWWforEurope_WPS_no010_MS99.pdf.

Dustmann, C. and Glitz, A. (2005) *Immigration, Jobs and Wages: Theory, Evidence and Opinion*. London: CEPR-CReAM Publications.

Dustmann, C., Glitz, A and Frattini, T. (2008) The labour market impact of immigration. *Oxford Review of Economic Policy* 24: 477–494.

Fujita, M. and Weber, S. (2004) *Strategic Immigration Policies and Welfare in Heterogeneous Countries*. FEEM working paper no. 2. Milan: Fondazione Eni Enrico Mattei.

Glaeser, E. L., Kallal, H. D., Scheinkman, J. A. and Shleifer, A. (1992) Growth in cities. *Journal of Political Economy* 100: 1126–1152.

Gupta, V., Hanges, P. J. and Dorfman, P. (2002) Cultural clusters: methodology and findings. *Journal of World Business* 37: 11–15.

Harrison, D. A. and Klein, K. J. (2007) What's the difference? Diversity constructs as separation, variety, or disparity in organizations. *Academy of Management Review* 32: 1199–1228.

Harrison, D. A. and Sin, H.-S. (2006) What is diversity and how should it be measured? In A. M. Konrad, P. Prasad and J. K. Pringle (eds), *Handbook of Workplace Diversity*, 191–216. London: Sage Publications.

Hoogendoorn, S. and van Praag, M. (2012) *Ethnic Diversity and Team Performance: A Field Experiment*. Discussion paper TI 2012-068/3. Amsterdam: Tinbergen Institute.

Hunt, J. and Gauthier-Loiselle, M. (2010) How much does immigration boost innovation? *American Economic Journal: Macroeconomics* 2: 31–56.

Jacobs, J. (1969) *The Economy of Cities*. New York: Random House.

Keely, L.C. (2003) Exchanging good ideas. *Journal of Economic Theory* 111: 192–213.

Kemeny, T. (2014) Immigrant diversity and economic development in cities: a critical review. *International Regional Science Review* (online first: doi: 10.1177/01600176 14541695).

Lazear, E. P. (2000) Diversity and immigration. In G. J. Borjas (ed.), *Issues in the Economics of Immigration*, 117–142. Chicago, IL: University of Chicago Press.

Longhi, S., Nijkamp, P. and Poot, J. (2008) Meta-analysis of empirical evidence on the labor market impacts of immigration. *Région et développement* 27: 161–191.

Manacorda, M., Manning, A. and Wadsworth, J. (2012) The impact of immigration on the structure of wages: theory and evidence from Britain. *Journal of the European Economic Association* 10: 120–151.

Maré, D. C., Fabling, R. and Stillman, S. (2014) Innovation and local workforce. *Papers in Regional Science* 93: 183–201.

Niebuhr, A. (2010) Migration and innovation: does cultural diversity matter for regional R&D activity? *Papers in Regional Science* 89: 563–585.

Niebuhr, A. and Peters, J. C. (2012) Labour diversity and firm's innovation: evidence from Germany. Paper presented at Economic Impacts of Immigration and Population Diversity workshop, University of Waikato, 11–13 April.

Nijkamp, P. (2012) Migration impact assessment: a review of evidence-based findings. *Review of Economic Analysis* 4: 179–208.

Nijkamp, P. and Poot, J. (2012) Migration impact assessment: a state of the art. In P. Nijkamp, J. Poot and M. Sahin (eds), *Migration Impact Assessment: New Horizons*, 3–64. Cheltenham: Edward Elgar.

Østergaard, C. R., Timmermans, B. and Kristinsson, K. (2011) Does a different view create something new? The effect of employee diversity on innovation. *Research Policy* 40: 500–509.

Ottaviano, G. I. P. and Peri, G. (2005) Cities and cultures. *Journal of Urban Economics* 58: 304–337.

Ottaviano, G. I. P. and Peri, G. (2006) The economic value of cultural diversity: evidence from US cities. *Journal of Economic Geography* 6: 9–44.

Ottaviano, G. I. P. and Peri, G. (2012) Rethinking the effect of immigration on wages. *Journal of the European Economic Association* 10: 152–197.

Ozgen, C. (2013) *Impacts of Immigration and Cultural Diversity on Innovation and Economic Growth*. Research series no. 565. Amsterdam: Tinbergen Institute.

Ozgen, C., Nijkamp, P. and Poot, J. (2012) Immigration and innovation in European regions. In P. Nijkamp, J. Poot and M. Sahin (eds), *Migration Impact Assessment: New Horizons*, 261–300. Cheltenham: Edward Elgar.

Ozgen, C., Nijkamp, P. and Poot, J. (2013) The impact of cultural diversity on firm innovation: evidence from Dutch micro-data. *IZA Journal of Migration* 2: 1–24.

Ozgen, C., Peters, J. C., Niebuhr, A., Nijkamp, P. and Poot, J. (2014) Does cultural diversity of migrant employees affect innovation? *International Migration Review* 48: S377–S416.

Parrotta, P., Pozzoli, D. and Pytlikova, M. (2012) *Does Labor Diversity Affect Firm Productivity?* IZA discussion paper no. 6973. Bonn: Institute for the Study of Labor.

Parrotta, P., Pozzoli, D. and Pytlikova, M. (2014) The nexus between labour diversity and firm's innovation. *Journal of Population Economics* 27: 303–364.

Peri, G. (2012) The effect of immigration on productivity: evidence from US States. *Review of Economics and Statistics* 94: 348–358.

Romer, P. M. (1990) Endogenous technological change. *Journal of Political Economy* 98: S71–S102.

Stock, R. (2004) Drivers of team performance: what do we know and what have we still to learn? *Schmalenbach Business Review* 56: 274–306.

Suedekum, J., Wolf, K. and Blien, U. (2014) Cultural diversity and local labour markets. *Regional Studies* 48: 173–191.

Trax, M., Brunow, S. and Suedekum, J. (2015) Cultural diversity and plant level productivity. *Regional Science and Urban Economics* 53: 85–96.

United Nations (2013) *Trends in International Migrant Stock: The 2013 Revision*. New York.

Zimmermann, K. F. (2005) European labour mobility: challenges and potentials. *De Economist* 153: 425–450.

8 A reality check to migrant entrepreneurs

The case of German–Turkish entrepreneurs

Canan Balkır and Kevin van Hove

Introduction

In Germany, with a population of about 80 million people, about 20 per cent of the population has a migration background. Of the nationalities with a migration background, Turks comprise the biggest group, with close to 4 million. According to Zentrum für Türkeistudien, while in 1975 only 100 Turks were entrepreneurs, currently more than 80,000 people with a Turkish background are entrepreneurs (Die Welt 2012). This rising trend raises a lot of questions, such as:

- *What explains the strong rise of Turkish entrepreneurship in Germany?*
- *What are the problems Turkish migrant entrepreneurs face?*

These questions can contribute to an understanding of the entrepreneurship trend, as the second and third generation migrant entrepreneurs are supposed to face less problems than the first generation. A third question can be about the business associations, representing the interests of the migrant entrepreneurs. Hence the question *Do migrant entrepreneurs organize themselves in business associations?* is followed by the question *What is the role of these business associations in terms of networks?* The entrepreneurs understandably want to have their interest well represented, but it is equally important that German society regards these business associations positively and incorporates them in the policy process, especially in terms of labour market integration. It is also relevant to find out the position of the European Union on migrant entrepreneurship. *Does it promote migrant entrepreneurship and if so how does it do that?* The answers to all these questions will provide a reality-check to the positive image that is attributed to migrant entrepreneurship. But before this, a short literature review of migrant entrepreneurship will be presented, to give background information for the discussion.

Migrant entrepreneurship as an economic force

International migrants, according to a widely used definition, persons who have been outside their country of birth or citizenship for a period of 12 months or longer, have become a key feature of a modern open society (Sasse and Thiele-mann 2005). Several studies show that in the short-run migration provides many benefits and contributes to economic growth and the creation of new jobs in Europe. Far less is known about the long-run economic impact. In any sense, for these benefits to be long term they have to be supported by appropriate policies of the host country (Desiderio 2014). The preference of many host countries to recruit highly-skilled workers, as revealed by their selection processes, is grounded in the belief that such workers will integrate more easily, reduce the amount of public funding for education and training, and boost long-run economic growth. Migration is likely to boost economic growth through five mechanisms: the population size effect, the population density effect, the migrant share effect, the skill composition effect and the migrant diversity effect (Özgen *et al.* 2011). However, high immigrant unemployment rates damage the welfare state's finances and undermine the role of migration as a solution to the ageing of the population and declining ratio of workers to pensioners. Thus the unemploy-ment rate of immigrants have been an important issue in the policy agendas of European countries. Moreover immigrant employment has been a pivotal feature in the discussion on immigrant integration as it determines material well-being, social integration and the integration of future generations of immigrants (Kesler 2006).

Within the field of migrant employment, one important feature has been the increasing entrepreneurial behaviour of many migrant groups (Baycan-Levent and Nijkamp 2009). While these migrant entrepreneurs originally remained invisible as they were viewed as workers, often as "factory fodder" in sunset industries or at the bottom end of the post-industrial service economy (Rath 2011), over the years their increasing number has led to the rise of a new pheno-menon called "migrant entrepreneurship" or "ethnic entrepreneurship", which is considered to be a factor in the economic dynamism of many countries. Follow-ing the work of Feldman and Audretsch (1999), who showed that regions with more diversity will facilitate the spillover of knowledge, which in turn should trigger more entrepreneurial activity, Niebuhr (2010) claims that migrants and native workers of different cultural backgrounds possessing fairly diverse abilities and knowledge may create skill complementarities in addition to those among workers of the same qualification levels. This has a potential for inno-vation, as innovation is defined as "a product of interaction between actors that have sufficiently different knowledge in order to make Schumpeterian new combinations" (Boschma and Martin 2010: 142). The high importance given to innovation as an engine for economic growth in the EU has been translated into an Innovation Union. This goal is strongly supported by the emergence of innovation networks, described as primary environments within which actors exchange knowledge and experience in an easier and less costly way (Gilbert 2001; Buchmann and Pyka 2011). The knowledge transfer takes place in innovation networks which are spawned between the core and periphery by these entrepreneurial individuals and their economic engagement in both regions (Saxenian 2006).

The migrant entrepreneurship has played a crucial role in increasing the employment opportunities for ethnic segments in the urban population not only for themselves but also for others. They create on average between 1.4 and 2.1 additional jobs (EESC 2012) and employ an average of at least 2.4 per cent of the total employed population in OECD (OECD 2010). They have also played a crucial role in resolving social tensions and problems (Rath 2011). They can enhance the vitality of particular streets or neighbourhoods in cities or of specific economic sectors; and most of all, they play their part in the "natural" process of succession and renewal of the total corpus of entrepreneurs (Rath 2011). It has also become one of the driving forces for the growth of national and regional economies, particularly in the USA and in many European countries. In fact, migrant entrepreneurship is increasingly seen as a powerful economic force and a contributor to solving structural labour market imbalances in many industrialized countries (Baycan-Levent and Nijkamp 2009).

Semantics behind migrant versus ethnic entrepreneurship

The rise of migrant entrepreneurship has drawn public attention as early as 1970 (Kloosterman and Rath 2003) and it has been an important field of study, especially in traditional immigration countries such as the United States ever since (Light 1972; Waldinger *et al.* 1990), where it originally mainly focused on Asian entrepreneurship (Jones and Ram 2013) and also in several European countries since the late 1980s (see Kloosterman and Rath 2003; Dana *et al.* 2008; Jones and Ram 2013; Rath 2011). In the academic literature there is no unanimity about the usage of the term (im)migrant entrepreneurship. Some authors consider migrant entrepreneurship to be a synonym of ethnic (minority) entrepreneurship (Kloosterman and Rath 2003), while others deny this and prefer the solely usage of the term ethnic entrepreneurship. According to the last group, entrepreneurs in question are not always immigrants in the true sense in that they were not always born in another country, notably many are second- and third-generation migrants. The definition of migrant entrepreneurship generally also includes the offspring of immigrants, the second generation or the native born children of the first generation (IMES Triodos 2008). Many authors also assume without further reflection that just because they are dealing with immigrants, there are real "ethnic" differences, and that these "ethnic" differences pertain to the entire immigrant population and that these "ethnic" differences never change (Rath 2000; Kloosterman and Rath 2003). Another problematic issue is that migrants, notably of the second generation, receiving citizenship of the country of residence, as in France and Belgium for instance, disappear from the national immigration statistics. In Germany dual citizenship is only allowed to EU citizens and citizens of Switzerland and (unless one of the parents is German) any other national has to renounce its former nationality to be able to receive the German citizenship. As a result many Turks for instance are registered as immigrant (Ausländer) while people from Central and Eastern Europe are not.

Defining an entrepreneur, IMES Triodos (2008) describe it as a person in effective control of a commercial undertaking for more than one client over a significant period of time. These entrepreneurs generally own and manage the firm, but these two roles may sometimes be performed by different individuals. Masurel *et al.* (2004) call it a broad concept which refers to business activities in a certain area driven or undertaken by people of a different ethnic or cultural (including religious) origin than the indigenous population. Some entrepreneurs are also referred to as "commuting entrepreneurs" (Saxenian 2006) or "transnational entrepreneurs", when they are involved in border crossing business activities (Man Yip 2011). The European Economic and Social Committee (EESC 2012) defines a migrant entrepreneur as a business owner born outside the EU who seeks to generate value through the creation or expansion of economic activity. The entrepreneur can be self-employed, such as employing only himself, or employ staff.

Profile of migrant entrepreneurs

Migrant entrepreneurs have a multi-dimensional profile in terms of generation, gender, age groups, migration reasons, language skills, opinions and religious beliefs, education and so forth. The majority are poorly educated, lacking proficiency in the host country's language, and lacking access to financial resources. This pushes many ethnic entrepreneurs to the lower end of the market. In these markets, production is mainly small in scale, low in value added, and usually labour intensive; earnings are typically low, and days are long and hard (Kloosterman 2010). Moreover there is an immense variation between countries and within countries, between cities and within cities, neighbourhoods, and also between economic sectors (Kloosterman 2010; Rath 2011). While data on immigrant entrepreneurship is in general limited, there is evidence that in many developed countries immigrants are indeed over-represented among entrepreneurs. This largely depends on the background of the migrants and the opportunity structure in the country of destination (Marchand and Siegel 2014). Within the EU, it can be seen that immigrants are more likely to be self-employed than native citizens in the Czech Republic, Poland, Hungary, the United Kingdom, Germany, Malta and Belgium. The opposite is the case in the remaining member countries. Therefore generalizations concerning the entrepreneurial nature of immigrants are risky.

In countries such as the United Kingdom, France, Belgium, Denmark, Sweden and Norway, and also the United States, the share of entrepreneurs in total employment of immigrants is somewhat higher for first-generation immigrants compared with natives. In other countries, namely Portugal, Spain, Italy, Greece, Ireland, Germany, Austria and Switzerland, the share of first-generation immigrants in self-employment is lower (Rath 2011; EESC 2012). Between countries and within one country, the survival rates of enterprises among different ethnic groups also show a high dispersion (Masurel *et al.* 2004). This also holds for the survival rates per economic sector, which also appear to differ significantly

(Baycan-Levent and Nijkamp 2009). Specific immigrant groups are viewed as making special contributions, which applies to Asian and Turkish immigrants in France (Boubakri 1999) and there are similar findings in Germany (Özcan and Seifert 2000).

Ethnic groups tend to cluster in large cities as a result of network externalities (Carrington *et al.* 1996). While cities represent a strong social network of migrants in promoting entrepreneurship, provincial towns represent a less dense social network. The role ethnicity plays in the entrepreneur's action, the dynamics of business start-ups run by migrants or their descendants and upward social mobility of migrants in relation to the impact of social networks varies from case to case. Despite their growing importance in Europe, in most cities studied, migrant entrepreneurship had not played a major role in the overall strategy supporting the integration of immigrants. Attention, if any, is given to wage labour. And to whatever extent ethnic entrepreneurship is actually promoted, it rarely forms part of a bigger economic agenda. Various reasons account for this. First, in a number of cases, immigrants have not actually entered the entrepreneurial market, so there seems little need for specific policies. Second, it is sometimes believed that ethnic minorities are not suffering from any form of disadvantage that would justify special measures. Third, integration policy rarely has an economic or socioeconomic orientation. It is mostly about language acquisition, social cohesion, security, norms and values, and only marginally about finding a job, embarking on a career, or setting up a business. Fourth, the assumption prevails that group-specific measures are "not done", and measures should be colour-blind, should not give "preferential treatment" to one group over another, and should not discriminate against any group (Rath 2011).

Migrant entrepreneurs may have expert knowledge on specific demands or specific sources of supply relating to foreign products. In many cases this expertise can be based on first-hand knowledge from back home, or it can be generated through transnational networks that bridge the country of origin and the sometimes extensive diaspora (Portes 1995). By introducing new products and new ways of marketing, even the migrant entrepreneurs at the bottom end of a market can become innovators. The introduction of the "döner kebab" by Turkish entrepreneurs in Germany has been cited as a case in point (Rudolph and Hillmann 1997).

Culturalist and structuralist approaches on migrant entrepreneurship

An important distinction in the literature on migrant entrepreneurship is the one between cultural and structural factors explaining the opportunities and the barriers, by identifying critical success or performance conditions for migrant entrepreneurs (see Ward and Jenkins 1984; Portes 1995; Kloosterman 2010). By and large the first wave of literature used a *culturalist* approach (see Light 1972; Barrett, Jones and McEvoy 1986), which sees migrant entrepreneurship positively as a viable route to upward social mobility and can be referred to as the socio-economic progress approach (Jones and Ram 2013). This approach suggests migrants to possess ethnic or culturally determined features which are prerequisites for economic success and entrepreneurial attitudes, such as particular values, skills, flexibility, the dedication to work, the membership of a *strong social network* and flexible financing arrangements, etc. , which may place them in some respects in a relatively favourable position (Light 1972). Many experts point first and foremost to the social cohesion of ethnic communities and the importance of ethnic solidarity and relations of trust. For them, networks are instrumental in acquiring knowledge, distributing information, recruiting capital and labour, and establishing strong relations with clients and suppliers (Waldinger *et al.* 1990; Portes and Sensenbrenner 1993; Jones and Ram 2013).

This social embeddedness[1] enables these entrepreneurs to reduce their transaction costs by eliminating formal contracts, giving privileged access to economic resources. Particularly in cases where the entrepreneurs' primary input is cheap and flexible labour, the reduction of transaction costs by mobilizing social networks for labour recruitment seems the key issue. Granovetter (1985) makes a distinction between two types of embeddedness; the relational embeddedness referring to "economic actors" and to the personal relations migrant entrepreneurs have with customers, suppliers, banks, competitors, and, law enforcers. Structural embeddedness relates to the broader network to which these actors belong, transcending direct personal relations.

Already in an early stage following the realization of some paradoxical aspects of ethnic entrepreneurship, the culturalist approach was countered by the *structuralist* approach. In general the structuralist approach (see Aldrich *et al.* 1981; Miles 1982; Waldinger *et al.* 1990; Jones *et al.* 1992; Rath 2011; Jones and Ram 2013) stresses the external environment of the migrants as the decisive player and claims that ethnic entrepreneurship is done out of necessity and a response to social exclusion, discrimination and blocked opportunities in the general labour market. Self-employment is less of a voluntarily chosen occupational specialization and more of a reactive survival mechanism for a newly arrived group suffering high unemployment rates, job discrimination and lacking viable options elsewhere in the economy.

The structuralist approach views self-employment as an economic dead-end for immigrants and a continuation of subordinate status rather than an escape from it. Long working hours, unpaid family labour and low incomes are some of the indicators that support this dead-end hypothesis. It also emphasizes the structure of the receiving society, in terms of economic, social and political conditions that immigrants encounter and force migrants to start a business. The vital point is how and to what degree agency and structure influence the development of migrant entrepreneurship (IMES Triodos 2008).

A *third approach* creates a more balanced synthesis of agency and structure and can hence be viewed as an intermediate approach between the culturalist and structuralist theories. Bonacich (1973) developed the middleman minority theory based on a combination of socio-economic exclusion and entrepreneurial spirit as the source of ethnic entrepreneurship. Building on this theory, Waldinger *et al.*

(1990) developed a so-called interaction model explaining ethnic entrepreneurship through a dynamic match between local market opportunities and the local demand on the one hand and the specific available ethnic resources on the other hand. The interaction model comprises three classes of factors, namely the opportunity structure, the group characteristics and the ethnic strategy. The model faced several amendments, of which Kloosterman *et al.*'s (1999) more dynamic model of mixed embeddedness has been particularly influential. Not only is the ethnic firm thoroughly embedded in its own social networks, this has to be placed in its external political-economic context. Political and economic institutions are considered crucial in understanding both the obstacles and opportunities for aspiring entrepreneurs to start their own business (see Kloosterman 2000; Engelen 2001; Kloosterman and Rath 2003). As the label "mixed embeddedness suggests, it acknowledges a strong significance for embeddedness" as the ethnic network is vital as a means of raising capital, mobilizing workforce and draw together support for business (Kloosterman 2010). However, the very fact that the informality of ethnic channels enables entrepreneurs to by-pass the costs and possible unfavourable bias of official channels like banks, is a heavy reminder that ethnic entrepreneurs and their community cannot be taken in isolation from that which surrounds them. The "mixed embeddedness" also suggests that the firm is grounded at more than one level and its fate is determined by the interplay between its own community and the structure of market and state.[2] For ethnic entrepreneurship firms in an advanced economy this interplay is by and large between a small under-resourced agent on the one hand; and a structure dominated by large corporate entities and rendered still more hostile by racist bias and discrimination (Jones and Ram 2013). Thus the immigrant's process of incorporation is not just determined by the resources he/she can mobilize, but is also decided by the time-and-place of specific opportunity structure. With the transition from industrial to post-industrial economies, the profile of the opportunity structure changed significantly and improved the opportunities for smaller firms.

Thus, building on his earlier work, Kloosterman (2010) presented an innovative analytical framework for the analysis of (migrant) entrepreneurship from a mixed embeddedness perspective. It combines the micro-level of the individual entrepreneur (with his/ her resources), with the meso-level of the local opportunity structure and links the latter, in a more loose way, to the macro-institutional framework. Within this framework, significant changes in the supply side (i.e. more high-skilled migrants from non-OECD countries) and demand side (new opportunities which arise due to the post-industrial transformation of urban economies that has increased opportunities for small firms due to the shift to services, outsourcing, market fragmentation and the availability of low-cost information and communication technology (ICT) in the last two decades, are integrated. Linking the micro-level of the entrepreneur and meso-level of the opportunity structure, shows that there are reasonably good chances of upward social mobility for low-skilled workers in post-industrial entrepreneurship and very good chances of upward social mobility for high-skilled workers in post-industrial entrepreneurship. Kloosterman identifies four ways in which the institutional framework may impact on the opportunity structure; namely, the differences in ways of provision, regulations regarding labour, regulations regarding businesses and webs of interrelationships of firms and relevant actors. However, here the relationships are much more open than in the case of the links between the micro- and the meso-level. According to Marchand and Siegel (2014) when using the mixed embeddedness approach it is important to understand the context of each individual case, especially the opportunity structure and the social environment of the entrepreneur.

Different generations of migrant business

First-generation immigrants seem to be more entrepreneurial than others, males are more so than females, and some ethnic groups are more so than other ethnic groups. In recent years the second and third generation of ethnic migrants tends to be involved in professional service provision and business consultancy, a trend owing to acquiring higher education. First generation immigrants often serve their own ethnic community in cities with products or services and thereby develop their own "ethnic market". From an economic perspective such an urban clustering has two major advantages: (i) the presence of a critical mass of potential customers of the same ethnic origin leading to viable market niches, and (ii) the rise of informal networks of a sufficient size which facilitate the recruitment of low-cost personnel, up-to-date information or inexpensive financing capital (Borjas 1992). These migrant entrepreneurs are strong in classic vacancy-chain sectors such as lower-end retailing, wholesaling, restaurants and catering. Those who risk unemployment or unattractive labour conditions are pushed rather than pulled to these less promising market segments. These enterprises however will soon realize the economic limits because of the size of the ethnic market and need to break out of the ethnic market in order to succeed.[3] However, for breaking out of the ethnic market one needs to possess enough familiarity with the bigger local markets and business environment as well as being able to deal with the bureaucracy. Thus, second generation entrepreneurs with better educational qualifications and better host country language skills broke out of the ethnic market, having clients of all origins and diversification of products.

The opportunity structure for (ethnic) entrepreneurs in cities is the basis to understand their performance. The growth of service economy accompanied by the decline of manufacturing industries has generated a demand for low-end activities, and that is fulfilled by outsourcing and a rise of small businesses with labour-intensive production and high flexibility. A second or third generation immigrant business may either continue to occupy a niche market using ethnic origin for sign value or increasingly venture out to growth sectors such as personal and business services. There can also be immigrant business catering to other immigrants, or immigrant businesses from diverse origins clustered together, either by tradition or by design, as in the recent trend of ethnic shopping malls.[4] Migrant entrepreneurs are increasingly to be found outside working-class ethnic neighbourhoods, in the central business districts and suburbs. This enables them to serve a larger number of and wealthier clientele. In the case of a middleman minority, this mainly concerns business with long opening hours, such as night shops, and activities in which the profits are rather low so that ethnic entrepreneurs meet few native competitors.

Currently, there is increasingly another kind of ethnic entrepreneur who fits Waldinger *et al.*'s (1990) description of "economic assimilation"; the aspiring or fledgling entrepreneur who tends to be highly educated and connected to different social networks, who is better qualified to operate in post-industrial growth markets such as finance, information and communication technology, insurance, real estate, media and tourism. Entrepreneurs from the second generation of immigrants, often being better educated than their parents, are able to position themselves in those profitable markets. Thus, they are pulled rather than pushed to these markets and because of their higher levels of human and social capital, they better fit the requirements of post-industrial economy.

EU policy towards migrant entrepreneurship

Despite their contrasting logics, since the early 1980s neoliberalism and the social democratic project of the Keynesian era have existed concurrently in the European Union (see Hay and Rosamond 2002; Dinan 2004; Mitchell 2006). The neo-liberalist project has been given expression with the common market, and a monetary policy based on price stability and an anti-inflationary mandate rather than on growth and development, and the Stability and Growth Pact which makes state-sponsored development targeted at the eradication of specific internal inequalities or the protection of particular sectors in society, by deficit spending increasingly difficult. Alongside a rhetoric of globalism, a discourse on competition and individual entrepreneurialism developed. The social democratic project has been given manifestation at the regional scale through geographical redistribution programs and social funds such as the European Regional Development Fund (ERDF) and the European Social Fund (ESF) (see Hay and Rosamond 2002; Mitchell 2006).

Ever since the Lisbon European Council decided in March 2000 to improve the EU's performance in the areas of employment, economic reform and social cohesion, promoting entrepreneurship in Europe became a core objective. Today the European Commission strongly advocates the creation of an environment conducive to the starting-up and development of entrepreneurship; in particular the small and medium-enterprise (SME)[5] sector. Representing 99 per cent of all businesses in the EU, and having created around 85 per cent of new jobs and providing two-thirds of the total private sector employment in the EU, the European Commission considers SMEs and entrepreneurship as the backbone of Europe's economy and key to ensuring economic growth, innovation, job creation, and social integration in the EU (European Commission 2015b). Hence Europe needs migrant entrepreneurs. In literature and policy making entrepreneurship development is commonly seen as a solution for the problems created by the economic crisis (Vasilescu 2014). A Eurobarometer report on entrepreneurship shows this vision is shared by the majority of the Europeans, as 87 per cent consider entrepreneurs as job creators, while 79 per cent agree that entrepreneurs create new products and services that benefit all (European Commission 2012). However, since 2004, the share of people preferring self-employment to being an employee has dropped in 23 EU member countries and in comparison to the USA and China much less people prefer to work as self-employed in the Union. The Commission claims that to make entrepreneurship the growth engine of the EU's economy, Europe needs a thorough, far-reaching cultural change. For this reason the principle of "think small first" must become the touchstone of European and national policies, under a co-ordinated action at European, national and regional levels.

Besides publicly recognizing the general contribution of migrants to sustainable growth and the creation of new jobs in the European Agenda for the Integration of Third-Country Nationals (European Commission 2011), the EU Labour Force Survey (1998–2008) highlights the positive contribution of migrant entrepreneurs to employment. The migrants are recognized as an important pool of potential entrepreneurs more likely to start businesses than natives and can substantially contribute to growth and job creation in the EU (European Commission 2015d). The European Commission aimed to illustrate this with the launch of the Europe 2020 strategy in 2010, which sets out a clear need to pave the way for economic migration in sectors in which labour and skills shortages are emerging, as well as to attract highly skilled third-country nationals in order to keep up with the global competition.

It is a known fact that immigrants founded 52 per cent of start-ups created in Silicon Valley, USA, between 1995 and 2005. Israel owes much of its success to its immigrant population. However, in the EU these migrant businesses are mainly micro-businesses,[6] with very few employees, a smaller turnover and low profits in comparison with indigenous businesses and fail more often due to a lack of information, knowledge and language skills (European Commission 2015a) and it has become the individual's responsibility to integrate effectively and the failure to do so is projected as a question of individual choice, under the discourse and practices of neoliberal governmentality. This is part of a broader delegation of responsibility to the *individual immigrant* for assimilating effectively into the labour market, the host nation and European society at large (Mitchell 2006; Hay and Rosamond 2002).

A number of programmes have been developed in the field of entrepreneurship by the European Commission's Directorate General for Internal Market, Industry, Entrepreneurship and Small and Medium Enterprises. However, according to the network of Cities for Local Integration Policy, migrant entrepreneurship is not an important part of the European integration policy for migrants (CLIP 2011), an area in which the EU has no competence to legislate and mainly focuses on assisting national, regional and local organizations and authorities in identifying and sharing best practices and benchmarking on successful integration strategies with each other (Malmstrom 2014). While during the last years migrant entrepreneurs have been targeted more by EU's entrepreneurship policies, these policies generally do not target immigrants explicitly (European Commission 2015c). Yet, nearly all the programmes have been accessible on grounds of residence and hence include legally-residing immigrants in one of the participating countries. An exception to this was the Blue Card directive (Council Directive 2009/50/EC)[7] with which, in accordance with the Europe 2020 Strategy, the European Commission aims to create policy that helps to attract talented would-be entrepreneurs from non-EU countries and ensure that business support services reach all potential entrepreneurs. However, considering the very low number of awarded Blue Cards, this can hardly be called a success. A second exception forms the Entrepreneurship 2020 Action Plan, adopted in January 2013 and which set out a renewed vision and a number of actions to be taken at both EU and Member States' level to support entrepreneurship in Europe under three pillars: developing entrepreneurial education and training and creating the right business environment; role models, a third one; reaching out to specific groups, one of which are migrant entrepreneurs. This can be interpreted as a step towards a bigger recognition and promotion of migrant entrepreneurship as part of wider integration policies.

A lot of effort has been done in the last two decades regarding the financing and innovation support to SME's. Today, access to finance, entrepreneurs and innovation of SMEs are at the core of the EU 2020 strategy and its major instruments COSME,[8] HORIZON 2020 and Regional Funds. As mentioned before, no special provision was made to migrant entrepreneurs, but as a legal resident in one of the partner countries, they can benefit from these programs and services as well (European Union 2015). COSME *supports actions to improve the framework conditions in which enterprises operate*, in particular SMEs, by reducing unnecessary administrative and regulatory burdens and it also *encourages an entrepreneurial culture*. An example in case is the Erasmus for Young Entrepreneurs program, which was launched in 2009 with 37 partner countries, within the framework of the Small Business Act (SBA) for Europe (European Commission 2015d). Legally residing migrants in one of the countries can also benefit from the HORIZON 2020 project,[9] the EU Research and Innovation Program. Moreover, 15.6 per cent of the economic, social and territorial cohesion fund was awarded to competiveness, highlighting the EU's strong emphasis on competitiveness (European Commission 2013c).

Turkish migrant entrepreneurs in Germany

Turkish migration outflows to Germany were a result of labour migration in the 1960s, family reunification in the 1970s–1980s, refugees and asylum seekers in the 1990s, and irregular migration in the 2000s (Sirkeci *et al.* 2012). Turks in Europe are more often unemployed than other migrant groups, although the Turkish community in Europe is made up of a significantly younger population when compared to the EU population. Many researchers claim there are *structural* reasons for their self-employment (see Miles 1982; Jones *et al.* 1992;

Waldinger *et al.* 1990: 13–16, Rath 2011; Jones and Ram 2013), which began as an alternative employment path for many first-generation redundant guest workers and received a significant response from second-generation youth, often assisted by parents who had in mind securing the future livelihoods of their children.

After already having signed a recruitment agreement with Italy in 1955, at the beginning of the 1960s, the Federal Republic of Germany signed bilateral agreements on guest workers first with Spain and Greece in 1960, then with Turkey in 1961, while other Mediterranean countries soon followed. "Blood" was a label for ethnicity in Germany, which meant that a person could only obtain German nationality by being born into the German community. Thus, foreign workers and their families as well as non-German refugees were not granted German citizenship but provided with naturalization entitlements. Later in the late 1990s, the Social Democrat/Green coalition (1998–2005), introduced *ius soli* (the law of the birthplace/soil) to children of foreigners born in Germany, but the proposal was not accepted. Eventually, children of non-EU immigrants born in Germany have been automatically German nationals at birth but at the age of 18, (unless one of the parents is German) they have to renounce the nationality of their parents, to be able to maintain the German citizenship. Today, almost 20 per cent of Germany's population has a migration background and Turks comprise the biggest migrant group with more than 3.5 million.

From the signing of the first bilateral agreements concerning guest workers with Italy in 1955 until the formal end of this policy in 1973, most migrant workers in Germany were recruited by government agencies. In order to avoid permanent immigration and to fulfil the objective of a rotation system, the number of workers was controlled by the issue of temporary work and residence permits. Work permits were usually prolonged as employers were reluctant to provide training for new workers (Rudolph 1994: 119–122). The employment of foreign workers was considered to be a short-term solution to bridge periods of labour shortage by keeping the foreign labour force flexible and adaptable to the demand of the German labour market. The rotation system was meant to benefit all participating parties. First, the cheap labour supply would meet the high demand of low-skilled workers in Germany. Second, immigrant workers were assumed to acquire knowledge and skills along with relatively high wages. Third, the employment abroad would help reduce the unemployment rate in sending countries (Rudolph 1994; Man Yip 2011). Specifically, Turkish migrants were in the lowest segment of the labour market (Bender and Seifert 1998: 99). Most of them were employed in sectors of agriculture, mining and construction. The first businesses appeared in the early 1960s, catering to Turkish labour migrants' special needs such as restaurants and cafés, translation services, travel agencies, and such (ibid.). Owing to the industrial restructuring in the late 1980s, many of the Turks who arrived during the late 1960s and early 1970s with low or no skills and engaged into the industrial sector became unemployed. Nevertheless, some of them later successfully started their own business in Germany (Martin 1991: 80–81, 83–84).

When the oil prices quadrupled at the beginning of the 1970s, the German federal government imposed a moratorium on recruiting foreign workers from non-European Community member states, such as Turkey. A remarkable drop in the proportion of workforce was immediately witnessed, with a parallel decrease in the Turkish population in Germany. However, from the mid-1970s onwards, despite the introduction of a return programme with financial incentives, many of migrant workers did not return to their home country when the contract was ended due to the economic outlook and political unrest in their homeland and out of for fear of being denied re-entry. They began to bring their families to join them, which ultimately led to an upsurge in family union. Among the migrant workers who chose to stay, Turks were the largest group. The family reunification had enlarged the needs of the immigrants and business activities began to expand. While Turkish guest workers became entitled as foreign residents, official policy – on the Federal as well as on the Länder level – refrained from any attempt to foster integration.[10] Following the 1980 military coup in Turkey, which enforced many Turkish migrants to reconsider their return plans, and the arrival of new Turkish asylum-seekers, the Federal Parliament passed the "Act on Promoting the Return of Foreign Nationals", which came into force on 1 December 1983 and provided many financial advantages for returning foreign nationals. However, the law had a lesser quantitative impact than originally assumed and was discontinued (Weinar and Schneider 2015).

The 1980 stabilization and structural adjustment programme brought radical changes to Turkey's economic structure and the Western-oriented business community, which already had begun voicing the full membership application to the EU. It also encouraged the Turkish immigrants in Germany to invest their savings back in Turkey. This gave rise to an increase in trade activities and circulation of products between the two countries. Moreover, while unemployment problems had already pushed many German Turks into independent business, acquiring German citizenship[11] enabled an easier access to self-employment (Şen and Goldberg 1996).

By the end of the eighties, several tendencies appeared which constitute the crucial features of the German–Turkish economy. The target market, size and duration of the enterprise and educational and professional skills of the second generation entrepreneurs were distinct from the first generation. According to Pécoud (2002) these can be illustrated under five categories: heterogeneity, hybridity, professionalism, internationalization, and state interest. The first characteristic of the new trend was "*heterogeneity*", reflecting the growing economic differentiation between enterprises in terms of scale and purpose. While in the previous decade, as the first generation entrepreneurs targeted members of the Turkish community, serving products of ethnic nature was concentrated in mainly in three sectors, namely, retail; restaurant/ takeaways; and the service sector, the second generation entrepreneurs with better educational qualifications became active in various fields, having clients of all origins. By the beginning of the 1990s, diversification into other areas with greater control over value-added parts of the commodity chain, such as retail, tourism, textile, catering, telecommunication, internet and computer industry became imminent. Despite these new developments, trade and gastronomy still remained the main sectors for Turkish entrepreneurs to do business in (Şen *et al.* 2007).

Another source of heterogeneity has been the "gender" issue, signifying the increasing number of immigrant women entrepreneurs. Compared to men, they try to avoid running a "Turkish" shop in a "Turkish" neighbourhood and mostly speak German to avoid giving the impression of a "typically Turkish" shop and to make non-Turkish customers feel comfortable. The second characteristic is *"hybridity"*. While in the early stages of their existence, German–Turkish entrepreneurs were relying on the "protected market" constituted by Turkish migrants' special needs, they now have more and more contacts with the mainstream economy. Turkish entrepreneurs have thus gone "from the niche to the market" (Duymaz 1989). The protected market was losing its importance because German–Turkish customers and shops have mutually adapted their supplies and demands to one another. Thus the generally limited size of the ethnic market and the evolution of the business had made them realize the need to break out of the niche to the bigger market (see Waldinger *et al.* 1990; Borjas 1992; Barrett, Jones and McEvoy 1996).

The establishment of associations representing the interests of the migrant entrepreneurs distinguish another characteristic of the new era, named *"professionalism"*. This tendency towards professionalism manifests itself in the emergence of business elite mostly in charge of these associations. An early example is the "Türkische–Deutsche Unternehmervereinigung Berlin-Brandenburg/Turkey–German Entrepreneurs' Association Berlin-Brandenburg". The main goal was to contribute to German Turks' integration in Germany by facilitating their business activities. Similar associations were established in most big German cities.

The other attribute is *"internationalization"*. In fact, businessmen of Turkish origin have always carried trade activities and circulated products between Turkey and Germany, but in time other countries also became target markets of these activities. However, apart from the sizeable growth of the SMEs, only a minority of German–Turkish entrepreneurs have undergone significant transformation and developed multiple economic linkages with different countries and set up transnational firms across the globe (Şen and Goldberg 1996). Finally, the *"state interest"* for Turkish entrepreneurship has been part of a more general recognition of the German Turks' position in the German society.

Germany-wide statistical information on the self-employment of Turkish immigrants is mostly based on publications of the *Zentrum für Türkeistudien*. According to the numbers from this centre in 1975 only 100 Turks were entrepreneur. This number saw a steep rise to 22,000 in 1985, and the rising trend has continued ever since, albeit more moderately. By the year 2000, 60,000 Turks were entrepreneur, in 2010 about 80,000 employing about 400,000 people. In 2010, all the Turkish entrepreneurs in Germany together had a turnover of about €36 billion, up from €25.4 billion in 1997 (Die Welt 2012). According to the same source 9.6 per cent of the foreigners in Germany are entrepreneurs, 10.2 per cent of the Turkish origin are self-employed, compared to only 9.4 per cent of Germans (Weinar and Schneider 2015). Citing from the data of the Chamber of Commerce and Industry, with Berlin Turks comprising one in every five migrants in Berlin, 28 per cent of enterprises established by people of foreign origin are from Turkey (Die Welt 2012).

Push and pull factors in self-employment

German–Turkish businessmen are now present in almost all sectors of the German economy, including competitive sectors like software and new technologies, but the number of successful migrant entrepreneurs in the main economy is not big. According to Abadan-Unat (1997), assessing ethnic business solely as a healthy sign of successful integration in the host society is a serious mistake. In fact, the decision to become self-employed has been significantly influenced by the push factor "unemployment", as the higher the unemployment rate, the higher the rate of self-employment (see Bögenhold and Staber 1990; Waldinger *et al.* 1990; Portes 1995; Rath 2000). Turkish workers have generally been addressed in the official German discourse as *gastarbeiter* (guest-worker), *ausländer* (foreigner) or *mitbürger* (co-citizen) – terms that underline their "otherness" and displacement (Kaya 2001). Thus being discriminated against in work life has been decisive for many Turks to establish their own business. Turks of lower social status were also the first ones to be affected by deindustrialization, a situation which was problematic even more by the arrival of new immigrants after the early 1990s. Hence many researchers point to the fact that there have been structural reasons for self-employment (see Miles 1982; Jones *et al.* 1992; Waldinger *et al.* 1990: 13–16; Rath 2011; Jones and Ram 2013). Studying the individual self-employment decision, Öztürk (2001) concludes that not only existing unemployment but even the threat of job loss increases the chances to choose self-employment. At the same time the niche market is assumed to have facilitated migrants' start-ups (Waldinger *et al.* 1990) and has functioned as a pull factor. The migrant population have different consumption preferences and thus created a specific demand which is provided by the people who have the cultural competency to fill the resulting niche market (Goldberg *et al.* 1999). Although the second and the third generation of Turks in Germany are better educated than the first generation of immigrants, they are still mostly positioned in sectors and branches that are badly paid and not very prestigious (Fassman and Içduygu 2013).

Restrictive approach to entrepreneurship

Due to its highly restrictive approach to entrepreneurship, Germany has been known for its low rate of self-employment of natives and migrants (Constant *et al.* 2003: 6). The share of first-generation immigrants in self-employment is lower compared to countries such as United Kingdom, France, Belgium, Denmark, Sweden, Norway, and the United States (Rath 2011). There is no doubt that the difficult economic situation starting in the beginning of the 1990s which affected migrants strongly fostered the path into self-employment. Beside this, the free movement introduced through the EU's enlargement in May 2004 has led to a general increase of migration and in self-employment of persons from East European countries, especially the Polish. At the same time, policy makers and stakeholders have been praising migrant entrepreneurs for their contribution to the national economy (El-Cherkeh and Tolciu 2009).

Entry barriers on the labour market are multifaceted and empirical evidence about these barriers including market entry and re-entry for ethnic minorities is provided by Seifert (2001), Goldberg *et al.* (1995) and Bruder and Frosch (2006). The first generation of entrepreneurs faced a lot of difficulties stemming both from themselves and from the German community (see Waldinger *et al.* 1990; Portes 1995; Rath 2000). They faced problems due to legal conditions set by immigration law, as well as other legal requirements and funding problems related to the lack of familiarity with the local market, and owing to lack of German-language skills. For the second and the third generation of entrepreneurs especially the latter two are still considered a problem. These problems are comparable to the challenges faced by migrant entrepreneurs in other OECD countries (Desiderio 2014).

Although there were no formal restrictions set by immigration laws for Turks in Germany, the legally embodied norms limited the freedom of action and the prohibition of self-employment without a German passport. Hence the first pioneer entrepreneurs had to establish their businesses with German partners (Bruder and Räthke-Döppner 2008). The second legal restriction was the regulation of various career fields, as most jobs required workers who had followed a specific professional training (*Ausbildung*) and the formal education and qualifications in Turkey were generally not approved (Bender *et al.* 2000: 81; Kogan 2003: 20). Thus with respect to human capital, the first generation did not have enough expertise and education to be successful. At the end of the 1980s, the legal situation had improved with the amendment of the crafts code, as the title of master craftsman became no longer a precondition for setting up a business in a range of crafts. Another law in 1991 granting foreigners with a right to residence also the right to earn an independent living, opened up business opportunities for ethnic minorities, including Turks (Bruder and Räthke-Döppner 2008).

Funding availabilities has always been an important barrier. A survey conducted in 2006 among 3,000 native and migrant entrepreneurs in Germany showed that entrepreneurs with a migration background are more likely to be denied credit or to obtain smaller loan amounts than requested (58% versus 39%) and less likely to finance their start up by bank loans (26% versus 45%) in comparison to native entrepreneurs (Bruder and Räthke-Döppner 2008). Thus they finance their start-ups more often with own capital and loans from their family and friends. Credit access is also hampered by the fact that foreign assets are not accepted as collateral. These financial constraints in combination with constraints in human capital have restricted access of migrants to capital-intensive industries, and have pushed them into industries with low entry barriers (Lofstrom and Wang 2006).

Migrant entrepreneurs and social networks

Ethnic groups tend to cluster in large cities as a result of network externalities (Carrington *et al.* 1996). The social networks are based on cultural, occupational or familial ties and shape entrepreneurial decisions and create opportunities for ethnic business (Portes 1995: 8). Portes defines the capacity of individuals to gain access to scarce resources by virtue of their membership of social networks or broader social structures. Examples for such scarce resources are information about business opportunities and business premises or loans from family members. The ability of the individual to mobilize these resources on demand is one of the crucial aspects of the social capital concept. Thus social relations and networks become "capital" assets that can be employed for income generation. Putnam (1993: 67) gives a wider definition of social capital as "features of social organization such as networks, norms and social trust that facilitate coordination and cooperation for mutual benefit". Networks utilized by skilled migrants often tend to be of a different nature, and may have different migratory outcomes, than those characterizing low or unskilled migrants. They enhance the flow of tacit knowledge and support the creation of new ideas and knowledge (Meyer 2007: 6).

According to Abadan-Unat (1997), German Turks' business activities are not so much a socio-economic but rather a cultural and political matter. Thus, the setting up of collective organizations and eventually "cultural" associations pursue home-oriented goals, rather than job creation. She relates the close links that exist between Islamic leaders in Turkey and Turkish firms in Germany and concludes that "the growth of political Islam is substantially influenced by the economic infrastructure built up by ethnic businesses". However, according to Pécoud (2000), Turkishness plays a role in the shaping of German–Turkish businessmen's identities, but should not be overestimated as their identities are not only determined by their ethnicity but also by the nature of their job and the complexity and heterogeneity of the contexts they are confronted with. Richter (2008: 173–174) found that Turkish transnational entrepreneurs have weak connections with Turkey or ethnic organizations in Germany, and had a minimal reliance on ethnic networks or resources in operating their companies. Thus, compared to other transnational entrepreneurs, Turkish transnational entrepreneurs are more able to be embedded in a broad social network of social relations between market actors in numerous countries and manage to create transnational enterprises that compete effectively with other corporations.

One of the most important social networks of migrant entrepreneurs in Germany are the associations.[12] According to Pries (2013), citing 2001 data, out of the roughly 16,000 associations of foreigners, approximately 11,000 can be regarded as associations dominated by people of Turkish origin. Many of these Turkish organizations keep up strong ties with Turkey and deal with its domestic and foreign policy agenda, maintain contacts to political representatives in both Germany and Turkey, but due to serious ideological divisions among themselves, they cannot come up to collective action (Amelina and Faist 2008; Weinar and

Schneider 2015). There are more than 20 umbrella organizations alone, most of which focus on fostering integration, although not exclusively (Weinar and Schneider 2015).

To almost all of these associations, the term "integration" has a dual meaning, one is the integration of immigrants of Turkish origin in Germany, and the second is the accession of Turkey in the EU. Beside this they attribute their activities to differing aspects of the *needs* of migrants. In a study made by Weinar and Schneider (2015) of 27 Turkish migrant associations the main activity areas were political participation, education, language support and labour market integration. Many of them, such as TGD (Türkische Gemeinde in Deutschland–Turkish Community in Germany), founded in 1992 and represents medium- and large-sized Turkish-origin enterprises, define themselves as "an advocate of Turkish entrepreneurship in Europe". These associations are crucial for the migrants to acquire necessary economic knowledge and expertise in order to be included in the main economy, and also essential for the adjustment of the economy at large for this new category of entrepreneurs.

Turkish migrant associational activity in Germany began in the 1960s and reflected the increasing numbers and the increasing diversity of the immigrants in the 1970s and 1980s. While these associations were initially established as student associations and trade unions, gradually, religious organizations became prominent.[13] The early associations were founded by professional translators and were limited to service provision, which focused mainly on translation and consultation on working and housing conditions. In the early 1970s, the first umbrella organization was established as the federation of students' associations, ATOF (Almanya Türk Öğrenci Dernekleri Federasyonu – Federation of Turkish Students' Association in Germany), which addressed mainly the problems of the student population. As a consequence of the 12 March 1971 military intervention in Turkey, when many Turks from all ends of the political spectrum fled to Germany, Turkish migrant associations started to be politically fragmented.[14] This trend was repeated after the military coup in Turkey on 12 September 1980, when another wave of political refugees and asylum seekers fled to Germany. This new wave of migrants easily became part of the already existing associations, due to the fact that the agendas of these organizations were already dominated by Turkish politics. But as the associations became politicized and distanced themselves from service provision, they lost their substance by the late 1980s.

The German reunification in 1990 and the emergence of anti-immigrant violence in Rostock, Mölln and Solingen in the early 1990s affected the ways in which immigrant populations operated and led to changes in the strategies of both the German government and the immigrant associations. The German government during the Kohl coalition aimed to limit immigration and asylum, by instigating policies intended to reduce social welfare benefits. The unemployment rate increased for the whole population, and even more so for the immigrant population. Excluding non-European immigrants, especially Turks, led to a turn toward more homeland-based and religious associations among the immigrant youth (Dörr and Faist 2003).

Concerning the role of the business associations run by German Turks in innovation networks and knowledge transfer, so far there has been little study. Nonetheless, within the TGIN project, already a few cases exist in considering patent data, which indicate the rich possibilities for the development of Turkey–German innovation networks. However, the questionnaire directed to almost forty business associations run by German Turks received limited number of replies, and did not allow finding out their role in promoting innovation networks. It only showed that they promote entrepreneurial activities of their members, support activities between Turkish businesses and German economic and political institutions, promote vocational training programmes and training/apprenticeship for young Turkish migrants, working closely with the Federal Ministry of Economy, Technology and Research. They also have contacts and communication channels with bureaucracy, private sector, and political sphere in Turkey. The associations also offer their members a discussion forum through workshops and business seminars. They support innovative ideas and MUSIAD-Berlin's "Hello Partner" is a well-known example. As the integration of Turkish-origin enterprises in Germany is seen as a vital contribution to Turkey's accession to the EU, these associations representing mainly SMEs identify themselves as a bridge between Turkey and Germany, and the EU. The most cited enterprises carrying out social network function for the entrepreneurs included the following:

- ATIAD (Verband türkischer Unternehmer und Industrieller in Europa e.V /Avrupa Türk İş Adamları ve Sanayicileri Derneği/ ATIAD);[15]
- MÜSIAD-Berlin e.V (Independent Industrialist and Businessmen's Association/ Müstakil Sanayici ve İşadamları Derneği);[16]
- TUMSİAD (All Industrialists and Businessmen's Association/ Tüm Sanayici ve İşadamları Derneği);
- TDU-Berlin (Türkisch-Deutsche Unternehmervereinigung Berlin-Brandenburg/Türk-Alman Girişimciler Derneği/ TDU);[17] and
- TD-IHK (Türkisch-Deutsche Industrie- und Handelskammer/Türk-Alman Ticaret ve Sanayi Odası).

Conclusion

In Germany, with a population of about 80 million people, about 20 per cent of the population has a migration background. Of these nationalities with a migration background with close to 4 million, Turks comprise the biggest group. Fronting a high rate of unemployment and being pushed towards entrepreneurship, they have been facing many difficulties stemming both from themselves and from the host community. Over time, they organized themselves in business organizations, but these have not become an important leverage for successful economic and political integration yet. Many studies show that immigrants have the potential to provide different types of knowledge other than the provided knowledge by the native population and hence are likely to contribute to innovation through their economic engagement in both the country of origin and the host country. Although the historical long-term Turkey–German relationships bear a large potential for knowledge and innovation driven dynamics, the identification of the role of German–Turkish entrepreneurs in innovation networks, connecting core European country Germany with Turkey, is in its infancy and needs further study.

Notes

1   For detailed analyses see Granovetter (1985), Waldinger (1986) and Portes and Sensenbrenner (1993).
2   See Archer (2003) on the general sense of agency/structure.
3   See detailed studies in Waldinger *et al.* (1990), Borjas (1992) and Barrett, Jones and McEvoy (1996).
4   According to Choenni (2000), "ethnic" has the popular meaning of non-western and does not refer to a single ethnicity but, on the contrary, to the combination of various cultural groups.
5   The definition of SMEs in the EU: the companies employing less than 250 people, with a turnover of maximum of €50 million or a balanced sheet total of maximum €43 million (European Commission 2003).
6   According to the EU, a micro-business is an enterprise with fewer than 10 employees, and a turnover of below €2 million or a balance sheet total of below €2 million (European Commission 2003).
7   Denmark, Ireland and the United Kingdom did not participate in the adoption of the Directive 2009/50/EC and are not bound by it or subject to its application (European Union 2009).
8   For the period 2014–2020, €2.3 billion was awarded to COSME, the EU programme for the Competitiveness of Enterprises and SMEs. With the single portal on Access to Finance, the COSME programme explicitly supports SMEs in facilitating access to finance, in different phases of their lifecycle. COSME supports internationalization and access to markets, funds web tools specifically designed for enterprises development and provides entrepreneurs with information and interactive services that help them expand their business in another member state and foreign markets (European Commission 2013b).
9   The HORIZON 2020 project stimulates SME participation with a particular focus on close-to-market support. With a budget of close to 3 billion EUR over the period 2014–2020 a SME-exclusive instrument targets highly innovative SMEs that cannot find financing on the market because of their high-risk character, but which are showing a strong ambition to develop, grow and internationalize, regardless of whether they are high-tech and research-driven or non-research conducting, social or service. Beside this direct support to SMEs, the Horizon 2020 specific objective Innovation in SMEs boosts the innovation capacity of SMEs, including through the Eurostars Joint Programme which will continue to promote transnational collaboration of R&D performing SMEs. About one third of the Access to Risk Finance budget under Horizon 2020 was awarded to SMEs and small midcaps (European Commission 2013d).
10 Instead, integration took place at the local level and at the workplace; through political groups, the trade unions, and associations. However since 2004 specific measures to promote integration have been enshrined in federal legislation, one of which are

integration courses in which all Turkish-originated migrant workers, self-employed persons and family members have a legal claim to participate (Weinar and Schneider 2015).

11 Many Turkish origin migrants benefited from more liberal German citizenship acquisition rules during the government of the Social Democrat/Green coalition from 1998 to 2005. In the year 2000 alone 100,000 Turkish origin migrants acquired German citizenship (Weinar and Schneider 2015).

12 For a detailed description of the role of different migrant associations and their evolution see Özcan (1992).

13 In the 1970s, the number of religious organizations increased and the IKZs (Islamischer Kultur Zentrum – Islamic Cultural Centers) were established. Observing the emergence of extremist Islamic organizations in Europe, the Turkish state intervened through the Turkish Piety Foundation, an organization for regulating religion under the control of the Turkish state, and established the DTB (Türkische–Islamische Union der Anstalt fur Religion e.V. – Piety Foundation Turkish–Islamic Union).

14 Such as TDF (Föderation Demokratischer Vereine der Arbeiter aus der Türkei in Europa – European Federation of Turkish Democratic Workers' Associations), the ATDF (Europäische Föderation Türkischer Sozialisten – The European Federation of Turkish Socialists).

15 See www.atiad.org.

16 See www.muesiad-berlin.de.

17 See www.tdu-berlin.de.

References

Abadan-Unat, N. (1997) Ethnic business, ethnic communities and ethno-politics among Turks in Europe. In E. Uçarer, and D. J. Puchala (eds), *Immigration into Western Societies: Problems and Policies*, 229–251. London: Bloomsbury.

Aldrich, H., Cater, J., Jones, T., *et al.* (1981) Business development and self-segregation: Asian enterprise in three British cities. In C. Robinson, V. Smith and S. Peach (eds), *Ethnic Segregation in Cities*, 170–190. London: Croom Helm.

Amelina, A. and Faist, T. (2008) Turkish migrant associations in Germany: between integration pressure and transnational linkages. *Revue européenne des migrations internationals* 24: 91–120.

Archer, M. (2003) *Structure, Agency and the Internal Conversation*. Cambridge: Cambridge University Press.

Barrett, G., Jones, T. and McEvoy, D. (1996) Ethnic minority business: theoretical discourse in Britain and North America. *Urban Studies* 33(4–5): 783–809.

Baycan-Levent, T. and Nijkamp, P. (2009) Characteristics of migrant entrepreneurship in Europe. *Entrepreneurship and Regional Development* 21(4): 375–397.

Bender, S. and Seifert, W. (1998) Migrants in the German labour market: nationality and gender specific labor market opportunities. In H. Kurthen, J. Fijalkowski and G. Wagner (eds), *Immigration, Citizenship and the Welfare State in Germany and the United States*, 95–117. Greenwich, CT: JAI Press.

Bender, S., Haas, A. and Klose, C. (2000) The IAB employment subsample 1975–1995: opportunities for analysis provided by the anonymised subsample. *Journal of Applied Social Science Studies* 120: 649–662.

Bögenhold, D. and Staber, U. (1990) Selbständigkeit als ein Reflex auf Arbeitslosigkeit? *Kölner Zeitschrift für Soziologie und Sozialpsychologie* 42: 265–279.

Bonacich, E. (1973) A theory of middleman minorities. *American Sociological Review* 38(5): 583–594.

Borjas, G. (1992) Ethnic capital and intergenerational mobility. *Quarterly Journal of Economics* 107(1): 123–150.

Boschma, R. and Martin, R. (2010) *The Handbook of Evolutionary Economic Geography*. Cheltenham: Edward Elgar.

Boubakri, H. (1999) Les entrepreneurs migrants d'Europe: dispositifs communautaires et économie ethnique. *Cultures and Conflicts* 33–34: 69–88.

Bruder, J. and Frosch, K. (2006) *Foreign Nationality and Age: A Double Drawback for Reemployment in Germany?* Thünen series of applied economic theory no. 63. Rostock: University of Rostock, Institute of Economics.

Bruder, J. and Räthke-Döppner, S. (2008) *Ethnic Minority Self-Employment in Germany: Geographical Distribution and Determinants of Regional Variation*. Thünen series of applied economic theory no. 100. Rostock: University of Rostock, Institute of Economics.

Buchmann, T. and Pyka, A. (2011) Innovation networks. In M. Dietrich and J. Krafft (eds), *Handbook on the Economics and Theory of the Firm*, 466–482. Cheltenham: Edward Elgar.

Carrington, W. J., Detragiache, E. and Vishwanath, T. (1996) Migration with Endogenous Moving Costs, *American Economic Review* 86(4): 909–931.

Choenni, C. E. S. (2000) *Ontwikkeling voor het rijksoverheidbeleid voor etnische minderheden 1975–2000*. The Hague: Werkverband periodieke bevolkingsvraagstukken.

CLIP (2011) CLIP – Ethnic entrepreneurship. Available at www.eurofound.europa.eu/clip-ethnic-entrepreneurship (accessed 1 November 2015).

Constant, A., Shachmurove, Y. and Zimmerman, K. (2003) *What Makes an Entrepreneur and Does it Pay? Native Men, Turks and Other Migrants in Germany*. Berlin: German Institute for Economic Research.

Dana, L. P., Welpe, I. M., Han, M. and Ratten, V. (2008) *Handbook of Research on European Business and Entrepreneurship: Towards a Theory of Internationalization*. Cheltenham: Edward Elgar.

Desiderio, M. V. (2014) *Policies to Support Immigrant Entrepreneurship*. Washington, DC: Migration Policy Institute.

Die Welt (2012) Zuwanderer zeigen großen Ehrgeiz als Unternehmer. Available at www.welt.de/politik/deutschland/article107259023/Zuwanderer-zeigen-grossen-Ehrgeiz-als-Unternehmer.html (accessed 15 July 2015).

Dinan, D. (2004) *Europe Recast: A History of European Union*. Basingstoke: Palgrave Macmillan.

Dörr, S. and Faist, T. (2003) Institutional conditions for the integration of immigrants in welfare states: a comparison of the literature on Germany, France, Great Britain and the Netherlands. *European Journal of Political Research* 31(4): 410, 414.

Duymaz, I. (1989) *Türkische Unternehmensgründungen: Von der Nische zum Markt?* Opladen: Leske+Budrich.

EESC (2012) Opinion of the European Economic and Social Committee on "The contribution of migrant entrepreneurs to the EU economy". 2012/C 351/04. *Official Journal of the European Union*.

El-Cherkeh, T. and Tolciu, A. (2009) *Migrant Entrepreneurs in Germany: Which Role Do They Play?* HWI policy paper 3–8. Hamburg: Hamburg Institute of International Economics.

Engelen, E. (2001) 'Breaking in' and 'breaking out': a Weberian approach to entrepreneurial opportunities. *Journal of Ethnic and Migration Studies* 3: 203–223.

European Commission (2003) Commission recommendation of 6 May 2003 concerning the definition of micro, small and medium-sized enterprises. Available at http://eur-lex.europa.eu/legal-content/EN/TXT/PDF/?uri=CELEX:32003H0361&from=EN (accessed 1 November 2015).

European Commission (2011) Communication from the Commission to the European Parliament, the Council, the European Economic and Social Economic Committee and the Committee of the Regions: European agenda for the integration of third-country nationals. Brussels.

European Commission (2012) Flash Eurobarometer 354: entrepreneurship in the EU and beyond. Brussels.

European Commission (2013a) Communication from the Commission to the European Parliament, the Council, the European Economic and Social Committee and the Committee of the Regions, Entrepreneurship 2020 action plan: reigniting the entrepreneurial spirit in Europe. Brussels.

European Commission (2013b), COSME: Europe's programme for SME's leaflet. Brussels.

European Commission (2013c), Multiannual financial framework 2014–2020 and EU budget 2014: the figures. Luxemburg.

European Commission (2013d), HORIZON 2020: SMEs. Available at http://ec.europa.eu/programmes/horizon2020/en/area/smes (accessed 1 November 2015).

European Commission (2015a) migrant integration: the mandate to promote integration. Available at https://ec.europa.eu/migrantintegration/index.cfm?action=furl.go&go=/the-eu-and-integration/the-mandate-to-promote-integration (accessed 30 October 2015).

European Commission (2015b) Entrepreneurship and Small and medium-sized enterprises (SMEs). Available at http://ec.europa.eu/growth/smes (accessed 3 November 2015).

European Commission (2015c) European Website on integration: integration in different policy areas. Available at https://ec.europa.eu/migrant-integration/the-eu-and-integration/integration-in-other-policy-areas (accessed 30 October 2015).

European Commission (2015d) Migrant entrepreneurs. Available at on http://ec.europa.eu/growth/smes/promoting-entrepreneurship/we-work-for/migrants/index_en.htm (accessed 3 November 2015).

European Union (2009) Council directive 2009/50/EC of 25 May 2009 on the conditions of entry and residence of third-country nationals for the purposes of highly qualified employment. *Official Journal of the European Union.* Available at http://eur-lex.europa.eu/legal-content/EN/TXT/PDF/?uri=CELEX:32009L0050&from=EN (accessed 25 October 2015).

European Union (2015) Erasmus for young entrepreneurs. Available at www.erasmus-entrepreneurs.eu/index.php?lan=en (accessed 1 November 2015).

Fassman, H. and Içduygu, A. (2013) Turks in Europe: migration flows, migration stocks and demographic structure. *European Review* 21(3): 349–361 (doi:10.1017/S1062798713000318).

Feldman, M. P. and Audretsch, D. B. (1999) Innovation in cities: science-based diversity, specialization and localized competition. *European Economic Review* 43(2): 409–429.

Gilbert, N., Pyka, A. and Ahrweiler, P. (2001) Innovation networks: a simulation approach. *Journal of Artificial Societies and Social Simulation* 4(3). Available at http://jasss.soc.surrey.ac.uk/4/3/8.html.

Goldberg, A., Mourinho, D. and Kulke, U. (1995) *Labour Market Discrimination against Foreign Workers in Germany*. International Migration Papers 7. Geneva: International Labour Organization.

Granovetter, M. S. (1985) Economic action and social structure: the problem of embeddedness. *American Journal of Sociology* 91(3): 481–510.

Hay, C. and Rosamond, B. (2002) Globalisation, European integration and the discursive construction of economic imperatives. *Journal of European Public Policy* 9(2). Available at http://users.ox.ac.uk/~ssfc0041/globalisation.pdf.

IMES Triodos (2008) *Examination and Evaluation of Good Practices in the Promotion of Ethnic Minority Entrepreneurs, European Commission Entrepreneurial Diversity in a Unified Europe: Ethnic Minority/Migrant Entrepreneurship*. Final report, Brussels, 5 March. Amsterdam: Institute for Migration and Ethnic Studies (IMES), University of Amsterdam and Triodos Facet.

Jones, T. and Ram, M. (2013) *Entrepreneurship as Ethnic Minority Liberation*. Research paper no. 11. London: Enterprise Research Centre.

Jones, T., McEvoy, D. and Barrett, G. (1992) *Small Business Initiative: Ethnic Minority Component*. Swindon: Economic and Social Research Council.

Kaya, A. (2001) *Sicher in Kreuzberg, Constructing Diasporas: Turkish Hip Hop Youth in Berlin*. Bielefeld: Transcript Verlag.

Kesler, C. (2006) Social policy and immigrant joblessness in Britain, Germany and Sweden. *Social Forces* 85(2): 743–770.

Kloosterman, R. (2000) Immigrant entrepreneurship and the institutional context: a theoretical explanation. In J. Rath (ed.), *Immigrant Businesses: The Economic, Political and Social Environment*, 90–106. Basingstoke: Macmillan/St Martin's Press.

Kloosterman, R. (2010) Matching opportunities with resources: a framework for analyzing (migrant) entrepreneurship from a mixed embeddedness perspective. *Entrepreneurship and Regional Development* 22(1): 25–45.

Kloosterman, R. and Rath, J. (2003) Introduction. In R. Kloosterman and J. Rath (eds), *Immigrant Entrepreneurs: Venturing Abroad in the Age of Globalization*, 1–16. Oxford: Berg.

Kloosterman, R., Van der Leun, J. and Rath, J. (1999) Mixed embeddedness: immigrant entrepreneurship and informal economic activities. *International Journal of Urban and Regional Research* 23: 253–267.

Kogan, I. (2003) *A Study of Employment Careers of Immigrants in Germany*. Working paper no. 66. Mannheim: Mannheimer Zentrum für Europäische Sozialforschung, Universität Mannheim.

Light, I. (1972) *Ethnic Enterprise in America*. Berkeley CA: University of California Press.

Lofstrom, M. and Wang, C. (2006) *Hispanic Self-Employment: A Dynamic Analysis of Business Ownership*. IZA discussion paper no. 2101. Bonn: Institute for the Study of Labor

Malmstrom, C. (2014) *EU Migration Policy: New Realities, New Opportunities*. Brussels: European Policy Centre.

Man Yip, C. (2011) Transnationalism in Germany: the case of Turkish transnational entrepreneurs. Dissertation, Humboldt University, Berlin.

Marchand, K. and Siegel, M. (2014) *Migrants and Cities: New Partnerships to Manage Mobility*. World Migration Report 2015. Geneva: International Organization for Migration.

Martin, P. L. (1991) *The Unfinished Story: Turkish Labour Migration to Western Europe, with Special Reference to the Federal Republic of Germany*. Geneva: International Labour Organization.

Masurel, E. Nijkamp, P. and Vindigni, G. (2004) Breeding places for ethnic entrepreneurs: a comparative marketing approach. *Entrepreneurship and Regional Development* 16: 77–86.

Meyer, J.-B. (2007) *Building Sustainability: The New Frontier of Diaspora Knowledge Networks.* Working paper no. 35. Bielefeld: COMCAD Arbeitspapiere.

Miles, R. (1982) *Racism and Migrant Labour.* London: Routledge and Kegan Paul.

Mitchell, K. (2006) Neoliberal governmentality in the European Union: education, training and technologies of citizenship. *Environment and Planning D Society and Space* 24: 389–407.

Niebuhr, A. (2010) Migration and innovation: does cultural diversity matter for regional R&D activity? *Papers in Regional Science* 89(3): 563–585.

OECD (2010) Main findings of the conference on entrepreneurship and employment creation of immigrants in OECD countries, 9–10 June 2010, Paris. In OECD (ed.), *Open for Business: Migrant Entrepreneurship in OECD Countries,* 13–19. Paris: OECD Publishing.

Özcan, E. (1992) *Türkische Immigrantenorganisationen in der Bundesrepublik Deutschland.* Berlin: Hitit-Verlag.

Özcan, V. and Seifert, W. (2000) Self-employment of immigrants in Germany: exclusion or path to integration? *Soziale Welt* 51(3): 289–302.

Özgen, C., Nijkamp, P. and Poot, J. (2011) *Immigration and Innovation in European Regions.* Migration discussion paper No. 2011-8. The Hague: NORFACE.

Öztürk, Y. N. (2001) *400 Fragen zum Islam – 400 Antworten: Ein Handbuch.* Düsseldorf: Grupello Verlag.

Pécoud, A. (2000) *Cosmopolitism and Business: Entrepreneurship and Identity among German–Turks in Berlin.* WPTC-2K-05. Oxford: Oxford University.

Pécoud, A. (2002) Weltoffenheit schafft jobs: Turkish entrepreneurship and multi-culturalism in Berlin. *International Journal of Urban and Regional Research* 26: 494–507.

Portes, A. (ed.) (1995) *The Economic Sociology of Immigration: Essays on Networks, Ethnicity, and Entrepreneurship.* New York: Russell Sage Foundation.

Portes, A. and Sensenbrenner, J. (1993) Embeddedness and immigration: notes on the social determinants of economic action. *American Journal of Sociology* 98: 1320–1350.

Pries, L. (2013) *Shifting Boundaries of Belonging and New Migration Dynamics in Europe and China.* New York: Palgrave Macmillan.

Putnam, R. D. (1993) *Making Democracy Work: Civic Traditions in Modern Italy.* Princeton, NJ: Princeton University Press.

Rath, J. (2000) Introduction: immigrant businesses and their economic, politico-institutional and social environment. In J. Rath (ed.), *Immigrant Businesses: The Economic, Political and Social Environment,* 1–19. Basingstoke: Macmillan/St Martin's Press.

Rath, J. (2011) *Promoting Ethnic Entrepreneurship in European Cities.* Luxemburg: Publications Office of the European Union.

Richter, R. (2008) On the social structure of markets: a review and assessment in the perspective of the new institutional economics. In A. Ebner and N. Beck (eds), *The Institutions of the Market: Organisations, Social Systems, and Governance,* 157–179. New York: Oxford University Press.

Rudolph, H. (1994) Dynamics of immigration in a non-immigrant country: Germany. In H. Fassman and R. Münz (eds), *European Migration in the Late Twentieth Century,* 113–126. Cheltenham: Edward Elgar.

Rudolph, H. and Hillmann, F. (1997) Döner contra Boulette: Berliner türkischer Herkunft als Arbeitskräfte und Unternehmer im Nahrungsgütersektor, Zuwanderung und Stadtentwicklung. *Sonderheft Leviathan* 17: 85–105.

Sasse, G. and Thielemann, E. (2005) A research agenda for the studies of migrants and minorities in Europe. *Journal of Common Market Studies* 43(4): 655–671.

Saxenian, A. L. (2006) *The New Argonauts: Regional Advantages in a Global Economy.* Cambridge, MA: Harvard University Press.

Seifert, W. (2001) *Berufliche Integration von Zuwanderen in Deutschland: Expertise for the Federal Commission on Migration to Germany.* Berlin: Federal Ministry of the Interior.

Şen, F. and Goldberg, A. (eds) (1996) *Türken als Unternehmer, eine Gesamtdarstellung und Ergebnisse neuerer Untersuchungen.* Berlin: Springer.

Şen, F., Ulusoy, Y. and Şentürk, C. (2007) *Avrupa Birliği ve Almanya'da Türk Girişimcilerin Ekonomik Gücü.* Duisburg: Stiftung Zentrum für Türkeistudien, Institut an der Universität Duisburg-Essen.

Sirkeci, I., Cohen, J. H. and Yazgan, P. (2012) The Turkish culture of migration: flows between Turkey and Germany, socio-economic development and conflict. *Migration Letters* 9(1): 33–46.

Vasilescu, L. (2014) Accessing finance for innovative EU SMEs: key drivers and challenges. *Journal of Economics and Business* XII(2): 35–47.

Waldinger, R. (1986) *Through the Eye of the Needle: Immigrants and Enterprise in New York's Garment Trades.* New York: New York University Press.

Waldinger, R., Aldrich, H. and Ward, R. (eds) (1990) *Ethnic Entrepreneurs: Immigrant Business in Industrial Societies.* London: Sage.

Ward, R. and Jenkins, R. (1984) *Ethnic Communities in Business: Strategies for Economic Survival.* Cambridge: Cambridge University Press.

Weinar, A. and Schneider, J. (2015) *Corridor Report Germany.* INTERACT RR 2015/02. San Domenico di Fiesole: Robert Schuman Centre for Advanced Studies, European University Institute.

9 Antecedents of transnational entrepreneurial behaviour

Evidence from Turkish–German firms

Gönenç Dalgıç, Andreas Kuckertz and Çağrı Bulut

Introduction

Numerous technological and societal developments of the early twenty-first century (i.e. changes in production, information, communication, international logistics and transportation facilities, which lead to reduction of transaction costs) make it possible even for small enterprises with limited resources to enter the international arena among multinational competitors (Knight and Cavusgil 2004). The root of this perspective in the business arena is embedded in the dispersion of globalization since it penetrates into the world economy and thus, a growing number of firms engages in international activities regardless of the firm size. In addition to these developments, international entrepreneurship has been increasingly drawing attention of scholars over the past two to three decades (Zahra and George 2002). We recognize the remarkable studies of McDougall and Oviatt, who define international entrepreneurship as "a combination of innovative, proactive, and risk-seeking behavior that crosses national borders and is intended to create value in organizations" (McDougall and Oviatt 2000: 903) and describe the concept as "the intersection of international business and entrepreneurship" (ibid.: 902). Conceptually similar to international entrepreneurship, transnational (or cross border) entrepreneurship which can be described as "entrepreneurial activity across international borders, which typically involves some form of cooperation or partnership" (Smallbone and Welter 2012: 95), has been increasingly discussed in academic debates from the 1990s to date.

Thus, transnational entrepreneurial activities are performed by actors who are at least embedded in two different social and economic domains (Drori, Honig and Wright 2009: 1001). Therefore, the critical difference between international entrepreneurship and transnational entrepreneurship lies at the core of the context that transnational entrepreneurship has a culturally oriented aspect which is related with the strong ties or dual affiliation among the entrepreneurs, ethnicity, or entrepreneurial relationships among a particular community (Sequeira, Carr and Rasheed 2009). In addition, the term transnational entrepreneur is generally used to describe individuals who have a migrant background and initiate entrepreneurial activities and business related linkages with their country of origin in the host country that they migrate to (Drori, Honig and Wright 2009: 1001).

Germany is a good place to study transnational entrepreneurship, since it has a strong immigration tradition (Constant, Shachmurove and Zimmerman 2005). The population in Germany, based on the 2013 Microcensus, comprises 16.5 million people with a migrant background. Country of origin of the migrant background population is sequenced as Turkey (12.8%), Poland (11.4%) and the Russian Federation (9.0%), Italy (4.0%), Greece (2.1%).

As the statistical data points to, immigrants with Turkish origin in Germany present a large number considered in comparative relation to the whole. The influx of immigrants from Turkey to Germany started following the signing of bilateral labour recruitment agreement between German and Turkish authorities in 1961 (İçduygu 2012). Guest workers (in German: *Gastarbeiter*) who left their home country to work in Germany constitute the first wave of immigration (Mueller 2014) and from the early 1960s to date, the population has grown substantially. This development not only led to a great number of academic studies from several scholarly fields, but also coined a specific term to identify this population: "Almancı". According to Pusch and Splitt (2013), Almancı is a popular term and "is composed by the noun Alman (German) and the denominal suffix -cı, which is used to form agent nouns having a certain occupation or a habit". We support the idea to use a specific term to describe immigrants with Turkish background, but we conceive that the term has expanded its own linguistic meaning and its scope has broadened from Germany towards Europe as well – including, for example, Belgium, Netherlands, and Switzerland. Therefore, we employed the term "Germaner", as a new English version of Almancı. Accordingly, Germaner comprises two main aspects simultaneously. First, the term describes a person who was born in Turkey and then migrated from Turkey to a European country (first generation) or who was born in a European country and whose parents have a Turkish background (second and following generations). Second, the term, at firm level, refers to Turkish–German firms that have been founded by entrepreneurs with a Turkish background in Germany. Consequently, Germaner can be used both at the individual level and also for Turkish–German firms of our study at firm-level.

When the entrepreneurial spirit of Germaners in Germany is analysed, more than one-fifth of all entrepreneurial initiatives (21%) from 2008 to 2013 are carried out by entrepreneurs having a migrant background (KfW 2014). Among those, entrepreneurs having Turkish origin represent the largest group (21%) on average during 2008 to 2013. Other migrant business founders from Russia (10%), Poland (7%) and Italy (5%) have a relatively lower share compared with Turkish–German entrepreneurs. In the present chapter, we focus on the most dominant and hence the most important group of entrepreneurs in Germany with a migrant background (i.e. Turkish–German entrepreneurs; (Constant, Shachmurove and Zimmerman 2005).

Turkish–German entrepreneurs, who constitute a huge population in Germany, take our interest with their inherently transnational features deriving from entrepreneurs' origins, networks, past experiences or business efforts. Moreover, the case of Turkish entrepreneurs in Europe has been subject to many research questions from different academic disciplines including management, economics, and sociology. In terms of business studies and particularly of entrepreneurship (Kuckertz 2013), the term immigrant entrepreneurship (e.g. Fertala 2006; Mueller 2014) is used to a large extend to describe the entrepreneurial activities of Germaners. In addition, limitedly, ethnic entrepreneurship is also used to address the same concept (e.g. Kostos 2003). In the light of previous descriptions and definitions, we recognize Turkish–German entrepreneurs as entrepreneurs with Turkish origin and living in Germany who start, build, conduct and manage their own businesses in Germany, where they have migrated for a life time residence (Pınar 2013). In addition, they are both a significant part of the German economy (Baycan-Levent and Kundak 2009) and also drivers of transnational practices (Morawska 2004), helping to establish and maintain the notable Turkish–German nexus that has developed starting in the 1960s when the first Turkish foreign workers migrated to Germany. Interestingly, Germaners are accepted with their remarkable entrepreneurial spirit (Constant, Shachmurove and Zimmerman 2005).

Previous literature provides many studies designed to identify economic, social or psychological motives of entrepreneurs of Turkish origin, or perform- ance (e.g. survival or success) conditions of Turkish-owned enterprises in Germany (Baycan-Levent and Kundak 2009). However, it is also assumed that Turkish–German entrepreneurs are not sufficiently studied in literature (Constant, Shachmurove and Zimmerman 2005). Moreover, as Yip (2013) suggests, Turkish entrepreneurs comprise an interesting population as some of their entrepreneurial activities have been transforming recently into building transnational firms through various connections in various countries. Under these circumstances, in order to contribute to the literature, we concentrate on the internationalization practices of Turkish entrepreneurs in Germany.

In this framework, the empirical study by Wang and Lui (2015) is remarkable as its results are convenient with our initial estimation that we start on our present chapter regarding transnational aspects of Turkish–German entrepreneurs. The researchers indicate that immigrants (or immigrant-owned firms) are more likely to internationalize their businesses and involve in transnational economic pra- ctices than non-immigrants (or non-immigrant-owned firms) in the US. Moreover, Yip (2013) states that entrepreneurs of Turkish background are more diverse and global rather than entrepreneurs in the US of different country of origin regarding transnational activities. Thus, moving one step further from this significant outcome, we recognize that Turkish–German entrepreneurs[1] have a natural propensity to internationalize as they are able to rely on their Turkish connections, social networks or social capital. We question whether strong ties regarding social capital, that Turkish–German entrepreneurs have, might facilitate getting information on international business and market opportunities, and utilize knowledge on critical competitive resources (e.g. innovation propensity). Given these discussions, we investigate the concepts associated with internationalization of Turkish entrepreneurs in Germany.

Therefore, the present chapter seeks to build a model on the determinants of internationalization among Turkish–German entrepreneurs through describing the causal chains on international entrepreneurial efforts. With this aim, it is arranged in the following sequence. The next section provides a brief presentation of the theoretical concepts of internationalization, innovation propensity, knowledge, opportunity recognition, and social capital and their respective theoretical relations. The methodology used in this research and the results are discussed, and the general drivers of Turkish–German entrepreneurs' transnational behaviours are highlighted. Finally, the conclusion and recommendations are presented.

Theoretical background

From innovation propensity to internationalization

Generally speaking, questions of internationalization are one of the most significant issues in current business research (Yu and Si 2012). Internationalization can be defined as the expansion of firms' involvement in international markets (Welch and Luostarinen 1988). The internationalization literature consists of a broad spectrum of different perspectives including the Uppsala model (Johanson and Vahlne 1977), resource based approaches (Peng 2001), innovation related models (Rogers 1962), and network approaches (Johanson and Mattsson 1986; Sharma and Blomstermo 2003) regarding multinational enterprises, new ventures, and small and medium-sized enterprises (SMEs) as well.

Since the 1990s, internationalization has been increasingly drawing attention of scholars from entrepreneurship research (McDougall and Oviatt 1996; Zahra and George 2002). The emerging field of international entrepreneurship can be understood as the intersection of international business and entrepreneurship and defined as "a combination of innovative, proactive, and risk-seeking behavior that crosses national borders" (McDougall and Oviatt 2000: 903). Gregorio, Musteen and Thomas (2008) view international entrepreneurship as a linkage of cross border individuals and opportunities. They argue that opportunities involve both resource combinations (i.e. association of skilled individuals and innovative capabilities, knowledge and / or networks) and market combinations (i.e. entrance to one or more cross-border market with a particular product or service). Dimitratos and Plakoyiannaki (2003: 193) expand the argument by introducing six dimensions of an international entrepreneurial culture in a particular firm namely "international market orientation", "international learning orientation", "international innovation propensity", "international risk attitude", "international networking dimension" and "international motivation".

The literature on international entrepreneurship leads us to recognize the significance of innovation and internationalization processes both of which aim to create value for enterprises. Yu and Si (2012: 526) define innovation as "the creation of better or more effective products, processes, services, technologies, or ideas that are accepted by markets, governments, and society". It has been identified as one of the major dimensions of entrepreneurial orientation that leads the development of new ideas, novelty and creative outputs (Lumpkin and Dess

1996). The current study relies on that innovation is viewed among intangible resources that a firm possesses (Hall 1993) and has great importance as it relates to the valuable, rare, non-substitutable and inimitable resources (Barney 1991) that are required for survival, success, and growth of enterprises. Moreover, innovation presents a multidimensional characteristic (Damanpour 1987; Manual 2005) that comprises product innovation, process innovation, technology innovation, administrative innovation, and market innovation all of which have respective influences in the internationalization process.

A broad range of empirical studies analysing the relationship between innovation and internationalization indicate that internationalization processes of a firm are positively affected by the innovation propensity of a given firm in different ways. First; two main challenges, namely the liabilities of newness and foreignness (Zahra 2005) while entering into international markets, can be overcome via applying innovative solutions (Evers and O'Gorman 2011). Second, product and process innovation lead to productivity gains which facilitate foreign market penetration and strengthen competitiveness not only in domestic markets but also in global markets (Becker and Egger 2013). Finally, innovative firms are more eager to discover new investment opportunities not only in domestic but also in foreign markets (Filippetti, Frenz and Letto-Gillies 2011). Hence:

H1   The higher the level of innovation propensity in a Turkish–German firm, the higher the level of internationalization in that firm.

From knowledge to innovation propensity

Since innovation is recognized as the successful implementation of creative ideas in an organization (Amabile *et al.* 1996), several researchers have discussed the antecedents of innovativeness in the organizations. This stream of literature highlights several concepts including absorptive capacity (Cohen and Levinthal 1990), learning orientation (Calantone, Cavusgil and Zhao 2002), learning capacity (Hernández-Espallardo, Sánchez-Pérez and Segovia-López 2011), organizational learning (Jiménez-Jiménez and Sanz-Valle 2011), and knowledge spillovers (Hashi and Stojcic 2013). Apart from pointing to the differences between these conceptually similar views which would be beyond the scope of the present chapter, we focus on the phenomenon of knowledge as the focal point with which above stated concepts are incorporated at least to some degree.

Whereby resource-based theory of the firm is developed and expanded (Barney 1991; Penrose 1959; Wernerfelt 1984), knowledge is accepted as a significant and competitive resource of a firm (von Krogh 1998). According to the knowledge-based perspective, knowledge assets can facilitate sustainable competitive advantage in a long period. Knowledge can be identified as an outcome or case of knowing, gathered through learning, experiencing or practicing (Alavi and Leidner 2001). Accordingly, what an organization needs is to empower and courage its employees to enhance their individual learning and personal knowledge and apply that knowledge consistent with the organizational aims and requirements (von Krogh 1998).

Knowledge can be both individual and shared (Zander and Kogut 1995). Grant (1996b: 109) conceptualizes a firm as "an institution for integrating knowledge". In addition, the knowledge, which is categorized as explicit (objective or codified) and tacit (experiential or implicit) knowledge (Polanyi 1967), is created and utilized in a firm through various ways (i.e. organizational culture, organizational processes, operating procedures and routines, and employees; Grant 1996a, 1996b; Spender 1996a, 1996b). For the effective implementation of the individual knowledge to organizational needs and the transformation of individual knowledge into shared knowledge, Zack (1999) suggests recognizing knowledge "both as object and process". According to Huber (1991), the knowledge process consists of four aspects: The first is the knowledge acquisition which refers to obtaining new information and knowledge in the firm. The second is knowledge distribution by which employees share information within the firm. The third is knowledge interpretation by which individuals give meaning to the information and transform it into new common knowledge. Finally, organizational memory expresses the tool of knowledge storage for further use.

Since the innovation process is accepted as the result from the combination of knowledge and other novel resources that a firm possesses (Cohen and Levinthal 1990; Kogut and Zander 1992), many studies have added knowledge as one of the antecedents of innovation (Calantone, Cavusgil and Zhao 2002; Carneiro 2000). Similarly, Baker and Sinkula (2002) state that knowledge increases innovativeness. Knowledge is related with both product and service innovation, and the development of overall innovation processes (Hernández-Espallardo, Sánchez-Pérez and Segovia-López 2011; Slavkovic and Babic 2013).

Meanwhile, sources of knowledge and their role take scholarly attention as well. Knowledge-based research states that sources of knowledge can be either internal or external (Fletcher and Harris 2012: 634). According to their classification, internal sources comprise direct experiences and internal information whereas external sources include indirect experiences such as indirect learning and grafting, and external search of information. However, the role of internal and external sources of knowledge on innovation is still under debate. For example, many scholars discuss the influence of external knowledge on innovation (e.g. Cohen and Levinthal 1990; Kang and Kang 2009). Whereas Cohen and Levinthal (1990) state that external knowledge is associated with the development of the innovative capability of a firm, Damanpour (1991) indicates that both professional knowledge of organizational members, which requires education and experience, and technical knowledge which is achieved by the organization's technical resources and technical potential have positive relationship with innovation.

In addition, Garriga, von Krogh and Spaeth (2013) highlight that firms apply to internal or external sources of knowledge in order to scan the environment and knowledge-rich environment improves the firm's ability to innovate. Thus, the innovativeness of a firm is influenced by the ability in the acquisition, distribution and interpretation of knowledge it possesses. Furthermore, Larrañeta, Zahra and

González (2012) point to the possible incompatibility of knowledge acquired from various sources, although it is mostly believed that there is a likelihood of developing and supporting new products, services and processes when an organization has access to varied knowledge sources. Therefore, the scholars recommend reconciliation and examination of information in the organization, utilization of the particular knowledge at hand, combining the different types of knowledge, and exploration of the best way to use knowledge to innovate.

Drawing from the previous literature, we assume that innovation propensity requires acquisition, distribution, and interpretation of knowledge effectively. Thus, our concern is the support of knowledge in innovation processes. Hence:

H2   The higher the level of knowledge in a Turkish–German firm, the higher the level of innovation propensity in that firm.

From knowledge to opportunity recognition, from opportunity recognition to innovation propensity

The entrepreneurship literature recognizes the concept of entrepreneurial opportunity as a scholarly study field (Park 2005). Entrepreneurial opportunities can be defined as "situations in which new goods, services, raw materials, markets and organizing methods can be introduced through the formation of new means, ends, or means-ends relationships" (Eckhardt and Shane 2003: 336).

Ardichvili, Cardozo and Ray (2003: 109–110) identify opportunity recognition as a process comprising three sub-processes of "perception, discovery, and creation". Accordingly, the term refers to "(1) sensing or perceiving market needs and/or underemployed resources, (2) recognizing or discovering a fit between particular market needs and specified resources, and (3) creating a new fit between heretofore separate needs and resources in the form of a business concept". Therefore, opportunity recognition requires not only the individual perception and capability regarding the presence of an entrepreneurial opportunity but also information about political, economic, commercial, regulatory, technological changes or developments in the business environment regarding underutilized resources or unfulfilled demands and/or needs (Shane and Venkataraman 2000).

Although many scholars claim that the opportunity recognition process is "still largely undeveloped" (Park 2005), to date, various views are discussed regarding the drivers of opportunity recognition (Kohlbacher, Herstatt and Levsen 2014) including prior knowledge (Shane 2000), cognitive processes (Sigrist 1999), and social networks (Hills, Lumpkin and Singh 1997). Obviously, each of these views focuses on one particular aspect of opportunity recognition rather than the complete phenomenon. Our theoretical model in the current study is built on understanding the nexus of knowledge with opportunity recognition.

The concept of knowledge has been associated with opportunity recognition including prior, existing and new knowledge, respectively. In addition to Shane (2000), Ucbasaran, Westhead and Wright (2009) concentrate on prior knowledge and experience that the entrepreneur has. The results of their study indicate that entrepreneurs are more likely to recognize more opportunities if they have previous knowledge and experience. Accordingly, they can exploit more innovative opportunities. Moreover, Haynie, Shepherd and McMullen (2009) argue that opportunity recognition can be pursued by the existing knowledge resources and individual knowledge acquisition skills that the entrepreneur has. Thus, the researchers state that "judgments as to the attractiveness of an opportunity will likely be influenced by the extent to which the entrepreneur has existing, related knowledge complementary to the opportunity" (ibid.: 341). In addition, Eckhardt and Shane (2003) suggest that opportunities emerge as a result of new information as well. In return, new knowledge leads to entrepreneurial opportunity creation in terms of providing new products and introducing new developments or techniques of sourcing, production or marketing.

Contrarily to the research on the relationship between knowledge and opportunity recognition, the literature is scarce in terms of studies conducted on the relationship of opportunity recognition and innovativeness. However, the question whether innovativeness is impacted by opportunity recognition process has not yet been fully answered. However, as every entrepreneurial opportunity goes along with an element of innovation (Kuckertz, Kohtamäki and Droege gen. Körber 2010), how small it may be, its relationship is at least from the theoretical point of view evident.

Therefore, we examine whether opportunity recognition can be viewed as a bridge connecting knowledge to innovativeness. We focus on the relationship between not only knowledge and opportunity recognition, but also the relationship between opportunity recognition and innovativeness as well. Hence:

H3   The higher the level of knowledge in a Turkish–German firm, the higher the level of opportunity recognition in that firm.

H4   The higher the level of opportunity recognition in a Turkish–German firm, the higher the level of innovation propensity in that firm.

From social capital to knowledge

Given the important influence of knowledge on several topics relevant to entrepreneurship, another research field shedding light on the antecedents of knowledge has increasingly taken attention. One of them is social capital, which Nahapiet and Ghoshal (1998: 243) define as "the sum of the actual and potential resources embedded within, available through and derived from the networks of relationships possessed by an individual or social unit". The researchers state that creation and maintenance of social ties in the network facilitate the combination and the exchange of resources and knowledge. Social capital is generally incorporated with strong social ties between partners and there is a link between strong ties and the usefulness of both tacit and explicit knowledge exchange (Levin and Cross 2004).

It is widely accepted that there is a positive relationship between social capital and knowledge. For example, Kogut and Zander (1992: 389) view knowledge acquisition as a predominantly social process and refer to social capital and links between multiple groups via promoting the term "common stock of knowledge". In the same vein, Swan and colleagues (1999) argue that networking as a social communication process, encourages the sharing of knowledge among communities. Researchers point to that knowledge which is required for innovativeness of a firm can be distributed either within (i.e. organizational units) or across (i.e. suppliers, consultants) the organizations and challenges faced in this process can be overcome by communication of knowledge through networks. Furthermore, the results of the studies by Yli-Renko, Autio and Sapienza (2001) and Yli-Renko, Autio and Tontti (2002) indicate that the social interaction and network ties dimensions of social capital are positively associated with knowledge acquisition and knowledge-based competitive advantage.

Subramaniam and Youndt (2005) state that social capital in a firm improves the quality of group work and the richness of information exchange among team members via facilitating interactions and exchange of ideas. Thus, social capital enables members of a firm either strengthen or transform the existing knowledge and therefore it supports the knowledge process. Furthermore, innovativeness of a firm is also positively affected by this process. This view is supported by the research of Pérez-Luño and colleagues (2011) as well. This study indicates that knowledge influences radical innovation and the impact of tacit knowledge seems only in combination with social capital.

We question whether social capital in Turkish–German firms positively associates with the knowledge. Drawing on the recent literature on the social capital theory, knowledge-based view of the firm and networking perspectives in innovation process, we hypothesize:

H5   The higher the level of social capital in a Turkish–German firm, the higher the level of knowledge in that firm.

Methods and results

Data and analytical approach

The sample for this study was constructed with the help of two different online database (i.e. the membership directories of the Association of Turkish–European Entrepreneurs, and the Turkish–German Chamber of Industry and Commerce). For the purposes of the study, we constructed our sample of Turkish–German entrepreneurs in three stages. At the first stage we excluded organizations which had no for profit business activities (i.e. sourcing, manufacturing, marketing, or sales in manufacturing or service sector and directed their operations into social, public or political issues – e.g. political parties, consulates, non-profit organizations). In the second stage, we drew a systematic sample from the comprehensive online database of stated organizations via their membership directories that contained all Turkish–German entrepreneurs involved in business activities in various industries. Finally, we verified the contact information by phone regarding the owner of the organization. At this stage firms which were not accessible or were shut down lately and owners who refused to share their contact information, had no e-mail accounts, or were not eligible for participation were naturally excluded from the sample. Subsequently, 279 Turkish–German business people each of whom represents one firm that he/she has founded or taken over from previous generation of family members were invited to participate in a personalized online survey. During the data collection process, two reminders were sent every two weeks following the initial contact. We received 86 usable responses corresponding to a satisfying response rate of 30.82 per cent.

As some indicators had some missing parts in some cases, the quality of the data needed to be assessed. For this purpose, we utilized missing value analysis (Little and Rubin 2002). Literature of statistics provides various alternatives rather than only one ideal approach to treat missing values. Little and Rubin (ibid.) suggest a statistical test, namely the MCAR-test which returned insignificant results in our study suggesting that the values were missing completely at random (MCAR). Therefore, the expectation maximization (EM) algorithm was facilitated in order to estimate the missing values and not to omit valuable information as, for instance, when only analysing complete cases.

We tested the research model using a nonparametric approach to structural equation modelling, known as the partial-least squares (PLS) approach (Chin 1998) via the software package SmartPLS 2.0 (Ringle, Wende and Will 2005). The main motive to apply PLS derives from the reason that the technique is well suited and works in a reliable way in particular with small samples to estimate causal models containing multiple independent and dependent constructs and examine all paths between them simultaneously.

Measures

Measures of social capital, knowledge, opportunity recognition, innovation propensity, and internationalization were employed in the present study. Key study variables (i.e. social capital, knowledge, opportunity recognition, innovation propensity) were measured on five-point Likert scales (1 = totally disagree, 5 = totally agree) that were adopted from prior studies. Social capital measurement scale was taken from Subramaniam and Youndt (2005).

To measure opportunity recognition, we utilized items originally developed by Kuckertz *et al.* (2013). Knowledge and innovation propensity were treated as multi-dimensional constructs based on Jiménez-Jiménez and Sanz-Valle (2011). Therefore, knowledge contained three dimensions as knowledge acquisition, knowledge distribution and knowledge interpretation. Innovation propensity comprised process innovation and administrative innovation. The dependent variable (i.e. internationalization) was measured with a multi-itemed formative scale including items indicating the owner's past experiences abroad and ongoing cross border business activities of the firm. Therefore, unlike the independent variables, items used to measure dependent variable were based on objective facts rather than subjective perceptions of the respondents.

We ran reliability analysis and computed alpha scores of the reflective constructs presented in Table 9.1. Measures are considered reliable as the scores exceed the recommended thresholds of 0.7 recognized by previous research (Nunnally and Bernstein 1994).

Table 9.1 Construct reliability measures.

Construct	Composite reliability	Cronbach's α
Social capital	0.9531	0.9384
Knowledge	0.9028	0.8648
Opportunity recognition	0.9350	0.9132
Innovation propensity	0.8815	0.8320

In addition to alpha statistics, discriminant validity and construct validity were also inspected. Prior studies recommend that each indicator at item cross loadings should exceed the acceptable limit of 0.7 (Chin 1998) and present the highest value on its core construct (Hulland 1999). Accordingly, three items measuring knowledge acquisition, one item measuring knowledge distribution, and one item measuring product innovation were dropped from the reflective constructs of this study. In order to ensure sufficient reliability of constructs, the average variance extracted (AVE) was examined as well. Previous studies indicated the acceptable limit of 0.5 for AVE (Bagozzi and Yi 1988; Chin 1998) that was exceeded in the present study. Table 9.2 presents AVE scores of the variables as italic diagonal elements. Moreover, off-diagonal elements indicate the squared latent variable correlations. The comparison of diagonal and off-diagonal elements reveals that discriminant validity is present in our study since AVE values indicate higher scores than squared latent variable correlations. Therefore, discriminant validity is stated both at the item level and construct level.

Table 9.2 Construct discriminant validity: squared latent variable correlations (off-diagonal elements) versus AVE (italic diagonal elements).

	Innovation propensity	Knowledge	Opportunity recognition	Social capital
Innovation propensity	0.5985			
Knowledge	0.3505	0.6506		
Opportunity recognition	0.3974	0.3547	0.7422	
Social capital	0.2827	0.6502	0.2852	0.8027

Results

The hypotheses of the present research are tested by employing a standard PLS algorithm and bootstrapping procedure with 500 resamples and consisting of the same number of cases as in the original sample ($n = 86$). Results obtained are presented in Figure 9.1.

Statistical calculations provide strong support for the hypothesized research model. The variables examined in our research have strong relationships presenting satisfactory path coefficients ranging from 0.3358 to 0.8047. R^2 values suggest a medium to large degree of explained variance since they are ranging from 0.2060 to 0.6476 (Cohen 1988). The model's goodness of fit (GoF) is 0.4961 which exceeds the threshold value of 0.36 for GoF$_{large}$ (Tenenhaus *et al.* 2005). Cohen's f^2 (Cohen 1988) calculations for effect size result in moderate to high degrees (Chin 1998). Therefore, all dependent variables are considered as presenting significant and meaningful effects on their associated dependent variables. Knowledge is highly affected by social capital (0.8047; $p \leq 0.001$; $f^2 =$ 1.8376) that a firm possesses. The effect of knowledge on innovation propensity (0.3358; $p \leq 0.001$; f^2 0.1407) is relatively lower than its effect on opportunity recognition (0.5956; $p \leq 0.001$; $f^2 = 0.5499$). Innovation propensity of a firm is affected moderately by the entrepreneurs' degree of opportunity recognition (0.4304; $p \leq 0.001$; $f^2 = 0.2300$). Finally, the results indicate that internationalization of business activities of Turkish–German entrepreneurs is significantly affected by innovation propensity (0.4539; $p \leq 0.05$; $f^2 = 0.2594$).

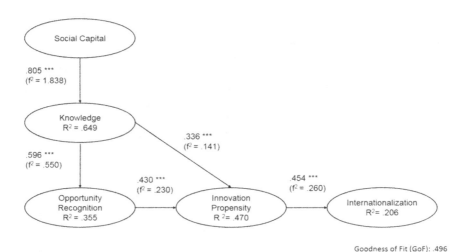

Goodness of Fit (GoF): .496

Figure 9.1 Results of the PLS analysis – path coefficients, significance and effect sizes (in parentheses).

Notes: •*$p \leq 0.001$; •$p \leq 0.01$; *$p \leq 0.05$ (one-sided test).

Conclusion and discussion

The aim of the present chapter was to highlight the drivers of Turkish–German entrepreneurs' internationalization. Against the background of international entrepreneurship and the Turkish–German nexus, the results obtained from the research imply an interesting causal chain through which internationalization activities are associated with social capital, knowledge, opportunity recognition and innovation propensity. Our findings reveal that internationalization of a Turkish–German firm is supported by the innovation propensity that the firm possesses. Innovation propensity is derived by process innovation and administrative innovation. Applying innovativeness to organizational processes and stages supports international activities and operations. Therefore, the study has been able to confirm the positive association between innovation propensity and internationalization.

Additionally, in the context of our study, due to the internationalization sequence of Turkish–German firms, the link from social capital to innovation propensity is critical for internationalization. In general, the results of the study suggest that social capital has positive effects on knowledge, and knowledge positively affects both opportunity recognition and innovation propensity. Furthermore, opportunity recognition has a significant role on innovation propensity as well. The integral model found by this study contributes also to the entrepreneurship literature.

Moreover, findings of our research have numerous implications for practitioners (i.e. entrepreneurs and managers) in terms of managing the roles of social capital, knowledge, innovation propensity, and opportunity recognition for internationalization. It is found that there is a sequence among the factors employed in this study. Social capital has significant effects on the distribution and interpretation of the existing knowledge. Moreover, the rise of innovation propensity is strongly associated with the degree of how members of the organization distribute and interpret the existing knowledge when social capital is an antecedent. On the other hand, the links between knowledge and opportunity recognition within Turkish–German firms have positive joint effects on their innovation propensity. Finally, innovation propensity was found to be an important factor as it stimulates the internationalization of Turkish–German firms as depicted in Figure 9.1. Therefore, practitioners' perceptions and abilities to discover entrepreneurial opportunities influence innovation propensity which has a positive impact on internationalization.

This research has focused on Turkish–German firms and has employed the term "Germaner", adapted from common usage, as a contribution to the entrepreneurship literature. It has been translated from the Turkish word called "Almancı" with the meaning of Germaner. The term has been commonly used within the Turkish culture for those who have immigrated to any European country either for working or entrepreneurship, or even for studying. So, a Germaner, as stated in the previous part, is a person who was born in Turkey and then migrated from Turkey to a European country (first generation) or who was born in a European country and whose parents have a Turkish background (second and following generations). Since all Germaners, including those living in France, Belgium, Netherlands, Switzerland, etc., have kept and preserved most of their cultural stereotypes and traditions from the early-comers to those countries, their culture differs dramatically from fast-developing Turkey. Consequently, findings of this study can also shed light upon Germaners' entrepreneurial behaviour.

We suggest several interesting avenues for future research. First, if social capital and knowledge arise from Turkey, then Turkish–German firms will have a higher tendency to recognize the investment and business opportunities in Turkey than in Germany. Because prior knowledge and recognized opportunities jointly motivate the internationalization process of Turkish–German firms, this time back to Turkey. This process can be viewed as a new research direction in future as "reverse international entrepreneurship of Turkish–German firms". Therefore, we suggest "reverse international immigrant entrepreneurship of Germaners" as an interesting field of study for future research regarding its antecedents, practices, impacts and outcomes. Second, derived from the findings of the current study, Germaners' entrepreneurial behaviour in other country contexts should be examined. Therefore, we suggest that the findings of our research which has been conducted in Germany can be controlled in other European countries. In doing so, similarities and differences regarding the entrepreneurial behaviour of Germaners living in other European countries can be analysed and compared. Third, entrepreneurial finance flows among Germaners over home and host countries can be a genuine field of study for the future as well. There is still a gap in the literature on the characteristics of entrepreneurial finance in terms of immigrant entrepreneurship and reverse international entrepreneurship. Fourth, studies can be conducted to indicate primary commercial and international trade fields among Germaners in order to make recommendations to international (entrepreneurial) trade policy makers. Therefore, international entrepreneurial opportunity maps towards commercial and economic potentials for Germaners could be developed for the future. Finally, we suggest questioning the business ethics of Germaners regarding the cultural differences between developing and developed countries taking into account host and home country cultures.

Note

1 Turkish–German entrepreneurs in this study comprise entrepreneurs who were born in Turkey, came to Germany in the 1960s or later and remained there, and entrepreneurs whose parents are Turkish and were either born or reside in Germany.

References

Alavi, M. and Leidner, D. E. (2001) Review: knowledge management and knowledge management systems: conceptual foundations and research issues. *MIS Quarterly* 25(1): 107–136.
Amabile, T. M., Conti, R., Coon, H., Lazenby, J. and Herron, M. (1996) Assessing the work environment for creativity. *Academy of Management Journal* 39(5): 1154–1184.

Ardichvili, A., Cardozo, R. and Ray, S. (2003) A theory of entrepreneurial opportunity identification and development. *Journal of Business Venturing* 18(1): 105–123.

Bagozzi, R. P. and Yi, Y. (1988) On the evaluation of structural equation models. *Journal of the Academy of Marketing Science* 16(1): 74–94.

Baker, W. E. and Sinkula, J. M. (2002) Market orientation, learning orientation and product innovation: delving into the organization's black box. *Journal of Market-focused Management* 5(1): 5–23.

Barney, J. (1991) Firm resources and sustained competitive advantage. *Journal of Management* 17(1): 99–120.

Baycan-Levent, T. and Kundak, S. (2009) Motivation and driving forces of Turkish entrepreneurs in Switzerland. *Innovation: The European Journal of Social Science Research* 22(3): 283–308.

Becker, S. O. and Egger, P. H. (2013) Endogenous product versus process innovation and a firm's propensity to export. *Empirical Economics* 44(1): 329–354.

Calantone, R. J., Cavusgil, S. T. and Zhao, Y. (2002) Learning orientation, firm innovation capability. and firm performance. *Industrial Marketing Management* 31(6): 515–524.

Carneiro, A. (2000) How does knowledge management influence innovation and competitiveness. *Journal of Knowledge Management* 4(2): 87–98.

Chin, W. W. (1998) The partial least squares approach to structural equation modeling. In G. A. Marcoulides (ed.), *Modern Methods for Business Research*, 295–336. Mahwah, NJ: Lawrence Erlbaum.

Cohen, J. (1988) *Statistical Power Analysis for the Behavioral Sciences*. Mahwah, NJ: Lawrence Erlbaum.

Cohen, W. M. and Levinthal, D. A. (1990) Absorptive capacity: a new perspective on learning and innovation. *Administrative Science Quarterly* 35(1): 128–152.

Constant, A., Shachmurove, Y. and Zimmerman, K. F. (2005) *The Role of Turkish Immigrants in Entrepreneurial Activities in Germany*. Working paper 05-029. Philadelphia, PA: PIER.

Damanpour, F. (1987) The adoption of technological, administrative, and ancillary innovations: impact of organizational factors. *Journal of Management* 13(4): 675–688.

Damanpour, F. (1991) Organizational innovation: a meta-analysis of effects of determinants and moderators. *Academy of Management Journal* 34(3): 555–590.

Dimitratos, P. and Plakoyiannaki, E. (2003) Theoretical foundations of an international entrepreneurial culture, *Journal of International Entrepreneurship* 1(2): 187–215.

Drori, I., Honig, B. and Wright, M. (2009) Transnational entrepreneurship: an emergent field of study. *Entrepreneurship Theory and Practice* 33(5): 1001–1022.

Eckhardt, J. T. and Shane, S. A. (2003) Opportunities and entrepreneurship. *Journal of management* 29(3): 333–349.

Evers, N. and O'Gorman, C. (2011) Improvised internationalization in new ventures: the role of prior knowledge and networks. *Entrepreneurship and Regional Development* 23(7–8): 549–574.

Fertala, N. (2006) Determinants of successful immigrant entrepreneurship in the Federal Republic of Germany. Doctoral dissertation, Eberhard-Karls-Universität, Tübingen.

Filippetti, A., Frenz, M. and Letto-Gillies, G. (2011) Are innovation and internationalization related? An analysis of European countries. *Industry and Innovation* 18(5): 437–459.

Fletcher, M. and Harris, S. (2012) Knowledge acquisition for the internationalization of the smaller firm: content and sources. *International Business Review* 21(4): 631–647.

Garriga, H., von Krogh, G. and Spaeth, S. (2013) How constraints and knowledge impact open innovation., *Strategic Management Journal* 34(9): 1134–1144.

Grant, R. M. (1996a) Prospering in dynamically-competitive environments: organizational capability as knowledge integration. *Organization Science* 7(4): July–August, 375–387.

Grant, R. M. (1996b) Toward a knowledge-based theory of the firm. *Strategic Management Journal* 17(S2): 109–122.

Gregorio, D. D., Musteen, M. and Thomas, D. E. (2008) International new ventures: the cross-border nexus of individuals and opportunities. *Journal of World Business* 43(2): 186–196.

Hall, R. (1993). A framework linking intangible resources and capabilities to sustainable competitive advantage. *Strategic Management Journal* 14(8): 607–618.

Hashi, I. and Stojcic, N. (2013) Knowledge spillovers, innovation activities, and competitiveness of industries in EU member and candidate countries. *Economic Annals* 58(198): 7–34.

Haynie, J. M., Shepherd, D. A. and McMullen, J. S. (2009) An opportunity for me? The role of resources in opportunity evaluation decisions. *Journal of Management Studies* 46(3): 337–361.

Hernández-Espallardo, M., Sánchez-Pérez, M. and Segovia-López, C. (2011) Exploitation-and exploration-based innovations: the role of knowledge in inter-firm relationships with distributors. *Technovation* 31(5): 203–215.

Hills, G., Lumpkin, G. T. and Singh, R. P. (1997) Opportunity recognition: perceptions and behaviors of entrepreneurs. *Frontiers of Entrepreneurship Research* 17: 168–182.

Huber, G. P. (1991) Organizational learning: the contributing processes and the literatures. *Organization Science* 2(1): 88–115.

Hulland, J. (1999) Use of partial least squares (PLS) in strategic management research. *Strategic Management Journal* 20: 195–204.

İçduygu, A. (2012) 50 years after the labour recruitment agreement with Germany: the consequences of emigration for Turkey. *Perceptions* 17(2): 11–36.

Jiménez-Jiménez, D. and Sanz-Valle, R. (2011) Innovation, organizational learning, and performance. *Journal of Business Research* 64(4): 408–417.

Johanson, J. and Mattsson, L. G. (1986) International marketing and internationalization processes: a network approach. In P. W. Turnbull and S. J. Paliwada (eds), *Research in International Marketing*, 234–265. London: Croom Helm.

Johanson, J. and Vahlne, J.-E. (1977) The internationalization process of the firm: a model of knowledge development and increasing foreign market commitments. *Journal of International Business Studies* 8(1): 23–32.

Kang, K. H. and Kang, J. (2009) How do firms source external knowledge for innovation? Analysing effects of different knowledge sourcing methods. *International Journal of Innovation Management* 13(1): 1–17.

KfW (2014) Migrants revive start-up activity in Germany. Press release. Available at www.kfw.de/KfW-Group/Newsroom/Aktuelles/Pressemitteilungen/Pressemitteilungen-Details_222784.html (accessed 24 November 2014).

Knight, G. A. and Cavusgil, S. T. (2004) Innovation, organizational capabilities, and the born-global firm. *Journal of International Business Studies* 35(2): 124–141.

Kogut, B. and Zander, U. (1992) Knowledge of the firm, combinative capabilities, and the replication of technology. *Organization Science* 3(3): 383–397.

Kohlbacher, F., Herstatt, C. and Levsen, N. (2014) Golden opportunities for silver innovation: how demographic changes give rise to entrepreneurial opportunities to meet the needs of older people. *Technovation* 39–40 (May–June): 73–82.

Kostos, M. (2003) Self-employment policies and migrants' entrepreneurship in Germany. *Entrepreneurship and Regional Development* 15(2): 119–135.

Kuckertz, A. (2013) Entrepreneurship education – status quo and prospective developments. *Journal of Entrepreneurship Education* 16: 59–71.

Kuckertz, A., Kohtamäki, M. and Droege gen. Körber, C. (2010) The fast eat the slow – The impact of strategy and innovation timing on the success of technology-oriented ventures. *International Journal of Technology Management* 52(1–2): 175–188.

Kuckertz, A., Kollmann, T., Krell, P. and Stöckmann, C. (2013) Opportunity recognition and opportunity exploitation – two validated scales. *Academy of Management Meetings*, Orlando, FL.

Larrañeta, B., Zahra, S. A. and González, J. L. G. (2012) Enriching strategic variety in new ventures through external knowledge. *Journal of Business Venturing* 27(4): 401–413.

Levin, D. Z. and Cross, R. (2004) The strength of weak ties you can trust: the mediating role of trust in effective knowledge transfer. *Management* Science 50(11): 1477–1490.

Little, R. J. and Rubin, D. B. (2002) *Statistical Analysis with Missing Data.* Hoboken, NJ: John Wiley.

Lumpkin, G. T. and Dess, G. G. (1996) Clarifying the entrepreneurial construct and linking it to performance. *Academy of Management Review* 21(1): 135–172.

Manual, O. (2005) *The Measurement of Scientific and Technological Activities: Proposed Guidelines for Collecting and Interpreting Technological Innovation Data.* Brussels: European Commission and Eurostat.

McDougall, P. P. and Oviatt, B. M. (1996) New venture internationalization, strategic change, and performance: a follow-up study. *Journal of Business Venturing* 11(1): 23–40.

McDougall, P. P. and Oviatt, B. M. (2000) International entrepreneurship: the intersection of two research paths. *Academy of Management Journal* 43(5): 902–906.

Morawska, E. (2004) Immigrant transnational entrepreneurs in New York: three varieties and their correlates. *International Journal of Entrepreneurial Behaviour and Research* 10(5): 325–348.

Mueller, E. (2014) Entrepreneurs from low-skilled immigrant groups in knowledge-intensive industries: company characteristics, survival and innovative performance. *Small Business Economics* 42(4): 871–889.

Nahapiet, J. and Ghoshal, S. (1998) Social capital, intellectual capital, and the organizational advantage. *Academy of Management Review* 23(2): 242–266.

Nunnally, J. and Bernstein, I. H. (1994) *Psychometric Theory.* New York: McGraw-Hill.

Park, J. S. (2005) Opportunity recognition and product innovation in entrepreneurial hi-tech start-ups: a new perspective and supporting case study. *Technovation* 25(7): 739–752.

Peng, M. (2001) The resource-based view and international business. *Journal of Management* 6(6): 803–829.

Penrose, E. T (1959) *The Theory of the Growth of the Firm.* New York: Wiley.

Pérez-Luño, A., Cabello Medina, C., Carmona Lavado, A. and Cuevas Rodríguez, G. (2011) How social capital and knowledge affect innovation. *Journal of Business Research* 64(12): 1369–1376.

Pinar, Y. (2013) A literature review on immigrant entrepreneurship. Post-graduate dissertation, Yaşar University, İzmir.

Polanyi, M. (1967) *The Tacit Dimension.* London: Routledge and Kegan Paul.

Pusch, B. and Splitt, J. (2013) Binding the Almancı to the "homeland": Notes from Turkey. *Perceptions* 13(3): 129–166.

Ringle, C., Wende, S. and Will, A. (2005) *Smart-PLS 2.0.* Hamburg: University of Hamburg.

Rogers, E. M. (1962) *Diffusion of Innovations*. New York: The Free Press.

Sequeira, J. M., Carr, J. C. and Rasheed, A. A. (2009) Transnational entrepreneurship: determinants of firm type and owner attributions of success. *Entrepreneurship Theory and Practice* 33(5): 1023–1044.

Shane, S. (2000) Prior knowledge and the discovery of entrepreneurial opportunities. *Organization Science* 11(4): 448–469.

Shane, S. and Venkataraman, S. (2000) The promise of entrepreneurship as a field of research. *Academy of Management Review* 25(1): 217–226.

Sharma, D. D. and Blomstermo, A. (2003) The internationalization process of Born Globals: a network view. *International Business Review* 12(6): 739–753.

Sigrist, B. (1999) Entrepreneurial opportunity recognition. A presentation at the Annual UIC/AMA symposium at Marketing/Entrepreneurship Interface, Sofia-Antipolis, France.

Slavkovic, M. and Babic, V. (2013) Knowledge management, innovativeness, and organizational performance: Evidence from Serbia. *Economic Annals* 58(199): 85–107.

Smallbone, D. and Welter, F. (2012) Cross-border entrepreneurship, entrepreneurship and regional development. *An International Journal* 24(3–4): 95–104.

Spender, J. C. (1996a) Making knowledge the basis of a dynamic theory of the firm. *Strategic Management Journal* 17(S2): 45–62.

Spender, J. C. (1996b) Organizational knowledge, learning, and memory: three concepts in search of a theory. *Journal of Organizational Change Management* 9(1): 63–78.

Subramaniam, M. and Youndt, M. A. (2005) The influence of intellectual capital on the types of innovative capabilities. *Academy of Management Journal* 48(3): 450–463.

Swan, J., Newell, S., Scarbrough, H. and Hislop, D. (1999) Knowledge management and innovation: networks and networking. *Journal of Knowledge management* 3(4): 262–275.

Tenenhaus, M., Vinzi, V. E., Chatelin, Y. and Lauro, C. (2005) PLS path modelling. *Computational Statistics and Data Analysis* 48: 159–205.

Ucbasaran, D., Westhead, P. and Wright, M. (2009) The extent and nature of opportunity identification by experienced entrepreneurs. *Journal of Business Venturing* 24(2): 99–115.

Von Krogh, G. (1998) Care in knowledge creation. *California Management Review* 40(3): 133–153.

Wang, Q. and Lui, C. Y. (2015) Transnational activities of immigrant-owned firms and their performances in the USA. *Small Business Economics* 44(2): 345–359.

Welch, L. S. and Luostarinen, R. (1988) Internationalization: evolution of a concept. *Journal of General Management* 14(2): 34–55.

Wernerfelt, B. (1984) A resource-based view of the firm. *Strategic Management Journal* 5(2): 171–180.

Yip, C. M. (2013) *Transnationalism in Germany: the case of Turkish transnational entrepreneurs*. Doctoral dissertation, Humboldt Universität zu Berlin, Berlin, Germany.

Yli-Renko, H., Autio, E. and Sapienza, H. J. (2001) Social capital, knowledge acquisition, and knowledge exploitation in young technology-based firms. *Strategic Management Journal* 22(6–7): 587–613.

Yli-Renko, H., Autio, E. and Tontti, V. (2002) Social capital, knowledge, and the international growth of technology-based new firms. *International Business Review* 11(3): 279–304.

Yu, X. and Si, S. (2012) Innovation, internationalization and entrepreneurship: A new venture research perspective. *Innovation: Management, Policy and Practice* 14(4): 524–539.

Zack, M. H. (1999) Managing codified knowledge. *Sloan Management Review* 40(4): 45–58.

Zahra, S. A. (2005) A theory of international new ventures: a decade of research. *Journal of International Business Studies* 36(1): 20–28.

Zahra, S. A. and George, G. (2002) International entrepreneurship: the current status of the field and future research agenda. In M. A. Hitt, D. R. Ireland, S. M. Camp and D. L. Sexton (eds), *Strategic Entrepreneurship: Creating a New Mindset*, 255–288. London: Blackwell Publishing.

Zander, U. and Kogut, B. (1995) Knowledge and the speed of the transfer and imitation of organizational capabilities: an empirical test, *Organization Science* 6(1): 76–92.

10 Turkish diaspora networks and innovation

Sylvie van Cour, Alexander Gerybadze and Andreas Pyka

Introduction

As a consequence of the increasing mobility of highly skilled professionals, innovation-promoting, transnational cooperation and communication structures, so-called diaspora networks, emerge. The term diaspora was originally used to describe a group sharing the same language, having the same ethnicity, belonging to the same religion and which builds a strong joint identity and solidarity abroad. Jewish migrants are the classic example of a diaspora in the above mentioned sense (see Cohen 2008). As a result of increasing international mobility, the term diaspora has come to be used and defined in a less narrow sense, and in particular has been used to describe groups of emigrants, which maintain relations with their homeland (ibid.). In this chapter, diaspora networks are understood to be cooperation structures of networking migrants building up communication channels and bridging the source and receiving countries, promoting knowledge transfer across national boundaries and implementing projects in the home country (see Kuznetsov 2006). The participation of strongly intrinsically motivated people can be seen as another characteristic of successful diaspora networks. As highly skilled international mobile people are called "Creators of Knowledge Roads" (Maier, Kurka and Trippl 2007), diaspora networks repeal the geographical limitation of knowledge spillovers and support the generation of innovation. Therefore not only the receiving country can benefit from mobile professionals in the sense of "Brain Drain", but also the receiving country in the sense of "Brain Circulation".

This chapter analyses the diaspora networks of highly skilled Turkish people and identifies special characteristics of Turkish diaspora networks. The categorization of diaspora networks in a general sense will be described in the following section, after which we concentrate on the functionality and impact of diaspora networks and migration on the generation of innovation. Knowledge migration of highly qualified Turkish people and Turkish diaspora networks in Germany are analysed, leading to a discussion of the nation-specific findings. Finally our key findings are summarized.

Categorization of diaspora networks

Kuznetsov (2006) characterized, identified and compared six different types of diaspora networks, depending on the conditions of the sending country on the one hand and the size, the maturity and degree of organization of the diaspora on the other hand (see Table 10.1).

Kuznetsov (2006) shows that even a sophisticated, mature and well-structured diaspora network is only able to influence positively the development of a country if the government simultaneously supporting the diaspora is open to change and establishes favourable structural conditions for the emergence of a knowledge-based economy (see Kuznetsov 2006; OECD 2008). According to this, Kuznetsov regards the diaspora networks as "mirrors of national development", which are

Table 10.1 Level of diaspora engagement based on country conditions and characteristics of the diaspora.

Characteristics of the diaspora	Country conditions		
	Unfavourable	*Moderately favourable*	*Favourable*
(a) Relatively large, mature and well organized (sophisticated) diaspora networks.			
Role of expatriates	Antennae and role models	Launching pad to move to knowledge-intensive value chains	Key resource in transition to knowledge-based economy
Activities	Engage diaspora in dialog about reform and engineer visible demonstration projects	Form brain circulation networks, encourage return migration	Form sophisticated brain circulation networks, encourage return migration
Country examples	Armenia, Bangladesh, Sri Lanka	El Salvador, India, Vietnam	China, Korea, Taiwan
(b) Relatively disengaged (emerging diaspora networks)			
Role of expatriates	Antennae and role models	Gradual engagement	Entry-point to knowledge-intensive growth
Activities	Engage diaspora in dialogue about reform and engineer visible demonstration projects	Create expatriate networks, initiate activities to encourage return of talent	Establish brain circulation networks, encourage return migration
Country examples	Colombia, Comoros, Nigeria, Russian Federation, Ukraine	Brazil, Mexico and other Latin American countries, Pakistan, South Africa, some transition economies	Croatia, Chile, Hungary, Slovenia, smaller Asian tigers (Malaysia, Thailand)

Source: adapted from Kuznetsov (2006: 234).

always influenced by the political and economic environment and therefore are not context-free (see Kuznetsov and Sabel 2006). Kuznetsov (2006) demonstrates the need to support the networks by describing the example of the Armenian Diaspora – a well-organized, mature and a relatively large diaspora network. However, due to enormous resistance of the former political and communistic elite, the diaspora cannot contribute to the economic development of Armenia (see Kuznetsov and Sabel 2006: 6. Former communistic bureaucrats, security officers or managers of state companies regard the diaspora network as rivalry, are afraid of the consequences of changes and refuse to cooperate with returning migrants (ibid.). The government wants to maintain its influence and therefore, programs for the promotion of FDI, that are much more difficult to control than long-term loans and humanitarian aid, are not supported. The example of Armenia thus shows the relevance of a cooperative-friendly infrastructure.

A very successful diaspora network is the Taiwanese diaspora, which is characterized by dynamic communication structures and the return of the highly skilled employees (see Kuznetsov 2006). Many returnees support and give advice to the Taiwanese government based on their accumulated knowledge and experience abroad, whereby measures to promote entrepreneurship and cluster structures have been adopted (see Saxenian 2005). Furthermore, since the 1980s thousands of qualified Taiwanese have returned from America and have transferred both the American model of venture capital funding and the Silicon Valley model (ibid.). The example of Taiwan thus illustrates the positive effects of brain circulation and shows that Taiwan's economic success can be traced back to the cooperation between returnees, government officials and policy advisors with the aim of creating institutions for the promotion of innovation and entrepreneurship.

While Indian and Taiwanese diaspora networks have been analysed in detail, there is less evidence regarding the effectiveness and characteristics of diaspora networks of foreign highly qualified workers in Germany. Nevertheless, Turkish diaspora networks can be characterized as emerging diaspora networks with moderately favourable country conditions.

Migration, diaspora networks and innovation

Theory of migration decisions

In recent decades, in different disciplines theories were developed in order to explain migration. In general, a distinction can be drawn between micro-, macro- and meso-theoretical approaches (see Ette and Sauer 2010). Micro-theoretical approaches define migration as an "individual decision to migrate" and as "a result of an individual search and optimization process" of rationally deciding people (ibid.). Macro-theoretical approaches consider migration as a collective phenomenon that arises as a consequence of regional disparities. People migrate for example due to income disparities, unequal unemployment rates, an exceptionally high population density, but also due to the gravitational force of urban areas and the presence of multinational companies (ibid.).

While meso-theoretical approaches regard migration decisions as influenced by social networks and institutional contexts, macro and micro theoretical approaches represent the classical and neoclassical view. For that reason meso-theoretical approaches can be assigned to more recent migration theories.

Corresponding to classical and neoclassical theories, migration is mainly influenced by economic factors. However, the importance of sociological reasons to explain the mobility of highly skilled employees is increasing strongly. According to Stark (1991), not only the individual actors, but also the networks they are woven in, have to be considered in the analysis of migration decisions. Thus, families are seen as collective actors of migration (see Baringhorst 2010). Furthermore, a new form of migration is becoming increasingly important, which can be described by the term "transnational migration" (see Ayudin 2010). Migration is no longer regarded as a unique and definitive change of location. Instead, migrants often change their place of residence.

Effects of diaspora networks

However, diaspora networks are not only becoming a relevant feature explaining the mobility of highly skilled individuals, but they are also relevant to explain the impact on the generation of innovation. Diaspora networks build social proximity and therefore they promote knowledge transfer even across national borders, especially if mobile highly skilled employees also connect to other new networks whereby they contribute their knowledge (see OECD 2008). This knowledge transfer can enhance further migration of highly skilled professionals from the home country (see Rath 2006). In general, the success of a diaspora and the emergence of knowledge transfer depend on several factors. These include for example the personality of the highly skilled professional, the reasons for migration, the political and economic situation of the sending country, income inequality and institutional structures (see Kapur 2001). However, mainly social ties seem to play an important role in order to enhance knowledge transfer and to support innovation (see Agrawal *et al.* 2006). Due to social networks, transaction costs can be reduced permanently (see Rath 2006). Furthermore, emigrants can use the knowledge of their home market to set up business activities and simultaneously transfer their knowledge of the foreign market. In this context Ghosh observed: "The diaspora can be a bridgehead for the Penetration by home country enterprises of markets of the host country, as exemplified by Korean Americans who helped to open markets in the US for Korean automobiles, electronics and other industries" (Ghosh 2005, cited in Rath 2006).

Relevance of mobile, highly qualified professionals for the emergence of innovations

The increase in productivity, innovation and growth as a result of an increased diversity was examined and confirmed in many different studies. According to

Ozgen, Nijkamp and Poot (2011) there are five mechanisms by which migration flows support the development of innovation (ibid.):

- the population size effect;
- the population density effect;
- the migrant share effect;
- the skill composition effect; and
- the migrant diversity effect.

The first three effects lead to an increased locally aggregated consumer demand – a driver of innovation. One the one hand, the response to such an increase of demand is an increase in export performance but, on the other hand, an increased diversified production of goods (see Mazzolari and Neumark 2009, quoted in Ozgen, Nijkamp and Poot 2011). In turn an expansion of production leads to employment and expansion effects and the emergence of new start-ups, which will stimulate innovation and increase the attractiveness of growing cities as destinations for highly skilled migrants. Such agglomeration effects increase the availability of heterogeneous skills, promote (cultural) diversity and are thus basis for the performance of enterprises, for economic development of regions and the emergence of innovations. However, the Skill Composition Effect and the Migrant Diversity Effect are the most important factors in order to explain an increase of the innovation potential (e.g. measured by patent analyses) caused by mobile highly skilled professionals.

Furthermore, mobile highly skilled employees contribute to the innovation potential both in the home and the host country, if brain circulation occurs. Figure 10.1 illustrates how mobile highly skilled staff has a significant impact on the science and innovation system of the home and the host country. If a highly qualified person decides to migrate, first of all the source country loses an important resource of knowledge and skills, especially if other highly qualified persons follow (followers). Consequently, interregional flows of knowledge occur, from which the recipient country can benefit. Abroad, the highly skilled emigrants build up new formal and informal network relationships and acquire new knowledge. Additionally, reciprocal flows of knowledge develop. If a highly skilled professional returns to his home country, the knowledge base will be expanded and positive influences on the knowledge and innovation system of the sending country can be observed.

Knowledge migration and Turkish diaspora networks in Germany

Qualification structure of the Turkish population in Germany

Since the recruitment agreement with Turkey in 1961 which aimed to cover the increasing demand for labour, a considerable Turkish diaspora network has developed in Germany. Today, about 1.6 million Turkish citizens and another approximately one million people with Turkish background are living in

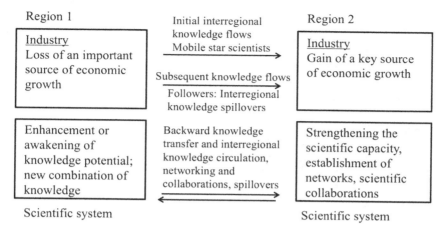

Figure 10.1 Importance of mobile highly skilled professionals.
Source: Modified from Maier, Kurka and Trippl (2007: 7).

Germany (see Statistisches Bundesamt 2011a). Approximately 10 per cent (100,000) of the highly qualified employees have a Turkish nationality according to ISCO 1–3 (see BAMF 2010, based on the data of the microcensus of 2009). In percentage terms and taking into account that still 75 per cent of the Turkish immigrants 2010 living in Germany have no education (see Statistisches Bundesamt 2011b), the qualification structure of Turkish immigrants in Germany is significantly worse than that of other highly skilled immigrants (see Statistisches Bundesamt 2011b). But in absolute terms, Turkey is the largest source of foreign highly qualified workers from third countries. Furthermore, the proportion of highly qualified Turks has increased since 2005. This fact stresses the importance of Turkish migrants as a major source of highly skilled human capital (see Statistisches Bundesamt 2011b).

By taking into account the number of foreign students in Germany the increasing relevance of Turkish human capital also becomes evident. With more than 25,000 Turkish students enrolled at German universities and colleges, Turkish students represent the largest group of foreign students in Germany (see Statistisches Bundesamt 2011c). The high number of Turkish students in Germany can also be explained by the presence of diaspora networks (see OECD 2010).

Brain drain from Germany to Turkey

Every year Turkish nationals living in Germany return to their home country. In 2009 and 2010, more Turkish nationals emigrated than immigrated. The net migration was –8,200 in 2009 and –4,200 in 2010 (see BMI 2012). The exact number of highly educated professionals among Turkish immigrants cannot be determined, but one can assume, that as the proportion of persons wishing to return is significantly high among Turkish academics in Germany, the share of

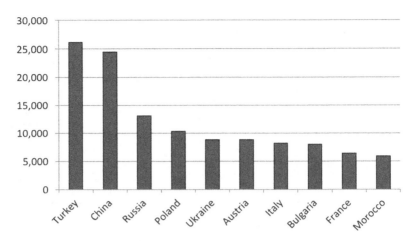

Figure 10.2 Foreign students in Germany by country of origin (winter term 2010/2011).
Source: Based on the data of the Statistisches Bundesamt (2011c).

highly educated professionals among emigrants is higher than among immigrants
from Turkey (see Sezer and Daglar 2009).

•   However, the migration of highly skilled Turkish people, who lived in
Germany, is not an expression of failed integration, but an expression of successful integration: The integrated emigrate. Since Turkish academics educated in
Germany are very well trained, often bilingual and versed in the Turkish labour
market, they are a vital source of human capital in Turkey. Accordingly, recruitment efforts to attract highly skilled Turkish staff are becoming increasingly
evident. For example, headhunter agencies were established in Germany in order
to support the career plans of Turkish professionals with the intention to return to
Turkey by establishing contacts and access to international companies in Turkey.
Additionally, the Turkish state recruits young Turkish-born researchers who work
in the US as a part of a project funded by the EU (see TUBITAK 2010). Further
initiatives to lure Turkish academics living in Europe back to their home country
are likely.

From a German perspective though, such initiatives will not necessarily lead
to migration flows in sense of the term "brain drain". Indeed, emigration leads to
a lower tax income and a reduced consumer demand, but since many of the
migrated professionals work in Turkish subsidiaries of German multinational
companies, the positive aspects of an emigration of highly skilled Turkish
employees in Germany should not be underestimated – especially since the direct
investment law in 2003 increased foreign direct investments and the number of
newly established foreign companies. Both German and Turkish companies in
Turkey fill key positions more often with young German–Turkish academics (see
Ayudin 2010). This in turn will lead to a stronger relationship between Germany
and Turkey and to the emergence of powerful diaspora networks.

The fact that skilled Turkish nationals who live abroad return to their home country is not a purely German phenomenon. The return motivation of highly qualified Turks in the US is significantly higher than that of other foreign highly skilled workers in the United States. The percentage of Turkish nationals, who remain in the US after receiving their PhD in the field of science and engineering, is slightly below average and has declined (see Güngör and Tansel 2011) in recent years to 42 per cent. This illustrates the strong connection of highly qualified Turks with their home country.

Factors influencing the mobility decision

The study of Turkish academics and students in Germany (TASD) examines the living, education and the labour market situation of 250 highly skilled Turkish persons, of which about three-quarters were born in Germany (see Sezer and Daglar 2009). The key finding is the fact that Turkish academics and students in Germany can be characterized by a strong double identity. They often identify themselves both with Germany and Turkey and are interested in the political events of both countries. According to the study, 38 per cent of Turkish academics in Germany are willing to emigrate, mainly due to professional reasons and because they don't feel home in Germany. The target region is Western Turkey, as cities such as Istanbul or Izmir reflect the European lifestyle.

The migration motives mentioned in the TASD study are confirmed by the results of 14 conducted interviews. The highly qualified Turkish respondents appreciate especially the diversity of Turkey, the high quality of life, the Mediterranean way of life and a sense of home.

Furthermore, many Turkish academics claim to have better career opportunities in Turkey. Based on qualifications acquired in Germany, a future position as general manager is much more likely in Turkey than in Germany, even if Turkish returnees – called "Almancı" because of a lack of Turkish language skills – are exposed to prejudices in Turkey, too, but to a lesser extent than in Germany. In addition, many Turkish migrants in Germany miss a welcome culture in Germany caused by bureaucratic hurdles (e.g. concerning university admission). This criticism of the German system is, however, directly related to one of the biggest advantages of Germany in the eyes of highly qualified Turkish persons. The low tuition fees and the international reputation of the universities are important pull factors. German education stands for quality, research-intensiveness, and a high budget for scientific studies. Moreover, the highly skilled interviewees criticize the poor infrastructure in Turkey, the high volume of traffic, lack of environmental awareness and associated with the fear of attacks the feeling of insecurity. These are pull factors influencing the emigration of highly skilled Turkish workers.

Diaspora networks

Diaspora networks are of great importance for Turkish emigrants and play a major role in mobility decisions. Highly skilled Turkish professionals are much more involved in different network activities than other groups of highly skilled foreigners in Germany. This implicit form of networking is more widespread and therefore more important for highly skilled Turkish than formal innovation networks with the aim of joint patenting.

Since more than 20 per cent of the Turkish population lives in Germany and since, in particular, many professionals live in Baden-Württemberg, the networks in the Stuttgart area are of special importance, especially for Turkish entrepreneurs. Figure 10.3 illustrates the most important political, cultural and corporate diaspora networks in the Stuttgart area and the identified interconnections.

Many of the network organizations are still relatively young and fast growing and will increasingly promote highly skilled Turkish professionals. The strong cross-linkage between the different networks is notable and while studying the diaspora activities of other skilled foreigners, this strong cross-linkage could not be observed to the same extent. This special characteristic of Turkish diaspora networks can be traced back to the large number of highly skilled Turkish professionals in Germany and to a pronounced double identity.

In the following, the most important network activities will be presented (see also Özdemir 2011).

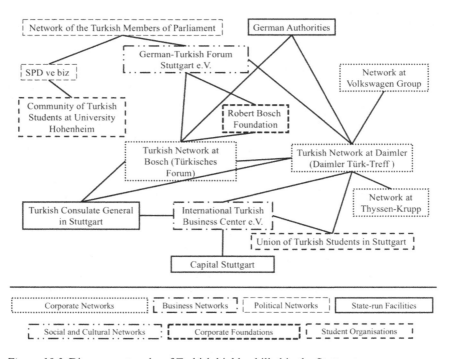

Figure 10.3 Diaspora networks of Turkish highly skilled in the Stuttgart area.

Political networks

Unlike other immigrant groups living in Germany, Turkish immigrants are also building networks in the political sphere. One example is the network of the Turkish members of parliament ("Netzwerk türkeistämmiger Mandatsträger"), an association of about 80 Turkish-born politicians in Germany, who transfer experiences across party lines. However, there are also networks within parties, for example "SPD ve biz", a loose association of about 200 of the 800 to 1,000 highly skilled Turkish workers within the Social Democratic Party of Germany pursuing the goal to involve Turkish immigrants in the democratic decision-making processes (see http://spd-vebiz.de).

Another political network is the Turkish Community in Germany (TGD), an umbrella organization of 267 individual diaspora associations nationwide head-quartered in Berlin and founded in 1995 in order to protect the interests of the Turkish population in Germany (see www.tgd.de). The TGD combats discrimination against immigrants in Germany and supports the integration of Turkish nationals in Germany while respecting their cultural identity. Achieving this aim involves the establishment of contacts with state agencies, foundations and companies in Germany and Turkey in order to solve environmental, social, political, scientific and economic issues.

Social and cultural networks

The most important social and cultural diaspora network in the Stuttgart area is the German – Turkish Forum Stuttgart e.V. (DTF), founded in 1999 by Germans and Turks and supported by the Robert Bosch Foundation. The main objective is the creation of dialogues and an improvement of the educational opportunities for young people from immigrant families by the organization of roundtables and mentoring (see www.dtf-stuttgart.de). The DTF follows the principle of networking and cooperates intensively with other network organizations, both with political and enterprise networks. Examples are internal networks at Daimler AG and Robert Bosch GmbH, as some of the DTF members are simultaneously involved in these employee networks.

Formal business networks of highly skilled Turkish professionals

A network of Turkish managers and academics from various industries with international importance is the International Turkish Business Centre Association (ITBC, www.itbcenter.com). It works closely with the Turkish Chambers of Commerce and with companies. In 2010, the Network organized a Turkish Business Forum focusing on economic cooperation between Turkey and Germany in cooperation with the city of Stuttgart and the Turkish Consulate General in Stuttgart. Potential investors were advised with regard to investment projects (mainly in the automotive and supplier industry) and provided with information concerning specific characteristics of business activities in Turkey.

Networks of returnees

Networks to exchange experiences are especially important for highly qualified Turkish employees, who grew up in Germany but returned to Turkey, and who have formed a distinctive double identity. The Round Table of returnees in Istanbul and the Turkish–German tandem club for solidarity and integration in Ankara organize socio-cultural activities, seminars, Turkish language courses for returnees and German language courses for Turkish nationals willing to emigrate. Furthermore, they assist Turkish, German and other European entrepreneurs in starting up a business in Turkey (see www.tandem.org.tr).

Corporate networks

In the last 10 years, the amount of FDI inflows in Turkey has increased almost tenfold. The total amount of foreign direct investment amounts US$186 billion in 2010. US$55 billion flow in the manufacturing industry, almost 20 per cent in the production of engines. Overall, in 2010 about 10 per cent of FDI inflows come from Germany (see OECD 2012). This illustrates the increasing importance of Turkey as an investment location and business partner. Accordingly, the relevance of Turkey for multinational German enterprises grows, which in turn increases the importance of highly skilled workers with German and Turkish language skills knowing both cultural realities and the corporate internal networks. In the following, Turkish networks within Daimler AG and Robert Bosch AG are presented.

The role of highly skilled Turkish employees at Daimler AG

With investments of over 650 million €, Daimler AG is one of the most important suppliers of foreign direct investment in Turkey (see MBTürk 2011). With a truck manufacturing plant employing 1,737 persons in the Anatolian city Aksaray and a factory for the production of coaches with 4,421 employees in Istanbul, Daimler AG is present in two Turkish cities (see www.daimler.com).

For a multinational operating company such as Daimler AG, the strategic use of expatriates plays a major role. Expatriates are sent to Turkey and, as part of their professional activities, Turkish highly skilled workers come to Germany. Concerning employee transfers to Turkey, Turkish or Germans with a Turkish migration background are not preferred initially. The decisive factor is the qualification for the aspired position in Turkey. But knowledge of the Turkish language and culture are important additional skills.

Ex- or inpatriates of Daimler AG are usually sent to a different country for three years. They can extend their temporary employment abroad for another two years, but then they either have to return to the home country or conclude a local contract – except a second contract with a different job title can be negotiated. Under these circumstances a highly qualified employee can stay abroad theoretically ten years in a row with an employment contract of the home country.

Important reasons for inpatriates from Mercedes-Benz Türk A.S. going abroad to the headquarters in Germany are the desire to work in a stable and geographically close economy, the chance to gain new experiences from the headquarters' perspective and the possibility to take on more strategic responsibilities. This possibility is given only at the corporate headquarters in Germany as in Turkey the market perspective dominates rather than the strategic perspective. Furthermore, Turkish inpatriates hope to improve their career opportunities.

However, Turkish inpatriates are facing one difficulty that should not be neglected: the dominance of the German language in the corporate headquarters of the multinational company. To simplify the integration, more and more internal corporate networks of highly skilled foreign workers emerge. Such a diaspora network of employees with a Turkish migration background is the "Daimler Türk-Treff" (DTT). Germany's oldest employee network was founded in 1992 by a non-formal gathering of six Turkish employees and today it consists of over 400 members, mainly academics and managers. Thus, the DTT is the largest organization of Turkish employees with a group-wide focus (see Özdemir 2011).

The DTT represents the affairs of the Turkish-born employees and tries to reduce social prejudices against the Turkish population, both within and outside the network (e.g. by joint theatre or sporting activities). The DTT is not just a simple employee network, but an Employee Resource Group: through the contacts and the informal communication between members of different departments, some business-related processes can be optimized and projects can be completed earlier than scheduled. In this way, the network makes a dynamic contribution to the company's success. The DTT is also working closely with several institutions within and outside the Daimler Group and with universities, professors, students, communities and political organizations. Furthermore, the DTT is in contact with the Turkish Consulate General in Stuttgart and the German authorities. Thus, the DTT affects the acceptance of Daimler AG in the public and an in-house cultural diversity in a positive way. The DTT can be seen as a model for the purposes of diversity and with its experience it is able to give advice to many internal company diaspora networks of other multinational companies. Therefore, for example, corresponding networks in the Volkswagen Group, at Robert Bosch GmbH and Thyssen-Krupp have been advised by DTT, through which cross-company networks have emerged at the same time.

The role of highly skilled Turkish at Robert Bosch GmbH

The Bosch Group started its operations in Turkey in 1910 by opening a branch office. In 1972 the first factory was founded in Bursa. Bosch Turkey operates in the areas of "Automotive Technologies", "Energy and Building Technology", "Durable Goods" and "Industrial Technology". In 2012, Bosch Turkey operates as one of the leading providers of technology and services sectors, employs 10,148 peoples and achieves a turnover of €2.1 billion and €1.25 billion export volume (see Robert Bosch GmbH 2014).

At Robert Bosch GmbH cultural diversity is of high importance. Bosch employs people from 200 different cultures and its research team is very international (see Robert Bosch GmbH 2010). In Germany, about 5,000 employees and thus 5 per cent of the total workforce in Germany are of Turkish origin. In the company's headquarters in Stuttgart–Feuerbach even one in five employees has a Turkish background. Among these are, on the one hand, many highly qualified employees and on the other hand, some inpatriates from Turkey.

Concerning employee transfers to Turkey, highly qualified Turkish are not favoured. As in the case of Daimler AG the decisive criterion is the technical expertise, except if special knowledge of the Turkish culture and language is required for the position to be filled. The expatriation takes two to five years.

In 2009 a Turkish internal diaspora network, the so-called Turkish Forum (TFB), was founded. With about 280 members, it is one of the largest employee networks in Germany and its three main objectives are: Promoting intercultural understanding and dialogue, education and supporting equal opportunities. Three project teams have been formed to achieve these objectives, whose members meet regularly in order to present their results and to support the reciprocal transfer of knowledge. For example, this includes an online journal and a brochure to inform non-Turkish colleagues about Ramadan. In this way, a mutual intercultural understanding can be created. Another result of the employee network is the nationwide introduction of Turkish weeks in the canteens (see Özdemir 2011).

The TFB works closely with several departments of the company and participates in international conferences of various foundations such as the Robert Bosch and the Heinrich Boell Foundation. Furthermore, the TFB has contact to other authorities, such as the Turkish Consulate General in Stuttgart or the State Ministry of Baden-Württemberg.

Characteristics of Turkish diaspora networks in an international comparison

Turkish diaspora networks are marked by special characteristics distinguishing them from diaspora networks of other nationalities.

First of all, according to Freinkman, Gonchar and Kuznetsov (2011) the diaspora networks of highly qualified employees can be divided into three categories: Advanced, Intermediate, and Young and Fast Growing. The first category includes the mature, professional and formalized diaspora networks of highly skilled workers from China, India, Taiwan and South Korea, which control significant amounts of venture capital and management resources. Diaspora networks of Russians, Argentinians and Iranians are less formalized and organized. For example, since mobile highly qualified Russians rather pursue a scientific activity and rarely work as executives in multinational companies or as entrepreneurs, the corresponding diaspora networks also have less access to the know-how of managers and venture capital – a situation that is even getting worse because of the little importance highly qualified Russians assign to diaspora networks. The third category includes the fast-growing diaspora networks of young Mexicans and Filipinos, although the share of highly educated workers is still relatively low (see Freinkman, Gonchar and Kuznetsov 2011). Turkish diaspora networks can be classified into the third category of fast-growing diaspora networks.

Secondly, it can be observed that social network ties are not of the same importance considering different groups of highly skilled people.[1] The social embeddedness of the Turkish highly skilled workers in transnational networks is mobility-promoting, while diaspora networks have little influence on the mobility of the high-skilled Germans. The fact that communication and cooperation structures of Indian, Chinese, Russian, Turkish and German highly skilled employees are nation-specific, is illustrated in Figure 10.4, showing the share of highly skilled employees being involved in network activities according to their nationality.

Qualified Chinese show the highest cross-linkages. All interviewees are involved in network organizations – but only after their arrival in Germany. The level of social capital is high but this, however, unfolds entirely abroad. Especially in countries with a high cultural distance, communication and cooperation structures within the Chinese community are important and influential. Highly qualified Turks have very high cross-linkages as well. Only 36 per cent of the respondents are not members of diaspora organizations. On the contrary, one-third of active users are members of at least two diaspora networks.

With a participation rate of 22 per cent, highly skilled Russian employees in Germany show the lowest networking intensity. On the one hand, there are significantly less network activities and organizations for highly qualified Russian workers – one reason why the analysis of Russian diaspora networks in the scientific literature is considered less relevant than the analysis of Indian and Chinese networks. On the other hand, many of the official Russian diaspora networks for high-skilled employees are often not perceived and do not

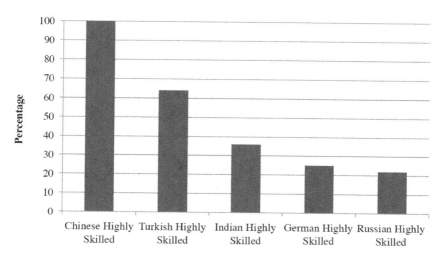

Figure 10.4 Involvement in network activities according to nationality (%).

experience the same importance as, for example, the highly skilled Turkish employees attach to their network activities. This result is consistent with the results of Freinkman, Gonchar and Kuznetsov (2011) who point out that the Russian diaspora is weak, because the cooperation with Russian institutions is hampered by structural deficits and an economically challenging environment. This includes the inflexibility and lack of cooperation willingness of the highly bureaucratic Russian institutions, but also the low demand for innovation because of the fact that the majority of economic activities is controlled by the Russian state. Thus, the competition in innovation is blocked by the lack of competitive pressure and, as a result, network activities and cooperation are considered as unnecessary (see ibid.).

Based on previous findings, the diaspora networks of foreign highly qualified workers in Germany can be structured according to their networking intensity and size. Figure 10.5 illustrates this graphically and shows that the two features' size and networking intensity are not correlated linearly.

Furthermore, highly qualified professionals can be characterized according to the strength of their attachment to the country of destination and to the home country. Figure 10.6 is based on Black and Gregersen (1992) who categorize expatriates according to their sense of belonging to the parent company and according to their commitment to the subsidiary abroad (see Berger and Böck 2010).

The interpretation of the matrix (Figure 10.6) is influenced by different factors. From the perspective of a host country "Going Natives" are much sought after. The objective is to prevent brain circulation, because in that case highly qualified employees leaving again would not be able to contribute to strengthening the economy of the recipient country. Accordingly, it is particularly important that highly trained foreign nationals are attracted and well-integrated into the society

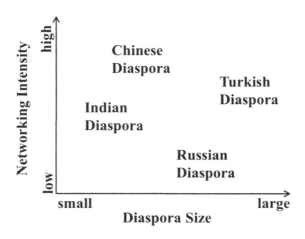

Figure 10.5 Diaspora networks in Germany according to their size and network intensity.

of the host country. This reduces the risk of losing them and benefits acquired and expanded knowledge in the host country. If brain circulation can be avoided, however, this implies a brain drain for the home country at the same time. Thus, from the perspective of a sending country, "Returnees" – or "Hearts at Home" derived from Black and Gregersen (1992) – are particularly attractive. They go abroad, but return with newly acquired knowledge to the home country, thereby promoting the local economy. Consequently, Returnees are not very attractive for the host country.

"Free Agents" are open to new cultures. Scientists are often Free Agents. They move to the country where the research conditions are particularly good and where their career can be promoted in the best way possible. Countries should be aware that they are competing with other potential recipient countries for Free Agents. Furthermore, it can be assumed that Free Agents are less often members of classical diaspora networks as "Dual Citizens". For scientists, networking with other scientists – regardless of their nationality and country of residence – is more important than networking with highly skilled employees of the same nationality in the host country. As Free Agents don't have a strong attachment neither to the home country nor to the host country, it is most likely that those modern nomads will move to a third country which will consequently lead to brain rotation – the superlative of brain circulation.

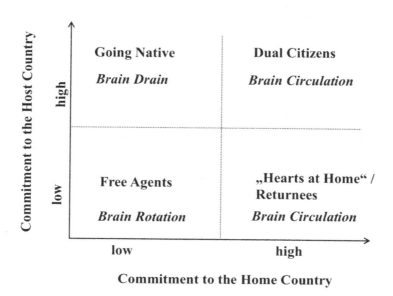

Figure 10.6 Categorization of highly skilled according to their attachment to the home and host country.

Source: based on Berger and Böck (2010).

Dual Citizens have a strong relationship to both their home country and to their host country. Accordingly, a further migration to a third country is unlikely, but multiple migrations between home and host country are very likely. They promote a circular transfer of knowledge between those two countries and thus they can support the development of both countries in a positive way. Due to their relevance as a source of knowledge and innovation potential, host and home country compete for Dual Citizens. Also from a multinational perspective, Dual Citizens are particularly attractive workers that can be deployed in both countries and integrated very well. They are much more settled than Free Agents who, on the one hand, can be deployed in any country, but may be less loyal and more mobile than Dual Citizens, on the other hand.

For the companies which favour highly trained foreign nationals to come as inpatriates for a limited time in order to gain experience, but which want them to go back to their home country, Returnees are particularly attractive. Thus, Returnees are of high interest, as they could become familiar with the corporate culture in the company's home country in order to transfer know-how concerning the strategies, structure and behaviour back to the subsidiary in the host country. In contrast, "Going Natives" are attractive for multinational firms, if the highly trained foreign nationals should be permanently displaced.

The commitment matrix of highly skilled professionals can also be used in order to characterize foreign highly skilled employees living in Germany based on interview results (see Figure 10.7).

Figure 10.7 illustrates, that highly skilled Turks are characterized by a pronounced double identity. They have a strong relationship both to Germany (the

Figure 10.7 The commitment matrix of foreign highly skilled employees living in Germany.

host country) and to Turkey (the source country) and thus they can be characterized as Dual Citizens. Furthermore, Indians living in Germany show a high probability of leaving again. Their binding to Germany is very low. They often have a high attachment to their homeland and subsequently, they can contribute to the Indian economy by supporting brain circulation. However, some of them also migrate to a third country. In this case, they can be characterized as Free Agents with a low binding to the sender and the recipient country. This shows, that the characterization of foreign highly qualified workers is not always a clear cut and may change over time. So it can be expected, that highly qualified Indians and Chinese are increasingly returning to their home country due to the current government initiatives promoting brain circulation and, accordingly, they can be increasingly characterized as Returnees in future. At present, China's highly skilled workers cannot be assigned unambiguously to a single category – quite in contrast to Russian highly skilled workers. Unlike highly skilled Turkish and Indians, highly qualified Russians have a high binding to Germany and a low binding to their home country. They are Going Natives and thus a symbol of brain gain from the German perspective and a symbol of brain drain from the Russian perspective.

Conclusion

This chapter dealt with the identification of key specifics of cooperation and communication structures of highly skilled Turkish workers. The analysis shows, that diaspora networks of highly skilled foreigners can affect the decision of mobility. For example, the mobility of highly qualified Germans is hardly determined by diaspora networks, while the transnational networks of highly skilled Turkish workers are extremely mobility-promoting. Thus, the strength of the impact of diaspora networks depends on nationality.

The diaspora networks of highly qualified foreign workers can be further characterized according to their relevance and networking intensity. Communication and cooperation structures are more relevant for highly skilled Turkish than for highly skilled Russian employees. In addition to the use and relevance of diaspora networks, the probability of return is nation-specific. Highly skilled Indians have a low probability to stay and thus to promote brain circulation rather than highly skilled Russians, who often do not want to return to their homeland, what corresponds to a brain drain from the Russian point of view. On the contrary, highly skilled Turks are characterized by a pronounced double identity. They have a strong relationship both to Germany (the host country) and to Turkey (the source country) and thus can be characterized as Dual Citizens promoting brain circulation and innovation in both countries.

Note

1   The following analysis and in particular the identification of the diaspora networks is based on the results of 67 interviews with German and foreign highly skilled workers.

Those interviews have been conducted during research activities and project seminars of the Department of International Management at the University of Hohenheim (see Berger and Böck 2010; Heisig and Ovchinnikova 2012; Matthes and Sattari 2011; Özdemir 2011; Parusheva and Fiechtner 2012; Xiang and Bian 2011). Specific characteristics of knowledge migration of different foreign highly qualified workers have been surveyed by nation-specific questions. Reasons for emigration, return plans, networking intensity and characteristics of diaspora networks have been examined.

References

Agrawal, A. *et al.* (2006) Gone but not forgotten: knowledge flows, labor mobility and enduring social relationships. *Journal of Economic Geography* 6: 571–591.

Ayudin, Y. (2010) *Der Diskurs um die Abwanderung Hochqualifizierter türkischer Herkunft in die Türkei.* Bremen: Hamburgisches WeltWirtschaftsInstitut.

BAMF (2010) *Deckung des Arbeitskräftebedarfs durch Zuwanderung, Studie der Europäischen Kontaktstelle für das Europäische Migrationsnetzwerk (EMN).* Working paper 32. Nürnberg: BAMF.

Baringhorst, S. (2010) Theorien der Migration, lecture summer term 2010, University Siegen. Available at www.fb1.uni-siegen.de/politik/mitarbeiter/baringhorst/dokumente/materialien_sose2010/(sose_10_theorien_der_migration_%5Bschreibgeschuetzt%5D).pdf (accessed 26 July 2011).

Berger, E. and Böck, W. (2010) Bedeutung und Rolle von hoch qualifizierten Migranten in der deutschen F&E Landschaft. Project seminar at the Chair of International Management at the University of Hohenheim, guided and supervised by Sylvie van Cour.

Black, J. and Gregersen, H. (1992) Serving two masters: managing the dual allegiance of expatriate employees. *Sloan Management Review* 33(4): 61–71.

BMI (2012) *Migrationsbericht des Bundesamtes für Migration und Flüchtlinge im Auftrag der Bundesregierung, Migrationsbericht 2010.* Berlin: BMI.

Cohen, R. (2008) *Global Diasporas: An Introduction.* Abingdon: Routledge.

Ette, A. and Sauer, L. (2010) *Auswanderung aus Deutschland, Daten und Analysen zur internationalen Migration deutscher Staatsbürger.* Wiesbaden: VS Verlag für Sozialwissenschaften.

Freinkman, L., Gonchar, K. and Kuznetsov, J. (2011) *How Can Talent Abroad Help Reform Institutions at Home: A study of Russian Technological Diaspora.* Working paper ID-493. Available at www.ungs.edu.ar/globelics/wp-content/uploads/2011/12/ID-493-Kuznetsov-Gonchar-Freinkman-Innovation-economic-development-and-inequality-from-a-syste.pdf (accessed 25 May 2012).

Güngör, N. D. and Tansel, A. (2011) *Brain Drain from Turkey: Return Intentions of Skilled Migrants.* Istanbul: Koç University, TÜSİAD Economic Research Forum.

Heisig, A. and Ovchinnikova, T. (2012) Knowledge Migration and Diaspora Networks of highly-skilled professionals from Russia. Project seminar at the Chair of International Management at the University of Hohenheim, guided and supervised by Sylvie van Cour.

Kapur, D. (2001) Diaspora and technology transfer. *Journal of Human Development* 2(2): 265–286.

Kuznetsov, Y. (ed.) (2006) *Diaspora Networks and the International Migration of Skills: How Countries Can Draw on Their Talent Abroad.* World Bank Development Studies. Washington, DC: World Bank.

Kuznetsov, Y. and Sabel, C. (2006) International migration of talent, diaspora networks, and development: overview of main issues. In Y. Kuznetsov (ed.), *Diaspora Networks and the International Migration of Skills: How Countries Can Draw on Their Talent Abroad*, 3–20. World Bank Development Studies. Washington, DC: World Bank.

Maier, G., Kurka, B. and Trippl, M. (2007) *Knowledge Spillover Agents and Regional Development: Spatial Distribution and Mobility of Star Scientists*. DYNREG working paper 17/2007. Vienna: Wirtschaftsuniversität Wien. Available at www.ifw-kiel.de/konfer/2007/agks/paper/maier_kurka_trippl.pdf.

Matthes, M. and Sattari, B. (2011) Knowledge migration: diaspora networks of highly-skilled professionals from India in Germany. Project seminar at the Chair of International Management at the University of Hohenheim, guided and supervised by Sylvie van Cour.

MBTürk (2011) Mercedes Benz Türk A.S.Hakkımızda. Available at www.mercedesbenz.com.tr/content/turkey/mpc/mpc_turkey_website/tr/home_mpc/passengercars/home/world/about.html (accessed 20 December 2011).

OECD (2008) *The Global Competition for Talent: Mobility of the Highly Skilled*. Paris: OECD Publishing.

OECD (2010) *Education at a Glance 2010: OECD Indicators*. Paris: OECD Publishing.

OECD (2012) OECD FDI statistics. Available at http://stats.oecd.org (accessed 5 June 2012).

Özdemir, A. (2011) Die Rolle türkischer Hochqualifizierter für den Wirtschaftsstandort Deutschland. Bachelor thesis, Chair of International Management, University of Hohenheim.

Ozgen, C., Nijkamp, P. and Poot, J. (2011) Immigration and Innovation in European Regions. Discussion paper IZA DP no. 5676. Bonn: Institute for the Study of Labor.

Parusheva, S. and Fiechtner, P. (2011) Knowledge migration of highly qualified germans and strategies to attract highly qualified Germans back to Germany. Project seminar at the Chair of International Management at the University of Hohenheim, guided and supervised by Sylvie van Cour.

Rath, J. (2006) Entrepreneurship among migrants and returnees: creating new opportunities. Paper presented at the International Symposium of International Migration and Development, Turin, Italy, 28–30 June.

Robert Bosch GmbH (2010) *Geschäftsbericht 2010*. Stuttgart: Robert Bosch GmbH.

Robert Bosch GmbH (2014) Bosch in Turkey. Available at http://bosch.com.tr/en/tr/about_bosch_home_2/about-bosch-in-turkey.php (accessed 1 June 2014).

Saxenian, A. L. (2005) From brain drain to brain circulation: transnational communities and regional upgrading in India and China. *Studies in Comparative International Development* 40(2): 35–61.

Sezer, K. and Dağlar, N. (2009) *Die Identifikation der TASD mit Deutschland –Abwanderungsphänomen der TASD beschreiben und verstehen*. Krefeld: Futureorg Institut.

Stark, O. (1991) *The Migration of Labour*. Oxford: Blackwell.

Statistisches Bundesamt (2011a) Ausländische Bevölkerung. Available at www.destatis.de/DE/ZahlenFakten/GesellschaftStaat/Bevoelkerung/MigrationIntegration/Auslaendisch eBevoelkerung/Tabellen/StaatsangehoerigkeitJahre.html (accessed 4 June 2012).

Statistisches Bundesamt (2011b) *Statistische Zeitreihen über die Wanderungen zwischen der Türkei und Deutschland 1962–2010: Schulischer und beruflicher Bildungsgrad von Migranten, Erwerbstätigkeit von Migranten 2005–2010*. Wiesbaden: Statistisches Bundesamt.

Statistisches Bundesamt (2011c) *Bildung und Kultur, Studierende an Hochschulen, Winter-semester 2010/2011: Fachserie 11 Reihe 4.1*. Wiesbaden: Statistisches Bundesamt.
TÜBITAK (2010) An Initiative in the US: destination Turkey. Available at www.fp7.org.tr/home.do?ot=5&rt=1&sid=5051&pid=547&cid=19872 (accessed 3 April 2012).
Xiang, G. and Bian, Q. (2011) Knowledge migration: diaspora networks of highly-skilled professionals from China in Germany. Project seminar at the Chair of International Management at the University of Hohenheim, guided and supervised by Sylvie van Cour.

11 International transfer of knowledge via Turkish re-migrants returning from Germany

Eberhard von Einem

Introduction

This chapter studies how Turkish re-migrants contribute to the transfer of knowledge from Germany to Turkey, shedding some light on those interlinked causal factors that allow Turkey's current economy to boom, both in manufacturing and services. The chapter starts from the assumption that Turkish re-migrants returning from Germany or other Western European countries help to improve the level of skills and competences in Turkish labour markets thus helping Turkey to development its industry from low to medium tech. Because knowledge, once generated is only imperfectly spilling over spatially, capabilities to generate and absorb both codified and tacit new knowledge is unevenly distributed among countries and regions worldwide.

This chapter is based on individual job biographies, randomly selected from those 2 million Turks that had gone back for work in Turkey within the last 50 years, excluding the other 2 million re-migrants, that return home as retired workers living on their pay checks from Germany´s social security system. The latter group was excluded from the research, as it exclusively concentrates on re-migrants at the age of 15–65, resulting in 40 semi-structured interviews with Turkish re-migrants after having returned back to Istanbul. In addition 32 managers from Turkish subsidiaries of German manufacturing companies (FDIs) were interviewed along with industry and trade associations and with other experts from government, universities and research institutes in Istanbul.

Turning the reader's attention to cross-border migration research, AnnaLee Saxenian (2005, 2006; Saxenian and Hsu 2001) has published explorative research on transnational migration of skilled computer experts allowing for a trans-pacific knowledge exchange. Re-migration of computer experts born in Asia and trained in the US, from Silicon Valley back to Taiwan and China, India and Israel have resulted in bi-polar innovation networks. The focus of this chapter is on testing the hypothesis, that a somewhat different transfer process of both technical skills and practical hands-on craft knowhow can be observed via re-migration of Turks returning from Germany and other EU countries to Turkey, in particular to Istanbul after having acquired advanced knowledge while working, going to school or attending universities abroad.

Upon reviewing research most publications concern disparities caused by migrating workers searching for a job within the limits of their home-countries (OECD 2005, 2008, 2014). Our research does not look at intra-national migration but at migration across European borders. Turkish–German migration patterns have mostly been researched one-way, not circular, focusing on in-migration into Germany, social discrimination and not-integrating into its wealthy society. Our research intends to look at the reverse process. It is assumed that in- and re-migration can be described as two sides of the coin. In- and out-migration are conceptualizes as a revolving process.

Occasionally research in Europe has addressed regional brain drain of students leaving their home-regions both for education and after graduation, with case studies concerning Sweden, Germany, UK and Italy (von Einem 1989; Faggian and Mc-Cann 2009). Recently the economic impact of south–north migration of high-skilled workers from the poor Mezzogiorno to Lombardy and other wealthy regions in the north of Italy have been investigated (Marinelli 2013; Fratesi 2014; Fratesi and Percoco 2014). Regions in the south, even after investing in higher education are losing through out-migration, whereas receiving regions gain from mobile new graduates entering prosperous regions, thus generating knowledge flows (Tripple 2013).

For more than 50 years Germany has attracted foreign workers as *gastarbeiter* (guestworkers) from countries such as Italy, Greece, Spain, former Yugoslavia, Poland, Romania and other Eastern Europe countries. However, Turkish *gastarbeiter* represent the largest group of in-migrants. Manufacturing firms have been recruiting Turkish labour mostly from rural Anatolia and Kurdistan as early as 1962. Many in-migrants became German citizens wishing to stay permanently in the country, others, among them Turks belonging to the second or third generation, had decided to return to Turkey after having lived and worked several years abroad. According to Turkish statistics 4 million Turks have been returning back from Germany over a period of five decades: 50 per cent had been coming back for retirement only, not counting those that returned from other European countries. Re-migrants returning for work have been easily integrated into the Turkish labour market or started their own business. Most of these second or third generation Turks are heading towards large megacities, especially Istanbul, Izmir, Ankara, Konya, Adana and other cities.

A decade ago migration patterns changed: the overall trend is different now. Since 2005 the number of re-migrants returning home from Germany exceeded those coming from Turkey first time. During the past 10 years more Turks have been going back to their home country overall compared with those leaving their home country. The stream of *gastarbeiter* coming for work to Germany has reversed (Aydin 2012; Griese 2013; Pusch 2013). Having said this, it is worth mentioning that only a few Turks are adding to the increasing number of refugees, very different from other Arabian and African countries

Three types of transnational migrants must be distinguished:

- Re-migrants with Turkish roots, born in Germany (two-thirds generation of *gastarbeiter*), emigrating from Germany back to Turkey after having visited school in Germany, after having acquired vocational training and/or after having gained additional work experiences over a number of years in German firms. Also about 10 per cent have been successfully earning an university degree.

- Young Turks that had been growing up in Turkey and then having been on leave from their home country for at least one year or more looking for a job outside Turkey or joining as students or visiting scholars the educational system both in Europe and North-America before returning home with accumulated knowledge, skills and competence gained abroad.
- The most talented enter the small group of circular migrants working both in OECD countries and in Turkey. After graduation from one of Turkish (mostly private) elite universities they have typically applied for a grant to specialize at one of Western Europe's or US universities as post-graduates. Going abroad is a cornerstone in many job biographies (Sunata 2010).

Re-migrants filling a gap in the Turkish labour market

Turkey, with its population of 73 million (mostly young) residents is an interesting case, because it allows a better understanding of what stages the economy of a developing country has to master in order to upgrade its GDP, to achieve higher technical standards and to gradually improve wealth. Upon a closer look the Turkish case provides evidence, what thresholds have to be successfully passed on its way up. Without increasing skill levels of regional labour markets, either through improved education, through FDI, foreign direct investments or via re-migration the dynamics of the Turkish economic development (2001–2014) would not have been possible. Up-grading local labour market profiles is a necessary precondition, to support the performance of any developing country, including Turkey.

Contrary to those few leading OECD countries, generating the vast majority of new patents via research and development this option is of rather limited importance for most developing countries. Instead absorbing and adopting new knowledge fast that in the first place has been created elsewhere becomes a promising option. This strategy, however, requires an answer to the following question: under what circumstances is knowledge mobile, and in particular transnationally mobile? Is there a difference concerning codified knowledge versus uncodified knowledge, so called tacit knowledge, or – as Meric Gertler puts it, "Can tacit knowledge be effectively shared over long distances?" (Gertler 2006).

Distinguishing codified from uncodified knowledge is at the core of this issue. Is the latter remaining to be locally bounded (Bathelt, Malmberg and Maskell 2004; Markusen 1996; Bahar, Hausmann and Hidalgo 2014)? In other words: To what extent is knowledge creation and diffusion remaining to be sticky in geographic terms, bounded to certain locations, to people, institutions and organisations in cities and city-regions? What has changed in terms of distances in the light of an ever widening globalisation and accelerating digital revolution? In search for the relevant mix of multi-causal relations, explaining different economic and social dynamics of cities and regions, it is frequently asked: "How can innovation and learning take form beyond the local territory?"

According to Mark Lorenzen there are several pipelines for the diffusion of new knowledge across national borders (Lorenzen 2007; Maskell 2014). Re-migration is one among several knowledge pipelines. First, databanks, computer, internet, smart-phones instantly provide data, information and codified knowledge worldwide. Although constantly improved it still does not cover the whole spectrum of all knowledge-elements. In particular tacit knowledge is still largely depending on personal contacts such as teaching, mentoring, and supervision. Second, Although German–Turkish innovation alliances (comparable to bi-polar networks Silicon Valley–Taiwan/China/India/Israel) are still rare examples (see Chapter 3 of this book), foreign direct investments (FDI) proves to be an efficient knowledge pipeline via off-shoring and sending experts from home countries to start a new subsidiary factory abroad thus transferring knowledge targeted to specific firms and locations (Dicken 2007; Yeung 2010). Third, knowledge intensive business services (KIBS) acting as consultants through their worldwide networks provide knowledge to clients supporting their ability to adapt via tailoring expertise to specific business needs. KIBS help to apply high end knowledge for solving problems locally (Simmie and Strambach 2006; Strambach 2008; Corrocher and Casmano 2014).

Confronted with a high qualification gap, the Turkish government has heavily invested to improve its educational system. By now in metropolitan areas eight years of basic schooling is obligatory. This is a success, if one takes into account that in 1924 the rate of illiteracy has been 71 per cent for males and 90 per cent for females. Schooling has been a cornerstone in Atatürk's policy, to radically modernise the old Ottoman Empire. In 2010 these figures are down nationwide to 2.6 per cent (for males) and 22.4 per cent (for females), mostly in remote rural areas (Akkaya, Özbek and Sen 1998).

A different picture concerns education at the university level. In 2013 about 10 per cent of each Turkish age cohort earns a university degree. There are almost 1 million students enrolled (2005: 590,000); 1.7 million have applied to the ÖSS test, which must be passed successfully to be eligible for entering any college in Turkey resulting in long waiting lists. A number of new universities had been found in recent years. By now, there are 172 universities in Turkey, 39 of them in metropolitan Istanbul. Because of budget constraints, 70 universities are private, set up by wealthy persons or profit seeking conglomerates, such as Koc and Sabanci, with excellent networks to both European and US universities. Given a limited number of scholarships, private universities are demanding tuition, most Turkish families, although supporting their children is a must, cannot afford. Thus private universities are trying to attract new students from oil-rich Arab countries, Russia, North Africa and the Balkans. This is a big leap forward. Prior to 1930 Turkey did not have a single full university. In 1933 Istanbul started its first university (Istanbul University) – with the help of 38 professors, who emigrated from Nazi Germany; this proved to be an early case of knowledge transfer via out-migration.

Despite tremendous improvements, the Turkish educational system has a long way to go. It is still far from meeting European standards, with only a few patents issued each year. Turkish students participating in PISA tests, still perform rather bad. In comparison to the EU average Turkish youngsters received grades at the bottom line in mathematics, reading and natural science (OECD 2014; DIW 2011).

Aside from schooling and universities one single main deficit remains: Turkey misses – with the exceptions of its technical schools – any systematic vocational training scheme (in crafts, technical, commercial and administrative professions) for the majority of the untrained youngsters. 35 per cent of each age cohort remain unemployed. Others are unvoluntarily forced to take up low paid jobs both in manufacturing and services. Lacking basic vocational skills, they may eventually gain experience on the job or fail, thus dropping out of the regular labour market, remaining poor, tied to the lower end of the workforce. Others end up as helping hands in one of the many family businesses, often without any pay in sectors such as retail, restaurants, construction industry, transport, cleaning or tourism.

In strategy meetings both businesses mangers and policy makers again and again claim (OECD 2014) that it is extremely important to focus on human capital development, schooling and education as well as on further research and development to gain innovation. Education – although on different levels – seems to be the main essential policy in both high- and in low-wage countries. In fact, "although there are many factors that impede successful transition, one that stands out in the literature is the shortage of skilled labour demanded by firms in technology based manufacturing sectors" (Goldstein *et al.* 2012: 106). In order to gradually shift the spectrum of manufacturing and services upwards towards improving productivity and Turkish competences required for producing technical more advanced goods and services, developing countries have to upgrade their labour force (Glaeser 2014). "The quality of the labour force in a locality is the single most important aspect of local competitiveness" (Simmie *et al.* 2002; see also Lawton Smith and Waters 2011).

Re-migrants contribute to fill the gap that opens up in most industry sectors once advanced technologies are applied. Coming from agriculture, each level of Turkey's improved industrialisation requires a certain mix of skills und competences. Any developing country, including Turkey, aiming at enhancing its industrial base needs parallel improvements of its skills and competences. That said, only a few policy-options remain to meet these expectations. As is the case of Turkey, re-migration is but one of them, up-grading the level of human capital. In fact re-migrants contribute to regional labour markets, suffering still from having too few professional services, technicians, media specialists and managers.

Cross-national knowledge transfer cannot fully be explained by transmitting data and information via publications, computers, smart phones and the internet only, because it also involves personal knowledge exchange such as teaching, reading, training, conferences and cooperation in networks (Malmberg and Maskell 2002; Bathelt, Malmberg and Maskell 2004), in particular with respect to transferring tacit knowledge and reflexive reasoning (Almeida and Kogut 1999; Gertler 2006).

The performance of both the Turkish manufacturing and service industry depend on advanced knowledge, originally created outside the country, thus knowledge absorption is critical (Cohen and Levinthal 1990). However, receiving countries such as Turkey, wanting to specialize in middle-tech products can only be successful in those city-regions that had already invested sufficiently in schooling, professional training and its university system in the past. Compared to Taiwan, Korea, China and India, as well as Israel, Brazil and Mexico, Turkey, although on a smaller scale, also seems to have pushed its industry successfully into production and service lines of a middle-tech level. In doing so, the Turkish economy benefits from the skill and competences of its re-migrants that had spent a number of years abroad, in particular, after graduation from one of Western Europe's universities and – in addition – after having gained work experiences based on solid professional training, re-migrants are welcomed as they contribute to upgrade the Turkish labour market.

In the globalising world metropolitan cities in OECD countries can no longer claim, that research and development, break through inventions and product/process innovations still remain their sole domain. Developing nations are catching up, enjoying annual rates of growth outpacing Europe, Japan and North America.

In this context transnational migrants seem to be an important knowledge pipeline. Receiving countries benefit. After having been educated abroad, Turkish re-migrants help to improve labour markets in particular in large metropolitan areas such as Istanbul, enriching qualification profiles. They are contributing to and compensating for still persistent deficits of the professional training schemes in Turkey.

If one conceptualizes knowledge not as a fixed stock that is freely flowing across national borders at no costs, but rather as a bundle of several knowledge-elements that must be absorbed, assembled and learned, it becomes obvious that transferring knowledge requires more than disseminating data and information via the internet. Because competitiveness depends on being ahead of others in terms of technology, product and process development, it is not sufficient to draw on data, information and codified knowledge provided by the Internet only. The computer is a leveller eroding acquired knowledge to the ubiquitous public.

Codified knowledge received via electronic media does not help to transfer the full set including every relevant knowledge-element. The bundle of knowledge needs to cover the whole spectrum, not just pieces. It must cover all multi-discipline elements, codified and un-codified, hard and soft. Each of these elements is transmitted differently. In particular the tacit elements of the bundle cannot be learned or absorbed without assistance and personal tutoring. Thus most developing countries, including Turkey, rather depend on adopting new knowledge instead of inventing new knowledge. Education is a pre-condition not only for generating innovation, but also for the absorbing new knowledge, created elsewhere (Cohen and Levinthal 1990).

According to the work of M. Polanyi (1966) tacit knowledge is defined as those elements that cannot be articulated or verbalized. Thus tacit knowledge cannot easily be transmitted via publications, documents, graphs, pictures and the computer. It must be gathered and accumulated through practical experience. Psychiatrists specializing in brain research have pointed out that every single lesson of new knowledge must be learned building of previous lessons. Its application must be repeated and trained in practice in order to be performed with routine (Pöppel 2006). Re-migrants can be helpful because they bring with them advanced levels of understanding, technical und social expertise, and can engage in training other workers on the job. In particular they seem to be helpful to diffuse tacit knowledge, such as craftsmanship, hands-on know-how in practical services, organisational and management skills as well as language competences (von Einem 2011). Re-migration contributes to this process in several ways, including the transfer of tacit knowledge (Nonaka and Takeuchi 1995; Roberts 2000). Because experts moving across regional and – even more important – across national borders, bring their skills and knowledge to the receiving countries they improve the level of local knowledge, its absorption capacity and its competences for tailoring and adopting new knowledge to local needs.

Turkey is still far from joining those few advanced OECD nations that successfully focus on inventing, patent development, new high end products and services. Instead developing countries have to rely early on knowledge absorption. Under time constrains picking up new ideas, concepts and technical innovations instantly becomes a critical competence in its self. This, however, is not so easy, because knowledge absorption requires both a certain level of prior existing knowledge – including language skills – in order to be able to comprehend the essence of any new invention. Thus knowledge absorption is depending on prior related knowledge that must be ready available locally in the first place. If such prior related knowledge is missing, neither firms nor individuals nor any research and development team can understand and grasp the importance of a new idea or innovation, thus being unable to communicate within the networks of international professionals. Without such prior related knowledge it is not possible to participate in relevant global scientific dialogs. So, again, human capital is an essential; it must simply be there (von Hippel 1994; Cohen and Levinthal 1990; von Einem 2011).

Because endowments of human capital are unevenly distributed in geographic terms across nations and – more precisely – among city-regions within nations, the capacity of both knowledge creation and knowledge absorption is limited to those few cities and regions, that already had reached the necessary level of competence through improving its human resources in past decades. They are best performing candidates for knowledge absorption.

Istanbul: attractive for re-migrants

Upon returning re-migrants usually enjoy various opportunities to enter the Turkish job market both in top management or – even more important – in middle management positions. Also, re-migrants commanding expertise in various technical, fiscal, touristic, medical, social and business management professions, are welcomed. For applying a university job, a top or middle management position, as a consultant, in medical services and hospitals having studied or worked outside the country is regarded to be a necessity. Some expatriates become increasingly footless by joining the armada of international commuting experts that circulate between Istanbul and Western Europe.

Max Steinhardt (2012) has conducted research based on the SOEP (socio-economic panel, administered by the DIW, the German Institute for Economic Research). He investigated transnational migration patterns of Turks. His results provide evidence that trained Turks living in Germany are more mobile and ready to re-migrate to Turkey as compared to workers without vocational training. Because of its strong economy, re-migrants prefer city-regions such as Istanbul avoiding rural areas.

Why are re-migrants returning to Turkey? Barbara Pusch (Orient Institute Istanbul) has pioneered transnational migration research. She published her findings, based on interviews with transnational migrants from Germany as well as with circular migrants (Pusch 2013; Aydin 2012; Pries 2013). Our research on re-migrants confirms existing empirical findings on transnational migration patterns. Overall, there is no single motive, but rather a bundle of motives with a mix of the following elements:

• Push-factors: Discrimination and fear not being treated respectfully in Germany is a major motive. In almost every interview, partners report on having had problems searching for an adequate job, decent housing, or having been de-motivated in school in Germany. Many have not been accepted as qualified professionals but rather as auxiliary workers. In the view of those that decided to leave, these observations add up to discouraging experiences.
• Pull-factors: Istanbul is currently offering more attractive job-perspectives allowing for a broader spectrum of job opportunities und advanced carriers options. Some have initially been testing the labour market only, drawing on friends and family networks, before deciding to return. Businesses in Istanbul currently allow a wide range of both top and middle management jobs, although often with reduced wages. However re-migrant speaking two or three languages and bringing skills and competences in such critical areas as management, crafts, applied software or technical disciplines do not find it difficult to perform in new positions.
• Personal search for identity is the third motive, thus the decision of re-migrants often has an additional social-psychological aspect, because of some kind of national uncertainty: Where is my home country? Is it Germany or Turkey?

To give an impression of the broad professional spectrum of such knowledge transfer, three job biographies have been selected and documented in the following boxes.

Case study A

In 1965 at the age of 8 years A (male) moved along with his father to the city of Herne (Ruhr Area). His father worked as a *gastarbeiter* at a steel factory. A attended 9 years at school and completed 3 years apprenticeship as a steel mechanic. Thereafter he had a number of jobs, including a well-paid job assembling steel in the construction industry. At the age of 25 A re-migrated along with his father, who retired and lived in his Turkish hometown. A decided to make his living in Istanbul. He got married and lives with his family in an owner occupied condominium which he was able to buy with savings and a loan in 2001. The loan has been repaid by now. In Turkey he worked in the cement industry and was promoted as a leading mechanic in charge of navigating and controlling a partly auto-mated huge machine unit. In this position he had to supervise one of the factory's core production stages, including solving technical problems and repair in case of a sudden break-down. Further on A worked himself upwards into a middle manager position in the construction industry with a number of day-to-day responsibilities. The basis of his carrier has been his initial solid training in Germany when he was a youngster as a mechanic allowing him since to command the necessary basic technical competences. Based on these skills he gradually learned on the job to handle related tasks such as electrical engineering, software and adminis-trative competences.

Case study B

B (female) is a 42-year-old teacher living and working part time in Istanbul. She grew up in Istanbul. Her parents were shop-owners. She graduated from Marmara University. At the age of 20 she married her husband, also a teacher. He was born and educated in Germany as a second generation male with Turkish Gastarbeiter roots. He was working at that time at one of Istanbul's foreign schools. In 1994 he returned to Düssel-dorf and B moved with him. B came to Germany with high expectations. The reality was a series of discouraging shocks. First, contrary to her aca-demic background and her ambitions to teach at a German school, her Turkish examination in sports and languages was not accepted. The government had strict rules not allowing to employ Turkish teachers for the many second generation Turks living in North-Rhine Westphalia. Prohibited from working, she focused on her family and gave birth to two babies. The second shock was searching for decent housing in a neigh-bourhood that allowed her to raise her kids in a friendly, open minded and stimulating environment. She and her husband were judged and suspected belonging to the category of *gastarbeiter*. She felt to be discriminated. In the end the family moved north into a Duisburg neighbourhood with many foreign families. The third shock was applying for a good school for her kids. Instead of integrating in a bi-cultural school, her kids were send to a school reserved for kids of migrants from Turkey, Italy, Spain, former Yugoslavia and other foreign countries. B protested because she felt not to be accepted with her background, competences and expectations.

By then B and her husband had decided, to go back to Istanbul. In 2009 the family re-migrated. Both found it easy to find a well-paid job. B's husband became deputy director at a foreign school in Istanbul's city centre and B is happy also to work again part-time in her old profession and building on her improved double language skills as a teacher, specializing in multi-cultural programmes. B's parents helped to buy and finance an apartment on the Asian side of the Bosphorus, which results in two hours commuting down town every day. Together their family income is higher than in Germany. Also drawing on established family networks had been important for managing re-migration. Support from the wider family and investing in real estate is quiet usual in Turkey, because it is the common way to save money for the elderly.

B and her family are part of Istanbul's growing upper middle class with its strong orientation to culture and values from Western Europe and its democratic traditions. They still visit Düsseldorf annually to visit friends. B's kids claim that they intend to go back to Germany once having finished school for studying at one of Germany's tuition free university.

Case study C

C (female) is a 36-year-old lawyer with Kurdish roots working in one of Istanbul's law firms. C grew up in Offenbach (close to Frankfurt) as a second-generation daughter in a family, that had migrated as *gastarbeiter* in 1974 to Germany. She and her two brothers and two sisters attended local schools in Offenbach. Among her sisters and brothers C was most eager to learn. She insisted to further go on to Gymnasium. Her parents encouraged her, whereas her teacher at school took a discouraging standpoint advising her to drop out of school and to enter apprenticeship at a local leather processing firm. C. worked hard, passed her Abitur and enrolled at the University of Bielefeld, department of law. With five years she successfully passed the first law examination and graduated after another three years from the second law examination (with results at the rather lower end of the scale).

She got her first job as a lawyer in 2006 in a Bielefeld law firm. However, she was assigned with cases only that were concerned judicial problems of Turkish and other foreign clients, in conflict with Germany's complicated regulations for working or living in the country, including asylum cases. She felt that she had little chance to further develop her professional competence and to be allowed to gain experience in other fields of law.

A friend from the Bielefeld campus had already moved to Istanbul and in 2010 offered her a job as a lawyer in his new and expanding law firm. She accepted and out-migrated from Bielefeld to Istanbul too; however, before being accepted by the Turkish association of lawyers she had to pass another examination, after taking additional courses at Istanbul University.

Meanwhile she has been working as a lawyer for several years both in Germany and Turkey. At the Istanbul law firm she earns less per month compared to her previous job in Germany, but she has a much wider spectrum of assignments. Mostly she is in charge for a multitude of variant business cases, in particular advising and handling joint German – Turkish investment cases. With her graduation both from the University of Bielefeld and from the University of Istanbul, with speaking three languages fluently (Turkish, German, English) and almost 10 years practical experiences she feels confident to master her way up in Turkey. Recently, she had been offered to become partner in the law firm. The only resentment is that she occasionally feels being offended, because of her solidarity with the Kurdish people thus not always being fully accepted by her Turkish colleagues and neighbours.

Turkey is undergoing radical social changes, deeply divided into a pro-Western urban society on the one side and a more traditional conservative Islamic society on the other side. In fact, Turkey is characterized by an internal polarization. Its society is split into a growing, mostly urban middle class and still a majority of poor residents both urban and rural. There is evidence that the new urban middle class is catching up with Western Europe's attitudes, consumption patterns, working habits, communication technologies and life-styles. Along with rising incomes, Istanbul's young middle class has been shattered in terms of changing their traditional habits, religion, and values in a most turbulent and radical process of civil modernisation. Turkey with its autocratic government enjoys little democratic legitimacy. Turks that had spent some time abroad, are bringing home more liberal and democratic aspirations. They seem to be increasingly unwilling to accept Ankara's authoritarian government, with its harsh and strict regulations.

The megacity Istanbul, with its 17 million residents and its 25 million residents in the wider mega-region both sides of the Marmara Sea, is still growing annually by 0.4 million new entries leaving Anatolia, Kurdistan and Syria in search for a better live. Rural Turks still depend on agriculture (22 per cent share of the local work-force) and on small family businesses in the food industry, in textiles, construction and mining, are facing little or no prospects for improving their income. Most of these new residents come without any skills adding to the urban poor. They live in inner-city slums or in shanty towns at the urban fringe ("*gececondus*", built from wood, plastic and rubbish overnight), which serve as arrival cities (Saunders 2011). Turkey by now hosts 2 million Syrian refugees mostly in southeast border towns but also adding to Istanbul's population. 20 per cent of Istanbul's population has still not been able to escape the urban poor. According to Turkish sources, the poverty rate of Istanbul's metropolitan population is defined as having not enough regular food, no sufficient clothes or no protection from the cold in the winter. According to Turkish estimates, 3 million of Istanbul's rising population has still not succeeded to leave the urban poor. Poverty is the other side of the coin for Istanbul, contrasting with its shiny middle class prosperity.

Most families, however, even the poor ones, are eager to send their kids to school enabling them to earn at least a small income and eventually to improve the families collective budget ... thus allowing them to gradually escape the poverty trap. Even among the urban poor it is well received that the way up is through improving education for the next generation.

Istanbul on its way up in the global economy

In 2001 Turkey experienced a severe banking crisis that forced its new incoming AKP government to implement reforms following IFM- recommendations to reduce inflation from 70 per cent to 8 per cent annually and inducing investment both domestic and foreign. The Turkish economy has been going strong in recent years with GDP-growth rates of 3–10 per cent annually. The only exception has been 2008/09, when the Turkish economy – as most other countries – was severely hit by recession due to the worldwide fiscal crisis. Thereafter the Turkish economy experienced again an unprecedented boom both driven by domestic demand and export (2014: +3%).

According to a DIW report (DIW 2011), Turkey's GDP in 2010 has reached €7500 per capita, still far below the EU average of €24,500 per capita, but steadily improving, Household incomes have risen from €2500 to €10,000 per household due to increased labour participation rates.

For understanding Istanbul's economic performance one has to investigate its links and dependencies in the context of globalization; this requires an interpretation of its strengths and weaknesses within a wider perspective concerning the causes, conditions, technical preconditions, legal framework and restrictions on urban and regional change that drive the current stage of economic globalization.

In Europe off-shoring has initially been part of the EU policy intending to integrate core European countries. It got off the ground after the Rome treaty had been signed in the 1960s, starting with relocating the garment, shoe and food industry from Germany towards Italy, followed by shifting parts of motor vehicle manufacturing towards Spain. With the fall of the iron curtain in 1989 manufacturing firms in Western Europe immediately turned eastwards to Poland, the Czech Republic, Slovakia, Slovenia, and Hungary as well as to the Baltic states. Because of shorter distances to EU markets these countries had a clear advantage.

In the 2000s, Turkey became another prime candidate for off-shoring in search for both cheap labour and new markets.

Foreign direct investments towards Turkey have been soaring, as has been reported by YASED (2014). The number of German firms investing in Turkey increased from 1000 to 5500 within the last 15 years, not counting FDIs stemming from the US, UK, France, Italy, Spain, the Netherlands and Scandinavia (see Figure 11.1).

Developing countries usually tend to specialize in the production of technical rather mature, standardized, labour-intensive goods. Upon industrialization developing countries have a clear cost advantage in the production of labour intensive goods that require only minimum education (Porter 1990; Saxenian 1994; Schamp 2008; World Bank 2009; Storper 2008, 2013; Storper and Scott 2009). This split in the global division of labour is in accordance to both the Ricardian and the Heckscher-Ohlin paradigm, which forms the theoretical basis for the "classic" core-periphery model: Developing countries enjoy an advantage in labour intensive routine mass production.

Since the 1960s, off-shoring has concerned almost exclusively labour intensive mass-production of technically rather simple goods such as textiles, shoes, apparel and plastics, but also steel, petro-chemicals and rubber (Piore and Sabel 1984; Reich 1983; Camagni and Capello 2013; Glaeser 2014) Most routine

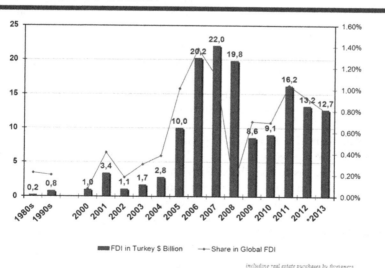

Figure 11.1 Foreign direct investment inflows to Turkey, including real estate purchases by foreigners.

products that could be packed in boxes and shipped over long distances had eventually been screened for relocation on a global scale (Mankiw, Romer and Weil 1992; Kromphardt 2001; McKinsey 2005; Statistisches Bundesamt 2006; Dicken 2007; Stiglitz 2007). Off-shoring has in addition been supported by technical innovations such as reduced costs for physical and digital transactions and transport. Manufacturing such standardized labour intensive items is requiring less transaction costs, as shipping costs have been declining due to containerization with ever larger vessels causing cheaper trans-ocean shipping rates. Also transactions costs have been falling due to expanding networks of air travel, aviation and improved telecommunication networks for transmitting and exchanging data, mails and information via the internet (Glaeser and Kohlhase 2004).

High-wage countries on the other hand specialize in precision and high-tech products at an early stage of their product life cycles requiring complexity and knowledge intensive inputs (Storper 2013), because an high level of education and training is needed in terms of human capital, advanced knowledge and faster absorption is needed (Glaeser and Maré 2001; Malecki 2010). Especially in high-tech and precision sectors, both hands on knowledge and knowledge intensive services are crucial. Drawing on clusters and regional labour pools that had been evolving over decades, certain regional clusters in OECD countries gained advantages in core technologies. Multi-national corporations (MNCs) tend to protect these knowledge assets against rivals in developing countries. Retaining and carefully developing such core competences at domestic home locations is valued as being an essential for sustaining competitiveness. This being said, strategies of western companies, competing on a global scale, focus on organizing manufacturing along the value chain with keeping core components, processing knowledge and R&D at home (Asheim, Lawton Smith and Oughton 2011). All these production stages require highly educated core personal. For constantly accumulating new knowledge for innovating new products and services, technically advanced industries insist on custom made solutions in their home countries (Sturgeon 2002, 2008; Glaeser and Kohlhase 2004).

For more than four decades the "classic" core–periphery model has been the dominant pattern analysing the dividing line, cutting through the global economy. Its perception seems to have been fairly stable and unchallenged. Upon second view, this model may be a too simple perception to reflect and explain more recent observations. Conditions are about to change. The "classic" core–periphery model may not capture every aspect of the growing causal complexity that has been driving global off-shoring processes more recently in all its economic social and political consequences (Labrianidis, Kalantaridis and Dunford 2011; Pickles and Smith 2011). The "classic" core–periphery model of globalisation works no longer as the sole and dominant global relocation theory. It implies a road model with extremes on both sides of the spectrum. In reality gradually shifting technical levels upwards can be observed among several developing countries, resulting in a continuum along a scale of technology and knowledge intensity with Turkey in the middle. Manufacturing both precision and high-tech products – including incorporated business services – is no longer remaining to be located geographically in Western Europe, North America and Japan. Low-tech labour intensive mass-production of mature technologies are no longer the only candidates to be off-shored towards fast growing developing countries as these countries improve both their infrastructure and skills.

Over time MNCs have been widening their global reach, demonstrating changing preferences in terms of not only relocating mature manufacturing facilities geographically. In the 2000s, three new aspects added to globalization resulting in a more complex picture, indicating a next stage of globalization.

- First, increasingly multi-national corporations have started considering to outsource and relocate not only simple manufactured goods, but also technically more advanced products to low wage countries. Not all of these FDIs were successful; quite a number had been returning to high wage countries after having experienced problems with quality control, precision, communication and time-to market logistics. Also as robots and automated processes were implemented, labour cost advantages of low wage countries started to vanish.
- Second, increasingly multi-national corporations offshore standardised service jobs too, such as book keeping, back-office banking and call-centres (Splitt 2013), followed by more demanding complex services, such as engineering and software. With improved IT technologies, services that do not require personal delivering or face-to-face contacts, are candidates for relocation (McKinsey 2005; Blinder 2006).
- Third, in some cases even research and development branches had been set up in developing countries. In particular, special teams optimizing process innovations and adapting knowledge to local needs are installed.

A new pattern of co-development targeted to various levels of knowledge, skills and competences is emerging along value chains. Some mega-cities in developing countries, including Istanbul, are among those challenging the classic core peripheral model. Its industry does not fit any longer the stereo-type of labour intensive low-tech mass production,

The classic model may still be valid for understanding globalisation in many countries, but not for understanding Turkey. It is overshadowed by another dynamic development, adding new aspects to the old picture, thus demonstrating that the global division of labour and markets is far from being without change. A next stage of globalization is on the horizon characterized by increasing technical competences in some developing countries.

Istanbul and its middle-tech industry

Istanbul is an example of rapid structural change of its industry from low-tech to middle-tech with re-migrants serving as catalysts.

The EU is still Turkey's most important partner for export, representing a 40 per cent share of its €175 billion per annum export volume. Germany's share is 13 per cent. Turkish exports had increased dramatically from €10 billion in the year 2000. In looking west Turkey was eager for many years to become the latest member of the EU. Talks with Brussels began in 2004, however, recently with little or no progress. Since 2010 both Turkey and the EU seem no longer to be willing to uphold negotiations. The envisioned treaty is stalemated and the bargain-process with the EU is stagnating, indicating conservative reservations among both Western European and Turkish politicians. Instead Turkey is more and more looking east and north: The focus is on the Middle East (Iraq, Iran, Syria, and the Gulf states etc.), on Russia, Ukraine and other former Soviet Union countries (Azerbaijan, Georgia, Armenia) as well as on North African states. The Islamic world alone counts for a growing market of 1.5 billion residents. These nations are becoming increasingly important for Turkey, exporting goods and services, because there are growing middle classes too. In particular, the Turkish building industry has been successful in acquiring contracts for large infrastructure projects and rebuilding facilities that had been destroyed during the Iraq war. Thus Istanbul is again – as it has traditionally been in earlier centuries – the focal, dominant marketplace, where the west meets the east. Istanbul is the city that governs this process trading with wealthy Arabs and Russians coming to Istanbul for shopping and investing.

Istanbul's economic upswing since 2001 and its involvement in global markets, has been impressive. The mega-region Istanbul alone contributes about 50 per cent to the national GDP and 75 per cent to Turkish exports. The case of Istanbul illustrates the rapid transformation towards the production of goods and services both for export and domestic markets, that might be labelled as middle-tech, in other words: no longer low-tech and not yet high-tech.

While manufacturing labour intensive textiles, for example, has by now been passed further on to low wage countries such as Bangladesh, India, Egypt and Morocco, Turkish manufacturers developed new markets for medium tech goods needed both by its own growing middle class and for export. Examples are low cost, easy to use machines, household appliances, dish washers, washing machines, refrigerators, electrical devices, TV sets, furniture, licensed automobiles and other technical components for export. In addition the building industry is booming, providing homes and modern infrastructures both for Istanbul's metro-system, but also for Cairo, Beirut, Baghdad, Teheran and other megacities. Within Istanbul's mega-region a third Bosphorus bridge, a third airport and an additional harbour are on the agenda. Along with these hard-ware infrastructure, consumer services are expanding including transport and logistics, banking, insurances and leasing, rental services, real estate, retail, engineering, legal and medical services, software, consulting, telecommunication, call centres and media services, not to forget hotels, restaurants, travel and tourism.

In a technological sense advanced middle-tech markets require not only international experienced top-management, but also excellence in engineering, trained technicians, fore-workers and middle managers commanding the implementation

of all the various stages of the value chain (Gereffi 2005; Sturgeon 2008) with sufficiently accumulated expertise. Implementation is a main threshold. Even adding
graduates from universities to local teams is not sufficient, to meet all the
expectations, that are necessary to perform multiple diverse tasks and to master the
production-process with perfection, including finance, legal matters and marketing.
Employing unqualified or poorly trained workers from rural Anatolia and
Kurdistan, some of them still illiterate, is not a feasible solution. Although
increasing numbers of graduates from local universities fill positions offered in
manufacturing, and in service industries, in government, in NGOs, in the media
and in culture institutions, this is not enough. There remains a shortage of expertise.

Re-migrants help to fill the gap. The author of this chapter argues that deficits
in vocational training are to some extend compensated by both re-migrants and
by expanding and improving the niveau of its universities. On the other hand,
Istanbul's manufacturing and services industries are still hindered, because of an
enduring shortage of skilled labour due to Turkey's still underdeveloped professional training schemes.

Confronted with the global competition for talent (Florida 2002, 2005; OECD
2008), both Turkish and foreign businesses that enter the Turkish market, focus
on re-migrants trained abroad. Also screening aggressively graduates from
Turkish universities with the help of head hunters is on the agenda. Shortage is
felt in occupations such as software, engineering, medical services, banking,
research and development and management.

Meanwhile the Turkish government has declared to further improve its
capacity in various fields of advanced technologies and precision products such
as Turkish made automobiles, aeroplanes, instruments and devices for high-tech
sectors. The Turkish government has declared its intensions, to manufacture not
only trucks and busses, but developing whole prototypes of motor vehicles in
Turkey including electronics. Also constructing fighters, warships, missiles and
other weapons is high on the agenda.

A closer look, however, reveals that the Turkish industry – with a few
exceptions – is not yet able, to perform sufficiently in high-tech markets. Success
in these industries is still limited, because there is still not enough expertise,
competences and routine both in its labour markets and its industrial facilities.
Turkish manufacturers claim for instances that although they can handle the
production of 70 per cent of all parts of an aeroplane and although the Turkish air
and aviation industry commands the necessary assembly lines, constructing and
testing a new plane completely within Turkish research and development centres
and manufacturing a plane completely within Turkish facilities is not yet feasible.
High-tech components still have to be imported.

Two examples for improving competitiveness are Siemens and SAP, that have
been setting up research and development branches at Gebse, 40 km outside east
of Istanbul with close access to the Sabiha Gokcen International Air Port,
employing 200 experts each. Teams are multi-discipline and multi-national,
including both software specialists and engineers, partly delegated to Istanbul
from German home destinations. The other half of these local teams had been

recruited from Turkish universities. In doing so, SAP and Siemens responded to the shortage of expertise both in Germany and in Turkey. Managers from both research and development centres reported that they could not find enough talented graduates in engineering and informatics in Western Europe, therefore setting up R&D facilities in greater Istanbul (for a similar case in Italy, see Lorena *et al.* 2013).

Their work assignments is not basic research. Instead they regularly focus on applying and recombining various skills and adapting basic technology, invented and developed in the EU or the US, to the specific needs of local Turkish customers and clients. For designing such customer-tailored solutions it is essential to precisely understand and listen to the client's needs. Creative adaption requires Turkish, German and English language skills along with technical and business competences. The working language in these teams makes it necessary to master two or three languages by every member in those teams. With their multi-lingual, multi-cultural, and multi-professional qualification profiles re-migrants are most welcomed to join the teams that critically depend upon qualified employees in order to increase their production both for domestic consumption and export.

Conclusion

The mega-region of Istanbul is still an island of knowledge within Turkey, along with Izmir, Ankara and a few other large cities, but very different from its rural areas lagging behind. Istanbul is the dominant motor of the rapidly growing Turkish economy. The city is increasingly becoming a hub connecting Western Europe and the Middle East. Its industrialized metropolitan region has specialized in manufacturing and services beyond mature, standardized labour intense items, requiring untrained labour only, often working under substandard conditions. Instead, Istanbul's regional economy gaining from knowledge infusion has been successful in specializing in a wide range of goods and services in the range of middle-technologies. Demand for such advanced items from the middle-tech segment is driven by both the Turkish middle class and exports to Western Europe as well as to Russia, Arabian and North African countries. In this sense, re-migrants serve both as agents of change for improving competitiveness as well as image figures speeding up modernisation and social change.

Acknowledgement

Research for this chapter has been gratefully funded by the German Science Foundation (DFG).

References

Akkaya, C., Özbek, Y. and Sen, F. (1998) *Länderbericht Türkei*. Frankfurt: Primus Verlag.
Almeida, P. and Kogut, B. (1999) Localization of knowledge and the mobility of engineers in regional networks. *Management Science* 45(7): 905–917.

Asheim, B., Lawton Smith, H. Oughton, C. (2011) Regional innovation systems: theory, empirics and policy. *Regional Studies* 45(7): 875–891.

Aydin, Y. (2012) *Transnational statt nicht integriert.* Munich: UVK Verlag.

Bahar, D., Hausmann, and R. Hidalgo, C. (2014) Neighbors and the evolution of the comparative advantages of nations: evidence of international knowledge diffusion. *Journal of International Economics* 92: 111–123.

Bathelt, H., Malmberg, A. and Maskell, P. (2004) Clusters and knowledge: local buzz, global pipelines and the process of knowledge creation. *Progress in Human Geography* 28: 31–56.

Blinder, A. (2006) The next industrial revolution. *Foreign Affairs* (March/April).

Camagni, R. and Capello, R. (2013) Regional competitiveness and territorial capital in the European Union. *Regional Studies* 47(9): 1385–1402.

Cohen, W. and Levinthal, D. (1990) Absorptive capacity: a new perspective on learning and innovation – technology, organisations, and innovation. *Administrative Science Quarterly* 35: 128–152.

Corrocher, N. and Casmano, L. (2014) The KIBS engine of regional innovation systems: empirical evidence from European regions. *Regional Studies* 48(7): 1212–1226.

Dicken, P. (2007) *Global Shift: Mapping the Changing Contours of the World Economy* (5th edn). New York: Guilford Press.

DIW (2011) *Türkei: Erfolgsgeschichte mit unsicherer Zukunftsperspektive.* Berlin: Deutsches Institut für Wirtschaftsforschung.

Faggian, A. and McCann, P. (2009) Human capital and regional development. In R. Capello and P. Nijkamp (eds), *Handbook of Regional Growth and Development*, 133–151. Cheltenham: Edward Elgar.

Florida, R. (2002) *The Rise of the Creative Class.* Christchurch, NZ: Harper Business.

Florida, R. (2005) *The Flight of the Creative Class: The Global Competition for Talent.* New York: Hazard Press.

Fratesi, U. (2014) The mobility of high-skilled workers. *Regional Studies* 48(10): 1587–1591, 1650–1668.

Gereffi, G. (2005) *The New Offshoring of Jobs and Global Development.* Geneva: International Labor Organization.

Gertler, M. (2006) Tacit knowledge and the economic geography of context or the indefinable tacitness of being there. *Journal of Economic Geography* 3: 75–99.

Glaeser, E. (2008) *Cities, Agglomeration and Spatial Equilibrium.* Oxford: Oxford University Press.

Glaeser, E. (2014) Cities, skills and regional change. *Regional Studies* 48(1): 7–43.

Glaeser, E. and Kohlhase, J. (2004) Cities, regions and the decline on transport costs. *Papers in Regional Science* 83: 197–228.

Glaeser, E. and Maré, D. C. (2001) Cities and skills. *Journal of Labour Economics* 19: 316–342.

Goldstein, H., Lowe, N. and Donegan, M. (2012) Transitioning to the new economy: individual, regional and intermediation influences on workforce retraining outcomes. *Regional Studies* 46: 105–118.

Griese, H. (2013) Hochqualifizierte TransmigrantInnen: Zum Wandel aktueller Bildungsbiographien im deutsch-türkischen Kontext. In B. Pusch (ed.), *Transnationale Migration am Beispiel Deutschland und Türkei*, 187–196. Wiesbaden: Springer VS.

Kromphardt, J. (2001) Herausforderungen der New Economy für Arbeitsmarkt und Bildungssystem. In L.-H. Röller and C. Weg (eds), *Die Soziale Marktwirtschaft in der neuen Weltwirtschaft*, 21–56. Berlin: Edition Sigma.

Labrianidis, L., Kalantaridis, C. and Dunford, M. (2011) Delocalization of economic activity: agents, places and industries. *Regional Studies* 45(2): 147–152.

Lawton Smith, H. and Waters, R. (2011) Scientific labour markets, networks and regional innovation systems. *Regional Studies* 45(7): 961–961.

Lorena, M., Agostino, D., Laursen, K. and Sentangleo, C. (2013) The impact of R&D offshoring on the home knowledge production of OECD investing regions. *Journal of Economic Geography* 13(1): 146–175.

Lorenzen, M. (2007) Social capital and localized learning: proximity and place in technological and institutional dynamics. *Urban Studies* 44(4): 799–817.

Malecki, E (2010), Global knowledge and creativity: new challenges for firms and regions. *Regional Studies* 44(8): 1033–1052.

Malmberg, A. and Maskell, P. (2002) The elusive concept of localization economies: towards a knowledge-based theory of spatial clustering. *Environment and Planning A* 34: 429–449.

Mankiw, D. Romer, P. and Weil, D. (1992) A contribution to the empirics of economic growth. *Quarterly Journal of Economics* 107: 407–437.

Marinelli, E. (2013) Sub-national graduate mobility and knowledge flows: an explanatory analysis of onward- and return-migration in Italy. *Regional Studies* 47(10): 1618–1633.

Markusen, A. (1996) Sticky places in slippery space: a typology of industrial districts. *Economic Geography* 72: 293–313.

Maskell, P. (2014) Accessing remote knowledge – the roles of trade fairs, pipelines, crowdsourcing and listing posts. *Journal of Economic Geography* 14(3): 883–902.

McKinsey (2005) *The Emerging Global Labor Market, Part 1: The Demand of Offshore Talent in Services*. Sydney: McKinsey Global Institute. Available at: www.mckinsey.com/global-themes/employment-and-growth/the-emerging-global-labor-market-demand-for-offshore-talent.

Nonaka, I. and Takeuchi, H. (1995) *The Knowledge-Creating Company: How Japanese Companies Create the Dynamics of Innovation*. Oxford: Oxford University Press.

OECD (2005) *Trends in International Migration*. Paris: OECD.

OECD (2008) *The Global Competition for Talent: Mobility of the Highly Skilled*. Paris: OECD.

OECD (2014) *International Migration Outlook 2013*. Paris: OECD.

Pickles, J. and Smith, A. (2011) Delocalization and persistence in the European clothing industry: the reconfiguration of trade and production networks. *Regional Studies* 45(2): 167–186.

Piore, M. and Sabel, C. (1984) *The Second Industrial Divide: Possibilities for Prosperity*. New York: Basic Books.

Polanyi, M. (1966) *The Tacit Dimension*. London: Routledge & Kegan Paul.

Pöppel, E. (2006) *Der Rahmen, ein Blick des Gehirns auf unser Ich*. Munich: Hanser.

Porter, M. (1990) *The Competitive Advantage of Nations*. New York: Free Press.

Pries, L. (2013) Neue Dynamiken inter- und transnationaler Migration: Herausforderungen für Wissenschaft und Politik. In B. Pusch (ed.), *Transnationale Migration am Beispiel Deutschland und Türkei*, 67–82. Wiesbaden.

Pusch, B. (2013) *Transnationale Migration am Beispiel Deutschland und Türkei*. Wiesbaden.

Reich, R. B. (1983) *The Next American Frontier*. New York: Penguin.

Roberts, J. (2000) From know-how to show-how? Questioning the role of information and communication technologies in knowledge transfer. *Technology and Strategic Management* 12(4): 429–443.

Saunders, D. (2011) *Arrival Cities*. Munich: Karl Blessing Verlag.

Saxenian, A. (1994) *Regional Advantage: Culture and Competition in Silicon Valley and Route 128*. Cambridge, MA: Harvard University Press.

Saxenian, A. (2005) From brain drain to brain circulation, transnational communities and regional upgrading in India and China. *Studies in Comparative Development* 40(2): 35–61.

Saxenian, A. (2006) *The New Argonauts*. Cambridge, MA: Harvard University Press.

Saxenian, A. and Hsu, J.-Y. (2001) The Silicon Valley–Hsinchu connection. *Industrial and Corporate Change* 10(4): 893–920.

Schamp, E. (2008) On the notion of co-evolution in economics geography. In R. Boschma and R. Martin (eds), Handbook of Evolutionary Economic Geography, Cheltenham: Edward Elgar.

Simmie, J. and Strambach, S. (2006) The contribution of knowledge-intensive business services (KIBS) to innovation in cities: an evolutionary perspective. *Journal of Knowledge Management* 10(5): 26–40.

Simmie, J., Sennet, J., Wood, P. and Hart, D. (2002) Innovation in Europe: a tale of networks, knowledge and trade in five cities, *Regional Studies* 36(1): 47–64.

Splitt, J. (2013) Transnationale Biographien deutsch-türkischer Callcenter Agents in Istanbul. In B. Pusch (ed.), *Transnationale Migration am Beispiel Deutschland und Türkei*, 253–266. Wiesbaden.

Statistisches Bundesamt (2008) *Unternehmen und Arbeitsstätten*. Wiesbaden: Statistisches Bundesamt.

Steinhardt, M. (2012) Does citizenship matter? The economic impact of naturalizations in Germany. *Labour Economics* 19(6): 813–823.

Stiglitz, J. (2007) *Making Globalization Work*. New York: W. W. Norton & Company.

Storper, M. (2008) Why does a city grow specialization, human capital, or institutions? Unpublished paper. London: LSE.

Storper, M. (2013) *Keys to the City*. Princeton, NJ: Princeton University Press.

Storper, M. and Scott, A. (2009) Rethinking human capital, creativity and urban growth, *Journal of Economic Geography* 9(2): 147–167.

Strambach, S. (2008) Knowledge-intensive business services (KIBS) as drivers of multilevel knowledge dynamics, *International Journal of Technology and Management* 10(2–4): 152–174.

Sturgeon, T. (2002) Modular production networks: a new American model of industrial organisation, *Industrial and Corporate Change* 11(3): 451–496.

Sturgeon, T. (2008) *From Commodity Chains to Value Chains, Interdisciplinary Theory Building in the Age of Globalization*. Working paper no. MIT-IPC 08-001, Cambridge, MA: MIT Industrial Performance Center.

Sunata, U. (2010) *Highly Skilled Labour Migration*. Münster: LIT Verlag.

Tripple, M. (2013) Scientific mobility and knowledge transfer at the interregional and intraregional level, *Regional Studies* 47(10): 1653–1667.

von Einem, E. (1989) Wirtschaftsstrukturpolitik: Hochschulen und regionale Arbeitsmärkte. In J. Hucke, H. Wollmann (eds), Dezentrale Technologiepolitik, 428–448. Basel: Birkhäuser.

von Einem, E. (2011) Wissensabsorption in Städten und Regionen. *Jahrbuch für Regionalwissenschaften* 31: 131–153.

von Hippel, E. (1994) Sticky information and the locus of problem solving: implications for innovation. *Management Science* 40: 429–439.

World Bank (2009) *World Development Report 2009: Reshaping Economic Geography*. Washington, DC: World Bank.

YASED (2014) *Investing in Turkey: Annual Report*. Istanbul: YASED.
Yeung, H. W. C. (2010) Transnational corporations, global production networks and urban and regional development: a geographer's perspective on multi-national enterprises and the global economy. *Growth and Change* 40(2): 197–226.

Part III

International innovation networks
The Germany–Turkey nexus

12 The comparative technological advantages and international patent network of Turkey and Germany

Dominik Hartmann and Tobias Buchmann

Introduction

A country's ability to generate, modify and distribute knowledge determines its level of economic development (Romer 1986, 1990; Lundvall 1992; Hanusch and Pyka 2007a, 2007b; Hartmann 2014). Recently, Turkey has made substantial improvements with respect to the diversification and sophistication of their export portfolio (see Chapter 3 of this book). It is unclear, though, to which extent this improvement in economic complexity is accompanied also by endogenous technological upgrading. In this chapter we will explore EPO patent data to reveal in which industrial technology fields Turkey is developing technological advantages and in which technology fields it is lagging behind in comparison to Germany and the average of 28 European economies between 1981 and 2010. Moreover we use methods from network analysis to identify key player – namely international partners, geographical regions, core technology fields, and key inventors and applicants – in the international patent networks of Turkey.

The following section provides a literature review on the role of innovation networks for economic-catch-up in both advanced countries and emerging economies. Subsequently, we present the data on patents and introduce methods that allow us to reveal technological advantages of countries and to identify key players in international patent networks. In the results section, we visualize the evolution of the technological strength and weaknesses of Turkey and Germany, and benchmark their performance with the average performance of all the European member states. We then use methods from social network analysis and complexity research to reveal the structure and key players in the Turkish–German patent. The results show that several large German and US companies play a major role in the technological upgrading of Turkey; moreover the spatial distribution of the patenting behaviour is highly skewed. Finally, we provide some concluding remarks and discuss the policy implications.

Literature review on international innovation networks and economic catch-up processes

Interactive learning and innovation are significant determinants of economic development (Schumpeter 1912, 1943; Romer 1986, 1990; Lundvall 1992; Hanusch and Pyka 2007a, 2007b). The Development and innovation economists have long argued that developing and emerging economies need to put more emphasis on R&D, endogenous innovation and economic diversification, in order to overcome a dependent position in the global production system and achieve higher levels of productivity and social welfare (Rosenstein-Rodan 1943; Singer 1950; Prebisch 1950; Abramowitz 1986). This line of research has argued that a productive structure based merely on low labour costs and resource exploitation activities might prevent developing and emerging countries from leaving a peripheral and dependent position in terms of the global production and value chains. While the central economies have innovated and diversified along the years, dependent economies remain supplying basic commodities to the central economies. However, specialization in basic commodities and natural resources is not enough for sustained economic development. Recent empirical studies have confirmed that innovation and economic diversification are crucial determinants of economic growth and social welfare (Fagerberg and Srholec 2006; Hidalgo *et al.* 2007; Hidalgo and Hausmann 2009; Hartmann 2014; Hartmann *et al.* 2015).

Recently, several developing and emerging countries have recently been able to diversify their economies and became significant sources of knowledge and innovation. Among other factors, this has been attributed to a mix of local technology upgrading, international knowledge networks, investment of foreign companies and brain circulation (Saxenian 2006; Fagerberg and Shrolec 2006; Immelt, Govindarajan and Timble 2009; Prahalad 2004; Hart 2010; Hartmann 2014). In particular, several Asian countries have diversified their knowledge base into more complex products and technology fields (Hartmann *et al.* 2016). Examples of this are the rise of the software industry in India, or the production of manufacturing products like computer parts and components in China, and East and South-East Asia. In this chapter we explore to which extent the emerging economy and EU accession candidates Turkey has been able to technologically catch-up, and what the key player are in the international innovation networks of Turkey.

International innovation networks between emerging and advanced economies

There is a significant amount of literature assessing the role of foreign direct investment as well as asset augmenting and asset exploiting activities of multinational enterprises in developing countries (see e.g. Cantwell *et al.* 2004; Dachs and Pyka 2009). For a long period of time, emphasis was put on the negative effects of the global production system, exploiting resources and low labour costs in developing countries and creating innovation and profits mainly in the centre or developed parts of the world economy (e.g. Wallerstein 2011; Sunkel and Girvan 1973). Recent work, though, highlights the economic win-win relationships that can results from of knowledge migration and international innovation networks (Saxenian 2006; Cantwell *et al.* 2004; Kuznetsov 2006). In her book *The New*

Argonauts: Regional Advantage in a Global Economy, Saxenian (2006) confronts the old core/periphery model of economic development with a new approach highlighting the role of individuals which entrepreneurially transfer competences from core to periphery regions. In the traditional core/periphery model, new technologies emerge in highly industrialized core countries that combine their endowment with high skills and high per capita incomes to develop new markets for innovations. The success in periphery countries strongly depends on these achievements in a trickling-down manner. These regions are destined to remain followers because cutting-edge skills remain in the companies and universities in the core. In contrast, Saxenian's observations of recent developments in high-tech cluster in the US show that "commuting entrepreneurs" are immigrating from peripheral regions to core regions for academic training and then create start-ups, business and social networks in core regions. Later in their career, though, they might stay in the core regions or return to their home periphery regions. In both cases they trigger the development of prolific network structures, knowledge transfer and economic transactions between both regions, and thereby can significantly push also development in their home regions. This knowledge transfer takes place in innovation networks which are spanned between the core and periphery by these entrepreneurial individuals and their economic engagement in both regions. In contrast to the established core/periphery model of economic development, Saxenian's approach can be considered as much more up-to-date, reflecting the changed conditions characteristic for knowledge-based economies. The network organization of knowledge-based economies strongly contributes to the mutual transfer of knowledge and competences, thereby positively contributing to a knowledge-driven catching up of the peripheral regions. The increasing knowledge intensiveness of economic production and the rapid technological progress triggered by new network production and communication technologies put special weight on innovation policies and international innovation networks. In an increasingly globalised world, firms and economies draw on both local and international knowledge sources to stay competitive by introducing new products, processes, applying new inputs or accessing new markets at home and in partner countries (e.g. Cantwell, Dunning and Janne 2004; Dachs and Pyka 2009; Immelt, Govindarajan, and Timble 2009; Prahalad 2004; Hart 2010). Thus, the knowledge transfer, commuting entrepreneurs and international innovation networks can be crucial for the technological catch-up and economic competitiveness of countries and regions.

Innovation networks and related knowledge bases

Innovation networks are primary environments where actors exchange knowledge and experience (Pyka 2002; Pyka and Buchmann 2011). The network ties they create between actors can have a positive effect on mutual learning and on the diffusion of knowledge (Gloor *et al.* 2006; Ahrweiler, Pyka and Gilbert 2011). Being embedded in innovation networks and accessing new knowledge sources offer a competitive advantage for firms. Therefore, firms establish collaborative arrangements to facilitate the transfer of knowledge (Echeverri-Carroll 1999). Additionally, investigating the relationships between organizations and individuals offers useful information for policy and decision makers which aim at enhancing competitiveness on the firm, the national and the regional level (e.g. Pyka, Gilbert and Ahrweiler 2007).

However, the success of innovation networks depends also on the complementarity and overlap between the knowledge bases of the involved actors. The impact of innovative networks on innovative performance depends strongly on the successful knowledge exploitation of different types of industrial knowledge bases (such as symbolic, synthetic and analytic knowledge bases; Moodysson, Coenen and Asheim 2008). For instance, Gülcan, Akgüngör and Kuştepeli (2009) showed that different knowledge bases and different institutional structures significantly affect the innovative performance of firms. Moreover, Boschma and Frenken (2009) and Akgüngör and Gülcan (2008) revealed that technological relatedness across industries and firms within a region facilitates knowledge transfer. More related knowledge bases allow to easier access knowledge created elsewhere through innovation networks between individuals, companies, research institutions and public agents. Therefore also related knowledge infrastructures are crucial for the success of catching up processes and affect the time path of the emergence of new industries in the peripheral regions.

Turkish–German linkages

The case of Turkey and Germany offers interesting insights into the evolution of technological advantages and innovation networks between a developed economy and a catching-up economy. Turkey and Germany are two countries with a long history of interactions, including political, military, economic, social, cultural and historical ties.

The long history of migration, investment and trade between both countries makes this a good case to explore the convergence and innovation networks between a technologically advanced EU member state and a catching-up EU accession candidate. The relationship between Turkey and Germany gained momentum within the framework of "Contract Labour Migration" signed by Turkey and Germany in 1961 which led several millions of Turkish citizens to migrate to Germany and creating multiple social, economic, political and technological ties between both countries. Such intensive multi-faceted relations continue today with strong international trade ties as well as a significant number of persons moving back and forth between Turkey and Germany.

It must be noted that while Turkey's export portfolio was limited to mainly agricultural products like cotton and fruits in the 1960s, today it exports a more diverse and complex set of products like textiles, car parts or electronic appliances (see atlas.media.mit.edu; and Chapter 3 of this book). It is unclear, though to which extent this diversification into more advanced industrial products co-evolved with technological upgrading, and which role international partners played in this process.

Data and methods

This section presents the data and the empirical methods used in this chapter. Our main data source is the EPO patent data from the OECD Regpat database (February 2015 release). OECD's Regpat database covers patent applications for 191 countries between the years 1978 and 2014, drawing on two primary sources: EPO's Worldwide Statistical patent database (Patstat, Autumn 2014) and the Inventors and Applicants records from EPO patents extracted from Epoline web (up to November 2014) services. The data contains patent application data, such as the addresses of applicants and inventors. These addresses have been used as an indicator for the nationality of the applicants and inventors.

Moreover, we used patent data to analyse strengths and weaknesses of Turkey, Germany and the average values in 28 Europe countries in 35 technology fields, according to the Schmoch Classification of Technology Fields (Schmoch 2008). This classification was developed for country comparisons and assigns all codes of the International Patent Classification (IPC) into 35 industrial technology fields (a list of all 35 technology fields can be found in the Appendix). The links between inventors, applicants and a country or region were established by matching the postal codes or town names, as part of the address, to regional units such as the NUTS3 regions and the two digit country code.

To understand the emergence or decline of technological strengths or weaknesses, it is important to know when the knowledge was created. In order to proxy the date of the invention, we used the so-called "priority year of the patent" that indicates when the applicant first filed a patent. We use this priority year because the final publication or grant date depends significantly on the specific administrative procedures of the evaluating patent authority and can last up to ten years after the patent (i.e. the invention) was initially applied.

Patents certainly have several shortcomings which must be taken into account. For instance, firms increasingly use strategic patenting (e.g. patents on small, but ubiquitous processes or designs) as a method to prevent competitors from entering into their markets. This so called strategic patenting can even impede knowledge generation and technological progress. It is also important to note that patents are not yet innovations. Innovations are inventions that are successfully applied in the markets. Additionally, some firms in an industry may not patent at all but still conduct R&D to understand what others are doing (Dosi 1988). Moreover, the question then arises to which extent patents are an adequate indicator for the technological competence profile of a region or country (e.g. Griliches 1990; Archibugi and Pianta 1992; Smith 2005). Obviously, not all the technological activities which shape the competence profile of a country or region can be found in patent statistics. Some industries for example draw on keeping the knowledge secret, instead of publishing them in patents. Or other industries may be mainly based on tacit knowledge that is difficult to codify. Nevertheless previous research shows that patents overall are indeed a valid indicator for the output, value and utility of inventions (Trajtenberg 1990; Hall, Jaffe and Trajtenberg 2005). They are a measure of inventiveness which is externally validated during the application process at a patent office, and since this process is time consuming and costly, firms most probably launch the application process only for inventions which have some sort of potential economic or strategic value (Griliches 1990). Also Hagedoorn and Cloodt (2003) show that patent statistics are a good indicator of innovation activities. In addition to being readily available, patents indicate the capability for appropriate returns from new knowledge and suggest the technological domains in which the firms in a region or country are active.

Measuring revealed technological advantages

We use the geographical information in the patent data to measure the revealed technological advantages (RTA) of regions and countries. Soete (1987), Cantwell (1989) and Patel and Pavitt (1991) developed and first used the so-called RTA Index, which can reveal the patterns of technological specialization and competences of regions and countries. This indicator was constructed by reformulating Balassa's Revealed Comparative Advantage Index (Balassa 1965) using patent data instead of export data (Cantwell *et al.* 2004). The rationale behind the RTAs is that if the share of a patent category in a country's entire portfolio of patents is higher (or lower) than the average share of this patent category in all countries patent portfolio, then the respective country has a revealed comparative advantage (or disadvantage) in the respective patent category.

Denoting P_{ij} as the number of patents of the country j in the industry i, the RTA for each country in that industry is defined as follows:

$$RTA = \frac{P_{ij} / \sum_j P_{ij}}{\sum_i P_{ij} / \sum_{ij} P_{ij}} \tag{12.1}$$

Having a value above one suggests a comparative technological advantage of a country in an industry, while having a value below one indicates a comparative technological disadvantage. We use these Revealed Technological Advantages to reveal in which fields Turkey is developing technological strengths.

Patent networks as indicators of innovation networks

We apply methods from network analysis to identify the key players and structure of the international patent networks of Turkey. Networks in general consist of nodes and ties linking the different nodes. In our patent networks, nodes are either inventors or applicants of patents, technology fields or geographic regions. The ties between them are established by their co-patenting, co-inventing and co-classification structure. Using network visualization techniques allows us to disentangle the complex architecture of the networks stemming from the various and multifaceted character of the links and nodes. Based on the information available in patent data, it is possible to construct various indicators for innovation networks.

Firstly, if more than one inventor is listed in a patent, it is likely that these agents have collaborated in one or another way in generating, developing, financing and distributing the new knowledge covered in the patent application. Hence, this collaborative relationship has successfully contributed to the generation of new knowledge because, a third actor – the applicant – invested resources to attain the intellectual property rights.

Secondly, the inventor's relationship with the applicant is an important feature of an innovation network as the location of competences is an essential information for managing successfully innovation projects. The inventor-applicant relationship can be described in a graphical representation of the network with two different types of nodes: the inventors and the applicants. Obviously, both play different roles in the generation, application and commercialization of the new knowledge.

Thirdly, where more than one applicant is listed in the patent, more than one firm is engaged in achieving legal property rights for the new knowledge. This suggests a technology related formal collaboration between the two applicants.

Fourthly, the technological competences of actors (e.g. inventors, applicants, regions or technology fields) can be identified with the technological classification in a patent document (IPC codes). Where more than one technological field is given to classify a patent document, a relationship can be established between these two fields (Saviotti 2009). This relationship indicates that the patent generated new knowledge, and thus created an interface between two different knowledge fields.

Finally, the geographic location of the inventors and applicants reveal the spatial distribution of technological capabilities and how international innovation networks connect different regions and create ties between regions with similar or complementary technology profiles. All these factors together allow us to gain a deeper knowledge about different facets of international innovation networks.

In order to identify the key player and understand the centrality of the nodes (i.e. the inventors, applicants, regions, countries and technology fields) in different types of networks (e.g. the geographic collaboration patterns, the most connected technology fields or the most central applicants in the entire networks), we calculate the degree centrality of the nodes in these networks. Degree centrality measures the number of direct connections a node has to the other nodes of the sample. Thus, degree centrality shows how well connected the individuals are and can be interpreted as representing the agent's direct influence (Borgatti *et al.* 2008).

The evolution of revealed technological advantages in Turkey, Germany and Europe

In this section we compare the Revealed Technological Advantages (RTA) and Disadvantages (RTD) of Turkey, Germany and the average in 28 European economies (see full list in the Appendix). Germany applied between 1978 and 2014 for over half a million EPO patents (i.e. 528,119 patents) and is hence responsible for 19.2 per cent of all applications at European Patent Office (EPO). In the same time span, Turkey applied for just 2386 patents, making it responsible for only 0.09 per cent of all EPO-patents. This large difference in the absolute number of patents must be taken into account when interpreting the RTAs. RTAs do not calculate the absolute technological strengths, but the relative specialization, strengths and weaknesses of countries. For example, Germany has significantly higher values than Turkey in all technology fields. In consequence, owing to the large absolute number of German patents in virtually all technology fields, the normalized values of the comparative advantages and disadvantages are comparatively low. In contrast, Turkey has comparatively few patents and thus in absolute terms is far behind in its technological capabilities behind technology leader in most areas, yet as we will show below, Turkey is starting to develop relative technological advantages in several fields.

Figure 12.1 compares the evolution to the total amount of patents and the revealed technological advantages of Turkey, Germany and the European average values in 35 technology fields between 1981 and 2010. Each technology field is represented by a time series graph. The evolution of Turkey's number of patents in each technology field is represented by dashed grey lines, Germany's patents by black lines, and the average number of patents in 28 European economies by dotted black lines. Moreover, RTAs are represented by solid up-pointing triangles, RTDs by white down-pointing triangles.[1] (A full list of all 28 European economies for which we calculated the average can be found in the Appendix). Figure 12.1 shows that Turkey has been catching-up in several technology fields and developed several technological advantages between 1981 to 2010, in fields like "pharmaceuticals" and "thermal processes and apparatus", and "civil engineering". In absolute terms, the number of patents of Turkey is rather small and significantly behind Germany as well as behind the average number of patents in the respective technology fields in 28 European economies. For instance the RTA of Turkey in the technology field "civil engineering" is based on only 42 patents, while Germany has in the same field 30,843 patents. However, the patent data provides useful information about nascent technological skills and promising investment in technological diversification. This allows us to observe in which technological fields Turkey is applying for patents, in which fields it is developing strength, and in which fields it is still lagging behind.

Next, we analyse the diversification and thus knowledge breadth of the patent portfolio of Turkey and Germany. The treemaps in Figure 12.2 compare the evolution of the diversity of the patent portfolio of both countries. We can observe a significant diversification of Turkey's patenting behaviour (Figure 12.2a–b). In the period 1981-1985, Turkey applied for just 14 patents in 9 technology fields, while in 2006–2010 it applied for 1753 patents in 35 technology fields. During the same period the patent portfolio of Germany continued at a high level of diversification (see Figure 2c–d). Germany applied for 59,285 patents in all 35 technology fields in 1981–1985, and 161,238 patents in 35 technology fields in 2006–2010. These results illustrate again that Turkey is still significantly behind Germany in absolute numbers of patents, however we can also see positive signs of technological upgrading and diversification which Turkey can further build upon.

Evolution of the Patents, Revealed Technological Advantages (RTA+) and Disadvantages (RTD-) of Turkey, Germany and the European Average in 35 technology fields between 1981-2010

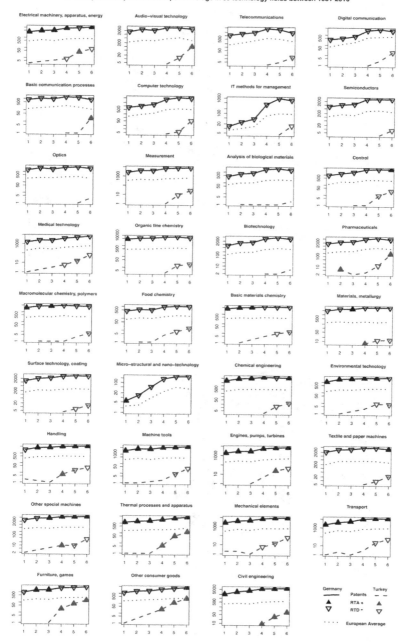

Figure 12.1 Evolution of patents and RTAs of Turkey, Germany and the European average in 35 technology fields between 1981 and 2010.

A. Turkey's patents 1981-1986

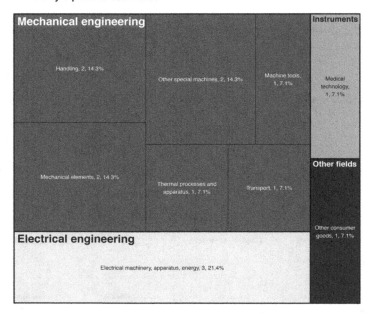

B. Turkey's patents 2006-2010

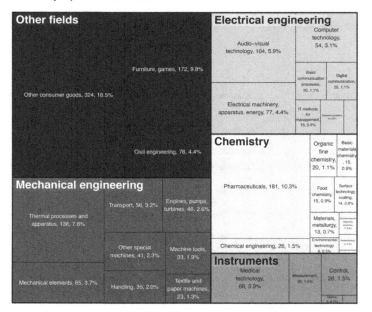

C. Germany's patents 1981-1986

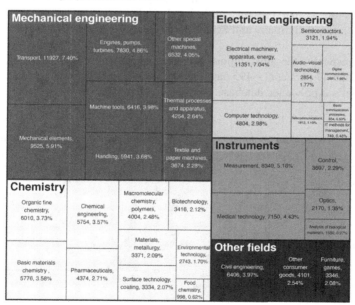

Chemistry

Organic fine chemistry, 4387, 7.40%

Chemical engineering, 3037, 5.12%

Macromolecular chemistry, polymers, 2784, 4.70%

Basic materials chemistry, 3825, 6.45%

Materials, metallurgy, 1918, 3.24%

Surface technology, coating, 1339, 2.26%

Environmental technology, 1110, 1.87%

Pharmaceuticals, 1683, 2.84%

Biotechnology, 763, 1.29%

Food chemistry, 414, 0.70%

Electrical engineering

Electrical machinery, apparatus, energy, 3641, 6.14%

Audio–visual technology, 1658, 2.80%

Basic communication processes, 826, 1.39%

Telecommunications, 1061, 1.82%

Semiconductors, 748, 1.26%

Computer technology, 752, 1.27%

Digital communication, 362, 0.61%

Instruments

Measurement, 2658, 4.46%

Optics, 1507, 2.54%

Medical technology, 1575, 2.66%

Control, 904, 1.52%

Analysis of biological materials, 399, 0.67%

Mechanical engineering

Other special machines, 2793, 4.71%

Transport, 2369, 4.00%

Handling, 2282, 3.85%

Textile and paper machines, 2069, 3.49%

Mechanical elements, 2631, 4.44%

Machine tools, 2319, 3.91%

Engines, pumps, turbines, 1893, 3.19%

Thermal processes and apparatus, 1246, 2.10%

Other fields

Civil engineering, 2128, 3.59%

Other consumer goods, 1177, 1.99%

Furniture, games, 987, 1.66%

D. Germany's patents 2006-2010

Mechanical engineering

Transport, 11927, 7.40%

Engines, pumps, turbines, 7830, 4.86%

Other special machines, 6532, 4.05%

Machine tools, 6416, 3.98%

Thermal processes and apparatus, 4254, 2.64%

Mechanical elements, 9525, 5.91%

Handling, 5941, 3.68%

Textile and paper machines, 3674, 2.28%

Electrical engineering

Semiconductors, 3121, 1.94%

Electrical machinery, apparatus, energy, 11351, 7.04%

Audio–visual technology, 2854, 1.77%

Digital communication, 2851, 1.86%

Computer technology, 4804, 2.98%

Telecommunications, 1912, 1.19%

Basic communication processes, 804, 0.50%

IT methods for management, 749, 0.46%

Instruments

Measurement, 8349, 5.18%

Control, 3697, 2.29%

Medical technology, 7150, 4.43%

Optics, 2170, 1.35%

Analysis of biological materials, 1580, 0.97%

Chemistry

Organic fine chemistry, 6010, 3.73%

Chemical engineering, 5754, 3.57%

Macromolecular chemistry, polymers, 4004, 2.48%

Biotechnology, 3416, 2.12%

Materials, metallurgy, 3371, 2.09%

Environmental technology, 2743, 1.70%

Basic materials chemistry, 5776, 3.58%

Pharmaceuticals, 4374, 2.71%

Surface technology, coating, 3334, 2.07%

Food chemistry, 998, 0.62%

Other fields

Civil engineering, 6406, 3.97%

Other consumer goods, 4101, 2.54%

Furniture, games, 3346, 2.08%

Figure 12.2 Evolution of diversity of the patent portfolio for (a) Turkey 1981–1986, (b) Turkey 2006–2010, (c) Germany 1981–1986 and (d) Germany 2006–2010.

Key players in the Turkish patent network

In this section, we analyse the key players in Turkey's international patent networks. For this purpose, we first identify the regions, countries, inventors, applicants and technology classes which have the highest network centrality in terms of degree centrality. Based on these results, we then use network visualization methods to illustrate the systemic connections between the key players in Turkey's patent network.

Spatial concentration and international key partners

Figure 12.3 shows the distribution of the degree centrality of (a) inventors and applicants and (b) regions in the international patent network of Turkey (IPNT). We can observe a highly skewed frequency distribution compared to a normal distribution (black line). This means that some regions and inventors/applicants have a large number of international ties, while most other regions and inventors/ applicant have very few international ties. Thus, the Turkey's international patent production is not distributed randomly, but shows a strong concentration in few key regions, applicants and inventors.

As expected due to its large size and strategic geospatial position, Istanbul has by far the highest degree centrality in the international patent network of Turkey (see Figure 12.4). Ankara, Artvin, Düzce, Osmaniye and Izmir, which follow Istanbul on the next places, have already significantly fewer connections. Interestingly, though is the strong presence of several foreign locations, like Munich and Ludwigshafen in Germany and Schenectady County in the US, in Turkey's patent network.

With respect to the most important partner countries (see Figure 12.5), we can observe that 47 per cent (= 495 patents) of Turkey's international patents included in Regpat's Applicants database (release February 2015) have been made in

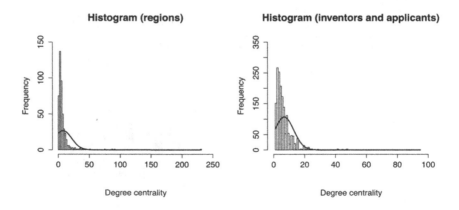

Figure 12.3 Histograms of the degree centrality of regions, inventors and applicants.

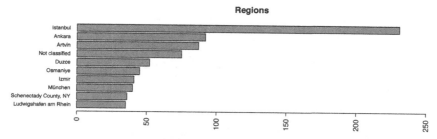

Figure 12.4 Top ten connected regions in Turkey's patent network.

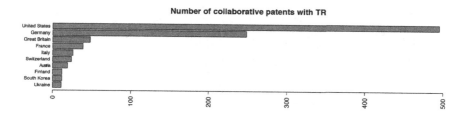

Figure 12.5 Top countries in terms of collaborative patents with Turkey.

collaboration with partners from the US. Germany follows with 23.6 per cent (or 248 patents) on the second place. Other European countries, like UK with 48 patents (= 4.6% of the total Turkish patents) and France with 39 patents (= 3.7%), have already significantly less importance in Turkey's patent networks.

If we look at the entire Turkish patent network, colouring Turkish applicants and inventors in white, German ones in black and other countries (in this case mainly US) in grey, again we can observe that partners from Germany and other countries play an important role across the entire network (see Figure 12.6).

More significantly, though, international companies like General Electric, Bosch and BASF are the most important applicants in Turkey's patent network (Figure 12.7). Strikingly, there is no Turkish firm among the top ten applicants of patents in Turkey. This points to a lack in the capacity of Turkish companies to generate and protect technological knowledge. Moreover, it means that the Turkish patent portfolio depends significantly on foreign multinational enterprises, especially from the US and Germany.

Core technology fields and systemic connections

Next, we connect our results about the key partners in Turkey's patent network with the most central technology fields in Turkey's patent networks. Among the

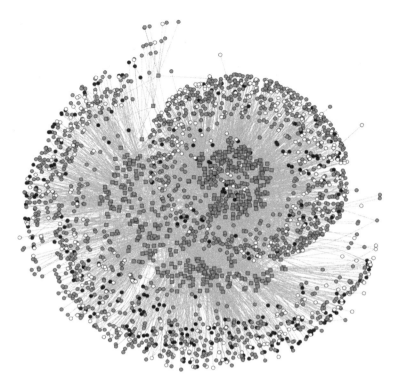

Figure 12.6 The Turkish patent network. White nodes indicate inventors or applicants from Turkey, black ones are from Germany, and grey ones from other countries.

most connected technology fields appear several technology fields related to chemistry, material sciences, and electrical machinery (Figure 12.8).

If we illustrate network of all key applicants, inventors, technology fields and regions, a clear structure and three main clusters emerge (see Figure 12.9). First (as seen on the top right of the network) a pharmaceutical and biotechnological cluster appears that is driven by inventors and a company located in Middlesex County in Massachusetts (MA). Second, on the left a material sciences and

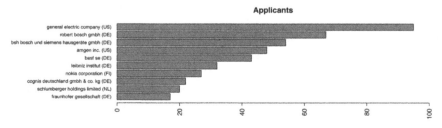

Figure 12.7 Top ten connected applicants.

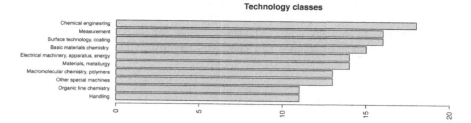

Figure 12.8 Top ten connected technology classes.

chemistry industry cluster can be revealed which is driven by German companies like Bosch or Fraunhofer from the Southern German regions like Stuttgart and Munich. Third (on the bottom), we can see an electrical and energy cluster related to General Electric (located in the Saratoga Country and Schenectady in the state of New York). Moreover we can also see a couple of key boundary spanner from Turkey, like Nomak, Arpac and Aksit, that are creating international innovation networks with foreign companies and technology sources. Thus, they are key player connecting Turkey to international knowledge sources.

In sum, making use of network analysis and visualization methods helps us to reveal the key players in Turkey's patent network. We can observe a strong spatial

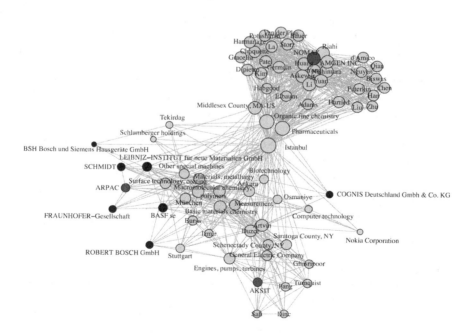

Figure 12.9 The network of key applicants, inventors, regions and technology fields.

concentration of the patenting behaviour on few core regions as well as a strong connectedness or even dependency on partner regions and applicants from US and Germany in several core technology fields for Turkey's technological upgrading like material science and chemistry, energy pumps and turbines, or pharmaceuticals.

Discussion and concluding remarks

In this chapter, we used EPO patent data to reveal the technological strengths and weaknesses of Turkey in comparison with Germany and the average values of 28 European economies in 35 technology fields between 1981 and 2010. While Turkey is still significantly lagging behind in the absolute number of patents, our results also shows that Turkey has been starting to diversify its patent portfolio and is developing comparative technological advantages in technology fields like "pharmaceuticals", "thermal processes and apparatus", "civil engineering", "energy, pumps and turbines", "audiovisual technologies", and "other consumer products".

Making use of network analysis techniques and showing the key players in Turkey's patent network, though, also shows a strong dependency of the Turkish patent network from large firms and technology companies in Germany and the US. Several firms and research institutions from Southern Germany (e.g. Stuttgart and Munich), like Bosch or Fraunhofer Institutes, are key players in several technology fields related to material sciences and chemical industries. Technological advantages in the networks of industries related to energy, pumps and turbines are strongly impacted by General Electric (GE), and the RTA in the pharmaceutical sector is strongly driven by the pharma-biotech company Amgen in the US.

It must be highlighted that several Turkish individuals, like Nomak, Arpac and Aksit, have an important role in creating knowledge bridges between Turkey, US and Germany. These boundary spanners are creating international innovation networks. Most strikingly though is that most patents in Turkey are actually applied by foreign companies. No Turkish companies feature among the top applicants in the Turkish patent network. We cannot properly know from our results to which extent this is due to (i) the mere lack of capabilities to generate technological and commercially useful knowledge in Turkey, (ii) the lack of capabilities to protect commercially useful knowledge, and/or (iii) the simple lack of emphasis of Turkish companies on patents. However, understanding the various factors leading to the low level of patenting constitutes an important path for future research on the international patent network and technological upgrading of Turkey as well as other emerging economies.

From a more general and innovation system perspective, it seems to be clear that there is a need for further emphasis on innovation networks between companies, research institutions and politics in Turkey to promote the generation and protection of technological knowledge. Mere emphasis on the exploitation of comparatively cheap labour or a booming construction sector is not enough to maintain future-oriented economic growth. Deliberate emphasis on technological upgrading, interactive learning and economic diversification is necessary. In order to create and establish prolific innovation systems, the variety of agents involved in the economic development process – such as companies, universities, the government and the civil society – need to jointly promote the generation, adoption, diffusion and appropriation of knowledge and technology. Accordingly, international partners and international innovation networks can help to access external knowledge sources, however there is also a need to further increase its endogenous innovation capabilities.

Summarizing, our findings suggest that Turkey can gain significantly from the cooperation with German and US companies and inventors, however it also illustrates a significant dependency of Turkey from foreign technologies and the need for further endogenous technological catch-up and diversification of technological capabilities.

Acknowledgements

The authors want to thank BMBF and TÜBITAK for their financial support as part of the TUR 10/65 project on Turkish–German Innovation Networks. Dominik Hartmann also would like to thank the Mercator IPC Initiative for his financial support as an IPC-Mercator fellow at the Istanbul Policy Center and the Marie Curie International Outgoing Fellowship no. 328828 within the 7th European Community Framework Programme. Moreover, we thank Fabian Stahl and Seda Aydin for their research assistance, and Andreas Pyka and the TGIN team for valuable comments. Any errors are the responsibility of the authors.

Appendix

Table 12A.1 Schmoch's classification of technology fields (2008).

No.	Field	No.	Field
1	Electrical machinery, apparatus, energy	19	Basic materials chemistry
2	Audio-visual technology	20	Materials, metallurgy
3	Telecommunications	21	Surface technology, coating
4	Digital communication	22	Micro-structural and nano-technology
5	Basic communication processes	23	Chemical engineering
6	Computer technology	24	Environmental technology
7	IT methods for management	25	Handling
8	Semiconductors	26	Machine tools
9	Optics	27	Engines, pumps, turbines
10	Measurement	28	Textile and paper machines
11	Analysis of biological materials	29	Other special machines
12	Control	30	Thermal processes and apparatus
13	Medical technology	31	Mechanical elements
14	Organic fine chemistry	32	Transport
15	Biotechnology	33	Furniture, games
16	Pharmaceuticals	34	Other consumer goods
17	Macromolecular chemistry, polymers	35	Civil engineering
18	Food chemistry		

Table 12A.2 List of European countries considered in Europe's average.

Austria	Estonia	Italy	Portugal
Belgium	Finland	Latvia	Romania
Bulgaria	France	Lithuania	Slovakia
Croatia	Germany	Luxembourg	Slovenia
Cyprus	Greece	Malta	Spain
Czech Republic	Hungary	Netherlands	Sweden
Denmark	Ireland	Poland	United Kingdom

Note

1   If the number of patents in a year in one of the technology field is smaller or equal five, the resulting RTA/RTD was not taken into account.

References

Abramowitz, M. (1986) Catching up, forging ahead, and falling behind. *Journal of Economic History* 46(2): 385–406.

Ahrweiler, P., Pyka, A. and Gilbert, N. (2011) A new model for university–industry links in knowledge-based economies. *Journal of Product Innovation Management* 28: 218–235.

Akgüngör, S. and Gülcan, Y. (2008) Textile cluster initiatives and related variety in Turkey. Paper presented at Regions: The Dilemmas of Integration and Cooperation, RSA Annual International Conference, Prague, 27–29 May.

Archibugi, D. and Pianta, M. (1992) *The Technological Specialization of Advanced Countries: A Report to the EEC on International Science and Technology Activities.* Boston, MA: Kluwer.

Balassa, B. (1965) Trade liberalization and "revealed" comparative advantage. *The Manchester School of Economics and Social Studies* 33: 99–123.

Borgatti, S. P., Halgin, D. and De Jordy, R. (2008). NIPS UCINET and NetDraw workshop: an introduction to UCINET and NetDraw. Seminar, Carroll School of Management, Boston College, Boston, MA. Available at www.hks.harvard.edu/netgov/files/NIPS/Halgin_NIPS_2008.pdf (accessed 19 June 2010).

Boschma, R. and Frenken, K. (2009) *The Spatial Evolution of Innovation Networks: A Proximity Perspective.* Papers in Evolutionary Economic Geography (PEEG) 0905. Utrecht: Utrecht University, Section of Economic Geography.

Cantwell, J. A. (1989): *Technological Innovation and Multinational Corporations.* Oxford: Blackwell.

Cantwell, J., Dunning, J. and Janne, O. (2004) Towards a technology-seeking explanation of US direct investment in the United Kingdom. *Journal of International Management* 10: 5–20.

Dachs, B. and Pyka, A. (2009) What drives the internationalization of innovation? Evidence from European patent data. *Economics of Innovation and New Technology* 19 (1): 71–86.

Dosi, G. (1988) Sources, procedures, and microeconomic effects of innovation. *Journal of Economic Literature* 26(3): 1120–1171.

Echeverri-Carroll, E. L. (1999) Knowledge flows in innovation networks: a comparative analysis of Japanese and US high-technology firms. *Journal of Knowledge Management* 3(4): 296–303.

Fagerberg, J. and Srholec, M. (2006) The role of "capabilities" in development: why some countries develop (while other stay poor). Paper presented at Innovation, Competition and Growth: Schumpeterian Perspectives, 11th ISS Conference, Université Nice/Sophia-Antipolis, France, 21–24 June.

Gloor, P., Paasivaara, M., Schoder, D. and Willems, P. (2006) Correlating performance with social network structure through teaching social network analysis. Paper presented at 7th IFIP Conference on Working Enterprises.

Griliches, Z. (1990) Patent statistics as economic indicators: a survey. *Journal of Economic Literature* 28(4): 1661–1707.

Gülcan, Y., Akgüngör, S. and Kuştepeli, Y. (2009) Regional innovation systems and knowledge generation in Turkish textile industry: a comparison of İstanbul and Denizli regions. 4th International Seminar on Innovation, Napier University, Edinburgh, 15–16 October.

Hagedoorn, J. and Cloodt, M. (2003) Measuring innovative performance: is there an advantage in using multiple indicators? *Research Policy* 32: 1365–1379.

Hall, B. H., Jaffe, A. B. and Trajtenberg, M. (2005) Market value and patent citations: a first look, *The Rand Journal of Economics* 36 (1): 16–38.

Hanusch, H. and Pyka, A. (2007a) The Principles of Neo-Schumpeterian Economics. *Cambridge Journal of Economics* 31: 275–289.

Hanusch, H. and Pyka, A. (eds) (2007b) *The Elgar Companion to Neo-Schumpeterian Economics*. Cheltenham: Edward Elgar.

Hart, S. L. (2010) *Capitalism at the Crossroads: Next Generation Business Strategies for a Post-Crises World*. Upper Saddle River, NJ: Wharton School Publishing.

Hartmann, D. (2014) *Economic Complexity and Human Development: How Economic Diversification and Social Networks Affect Human Agency and Welfare*. New York: Routledge.

Hartmann, D., Guevara, M. R., Jara-Figueroa, C., Aristarán, M. and Hidalgo, C. A. (2015) Linking economic complexity, institutions and income inequality. *arXiv* 1505.07907 [physics, q-fin], May. Available at http://arxiv.org/abs/1505.07907.

Hartmann, D., Jara-Figueroa, C., Simoes, A., Guevara, M. R. and Hidalgo, C. A. (2016) The Structural Constraints of Income Inequality in Latin America. *Integration & Trade Journal*, Washington, DC: IADB.

Hidalgo, C. A. and Hausmann, R. (2009) The building blocks of economic complexity. *Proceedings of the National Academy of Sciences* 106(26): 10,570–10,575.

Hidalgo, C. A., Klinger, B., Barabási, A.-L. and Hausmann, R. (2007) The product space conditions the development of nations. *Science* 317(5837): 482–487.

Immelt, J. R., Govindarajan, V. and Timble, C. (2009) How GE is disrupting itself. *Harvard Business Review* (October). Available at https://hbr.org/2009/10/how-ge-is-disrupting-itself/ar/1.

Kuznetsov, Y. (ed.). (2006) *Diaspora Networks and the International Migration of Skills: How Countries Can Draw on Their Talent Abroad*. Washington, DC: World Bank Publications.

Lundvall, B.-Å. (1992) *National Systems of Innovation: Towards a Theory of Innovation and Interactive Learning*.London: Frances Pinter.

Moodysson, J., Coenen, L. and Asheim, B. (2008) *Two Sides of the Same Coin? Local and Global Knowledge Flows in Medicon Valley*. CIRCLE electronic working paper series 2008–15. Lund: Centre for Innovation, Research and Competence in the Learning Economy, Lund University.

Patel, P. and Pavitt, K. L. R. (1991) Europe's technological performance. In C. Freeman, M. Sharp and W. Walker (eds), *Technology and the Future of Europe: Global Competition and the Environment in the 1990s*, ch. 3. London: Thomson Learning.

Prahalad, C. K. (2004) *The Fortune at the Bottom of the Pyramid: Eradicating Poverty through Profits*. Upper Saddle River, NJ: Wharton School Publishing.

Prebisch, R. (1950) *The Economic Development of Latin America and Its Principal Problems*. New York: United Nations.

Pyka, A. (2002) Innovation networks in economics – from the incentive-based to the knowledge-based approaches. *European Journal of Innovation Management* 5(3): 152–163.

Pyka, A. and Buchmann, T. (2011) Innovation networks. In J. Krafft and M. Dietrich (eds), *Handbook on the Theory of the Firm*, 466–483. Cheltenham: Edward Elgar.

Pyka, A., Gilbert, N. and Ahrweiler, P. (2007) Simulating knowledge-generation and – distribution processes in innovation collaborations and networks. *Cybernetics and Systems* 38: 667–693.

Romer, P. M. (1986) Increasing returns and long-run growth. *Journal of Political Economy* 94: 1002–1037.

Romer, P. M. (1990) Endogenous technological change. *The Journal of Political Economy* 98(5–2): S71–S102.

Rosenstein-Rodan, P. M. (1943) Problems of industrialisation in eastern and south-eastern Europe. *Economic Journal* 53: 202–211.

Saviotti, P. P. (2009) Knowledge networks: structure and dynamics. In A. Pyka and A. Scharnhorst (eds), *Innovation Networks: New Approaches in Modelling and Analyzing*, 19–41. Berlin: Springer.

Saxenian, A. (2006) *The New Argonauts: Regional Advantage in a Global Economy.* Cambridge, MA: Harvard University Press.

Schmoch, U. (2008) *Concept of a Technology Classification for Country Comparisons.* Final report to the World Intellectual Property Office. Karlsruhe: Fraunhofer ISI. Available at www.wipo.int/export/sites/www/ipstats/en/statistics/patents/pdf/wipo_ipc_technology.pdf.

Schumpeter, J. A. (1912) *Theorie der wirtschaftlichen Entwicklung.* Berlin: Duncker and Humblodt.

Schumpeter, J. A. (1943) *Capitalism, Socialism and Democracy.* New York: Allen and Unwin.

Singer, H. W. (1950) The distribution of gains between investing and borrowing countries. *The American Economic Review* 40(2): 473–485.

Smith, K. (2005) Measuring innovation. In J. Fagerberg, D. Mowery and R. R. Nelson (eds), *The Oxford Handbook of Innovation*, 148–178. Oxford: Oxford University Press.

Soete, L. L. G. (1987) The impact of technological innovation on international trade patterns: the evidence reconsidered. *Research Policy* 16: 101–128.

Sunkel, O. and Girvan, C. (1973) Transnational capitalism and national disintegration in Latin America. *Social and Economic Studies* 22(1): 132–176.

Trajtenberg, M. (1990) A penny for your quotes: patent citations and the value of innovations. *The Rand Journal of Economics* 21(1): 172–187.

Wallerstein, I. (2011) *The Modern World-System I: Capitalist Agriculture and the Origins of the European World-Economy in the Sixteenth Century.* Berkeley, CA: University of California Press.

13 Turkish–German innovation networks in the European research landscape

Irene Peschkov, Andreas Pyka and Barbara Heller-Schuh

Introduction

Innovation networks serve primarily as channels for knowledge creation and diffusion. Innovation networks offer access to scarce resources, create learning opportunities and are considered as means to share R&D costs as well as to cope with technological uncertainty. They are of particular importance for knowledge-intensive industries where the involved clients play a critical role in e.g. fast and new knowledge creation (Buchmann and Pyka 2011; Pyka 2002). In addition, besides their role in creating learning opportunities and their impact on knowledge transfer, innovation networks are also important for the development and integration of economies. As Saxenian (2006) has shown, Silicon Valley has significantly benefited from "transnational or commuting entrepreneurs" which transferred competences from the core to peripheral regions.[1] Thereby special innovation networks are created where knowledge is diffused that emerges due to local and international linkages of those transnational or commuting entrepreneurs.

Similar opportunities are offered in Europe by the Turkish-German-migration history where both economies may benefit from their long-lasting relation and brain circulation in innovation networks spanning actors from both countries (Hartmann *et al.* 2012). That is, Turkish commuting entrepreneurs may help their home country to overcome typical disadvantages[2] of latecomer economies by their experience and ties to leading high-tech regions. As a side effect, the Turkish–German innovation networks might support the European integration process. Simultaneously, like in the Silicon Valley case, the national frontiers bridging innovation networks transfer new knowledge into German innovation networks and diffuse market information of the highly dynamic Turkish economy.

An interesting case are European research networks created by the Framework Programmes (FPs) where since 1999 also Turkish actors are eligible to participate. A better understanding of these research networks in the European Research Area and in particular the specific relations between Turkish and German actors provides insights into the patterns of technology and knowledge transfer between Turkey and Germany. This in turn enables appropriate policy designs in order to foster knowledge flows and thus enhance technological integration, development and mutual understanding.

In order to improve the understanding of these research networks, this paper deals with the following research questions and will thus contribute to the scarce information available on Turkish-German research networks of the EU FPs and their knowledge diffusion. In essence, it is of utmost interest to reveal whether there are specific patterns of how Turkish actors find access to European research networks. Do German actors and the long-lasting Turkish–German relations play a specific role? Thereby it is assumed that Turkey connects with the most important actors in the EU (e.g. the German Fraunhofer Society)[3] according to the preferential attachment phenomenon. Furthermore, also the intensity of connections between Turkish and other actors (in particular German ones) is of interest.

In the present paper, research networks of the EU FPs are examined that are established by joint participation of organizations in EU funded research projects in which at least one Turkish organization participated in FP5, FP6 and FP7. The empirical analysis is restricted to knowledge-intensive technology fields such as Information and Communication Technologies (ICT), Biotechnology and Nanoscience, which stimulate collaborative innovation (Pyka and Saviotti 2005).

The remaining part of this chapter is structured as follows. First, we introduce the methodological approach and provide the empirical setting before the descriptive features of the networks are examined in more detail. Focus is placed on exploratory social network analysis in the following section, revealing structural and dynamic features of research networks with Turkish participation as well as the role and position of network members, putting emphasis on key German cooperation partners. Finally, we summarize key results and draw conclusions, providing suggestions for future research.

Methodological approach and empirical setting

Before introducing and analysing the network data, we introduce the formal and theoretical concepts, as well as the empirical setting. For this purpose, we begin with the theoretical concepts of social network analysis, before moving on introducing the data source implemented in this work, and finally presenting descriptive results of the examined network data.

Theoretical concepts of social network analysis

Network formation

Networks are formed and expanded by joint participation of organizations in research projects funded within the FPs. Knowledge is diffused between organizations, and new knowledge can jointly be discovered. The single sub-networks are linked via participation of organizations in *different* projects forming a FP network. The bipartite graphs with the two sets of vertices, organizations and projects, are drawn. These graphs are transformed to unipartite graphs where organizations are linked by undirected ties representing the joint participation of organizations in research projects.

The following paragraphs introduce important definitions of network metrics:

SIZE, DENSITY AND DEGREE OF ACTORS

Network size is determined by the number of vertices and ties which also determine the degree of connectivity of the network. Network size is important for the composition of social relations as it determines actor's resources for building connections within the network (Izquierdo and Hanneman 2006).

The ratio of all present ties expressed as a proportion of all possible ties describes the *density* of a network. It may serve as an estimation about the intensity of knowledge flows among actors (Jansen 2003).

The *degree of a node* represents the total number of ties linked to a vertex (total number of adjacent vertices) and measures the degree of interconnectedness of an actor (Jansen 2003; Izquierdo and Hanneman 2006).

The above introduced properties deal primarily with actors' immediate connections, but social neighbours of an actor may be as well of interest, as they can be useful in certain environments.

SOCIAL DISTANCE AND RELATED CONCEPTS

Pairs of vertices are reachable via *paths* (i.e. a sequence of links connecting two vertices). Paths are used to determine the distance between nodes (Jansen 2003; Izquierdo and Hanneman 2006). The *geodesic distance* captures the shortest path between two vertices in the network. The average geodesic distance in a connected graph is defined as the *average* (or *characteristic) path length*. The characteristic path length indicates a network's interconnectedness, i.e. its efficiency in knowledge diffusion. Thus low values of path length imply that information or knowledge is diffused efficiently as only a few intermediaries have to be surpassed (Barabási *et al.* 2002; Wasserman and Faust 1994). The graph *diameter* is defined as the largest geodesic distance between any two vertices in a connected network.[4]

LOCAL STRUCTURES IN NETWORKS

The *clustering coefficient* assesses the degree to which vertices in a graph tend to group together (i.e. the extent to which the friends of my friends are also my friends). Formally, the clustering coefficient of a vertex is determined by the ratio of present links that connect the neighbours of a vertex to each other, to all possible links among these vertices. The clustering coefficient of the network is determined by the mean clustering coefficient of all vertices. It is a measure of local density of a network denoting how close organizations are through direct and indirect ties (Watts and Strogatz 1998; Bornholdt *et al.* 2003; Heller-Schuh *et al.* 2011).

CENTRALITY AND POWER

One important property of a vertex is its position in the network. Vertex centrality allows for the identification and ranking of vertices according to their importance. Central actors possess extensive relations to other actors; they are assumed to have greater access and control over resources and are thus associated with greater innovative activity (Wasserman and Faust 1994; Jansen 2003; Izquierdo and Hanneman 2006). In the following, three different centrality measures are presented which can be normalized to guarantee comparability across networks of different sizes.

1   *Degree centrality* is a measure of prominence and power. It considers direct links of a vertex. Vertices with a high number of links are integrated stronger within a network and are therefore assumed to have many advantages: they are highly visible by others, can easily receive or diffuse information, or they may have better access to more resources.[5]
2   *Closeness centrality* takes into account the indirect ties of an actor (i.e. its reachability). It is defined as the inverse of the mean geodesic distance from one vertex to every other vertex (e.g. vertices having short distances from any other can obtain or spread new information more efficiently than more distant vertices). Higher closeness centrality scores indicate short distances. In the case of an only weak connected network, closeness centrality cannot be calculated since the distance between two disconnected vertices is infinite (Jansen 2003; Wasserman and Faust 1994; Krogmann *et al.* 2011).
3   *Betweenness centrality* examines the role of actors according to their importance as an intermediary within the network. Hence it may be interpreted as a measure of control of information flow, as actors lying on many shortest paths between actors, i.e. having high betweenness centrality, may act as gatekeepers without the necessity to maintain many direct ties. Hence actors with high betweenness centrality are important for the diffusion of information. As a consequence, information flows in networks with high scores of betweenness centrality are more likely to be disrupted through strategic behaviour of one of the gatekeepers (Jansen 2003; Izquierdo and Hanneman 2006; Wasserman and Faust 1994).

Network centralization

Degree centralization of a network measures the variation in the degree of vertices as a proportion of the maximal possible degree variation of a network of the same size. Hence, it reflects the relative dominance of single actors in the network (Jansen 2003; de Nooy *et al.* 2005).

Besides the discussed structural properties, real-world networks show certain common characteristics that also hold for networks of knowledge-intensive technology fields.

NETWORK CHARACTERISTICS

Small-world

Large real-world networks may show surprisingly short average geodesics, which can be attributed to the origin of the small-world phenomenon. A short average path length allows each vertex to reach another one in a few "steps" only. Networks that show small-world characteristics together with a high clustering coefficient are called *small-world networks* (Watts and Strogatz 1998). Small-worlds perform well in knowledge creation and diffusion, hence, contributing to the overall efficiency of a network (Bornholdt *et al.* 2003; Roediger-Schluga and Barber 2006).

Scale-free networks

Classical random networks assume complete randomness with respect to the establishment of new links. That is, vertices are linked to each other independent of the number of ties they already have, whereby the degree distribution follows a Poisson law. However, many large real-world networks have a highly skewed degree distribution (i.e. they follow a power-law and are referred to as *scale-free* networks). A high skewness indicates that the majority of vertices have only a small number of direct connections and only a few vertices possess many ties. This leads to the assumption that actors act according to different preferences for vertices, and thereby suggests that the probability is higher that a new vertex will link to another vertex which already has a high number of links. Thus, vertices with a high number of links get new connections at a higher rate which is also known as the *preferential attachment* phenomenon. Preferential attachment can explain the existence of a few actors having a high degree (hubs) and a large number of actors having a low degree (Barabási *et al.* 2002; Bornholdt *et al.* 2003). The power-law degree distribution is a property that has been identified in a wide range of different networks (e.g. the Internet, world wide web and research collaborations based on co-authorship of papers) and holds as well for knowledge-intensive industry networks as shown by Barabási and Albert (1999).

After the discussion of the theoretical background of the social network analysis, the next section is devoted to introduce the data analysed in this work.

Data source and terminology

Our analysis focusses on joint research projects with the European FPs in different technology fields that were executed during three different time periods (FP5: 1992–2002), (FP6: 2002–2006), (first half of FP7: 2007–2010.03). The analysis is restricted to knowledge-intensive technology fields: Information and communication technologies (ICT), Biotechnology (Biotech) and Nanoscience (Nano).

The data source that has been implemented in this analysis is the latest version of the EUPRO database provided by the Austrian Institute of Technology (AIT). The EUPRO database contains comprehensive information on research projects funded by the EU FPs and its participating organizations.[6] EUPRO was developed by the AIT and is based on data of the CORDIS projects database. The EUPRO version 7.1.1 used in this analysis covers all projects from FP1 to FP7 until March 2010, which corresponds to the latest update of the database, hence, only the first half of the FP7 period is covered.[7] CORDIS is a Community Research and Development Information Service of the European Union to support cooperation in European research and innovation projects. It contains information on all EU funded FP projects and project participants.[8]

For the present purpose of analysis, data from the EUPRO database was extracted that consists of joint research projects in which at least one Turkish organization participates. Data of the specific technology fields is thereby filtered as follows:

• ICT: All projects are selected of the programmes IST (in FP5 and FP6) and ICT (in FP7).
• Biotech: All projects in FP5 to FP7 are selected containing "biotech" in their subject index.
• Nano: In FP6 and FP7 all projects are selected of the programmes "NMP" (in FP6) and "Nanoscience and Nanotechnology" (in FP7).[9] In FP5 data was filtered containing "nano" in the field "other indexes". Thereby three projects were found in FP5, but with no Turkish participation.

Terminology

The terminologies about different networks in the analysed time frames are defined as follows: The *total* network in a specific Framework Programme *x* and the technology field *y* is specified as FPx-y. If it is referred to a network *with Turkish participation* (TUR) the respective terminology is then FPx-y TUR. The technology field (sector) ICT is consequently denoted and referred to here as:

• FPx-ICT: Total network of the ICT sector in FPx, with x = 5, 6, 7.
• FPx-ICT TUR: ICT network with Turkish participation in FP5, with x = 5, 6, 7.

Further, total networks of the technology fields Biotech and Nano are expressed as FPx-Biotech and FPx-Nano, respectively. Their counterparts with Turkish participation are defined as FPx-Biotech TUR and FPx-Nano TUR. Projects implemented in the respective technology field (ICT, Biotech or Nano) are referred to as "ICT projects", "Biotech projects" or "Nano projects". Projects containing Turkish participants are referred to as "ICT projects with Turkish participants", and respectively for the other two technology fields.

Descriptive features of the examined networks

A first overview of projects and organizations in the different technology fields and FPs is presented in Table 13.1 including the share of Turkish participation. This will provide insights on the frequency of Turkish participation in FP projects.

Table 13.1 Overview of projects (with and without Turkish participation) and organizations in the technology fields ICT, Biotech and Nano in FP5–FP7.

Technology-field	FPx	Projects			Organizations		
		Total	TUR	Share	Total	TUR	Share
IST	FP5	2,520	18	0.7%	7,154	14	0.2%
IST	FP6	1,224	56	4.6%	4,741	35	0.7%
ICT	FP7	686	22	3.2%	2,557	12	0.5%
Sum ICT		4,430	96	2.2%	11,254*	44*	0.4%
Biotech	FP5	638	1	0.2%	1,263	1	0.1%
Biotech	FP6	717	38	5.3%	2,954	33	1.1%
Biotech	FP7	535	10	1.9%	1,355	11	0.8%
Sum Biotech		1,890	49	2.6%	5,572*	45*	0.8%
Nano	FP5	3	–	–	n.s.	–	–
Nano	FP6	414	26	6.3%	2,589	24	0.9%
Nano	FP7	239	18	7.5%	1,739	16	0.9%
Sum Nano		653	44	6.7%	4,328*	40*	0.9%

Note: FP: Framework Program; TUR: 'with Turkish participation' (regarding projects) or Turkish (organizations); n.s.: not specified. *Total number of organizations over all FPs equals not to the sum of organizations over the single FPs as some organizations may participate in projects that go over several FPs. Data for FP7 available until March 2010.
Source: Own illustration according to data of EUPRO/AIT.

According to the data in Table 13.1, ICT is the largest technology field with 4,430 projects (implemented from FP5 to FP7) followed by Biotech and Nano comprising 1,890 and 653 projects, respectively. It has to be noted that the number of projects in FP7 is lower compared to FP6 in all technology fields, which is due to the not fully covered time period of FP7 in the present data source as mentioned above. Moreover, FP6 experienced a significant increase in the average project size which has to be attributed to new policy instruments – Integrated Projects (IP) and Networks of Excellence (NoE) – implemented in FP6 intending to cope with fragmentation of research capabilities and establish the critical mass of expertise and resources. In addition, average funding per project increased in FP6 (Heller-Schuh *et al.* 2011).

It is obvious that Turkey accounts for a relatively small share in EU funded FP projects (FP5-FP7) in all examined technology fields. Turkey's relatively small participation in European research projects in FP5 may find one reason in the funding and participation regulations of the EU FPs. Turkey was allowed to participate in EU FPs only in the last two years of FP5 (i.e. since it has been officially recognized as a candidate country of the EU in 1999). In addition, it has had to finance research projects on its own. This is confirmed considering the significant increase of its participation share in FP6 where Turkey could finally benefit from the funding mechanism of the EU FPs. Finally, Turkey's exceptionally high participation share in Nano projects (6.7%) requires further investigations.

Following the clarification of the theoretical background, rationales and the scope of this work, it is now possible to examine research networks within FP5, FP6 and FP7 due to collaborations in EU funded research projects in which at least one Turkish organization participated, focusing on the technology fields ICT, Biotechnology and Nanoscience.

Empirical evidence

The main purpose of this section is to provide insights into research networks that are established by joint participation of organizations in EU funded research projects in which at least one Turkish organization also participated. The analysis is based on methods used in social network analysis, applying the network analysis and visualization program Pajek (de Nooy *et al.* 2005).

Structural properties of the FPx-y TUR networks

This section examines structural properties of ICT,[10] Biotech and Nano networks (i.e. FP*x-y* TUR networks) in FP5, FP6 and FP7 that were generated due to collaborations in EU funded research projects in which at least one Turkish organization participated. The structural properties of FP*x-y* TUR networks are summarized in Table 13.2.

Table 13.2 Structural properties of FPx–y TUR networks.

Structural properties	ICT			Biotech			Nano		
	FP5	*FP6*	*FP7*	*FP5*	*FP6*	*FP7*	*FP5*	*FP6*	*FP7*
No. of vertices N	274	679	267	6	587	128		340	252
No. of edges	7,941	15,172	3,718	15	16,977	1,043		4,601	2,572
M with line value >1	11	1664	51	–	374	37		125	53
No. of components	4	2	2	1	3	2		1	5
N for largest component	254	678	182	6	582	96		340	173
Share of total N (%)	92.7	99.9	68.2	100.0	99.1	75		100	68.7
Diameter of largest component	5	4	4	1	5	4		5	5
Average path length of largest comp.	1.0	2.4	2.1	1.0	2.5	2.2		2.5	2.7
Density	0.21	0.07	0.10	1.00	0.10	0.13		0.08	0.08
Mean degree	58.0	44.7	27.9	5	57.8	16.3		27.1	20.4
Mean clustering coefficient	0.98	0.87	0.94	1.0	0.93	0.95		0.92	0.94
Degree centralization	0.39	0.38	0.29	0	0.29	0.17		0.28	0.16

Source: Own illustration according to data of EUPRO/AIT.

Information and communication technologies

Information and communication technology (ICT) networks with Turkish participation in FP5-FP7 are illustrated graphically in Figures 13.1–3 where Turkish and German organizations are illustrated in different shades of grey, respectively. All other countries are represented as white nodes. The node size reflects the degree centrality of actors.

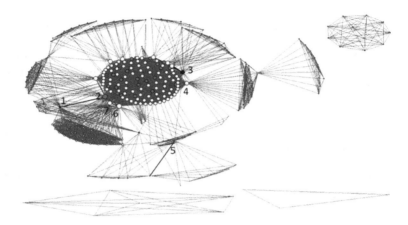

Figure 13.1 ICT network with Turkish participation in FP5.

Notes: 1 = TUBITAK; 2 = Helmholtz Association; 3 = Orta Dogu – Middle East Technical University; 4 = Swiss Federal Institute of Technology; 5 = Sabanci University; 6 = Bulgarian Academy of Sciences; 7 = Hungarian Academy of Sciences.
Source: EUPRO/AIT.

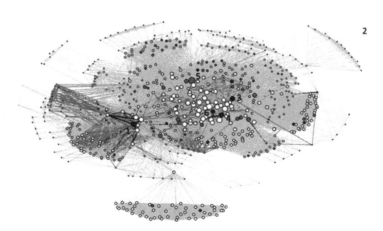

Figure 13.2 ICT network with Turkish participation in FP6.

Notes: 1 = TUBITAK; 2 = Technical University of Istanbul; 3 = Orta Dogu – Middle East Technical University; 4 = Bilkent University; 5 = Fraunhofer Society; 6 = Koc University.
Source: EUPRO/AIT.

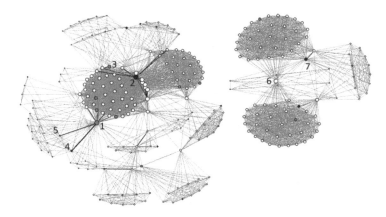

Figure 13.3 ICT network with Turkish participation in FP7.

Notes: 1 = Fraunhofer Society; 2 = Bilkent University; 3 = Berlin University of Technology; 4 = Koc University; 5 = Orta Dogu – Middle East Technical University; 6 = Polish Academy of Sciences; 7 = TUBITAK.

Source: EUPRO/AIT.

The FP5-ICT TUR network consists of one giant component containing 93 per cent of all vertices. A majority of actors (43%) is interconnected by participation in one large project EURON[11] (in the center) which is crucial for the determination of FP5-ICT TUR network characteristics; all other projects are relatively smaller.

FP6-ICT TUR can be described by many projects that are of smaller size compared to FP5-ICT TUR. Additionally, FP6-ICT TUR shows significantly many *repetitive* partners (11%) that participate in FP6 in more than one project together compared to the other two networks (i.e. edges with line value >1).

FP7-ICT TUR seems to be similar to FP5-ICT TUR showing several larger, rather separated projects instead of one very large one. Nevertheless, as the period of FP7 is not represented completely (only until March 2010) it is possible that it develops similar to FP6-ICT TUR by the end of FP7 when single organizations take part in projects of both components.

Biotechnology

FP6–FP7 Biotech TUR networks are illustrated graphically in Figures 13.4–5.

FP6-Biotech TUR consists of one giant component containing 99 per cent of all vertices. FP6-Biotech TUR can be described by one large project (European Leukemianet)[12] that comprises 25 per cent of all organizations and some relatively smaller ones. Moreover, not all central actors are located in the center of the network. For example, TUBITAK, the Scientific and Technical Research Council of Turkey in the lower left part of the network is an important actor in terms of betweenness centrality.

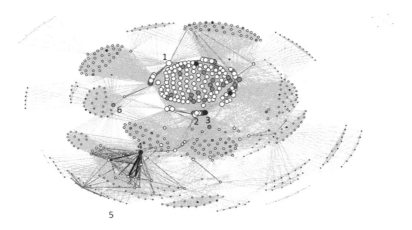

Figure 13.4 Biotech network with Turkish participation in FP6.

Notes: 1 = Karolinska Institute, Sweden; 2 = University of Helsinki; 3 = University of Ankara; 4 = TUBITAK; 5 = Orta Dogu – Middle East Technical University; 6 = Helmholtz Association.
Source: EUPRO/AIT.

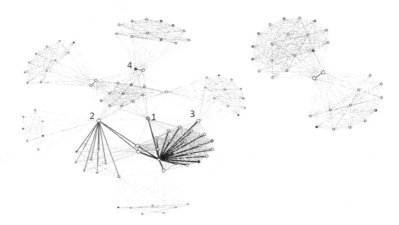

Figure 13.5 Biotech network with Turkish participation in FP7.

Notes: 1 = Leibniz Association; 2 = INRA – French National Institute for Agricultural Research; 3 = ISS – Italian Superior Health Institute; 4 = Sabanci University.
Source: EUPRO/AIT.

FP7-Biotech TUR is described by several relatively small, rather separated projects compared to FP6-Biotech TUR.[13]

Organizations in FPx Biotech TUR networks participate with the same partners in fewer projects, hence there are only few edges with line value >1. Finally, it is possible that FP7-Biotech TUR develops similar to FP6-Biotech

TUR by the end of FP7 if single organizations take part in projects of both components connecting them to a single one.

Nanoscience

FP6- and FP7 Nano TUR networks are illustrated graphically in Figures 13.6–7.

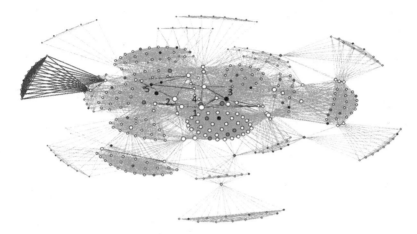

Figure 13.6 Nano network with Turkish participation in FP6.
Notes: 1 = VTT – Technical Research Centre of Finland; 2 = QUB – Queen´s University of Belfast; 3 = Orta Dogu – Middle East Technical University; 4 = Fraunhofer Society; 5 = Bilkent University.
Source: EUPRO/AIT.

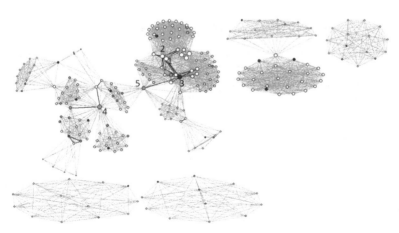

Figure 13.7 Nano network with Turkish participation in FP7.
Notes: 1 = Research Council of Norway; 2 = Tekes – Finish National Technology Agency; 3 = TUBITAK; 4 = Fraunhofer Society; 5 = Helmholtz Association.
Source: EUPRO/AIT.

First of all it is important to mention that Turkey did not participate in Nano-science projects in FP5. Further, network FP6-Nano TUR can be described by several relatively small projects with one project (Virtual Intelligent Forging – CA) which is slightly larger. Network FP7-Nano TUR is highly fragmented as it comprises five components implying a rather poor interconnectedness of organizations. Moreover, this network consists of several relatively small, rather separated projects. Additionally, FP7-Nano TUR shows some very central actors in terms of high betweenness centrality that connect organizations of different separated projects.

In fact, most structural properties in FP6- and FP7-Nano TUR networks are very similar. According to Table 2 organizations collaborate with the same partners in a few projects. That is, edges with line value >1 are marginal in both networks. Finally as already stated above, the separated components of FP7-Nano TUR may still get connected by the end of FP7 when organizations participate in projects of different components connecting them to one or more larger components.

Summarizing, as all examined networks exhibit specific properties such as high clustering coefficients and short average path lengths, they can be characterized as small-world networks according to the definition of Watts and Strogatz (1998). This implies that knowledge can diffuse rapidly and widely in the network and thus enhance local knowledge creation. Furthermore, scale-free properties in FPx-y TUR networks cannot be recognized as none of the networks shows a power-law degree distribution.[14] One reason may lie in the relative small size of the examined networks or the fact that only networks of projects with Turkish participants are examined whereby organizations may as well participate in other projects or cooperate with other partners.

Centrality and power of actors in FPx-y TUR networks

This section is devoted to identifying central players in FPx-y TUR networks considering measures of centrality (degree, closeness and betweenness) in FP5–FP7. Degree centrality is calculated for both kinds of networks: networks *with Turkish* participation FPx-y TUR and for the *total* FPx-y networks.[15]

Information and communication technologies

It is noticeable that most cooperation partners of Turkey in FPx-ICT TUR networks are central as well as important actors (in terms of high degree centrality) in the total ICT networks (FPx-ICT) implying that they may provide Turkish organizations with many other (indirect) contacts.[16] The most important organizations (with respect to a high degree centrality) in ICT TUR research networks are the BAS – Bulgarian Academy of Sciences (FP5-ICT TUR), the German Fraunhofer Society (FP6-ICT TUR) and the Turkish Bilkent University (FP7-ICT TUR) whereby the Fraunhofer Society is also central positioned (rank 1)[17] in the *total* FP6- and FP7-ICT networks. It is possible that BAS occurs more often as a partner of Turkish organizations due to its geographical proximity to Turkey and has therefore a higher degree centrality value.

Analysing Turkish actors in ICT projects (FPx-ICT TUR), three central Turkish actors are identified in the top 10 FPx-ICT TUR networks. Those are the METU – Middle East Technical University (FP5-ICT TUR), TUBITAK – the Scientific and Technical Research Council of Turkey (FP6-ICT TUR) and the Bilkent University where the latter is most central positioned in FP7-ICT TUR. Moreover, TUBITAK took part in 25 per cent (14 projects) of all ICT projects in FP6-ICT TUR achieving the largest participation share next to the Fraunhofer Society.[18] Moreover, it turns out that none of the Turkish actors are centrally positioned in the total ICT networks (FPx-ICT).

Biotechnology

In FP5-Biotech TUR all organizations have equal centrality values as they participate in one project and are all interconnected. Further, none of the project participants represents a central actor in the total Biotechnology network (FP5-Biotech). In comparison, FP6- and FP7-Biotech TUR show mainly central and important organizations that are as well of high importance with respect to a high degree centrality in the respective total Biotech networks (FP6- and FP7-Biotech).[19] Those are the Finnish University of Helsinki (rank 8)[20] and the German Leibniz Association (rank 14) in FP6- and FP7-Biotech TUR respectively. In general, the same organizations are identified as most central actors in the three different centrality measures (degree, closeness, betweenness) in FP5-, FP6- and FP7-Biotech TUR networks. The only (non-Turkish) outlier is the German Helmholtz Association (HHG) having a high betweenness centrality in FP6-Biotech TUR, but it is not centrally positioned with respect to the other two centrality measures.

Three central Turkish organizations are identified: MERKAT (FP5-Biotech TUR), the University of Ankara (FP6-Biotech TUR) and the Sabanci University (FP7-Biotech TUR). In addition, TUBITAK – the Scientific and Technical Research Council of Turkey is identified as a very central actor in terms of a high betweenness centrality in FP6-Biotech TUR.

Nanoscience

Most centrally positioned in FP6- and FP7-Nano TUR are the Technical Research Centre of Finland (VTT) (rank 7)[21] and the Research Council of Norway, respectively.[22] But, whereas most actors in FP6-Nano TUR (degree centrality) are also centrally positioned in the total FP6-Nano network, in FP7-Nano TUR only one single actor (Fraunhofer Society) is identified that constitutes simultaneously a central organization in the total FP7-Nano network. Moreover, the German Helmholtz Association (HHG) and the Fraunhofer Society are identified as particular central actors with respect to a high betweenness centrality in FP7-Nano TUR denoting that they are relatively more important as intermediaries in this network.

Examining Turkish actors, the Turkish Middle East Technical University (METU) and the Scientific and Technical Research Council of Turkey (TUBITAK) are identified in FP6- and FP7-Nano TUR, respectively. However, both organizations are not recognized as important players (in terms of high degree centrality) in the total FPx-Nano networks. METU participated in 19 per cent and 11 per cent, TUBITAK took part in 8 per cent and 22 per cent of all Nanoscience projects with Turkish participation in FP6 and FP7, respectively.

Finally, all centrality measures show a broad variety of organizations of different countries where research organizations and universities dominate.

Following the identification of central actors in FPx-y TUR networks, it is important to examine the connections to reliable partners in more detail as they may be used to exploit and deepen existing knowledge. Thereby emphasis is put on Turkey's key German cooperation partners.

Key German actors in FPx-y networks with Turkish participation

The final section of FPx-y TUR network analysis intends to provide evidence whether Turkey's key German cooperation partners are as well of particular importance in FPx-y networks and may therefore support Turkey's integration in ICT, Biotechnology and Nanoscience networks on the European level. A first overview considers measures of participation to provide an impression of Europe's (EU27 and Turkey) performance in research projects with Turkish participation in FPx-y TUR networks (Figure 13.8).[23]

German organizations had the highest involvement in research projects with Turkish participation in the ICT, Biotech and Nano sector from FP5 to FP7. However, the results may be a result of Germany's generally strong presence in European research projects. Unfortunately, the participation share of Germany in ICT-, Biotech- and Nano TUR projects compared to the overall participation share of Germany in the respective total networks cannot be validated, since for this study, detailed data is only provided for projects with Turkish participants in ICT, Biotech and Nano. Nevertheless, as Germany is of particular interest in this network analysis it is examined in more detail.

It becomes particularly apparent that Germany participated in the majority of ICT, Biotech and Nano research projects in the examined FPx-y TUR networks (with an increasing trend) in the following.

Information and communication technologies

Germany has the highest share (12%) in terms of participating organizations in FPx-ICT TUR networks, closely followed by Italy (10%) and France (9%). Thereby Germany participated in 50, 89 and 95 per cent of all ICT projects in the networks FP5-, FP6- and FP7-ICT TUR, respectively.[24] Appendix E illustrates these figures graphically considering exclusively German and Turkish cooperation partners.

Analysing the most important actors (in terms of a high degree centrality) in the FPx-ICT TUR networks (Appendix B) that are also centrally positioned in the

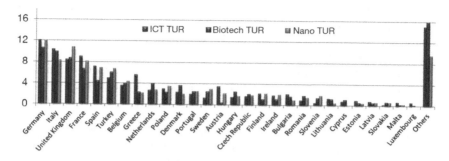

Figure 13.8 Share of Turkey's cooperation partners in ICT, Biotech and nano TUR
networks in FP5–FP7.

Source: Own illustration using data of EUPRO/AIT.

total FPx-ICT networks (Appendix D), only three organizations could be
identified in FPx-ICT TUR networks: namely the Helmholtz Association (in FP5-
and FP6-ICT TUR), the Fraunhofer Society (in FP6- and FP7-ICT TUR) and the
Berlin University of Technology (FP7-ICT TUR).[25] Most other central players in
the FPx-ICT TUR networks are not centrally positioned (in terms of a high degree
centrality) in the total FPx-ICT networks. This in turn implies that Turkey can
strengthen its position in the ICT sector by increasing its collaborations with
rather central German actors of the total FPx-ICT networks (e.g. Alcatel-Lucent
in FP7-ICT).

In conclusion, the Helmholtz Association and the Fraunhofer Society are
important with respect to their high degree centrality in FPx-ICT TUR and total
FPx-ICT networks, but also in terms of their participation rate in ICT projects in
FP5- to FP7-ICT TUR networks. Accordingly, Helmholtz and Fraunhofer
participated in 8 per cent (8 projects) and 30 per cent (29 projects) of all ICT
projects with Turkish participation, respectively, that were implemented in the
FPs 5-7. Within these research organizations, Helmholtz German Aerospace
Center (DLR) and the Fraunhofer Institute for Applied Solid State Physics (IAF)
are partners in the majority of the examined ICT projects in FPx-ICT TUR
networks.[26]

Biotechnology

Also in the Biotechnology sector Germany has the highest share (11%) of participating organizations in FP5- to FP7-Biotech TUR networks, closely followed by
Italy (10%) and the United Kingdom (9%). Hereby, Germany took part in 50 per
cent and 70 per cent of Biotechnology projects with Turkish participation in FP6
and FP7, respectively.[27] German organizations accounted thereby for 10 per cent
(61 organizations) and 12 per cent (16 organizations) in FP6- and FP7-Biotech
TUR. Appendix E illustrates these figures graphically considering exclusively
German and Turkish cooperation partners.

The most central German organizations in FPx-Biotech TUR (Appendix B) are also central positioned in the total FPx-Biotech networks (Appendix D), the Charite – University of Berlin and the Technical University of Munich in FP6-Biotech and the Leibniz Association with the Bonn University in FP7-Biotech. The results show that most central German cooperation partners of Turkey in FPx-Biotech TUR networks are rather less important (with respect to a high degree centrality) in the total FPx-Biotech networks. Most other central German actors of the total FPx-Biotech networks are less important in the FPx-Biotech TUR networks. This implies that Turkey can improve its position in the Biotechnology sector by strengthening its cooperation with those central German actors in the overall FPx-Biotech networks such as the Helmholtz Association. Moreover, Turkey can further enhance its position by cooperating with the Fraunhofer Society that is a central actor in the FPx-Biotech networks, with whom it did not yet collaborate.

In conclusion, Turkey seems to be strongly connected to the Leibniz Association which is a central actor in both, the FPx-Biotech TUR and the total FPx-Biotech networks. Another important German actor is the Helmholtz Association which accounted for the largest share of German organizations in Biotech projects in FPx-Biotech TUR networks although it is not central positioned there. Helmholtz and Leibniz participated in 12 per cent (6 projects) and 6 per cent (3 projects) of all Biotech projects with Turkish participation in FP6- and FP7-Biotech TUR networks.[28]

Nanoscience

As in the other two technology fields, German organizations have the highest share (12%) in FPx-Nano TUR networks, closely followed by the United Kingdom (11%), Italy (8%) and France (8%). Germany participated in almost every Nano project (77% and 89%) in which Turkey took part in FP6 and FP7 as well.[29] Appendix E illustrates these figures graphically considering exclusively German and Turkish cooperation partners.

Moreover, examining most central German actors (degree centrality) in FP6- and FP7-Nano TUR networks (Appendix B), that are also centrally positioned in the respective total FPx-Nano networks (Appendix D) shows that Turkey is already cooperating with more or less important German actors of the total Nano network in FP6, but not anymore in FP7). This implies that Turkey can improve its position in the Nanoscience sector by strengthening its cooperation with more central German actors of the FP7-Nanoscience network such as such as for instance the Dresden University of Technology or the Karlsruhe Institute of Technology – KIT. Finally, potential German cooperation partners for Turkey in the future are for instance the BASF AG or the Bayer AG as they constitute central actors in FPx-Biotech networks with whom Turkey did not yet collaborate in Nanos projects.

As stated above Fraunhofer and Helmholtz are the most important partners of Turkey (in terms of degree centrality) in FPx-Nano TUR and in the total

FPx-Nanoscience networks. Together they participated in 11 per cent (5 projects) and 18 per cent (8 projects) of all Nanoscience projects with Turkish participation in the FP6- and FP7-Nano TUR networks.[30]

Conclusions

The analysis of ICT, Biotech and Nano research networks with Turkish participation in FP5 to FP7 by social network analysis methods shows some interesting facts about the networks established under the EU FPs. As has been shown, Turkey accounts for a relatively small share in EU funded FP projects (FP5–FP7) in all examined technology fields. However, its participation share has been increasing over time since it was officially recognized as a candidate country of the EU in 1999 and could therefore gradually participate in European research programmes.

The empirical examination of structural properties of the examined networks reveals that all networks show a range of similarities in the three technology fields in each FP. All networks show very high clustering coefficients and short average path lengths and can thus be characterized as small-world networks implying fast knowledge diffusion and enhanced knowledge creation. Further, there is no clear sign of scale-free properties of the networks as a power-law degree distribution could not be assessed in any network. The similarities in the outcomes indicate that the networks (and their structure) seem to be significantly affected (and formed) by their participating organizations and are not specific to a technology field.

The identified central actors in all networks are primarily research organizations and universities (with respect to their participation rate and high degree centrality). German organizations have the highest share in terms of participating organizations in almost all examined ICT, Biotech and Nano networks with Turkish participation in FP5 to FP7. Analysing Turkey's key *German* collaboration partners (with respect to a high degree centrality) it turns out that only a few are centrally positioned in total ICT, Biotech and Nano networks. This implies that Turkey can improve its position in all three examined technology fields by strengthening its cooperation with rather central German actors of those total networks, as well with those with whom it did not collaborate yet.

The results support the assumption that German actors play a specific role in most examined research networks with Turkish participation in FP5 to FP7. Established connections to key German actors might foster Turkey's integration in research networks of the examined technology fields on the European level, but there is also potential to enhance and expand the connections to German actors (with regards to central positioned German actors in the total networks).

The present results suggest that further research is required to gain in-depth knowledge about the emergence of the relationships between Turkish and German actors. In particular, case studies of the implemented research projects or interviews with its participants could be considered in order to examine whether the Turkish–German-migration history is of particular importance for the identified collaborations and whether it triggered network formation. Furthermore, in addition to the analysis of project participation, results from the identified projects, such as patents or co-publications could be examined with respect to their Turkish and German inventors or authors. This allows for the analysis of the roles of commuting entrepreneurs and researchers and their performance in the Turkish-German research networks, and provides deeper insights into the patterns of technology and knowledge transfer between Turkey and Germany.

Appendix A Degree distribution of FPx-y TUR networks

All examined networks with Turkish participation (ICT, Biotech and Nano) do not show scale-free properties as none of the networks shows a power-law degree distribution. Figure 13A.1 illustrates the degree distribution for the giant components of ICT TUR networks developed in FP5, FP6 and FP7. Figure 13A.2 shows the degree distribution for the giant components of Biotech TUR networks developed in FP6 and FP7. Figure 13A.3 illustrates the degree distribution for the giant components of Nano TUR networks developed in FP6 and FP7.

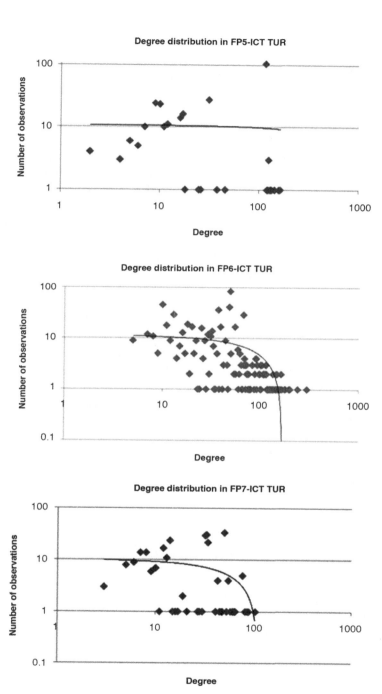

Figure 13A.1 Degree distribution of FPx-ICT TUR networks in FP5 to FP7.

Source: Own illustration using data of EUPRO/AIT.

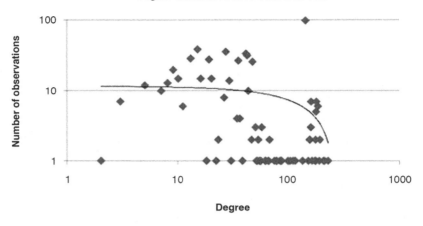

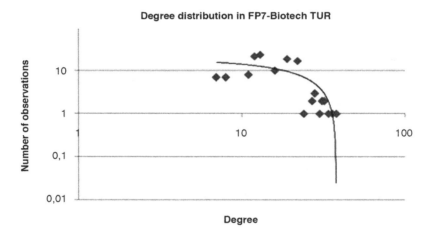

Figure 13A.2 Degree distribution of FPx-Biotech TUR networks in FP6 and FP7.
Source: Own illustration using data of EUPRO/AIT.

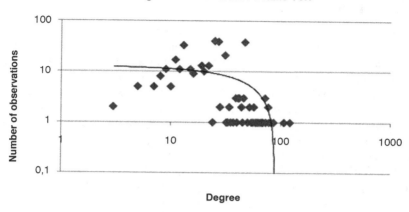

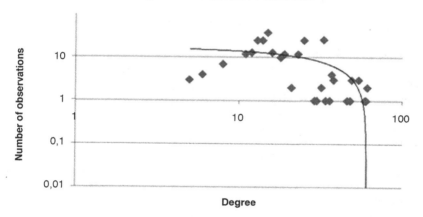

Figure 13A.3 Degree distribution of FPx-Nano TUR networks in FP6 and FP7.
Source: Own illustration using data of EUPRO/AIT.

Appendix B Degree centrality of FPx-y TUR networks (with Turkish participation)

Tables 13B.1–3 illustrate organizations with the ten highest degrees in FPx-y TUR networks in FP5 to FP7 (the empty fields indicate either that no organizations are listed further in the top 10 centrality measures in Pajek, or that there are more than the listed 10 organizations having equal values). One has to note, that the precise position of individual organizations in the ranking should not be overemphasized as centrality scores may depend on the project type. That is, participation in one large project increases centrality scores disproportionally (as seen in e.g. EURON in FP5-ICT TUR). Hence, single universities may appear in the higher ranks next to large research organizations (such as Fraunhofer Society or TUBITAK) although they did not participate in many projects but in single very large projects. Based on the data and the time frame of this paper, no further classification of the participating institutes was possible.

Table 13B.1 Overview of centrality measures in FPx-ICT TUR networks in FP5–FP7.

Degree centrality	T	Value	Closeness centrality	T	Value	Betweenness centrality	T	Value
FP5-ICT TUR								
Bulgarian Academy of Sciences (BAS)	R	0.60	Bulgarian Academy of Sciences (BAS)	R	0.71	Bulgarian Academy of Sciences (BAS)	R	0.18
Helmholtz Association (HHG), Germany (*)	R	0.58	Helmholtz Association (HHG)	R	0.70	Swiss Federal Institute of Technology	R	0.16
Magyar – Hungarian Academy of Sciences (MTA) (*)	R	0.53	Magyar – Hungarian Academy of Sciences (MTA)	R	0.67	Orta Dogu – Middle East Technical University (METU), Turkey	U	0.09
Orta Dogu – Middle East Technical University (METU), Turkey	U	0.49	Orta Dogu – Middle East Technical University (METU), Turkey	U	0.66	Helmholtz Association (HHG)	R	0.09
Swiss Federal Institute of Technology (*)	R	0.48	Swiss Federal Institute of Technology	R	0.66	National Technical University of Athens (NTUA), Greece	U	0.07

Degree centrality	T	Value	Closeness centrality	T	Value	Betweenness centrality	T	Value
AIT Austrian Institute of Technology GmbH	R	0.48	AIT Austrian Institute of Technology GmbH	R	0.64	University of Sofia Kliment Ohridski, Bulgaria	U	0.06
Polytechnic University of Milan, Italy (*)	R	0.46	Technical University Vienna (TU Wien), Austria	U	0.63	Magyar – Hungarian Academy of Sciences (MTA)	R	0.05
							R	0.05
National Technical University of Athens (NTUA) (*)	R	0.46	Politecnico di Milano, Italy	U	0.63	University of Amsterdam, Netherlands		
Technical University Vienna (TU Wien), Austria (*)	R	0.46	National Technical University of Athens (NTUA), Greece	U	0.63	Planet S.A., Greece	I	0.04

FP5-ICT TUR

Degree centrality	T	Value	Closeness centrality	T	Value	Betweenness centrality	T	Value
University of Amsterdam, Netherlands (*)	U	0.45	University of Amsterdam, Netherlands	U	0.63	AIT Austrian Institute of Technology GmbH	R	0.04

FP6-ICT TUR

Degree centrality	T	Value	Closeness centrality	T	Value	Betweenness centrality	T	Value
Fraunhofer Society, Germany (*)	R	0.44	Fraunhofer Society, Germany	R	0.61	Fraunhofer Society, Germany	R	0.14
French National Centre for Scientific Research (CNRS), France (*)	R	0.36	French National Centre for Scientific Research (CNRS), France	R	0.58	Vilnius University, Lithuania	U	0.13
Turkiye Bilimsel – Scientific and Technical Research Council of Turkey (TUBITAK)	R	0.30	Turkiye Bilimsel – Scientific and Technical Research Council of Turkey (TUBITAK)	R	0.58	Turkiye Bilimsel – Scientific and Technical Research Council of Turkey (TUBITAK)	R	0.11

Degree centrality	T	Value	Closeness centrality	T	Value	Betweenness centrality	T	Value
Polytechnic University of Catalonia (UPC), Spain (*)	U	0.29	Chalmers University of Technology, Sweden	U	0.57	Chalmers University of Technology, Sweden	U	0.06
VTT Technical Research Centre of Finland (*)	R	0.29	Budapest University of Technology and Economics (BME), Hungary	U	0.56	Orta Dogu – Middle East University (METU), Turkey	U	0.06
Technical University Vienna (TU Wien), Austria (*)	U	0.27	Polytechnic University of Catalonia (UPC), Spain	U	0.55	Budapest University of Technology and Economics (BME), Hungary	U	0.05
Chalmers University of Technology, Sweden	U	0.26	VTT Technical Research Centre of Finland	R	0.55	VTT Technical Research Centre of Finland	R	0.03
Royal Institute of Technology (KTH), Sweden (*)	U	0.25	Technical University Vienna (TU Wien), Austria	U	0.54	Institute for Systems and Computer Engineering (INESC), Portugal	R	0.03
Bilkent University, Turkey	U	0.24	Orta Dogu – Middle East Technical University (METU), Turkey	U	0.54	Magyar – Hungarian Academy of Sciences (MTA)	R	0.03
Orta Dogu – Middle East Technical University (METU), Turkey	U	0.24						

FP7-ICT TUR

Degree centrality	T	Value	Closeness centrality	T	Value	Betweenness centrality	T	Value
Bilkent University, Turkey	U	0.39	Polish Academy of Sciences (PAS/PAN)	R	0.82	Fraunhofer Society, Germany	R	0.13
Fraunhofer Society, Germany	R	0.33	Turkiye Bilimsel – Scientific and Technical Research Council of Turkey (TUBITAK)	R	0.73	Bilkent University, Turkey	U	0.08

Table 13B.1 Continued.

Degree centrality	T	Value	Closeness centrality	T	Value	Betweenness centrality	T	Value
National and Kapodistrian University of Athens (UOA), Greece (*)	U	0.32	Greek National Research and Technology Network Sa	R	0.69	Charles III University of Madrid (UC3M), Spain	U	0.04
Technical University Vienna, Austria (*)	U	0.31	Ministry of Education and Science, Montenegro	G	0.68	National Research Council (CNR), Italy	R	0.03
Ghent University (RUG), Belgium	U	0.29	Magyar – Hungarian Academy of Sciences (MTA)	R	0.66	T.X.T. E-Solutions Spa	I	0.03
Poznan University of Technology, Poland	U	0.29				National and Kapodistrian University of Athens (UOA), Greece (*)	U	0.03
Groupe des ecoles des Telecom-munications, France (*)	U	0.29				Polish Academy of Sciences (PAS/PAN)	R	0.03
Polytechnic University of Catalonia (UPC), Spain (*)	U	0.29				French National Centre for Scientific Research (CNRS), France	R	0.03
Technological Centre of Telecomuni-cacions of Catalunya – CTTC, Spain	R	0.29				Open University UK (OpenU)	U	0.03
Polish Academy of Sciences (PAS/PAN)	R	0.24				University of Bologna, Italy	U	0.02

Note: (*) Organization is also under the top 50 organizations with the highest degree centrality in the total ICT network. T: organization type; U: university; R: research organization; I: industry; C: consulting; G: government; O: other. The empty fields imply either that no organizations are listed further in the top 10 (in Pajek), or that there are more than the listed 10 organizations having equal centrality values.

Source: Own illustration according to data of EUPRO/AIT.

Table 13B.2 Overview of centrality measures in FPx-Biotech TUR networks in FP5–FP7.

Degree centrality	T	Value	Closeness centrality	T	Value	Betweenness centrality	T	Value
FP5-Biotech TUR								
Austrian Energy Agency	O	1	Austrian Energy Agency	O	1	Austrian Energy Agency	O	0
MERKAT, Turkey	C	1	MERKAT, Turkey	C	1	MERKAT, Turkey	C	0
EXERGIA, Greece	C	1	EXERGIA, Greece	C	1	EXERGIA, Greece	C	0
Green Land Reclamation Ltd, GBR	I	1	Green Land Reclamation Ltd, GBR	I	1	Green Land Reclamation Ltd, GBR	I	0
British Biogen Ltd	I	1	British Biogen Ltd	I	1	British Biogen Ltd	I	0
China Association of Rural Energy Industry	O	1	China Association of Rural Energy Industry	O	1	China Association of Rural Energy Industry	O	0
FP6-Biotech TUR								
University of Helsinki, Finland (*)	U	0.39	University of Helsinki, Finland	U	0.61	Scientific and Technical Research Council of Turkey – TUBITAK	R	0.11
Karolinska Institute, Sweden (*)	U	0.36	Justus Liebig University Gießen, Germany	U	0.57	Helmholtz Association (HHG), Germany	R	0.10
University of London – UOL (*)	U	0.35	Heinrich Heine University, Germany	U	0.57	Queens University of Belfast (QUB), GBR	U	0.08
University of Bologna, Italy (*)	U	0.33	Christian-Albrechts -University Kiel, Germany	U	0.57	University of Milan, Italy	U	0.07
Queens University of Belfast (QUB), GBR	U	0.33	University of Bari, Italia	U	0.57	University of Bologna, Italy	U	0.05
University of Perugia, Italy	U	0.32	University of Ankara (ankaraU), Turkey	U	0.57	University of Helsinki, Finland	U	0.05

Degree centrality	T	Value	Closeness centrality	T	Value	Betweenness centrality	T	Value
			University of Sheffield (SheffU), GBR	U	0.57	Academy of Sciences of the Czech Republic	R	0.04
			University of Bologna, Italy	U	0.57	University of London – UOL	U	0.04
			University of Newcastle upon Tyne (NCL), GBR	U	0.55	Wageningen University UR, Netherlands	U	0.04
			University of Aarhus (AU), Denmark	U	0.55	Karolinska Institute, Sweden	U	0.04
FP7-Biotech TUR								
Leibniz Association, Germany (*)	R	0.30	Leibniz Association, Germany	R	0.63	Institut National de la Recherche Agronomique (INRA), France	R	0.15
Institut National de la Recherche Agronomique (INRA), France (*)	R	0.27	Institut National de la Recherche Agronomique (INRA), France	R	0.61	Leibniz Association, Germany	R	0.12
Superior Health Institute (I.S.S.), Italy (*)	R	0.27	University of Milan, Italy	U	0.56	University of Milan, Italy	U	0.07
French Agricultural Research Centre (CIRAD), France	R	0.25	Scottish Agricultural and Biological Research Institutes (SABRIs), GBR	R	0.56	Sabanci University (SabanciU), Turkey	U	0.06
National Institute for Agriculture and Food Research and Technology (INIA), Spain	R	0.25	Sabanci University (SabanciU), Turkey	U	0.56	Scottish Agricultural and Biological Research Institutes (SABRIs), GBR	R	0.06
Chalmers University of Technology, Sweden	U	0.24	University of Bologna, Italy	U	0.56	University of Bologna, Italy	U	0.06

Table 13B.2 Continued.

Degree centrality	T	Value	Closeness centrality	T	Value	Betweenness centrality	T	Value
ETH Zürich – Swiss Federal Institute of Technology (*)	R	0.24	Biotechnology and Biological Sciences Research Council (BBSRC), GBR	R	0.56	Biotechnology and Biological Sciences Research Council (BBSRC), GBR	R	0.06
New University of Lisbon (UNL), Portugal	U	0.24				Superior Health Institute (I.S.S.), Italy	R	0.05
						New University of Lisbon (UNL), Portugal	U	0.05

Note: (*) Organization is also under the top 50 organizations with the highest degree centrality in the total ICT network. T: organization type; U: university; R: research organization; I: industry; C: consulting; G: government; O: other. The empty fields imply either that no organizations are listed further in the top 10 (in Pajek), or that there are more than the listed 10 organizations having equal centrality values.

Source: Own illustration according to data of EUPRO/AIT.

Table 13B.3 Overview of centrality measures in FPx-Nano TUR networks in FP5–FP7.

Degree centrality	T	Value	Closeness centrality	T	Value	Betweenness centrality	T	Value
FP6-Nano TUR								
VTT Technical Research Centre of Finland (*)	R	0.36	VTT Technical Research Centre of Finland	R	0.57	University of Ljubljana, Slovenia	U	0.11
Queen's University of Belfast (QUB), GBR (*)	U	0.32	Queen's University of Belfast (QUB), GBR	U	0.54	VTT Technical Research Centre of Finland	R	0.09
Orta Dogu – Middle East Technical University (METU), Turkey	U	0.25	University of Ljubljana, Slovenia	U	0.53	Queen's University of Belfast (QUB), GBR	U	0.08
University of Ljubljana, Slovenia	U	0.24	Orta Dogu – Middle East Technical University (METU), Turkey	U	0.52	Budapest University of Technology and Economics (BME), Hungary	U	0.07
Fraunhofer Society, Germany (*)	R	0.23	University of Birmingham (BirmU), GBR	U	0.52	National Physical Laboratory (NPL), GBR	U	0.07
University of Birmingham (BirmU), GBR (*)	U	0.23	Swerea IVF, Sweden	R	0.52	French National Centre for Scientific Research (CNRS), France	R	0.07
Swerea IVF, Sweden	R	0.23	University of Twente, Netherlands	U	0.52	Orta Dogu – Middle East Technical University (METU), Turkey	U	0.06
French National Centre for Scientific Research (CNRS), France (*)	R	0.22	Centre Technique des Industries Mecaniques – CETIM, France	R	0.51	Tekniker – Technological Centre of Spain	R	0.05
			Leibniz University of Hannover, Germany	U	0.51			
			Fraunhofer Society, Germany	R	0.51			

Degree centrality	T	Value	Closeness centrality	T	Value	Betweenness centrality	T	Value
FP7-Nano TUR								
Research Council of Norway	R	0.24	Helmholtz Association (HHG), Germany	R	0.55	Helmholtz Association (HHG), Germany	R	0.24
Tekes, National Technology Agency, Finland	G	0.24	Fraunhofer Society, Germany	R	0.50	Fraunhofer Society, Germany	R	0.18
Scientific and Technical Research Council of Turkey – TUBITAK	R	0.24	Scientific and Technical Research Council of Turkey – TUBITAK	R	0.47	French National Centre for Scientific Research (CNRS), France	R	0.06
Fraunhofer Society, Germany (*)	R	0.24	Research Council of Norway	R	0.46	Scientific and Technical Research Council of Turkey – TUBITAK	R	0.04
National Center of Management Programs, Romania	R	0.22	Tekes, National Technology Agency, Finland	G	0.46	National Interuniversity Consortium for the Technology Sciences of Matter – INSTM, Italy	R	0.04
Foundation for Science and Technology (FCT), Portugal	O	0.22	French National Centre for Scientific Research (CNRS), France	R	0.46	Research Council of Norway	R	0.04
SenterNovem – Netherland Agency for Energy and the Environment, Netherlands	O	0.22	Swedish Research Council for Environment, Agricultural Sciences and Spatial Planning, Sweden	R	0.45	Tekes, National Technology Agency, Finland	G	0.04

Table 13B.3 Continued.

Degree centrality	T	Value	Closeness centrality	T	Value	Betweenness centrality	T	Value
Swedish Research Council for Environment, Agricultural Sciences and Spatial Planning, Sweden	R	0.20	Latvian Academy of Sciences, Latvia	R	0.45	Swedish Research Council for Environment, Agricultural Sciences and Spatial Planning, Sweden	R	0.03
Institute for the Promotion of Innovation, Belgium	G	0.20						
The Technology Strategy Board, GBR	O	0.20						

Note: (*) Organization is also under the top 50 organizations with the highest degree centrality in the total ICT network. T: organization type; U: university; R: research organization; I: industry; C: consulting; G: government; O: other. The empty fields imply either that no organizations are listed further in the top 10 (in Pajek), or that there are more than the listed 10 organizations having equal centrality values.
Source: Own illustration according to data of EUPRO/AIT.

Appendix C Degree centrality of FPx-y networks (total networks)

The following lists provide degree centrality scores of the top 50 organizations in the total networks of the examined technology fields. Names of organizations are as stated in the EUPRO database. The degree centrality lists of total networks of all technology fields have been provided by the AIT.

Table 13C.1 Degree centrality of FP5–FP7 ICT networks (total networks).

FP5-ICT

Rank	Vertex	Value	Organization
1	24	0.1733	Fraunhofer-Gesellschaft zur Förderung der angewandten Forschung e.V.
2	309	0.0970	CENTRE NATIONAL DE LA RECHERCHE SCIENTIFIQUE – CNRS
3	77	0.0921	Siemens AG
4	21	0.0912	Consiglio Nazionale delle Ricerche (CNR)
5	17	0.0852	National Technical University of Athens (NTUA)
6	177	0.0829	Helmholtz-Gemeinschaft (HHG)
7	98	0.0785	Universitat Politecnica de Catalunya (UPC)
8	322	0.0756	Ecole Polytechnique Federale de Lausanne – EPFL – Swiss Federal Institute of Technology, Lausanne
9	25	0.0739	Institut National de Recherche en Informatique et en Automatique (INRIA)
10	380	0.0715	Magyar Tudomanyos Akademia – Hungarian Academy of Sciences (MTA)
11	134	0.0713	UPM Universidad Politecnica de Madrid/Madrid Polytechnical University
12	39	0.0708	Katholieke Universiteit Leuven
13	694	0.0700	CSIC – Consejo Superior de Investigaciones Cientificas/Higher Council for Scientific Research
14	830	0.0663	Universiteit van Amsterdam/University of Amsterdam
15	354	0.0636	Thales Group
16	339	0.0626	DaimlerChrysler AG
17	450	0.0609	Rheinisch-Westfälische Technische Hochschule (RWTH) Aachen/RWTH Aachen University
18	436	0.0600	ENEA – Ente per le Nuove tecnologie, Energia e Ambiente
19	796	0.0583	Politecnico di Milano
20	175	0.0576	University of Edinburgh (EdinburghU)
21	424	0.0573	Universiteit Twente
22	152	0.0571	Universita degli Studi di Genova/University of Genova
23	117	0.0570	Technische Universität Wien/ Technical University Vienna (TU Wien)
24	167	0.0570	University of London – UOL
25	81	0.0564	Philips NV
26	97	0.0563	Technical University of Denmark – Danmarks Tekniske Universitet (DTU)

Table 13C.1 Continued.

Rank	Vertex	Value	Organization
27	168	0.0557	University of Southampton (SotonU)
28	404	0.0541	Universita degli Studi di Bologna, University of Bologna
29	835	0.0539	UTL – Universidade Tecnica de Lisboa, Technical University of Lisbon
30	100	0.0537	University of Manchester (ManU)
31	135	0.0534	UPV Universidad Politecnica de Valencia – Politechnical University of Valencia
32	784	0.0524	Helsinki University of Technology, Teknillinen Korkeakoulu

FP5-ICT

Rank	Vertex	Value	Organization
33	219	0.0521	Atos Origin
34	368	0.0513	VTT Technical Research Centre of Finland
35	652	0.0510	Universitá di Roma La Sapienza, University of Rome La Sapienza
36	779	0.0497	Cranfield University (CranfieldU)
37	206	0.0490	Royal Institute of Technology – Kungliga Tekniska Högskolan (KTH)
38	367	0.0490	Telecom Italia SPA
39	607	0.0490	Delft University of Technology
40	223	0.0486	University of Cyprus – UCY
41	113	0.0473	ETH Zürich – Eidgenössische Technische Hochschule – Swiss Federal Institute of Technology
42	644	0.0471	Kings College London – KCL – UOL
43	35	0.0471	British Telecom PLC (BT)
44	612	0.0468	TNO – Netherlands Organisation for Applied Scientific Research
45	270	0.0463	France Telecom
46	537	0.0463	Universität Stuttgart/University of Stuttgart
47	96	0.0461	Politecnico di Torino
48	23	0.0460	FORTH, Foundation for Research and Technology – Hellas
49	473	0.0454	Universität Wien/University of Vienna (UNIVIE)
50	196	0.0453	Czech Technical University / CESKE VYSOKE UCENI TECHNIKE V PRAZE

FP6-ICT

Rank	Vertex	Value	Organization
1	20	0.3931	Fraunhofer-Gesellschaft zur Förderung der angewandten Forschung e.V.
2	143	0.2473	CENTRE NATIONAL DE LA RECHERCHE SCIENTIFIQUE – CNRS
3	99	0.1906	Siemens AG
4	340	0.1834	Consiglio Nazionale delle Ricerche (CNR)
5	56	0.1832	Ecole Polytechnique Federale de Lausanne – EPFL – Swiss Federal Institute of Technology, Lausanne
6	107	0.1788	National Technical University of Athens (NTUA)
7	139	0.1729	Royal Institute of Technology – Kungliga Tekniska Högskolan (KTH)
8	54	0.1710	VTT Technical Research Centre of Finland
9	274	0.1699	Thales Group

Rank	Vertex	Value	Organization
10	30	0.1658	Telefonica de Espana SA
11	70	0.1647	UPM Universidad Politecnica de Madrid/Madrid Polytechnical University
12	59	0.1610	Institut National de Recherche en Informatique et en Automatique (INRIA)
13	93	0.1514	ETH Zürich – Eidgenössische Technische Hochschule – Swiss Federal Institute of Technology
14	126	0.1455	COMMISSARIAT A LENERGIE ATOMIQUE (CEA)
15	57	0.1453	France Telecom
16	419	0.1429	Universität Stuttgart/University of Stuttgart
17	213	0.1370	Universitat Politecnica de Catalunya (UPC)
18	359	0.1347	Helmholtz-Gemeinschaft (HHG)
19	136	0.1347	Katholieke Universiteit Leuven
20	27	0.1344	Politecnico di Milano
21	191	0.1344	FIAT Gruppo
22	305	0.1227	TNO – Netherlands Organisation for Applied Scientific Research
23	55	0.1218	Center for Research and Technology Hellas – CERTH
24	176	0.1205	Budapesti Mueszaki es Gazdasagtudomanyi Egyetem – Budapest University of Technology and Economics (BME)
25	8	0.1203	Philips NV
26	103	0.1199	University of Surrey (SurreyU)
27	146	0.1166	FORTH, Foundation for Research and Technology – Hellas
28	22	0.1153	IMEC (Interuniversity Micro Electronics Center)
29	460	0.1138	University of Southampton (SotonU)
30	13	0.1122	Alcatel-Lucent
31	209	0.1116	Technische Universität Wien/ Technical University Vienna (TU Wien)
32	60	0.1105	Karlsruher Institut für Technologie/Karlsruhe Institute of Technology – KIT
33	109	0.1027	Telecom Italia SPA
34	413	0.1025	Polish Academy of Sciences / Polska Akademia Nauk (PAS/PAN)
35	132	0.1009	Groupe des ecoles des Telecommunications
36	660	0.1003	Universiteit Twente
37	447	0.1001	Universitá di Roma La Sapienza, University of Rome La Sapienza
38	101	0.0992	University of Cambridge (CU)
39	410	0.0985	Lund University
40	108	0.0981	Technical University of Denmark – Danmarks Tekniske Universitet (DTU)
41	834	0.0981	University of Patras
42	133	0.0966	Helsinki University of Technology, Teknillinen Korkeakoulu
43	159	0.0961	INESC – Instituto de Engenharia de Sistemas e Computadores/Institute for Systems and Computer Engineering
44	114	0.0957	University of London – UOL
45	168	0.0944	Universite de Geneve/University of Geneva (UNIGE)
46	138	0.0933	Rheinisch-Westfälische Technische Hochschule (RWTH) Aachen/RWTH Aachen University

Rank	Vertex	Value	Organization
47	207	0.0929	Magyar Tudomanyos Akademia – Hungarian Academy of Sciences (MTA)
48	147	0.0925	Imperial College London (ImperialCL)
49	187	0.0911	DaimlerChrysler AG
50	166	0.0901	Universita degli Studi di Genova/University of Genova

FP7-ICT

Rank	Vertex	Value	Organization
1	7	0.2735	Fraunhofer-Gesellschaft zur Förderung der angewandten Forschung e.V.
2	113	0.1727	CENTRE NATIONAL DE LA RECHERCHE SCIENTIFIQUE – CNRS
3	53	0.1602	VTT Technical Research Centre of Finland
4	117	0.1578	Thales Group
5	2	0.1534	COMMISSARIAT A LENERGIE ATOMIQUE (CEA)
6	67	0.1470	Consiglio Nazionale delle Ricerche (CNR)
7	194	0.1321	Institut National de Recherche en Informatique et en Automatique (INRIA)
8	211	0.1305	Telefonica de Espana SA
9	93	0.1189	Ecole Polytechnique Federale de Lausanne – EPFL – Swiss Federal Institute of Technology, Lausanne
10	94	0.1185	ETH Zürich – Eidgenössische Technische Hochschule – Swiss Federal Institute of Technology
11	26	0.1165	Technische Universität Wien/ Technical University Vienna (TU Wien)
12	96	0.1145	Helmholtz-Gemeinschaft (HHG)
13	190	0.1092	UPM Universidad Politecnica de Madrid/Madrid Polytechnical University
14	64	0.1092	Royal Institute of Technology – Kungliga Tekniska Högskolan (KTH)
15	176	0.1052	Alcatel-Lucent
16	60	0.1048	Politecnico di Milano
17	253	0.1036	Philips NV
18	29	0.1036	IMEC (Interuniversity Micro Electronics Center)
19	233	0.1008	Siemens AG
20	199	0.0988	National Technical University of Athens (NTUA)
21	145	0.0988	University of London – UOL
22	30	0.0980	Katholieke Universiteit Leuven
23	84	0.0980	Rheinisch-Westfälische Technische Hochschule (RWTH) Aachen/RWTH Aachen University
24	170	0.0960	Center for Research and Technology Hellas – CERTH
25	205	0.0952	Eindhoven University of Technology
26	13	0.0932	Chalmers University of Technology
27	102	0.0928	Universität Stuttgart/University of Stuttgart
28	33	0.0920	STMicroelectronics NV
29	41	0.0843	FIAT Gruppo

Table 13C.1 Continued.

Rank	Vertex	Value	Organization
30	122	0.0819	Karlsruher Institut für Technologie/Karlsruhe Institute of Technology – KIT
31	206	0.0819	France Telecom
32	151	0.0803	University of Cambridge (CU)
33	356	0.0791	Technische Universität Berlin/Berlin University of Technology
34	49	0.0779	TNO – Netherlands Organisation for Applied Scientific Research
35	351	0.0779	Universitat Politecnica de Catalunya (UPC)
36	316	0.0775	SAP AG
37	232	0.0747	National and Kapodistrian University of Athens (UOA)
38	456	0.0743	Universite de Paris VI (Universite Pierre et Marie Curie) (UPMC)
39	146	0.0707	University of Southampton (SotonU)
40	14	0.0703	Delft University of Technology
41	149	0.0703	Universita degli Studi di Bologna, University of Bologna
42	242	0.0691	Imperial College London (ImperialCL)
43	183	0.0687	Technische Universität München/Technical University of Munich
44	263	0.0687	Groupe des ecoles des Telecommunications
45	215	0.0683	UPV Universidad Politecnica de Valencia – Politechnical University of Valencia
46	381	0.0679	Alborg Universitet
47	1	0.0675	Budapest University of Technology and Economics (BME)
48	352	0.0667	FORTH, Foundation for Research and Technology – Hellas
49	210	0.0659	Politecnico di Torino
50	343	0.0655	IT – Instituto de Telecomunicacões/Telecommunications Institute

Table 13C.2 Degree centrality of FP5–FP7 Biotech networks (total networks).

FP5-Biotech

Rank	Vertex	Value	Organization
1	16	0.2366	CENTRE NATIONAL DE LA RECHERCHE SCIENTIFIQUE – CNRS
2	33	0.1644	Helmholtz-Gemeinschaft (HHG)
3	51	0.1492	CSIC – Consejo Superior de Investigaciones Cientificas/Higher Council for Scientific Research
4	18	0.1323	Institut National de la Sante Et de la Recherche Medicale – INSERM
5	44	0.1283	Max-Planck-Gesellschaft zur Förderung der Wissenschaften eV (MPG)
6	89	0.1187	Institut National de la Recherche Agronomique (INRA)
7	30	0.1131	University of Copenhagen – Koebenhavns Universitet (KU)
8	41	0.1131	Consiglio Nazionale delle Ricerche (CNR)
9	48	0.1059	Universiteit Leiden /Leiden University
10	70	0.1002	Universiteit Utrecht/Utrecht University
11	87	0.0978	University of London – UOL
12	38	0.0962	Karolinska Institutet
13	201	0.0954	Biotechnology and Biological Sciences Research Council (BBSRC)
14	191	0.0954	Wageningen UR (EDU)
15	91	0.0930	Rijksuniversiteit Groningen
16	19	0.0922	Lund University
17	63	0.0890	University of Manchester (ManU)
18	17	0.0842	Imperial College London (ImperialCL)
19	85	0.0778	Universität Zürich – University of Zürich (UZ)
20	32	0.0762	Eberhard Karls Universität Tübingen/Eberhard Karls University of Tuebingen
21	248	0.0730	Georg-August-Universität Göttingen/Georg-August-University Göttingen
22	79	0.0714	Federation Nationale des Centres de Lutte Contre le Cancer (FNLCC)
23	14	0.0690	University of Umea/ Umea Universitet
24	340	0.0690	Katholieke Universiteit Leuven
25	9	0.0690	Technical University of Denmark – Danmarks Tekniske Universitet (DTU)
26	131	0.0690	University of Uppsala
27	15	0.0682	Weizmann Institute of Science (Weizmann)
28	210	0.0658	VIB (Flanders Interuniversity Institute for Biotechnology)
29	66	0.0650	European Molecular Biology Laboratory (EMBL)
30	241	0.0642	University of Helsinki, Helsingin Yliopisto
31	102	0.0642	Universitá di Roma La Sapienza, University of Rome La Sapienza
32	114	0.0609	Polish Academy of Sciences / Polska Akademia Nauk (PAS/PAN)
33	415	0.0609	Radboud Universiteit Nijmegen

Rank	Vertex	Value	Organization
34	617	0.0609	CIEMAT – Centro de Investigaciones Energeticas, Medioambientales y Tecnologicas/Centre for Energy, Environmental and Technological Research
35	36	0.0609	University of Newcastle upon Tyne (NCL)
36	141	0.0609	University of Cambridge (CU)
37	31	0.0601	University of Dublin – Trinity College (TCD)
38	97	0.0601	University of York (YorkU)
39	238	0.0593	Swedish University of Agricultural Sciences (SLU)
40	25	0.0593	University of Oxford (OU)
41	251	0.0585	Wageningen UR (ROR)
42	206	0.0585	Technische Universität Wien/ Technical University Vienna (TU Wien)
43	330	0.0585	Hebrew University of Jerusalem (HUJ)
44	74	0.0585	Universita degli Studi di Milano, University of Milan
45	52	0.0569	Institut Pasteur
46	133	0.0561	ETH Zürich – Eidgenössische Technische Hochschule – Swiss Federal Institute of Technology
47	34	0.0553	Medical Research Council (MRC), UK
48	198	0.0545	Wissenschaftsgemeinschaft Gottfried Wilhelm Leibniz e.V.
49	208	0.0537	Universite de Paris XI (Universite Paris-Sud)
50	791	0.0537	National Technical University of Athens (NTUA)

FP6-Biotech

Rank	Vertex	Value	Organization
1	119	0.3109	Institut National de la Sante Et de la Recherche Medicale – INSERM
2	165	0.2739	Karolinska Institutet
3	159	0.2633	CENTRE NATIONAL DE LA RECHERCHE SCIENTIFIQUE – CNRS
4	157	0.2544	University of London – UOL
5	118	0.2437	Helmholtz-Gemeinschaft (HHG)
6	52	0.2314	Imperial College London (ImperialCL)
7	122	0.2036	Max-Planck-Gesellschaft zur Förderung der Wissenschaften eV (MPG)
8	465	0.2009	University of Helsinki, Helsingin Yliopisto
9	231	0.1933	CSIC – Consejo Superior de Investigaciones Cientificas/Higher Council for Scientific Research
10	287	0.1923	Universiteit Leiden /Leiden University
11	151	0.1916	Lund University
12	311	0.1796	Consiglio Nazionale delle Ricerche (CNR)
13	130	0.1762	University of Oxford (OU)
14	120	0.1759	Ludwig-Maximilians-Universität München
15	266	0.1748	Kings College London – KCL – UOL
16	187	0.1632	Katholieke Universiteit Leuven
17	209	0.1618	Universiteit van Amsterdam/University of Amsterdam
18	199	0.1615	Charite – Universitätsmedizin Berlin
19	197	0.1604	University of Uppsala

Table 13C.2 Continued.

Rank	Vertex	Value	Organization
20	194	0.1591	Universiteit Utrecht/Utrecht University
21	908	0.1577	Universita degli Studi di Milano, University of Milan
22	117	0.1553	Technische Universität München/Technical University of Munich
23	566	0.1546	University of Copenhagen – Koebenhavns Universitet (KU)
24	163	0.1519	Institut Pasteur
25	133	0.1508	Erasmus Universiteit Rotterdam/Erasmus University Rotterdam
26	128	0.1495	University of Aarhus – Aarhus Universitet (AU)
27	123	0.1491	Medical Research Council (MRC), UK
28	314	0.1491	Institut National de la Recherche Agronomique (INRA)
29	259	0.1488	COMMISSARIAT A LENERGIE ATOMIQUE (CEA)
30	139	0.1484	Albert-Ludwigs-Universität Freiburg
31	210	0.1478	European Molecular Biology Laboratory (EMBL)
32	289	0.1454	Academy of Sciences of the Czech Republic / AKADEMIE VED CESKE REPUBLIKY
33	101	0.1423	University of Cambridge (CU)
34	466	0.1416	University of Newcastle upon Tyne (NCL)
35	205	0.1399	Istituto Superiore di Sanitá (I.S.S.)
36	89	0.1378	University of Birmingham (BirmU)
37	283	0.1358	Radboud Universiteit Nijmegen
38	13	0.1344	Hebrew University of Jerusalem (HUJ)
39	506	0.1334	University of Göteborg
40	115	0.1323	Polish Academy of Sciences / Polska Akademia Nauk (PAS/PAN)
41	71	0.1310	Fraunhofer-Gesellschaft zur Förderung der angewandten Forschung e.V.
42	399	0.1296	Wageningen UR (EDU)
43	256	0.1286	Medizinische Universität Wien/Medical University of Vienna – MUW
44	206	0.1279	Ruprecht-Karls-Universität Heidelberg
45	386	0.1272	Technical University of Denmark – Danmarks Tekniske Universitet (DTU)
46	152	0.1262	Medizinische Hochschule Hannover/Hannover Medical School
47	328	0.1255	Universita degli Studi di Bologna, University of Bologna
48	126	0.1244	Universität Zürich – University of Zürich (UZ)
49	134	0.1200	Fondazione Centro San Raffaele del Monte Tabor
50	733	0.1179	Westfälische Wilhelms-Universität Münster

FP7-Biotech

1	27	0.2109	CENTRE NATIONAL DE LA RECHERCHE SCIENTIFIQUE – CNRS
2	11	0.1900	Institut National de la Sante Et de la Recherche Medicale – INSERM
3	75	0.1714	CSIC – Consejo Superior de Investigaciones Cientificas/Higher Council for Scientific Research
4	28	0.1528	Consiglio Nazionale delle Ricerche (CNR)
5	41	0.1505	Max-Planck-Gesellschaft zur Förderung der Wissenschaften eV (MPG)

Rank	Vertex	Value	Organization
6	201	0.1461	University of Oxford (OU)
7	29	0.1379	Institut National de la Recherche Agronomique (INRA)
8	106	0.1349	Wageningen UR (ROR)
9	49	0.1304	University of London – UOL
10	175	0.1267	Helmholtz-Gemeinschaft (HHG)
11	22	0.1237	Lund University
12	55	0.1230	Katholieke Universiteit Leuven
13	92	0.1192	University of Cambridge (CU)
14	171	0.1170	Wissenschaftsgemeinschaft Gottfried Wilhelm Leibniz e.V.
15	15	0.1148	ETH Zürich – Eidgenössische Technische Hochschule – Swiss Federal Institute of Technology
16	12	0.1133	Karolinska Institutet
17	19	0.1095	Universität Zürich – University of Zürich (UZ)
18	253	0.1088	Universita degli Studi di Bologna, University of Bologna
19	211	0.1080	Institut Pasteur
20	24	0.1058	University of Newcastle upon Tyne (NCL)
21	278	0.1036	Wageningen UR (EDU)
22	3	0.1028	Ecole Polytechnique Federale de Lausanne – EPFL – Swiss Federal Institute of Technology, Lausanne
23	445	0.1021	Universiteit Leiden /Leiden University
24	209	0.0946	University of Edinburgh (EdinburghU)
25	154	0.0946	Rijksuniversiteit Groningen
26	63	0.0939	Universita degli Studi di Milano, University of Milan
27	179	0.0931	Universiteit Utrecht/Utrecht University
28	53	0.0924	Imperial College London (ImperialCL)
29	264	0.0909	Technical University of Denmark – Danmarks Tekniske Universitet (DTU)
30	71	0.0872	Istituto Superiore di Sanitá (I.S.S.)
31	248	0.0864	University of Aarhus – Aarhus Universitet (AU)
32	130	0.0864	Albert-Ludwigs-Universität Freiburg
33	126	0.0827	University of Uppsala
34	244	0.0805	Fraunhofer-Gesellschaft zur Förderung der angewandten Forschung e.V.
35	259	0.0797	Department for Environment Food and Rural Affairs (DEFRA), UK
36	42	0.0790	Universita degli Studi di Padova/University of Padova
37	187	0.0782	Ruprecht-Karls-Universität Heidelberg
38	226	0.0768	Georg-August-Universität Göttingen/Georg-August-University Göttingen
39	128	0.0768	VTT Technical Research Centre of Finland
40	341	0.0760	Academy of Sciences of the Czech Republic / AKADEMIE VED CESKE REPUBLIKY
41	206	0.0738	Biotechnology and Biological Sciences Research Council (BBSRC)
42	440	0.0730	Kings College London – KCL – UOL

Table 13C.2 Continued.

Rank	Vertex	Value	Organization
43	266	0.0730	USC Universidade de Santiago de Compostela – University of Santiago de Compostela
44	111	0.0723	Medical Research Council (MRC), UK
45	10	0.0715	Weizmann Institute of Science (Weizmann)
46	298	0.0715	Radboud Universiteit Nijmegen
47	44	0.0678	Johann Wolfgang Goethe-Universität Frankfurt am Main
48	155	0.0678	University of Helsinki, Helsingin Yliopisto
49	301	0.0671	COMMISSARIAT A LENERGIE ATOMIQUE (CEA)
50	34	0.0671	Hebrew University of Jerusalem (HUJ)

Table 13C.3 Degree centrality of FP6–FP7 Nano networks (total networks).

FP6-Nano

Rank	Vertex	Value	Organization
1	114	0.3022	Fraunhofer-Gesellschaft zur Förderung der angewandten Forschung e.V.
2	171	0.2658	CENTRE NATIONAL DE LA RECHERCHE SCIENTIFIQUE – CNRS
3	172	0.2195	Consiglio Nazionale delle Ricerche (CNR)
4	173	0.2175	CSIC – Consejo Superior de Investigaciones Cientificas/Higher Council for Scientific Research
5	402	0.2021	TNO – Netherlands Organisation for Applied Scientific Research
6	196	0.1990	COMMISSARIAT A LENERGIE ATOMIQUE (CEA)
7	66	0.1955	VTT Technical Research Centre of Finland
8	151	0.1681	FIAT Gruppo
9	209	0.1499	Universiteit Twente
10	186	0.1437	Katholieke Universiteit Leuven
11	270	0.1430	Ecole Polytechnique Federale de Lausanne – EPFL – Swiss Federal Institute of Technology, Lausanne
12	282	0.1383	Royal Institute of Technology – Kungliga Tekniska Högskolan (KTH)
13	299	0.1291	Technical University of Denmark – Danmarks Tekniske Universitet (DTU)
14	85	0.1244	Universität Stuttgart/University of Stuttgart
15	245	0.1236	Fundacion INASMET Asociacion de Investigacion Metalúrgica del Pais Vasco
16	190	0.1229	EADS European Aeronautic Defence and Space Company
17	477	0.1182	ARMINES – Structure de Recherche Contractuelle
18	43	0.1148	Helsinki University of Technology, Teknillinen Korkeakoulu
19	16	0.1136	Rheinisch-Westfälische Technische Hochschule (RWTH) Aachen/RWTH Aachen University
20	158	0.1132	Polish Academy of Sciences / Polska Akademia Nauk (PAS/PAN)
21	184	0.1117	Helmholtz-Gemeinschaft (HHG)
22	237	0.1094	Karlsruher Institut für Technologie/Karlsruhe Institute of Technology – KIT
23	9	0.1094	Russian Academy of Sciences
24	109	0.1070	Centro Tecnologico Tekniker
25	382	0.11	Siemens AG
26	112	0.1039	Eidgenössische Materialprüfungs- und Forschungsanstalt/Swiss Federal Laboratoires for Materials Testing and Research – EMPA
27	144	0.1039	University of Cambridge (CU)
28	167	0.1020	Max-Planck-Gesellschaft zur Förderung der Wissenschaften eV (MPG)
29	213	0.1005	Joint Research Centre (JRC) – Commission of the European Communities
30	94	0.0993	Universidade do Minho – University of Minho
31	350	0.0916	Politecnico di Milano

Table 13C.3 Continued.

Rank	Vertex	Value	Organization
32	187	0.0896	Magyar Tudomanyos Akademia – Hungarian Academy of Sciences (MTA)
33	86	0.0866	University of Manchester (ManU)
34	1496	0.0842	DAppolonia SPA
35	179	0.0842	Technische Universität Darmstadt/Darmstadt University of Technology
36	131	0.0842	University College Cork, National University of Ireland, Cork (UCC)
37	92	0.0815	Queens University of Belfast (QUB)
38	327	0.0815	Linköping University (LIU)
39	258	0.0811	National Center for Scientific Research Demokritos (NCSR)
40	342	0.0796	Budapesti Mueszaki es Gazdasagtudomanyi Egyetem – Budapest University of Technology and Economics (BME)
41	67	0.0796	Academy of Sciences of the Czech Republic / AKADEMIE VED CESKE REPUBLIKY
42	160	0.0788	Technische Universität München/Technical University of Munich
43	219	0.0777	Lund University
44	133	0.0777	University of Patras
45	176	0.0773	Politecnico di Torino
46	312	0.0773	Technische Universität Wien/ Technical University Vienna (TU Wien)
47	95	0.0769	Imperial College London (ImperialCL)
48	383	0.0750	Slovak Academy of Sciences/Slovenska akademia vied
49	137	0.0750	Jozef Stefan Institute (JSI)
50	132	0.0750	University of Birmingham (BirmU)

FP7-Nano

Rank	Vertex	Value	Organization
1	99	0.2681	Fraunhofer-Gesellschaft zur Förderung der angewandten Forschung e.V.
2	2	0.1968	Consiglio Nazionale delle Ricerche (CNR)
3	1	0.1847	CENTRE NATIONAL DE LA RECHERCHE SCIENTIFIQUE – CNRS
4	48	0.1513	Technical University of Denmark – Danmarks Tekniske Universitet (DTU)
5	33	0.1461	COMMISSARIAT A LENERGIE ATOMIQUE (CEA)
6	538	0.1335	VTT Technical Research Centre of Finland
7	43	0.1243	Joint Research Centre (JRC) – Commission of the European Communities
8	215	0.1157	TNO – Netherlands Organisation for Applied Scientific Research
9	325	0.1122	Ecole Polytechnique Federale de Lausanne – EPFL – Swiss Federal Institute of Technology, Lausanne
10	55	0.1087	CSIC – Consejo Superior de Investigaciones Cientificas/Higher Council for Scientific Research
11	165	0.1076	Universität Stuttgart/University of Stuttgart
12	465	0.1053	SINTEF – Foundation for Scientific and Industrial Research at the Norwegian Institute of Technology/NTNU

Rank	Vertex	Value	Organization
13	262	0.1053	FIAT Gruppo
14	188	0.1024	DAppolonia SPA
15	314	0.0984	Swerea IVF
16	373	0.0955	Imperial College London (ImperialCL)
17	125	0.0915	Eindhoven University of Technology
18	104	0.09	BASF AG
19	132	0.0892	University of Cambridge (CU)
20	36	0.0875	Eidgenössische Materialprüfungs- und Forschungsanstalt/Swiss Federal Laboratoires for Materials Testing and Research – EMPA
21	129	0.0811	Academy of Sciences of the Czech Republic / AKADEMIE VED CESKE REPUBLIKY
22	61	0.0788	ETH Zürich – Eidgenössische Technische Hochschule – Swiss Federal Institute of Technology
23	183	0.0742	ACCIONA INFRAESTRUCTURAS SA
24	100	0.0736	Katholieke Universiteit Leuven
25	435	0.0725	Jozef Stefan Institute (JSI)
26	45	0.0725	National Center for Scientific Research Demokritos (NCSR)
27	87	0.0708	Helmholtz-Gemeinschaft (HHG)
28	366	0.0690	Technische Universität Dresden/Dresden University of Technology
29	12	0.0679	Karlsruher Institut für Technologie/Karlsruhe Institute of Technology (KIT)
30	74	0.0679	Max-Planck-Gesellschaft zur Förderung der Wissenschaften eV (MPG)
31	24	0.0673	National Technical University of Athens (NTUA)
32	398	0.0673	Chalmers University of Technology
33	673	0.0667	electricite de France (EDF)
34	145	0.0662	Rheinisch-Westfälische Technische Hochschule (RWTH) Aachen/RWTH Aachen University
35	115	0.0639	Politecnico di Milano
36	112	0.06	Bayer AG
37	702	0.0621	ARMINES – Structure de Recherche Contractuelle
38	300	0.0621	Bundesanstalt für Materialforschung und Materialprüfung/Federal Institute for Material Research and Testing
39	118	0.0616	University of Manchester (ManU)
40	357	0.0610	Steinbeis-Stiftung für Wirtschaftsförderung
41	469	0.0604	Universita degli Studi di Pisa/University of Pisa
42	374	0.0604	Politecnico di Torino
43	231	0.0593	Centro Tecnologico Tekniker
44	46	0.0593	National Institute of Public Health and Environment (RIVM)
45	139	0.0593	Universita degli Studi di Bologna, University of Bologna
46	277	0.0593	EADS European Aeronautic Defence and Space Company
47	190	0.0581	Det Norske Veritas A/S
48	11	0.0575	Helsinki University of Technology, Teknillinen Korkeakoulu
49	354	0.0575	Czech Technical University / CESKE VYSOKE UCENI TECHNIKE V PRAZE

Table 13C.3 Continued.

Rank	Vertex	Value	Organization
50	386	0.0564	Consorzio Interuniversitario Nazionale per la Scienza e Tecnologia dei Materiali (INSTM)

Appendix D Top 10 German organizations with the highest degree centrality values in total FPx-Nanoscience networks that collaborate with Turkey in FP6 and FP7

To identify whether Turkey's most central German collaboration partners (in terms of degree centrality, Appendix B) in FPx-ICT TUR networks are as well centrally positioned in the total ICT networks (Appendix C), Tables 13D.1–3 display German organizations with the ten highest degrees in the total FPx-y networks, restricted to organizations appearing as well in networks with Turkish participation (FPx-y TUR) in FP5–FP7.

Table 13D.1 Overview of German organizations with the highest degrees in total FPx-ICT networks that collaborate with Turkey in FP5–FP7.

Total ICT network – Degree centrality of German organizations

FP5				FP6				FP7		
Rank	Organization	T	Value	Rank	Organization	T	Value	Organization	T	Value
1	Fraunhofer Society	R	0.17	1	Fraunhofer Society (*)	R	0.39	Fraunhofer Society (*)	R	0.27
3	Siemens AG	I	0.09	12	Siemens AG	I	0.19	Helmholtz Association – HHG	R	0.11
6	Helmholtz Association – HHG (*)	R	0.08	15	University of Stuttgart	U	0.14	Alcatel-Lucent	I	0.11
16	DaimlerChrysler AG	I	0.06	23	Helmholtz Association – HHG (*)	R	0.13	RWTH Aachen University	U	0.10
17	RWTH Aachen University	U	0.06	27	Karlsruhe Institute of Technology – KIT	R	0.11	University of Stuttgart	U	0.09
67	University of Hamburg	U	0.04	30	RWTH Aachen University	U	0.09	Karlsruhe Institute of Technology – KIT	R	0.08
78	University of Bremen	U	0.04	33	DaimlerChrysler AG	I	0.09	Berlin University of Technology (*)	U	0.08
91	Rheinisch Friedrich-Wilhelms-University Bonn	U	0.04	43	Dresden University of Technology	U	0.08	Technical University of Munich	U	0.07
95	Albert-Ludwigs-University Freiburg	U	0.03	65	SAP AG	I	0.08	German Research Center for Artificial Intelligence – DFKI	R	0.05
				78	University Duisburg-Essen	U	0.08	University Duisburg-Essen	U	0.05

Note: (*) Organization is as well central in the top 30 FPx-ICT TUR network. T: organization type; U: university; R: research organization; I: industry; C: consulting.
Source: Own illustration according to data of EUPRO/AIT.

Table 13D.2 Overview of German organizations with the highest degrees in total FPx-Biotech networks that collaborate with Turkey in FP5–FP7.

Total Biotech network – Degree centrality of German organizations

FP5	FP6 Rank Organization		T value	FP7 Rank Organization		T
No German participation in FP5-Biotech TUR value	5	Helmholtz Association – HHG	R 0.24	10	Helmholtz Association – HHG	R 0.13
	7	Max Planck Society – MPG	R 0.20	14	Leibniz Association (*)	R 0.12
	14	Ludwig-Maximilians-University München	U 0.18	38	Georg-August-University Göttingen	U 0.08
	18	Charité – Berlin University of Medicine (*)	U 0.16	47	Johann Wolfgang Goethe-University Frankfurt am Main	U 0.07
	22	Technical University of Munich (*)	U 0.16	68	Rheinisch Friedrich-Wilhelms-University Bonn (*)	U 0.06
	30	Albert-Ludwigs-University Freiburg	U 0.15	77	Saarland University	U 0.05
	31	European Molecular Biology Laboratory (EMBL)	R 0.15			

Note: (*) Organization is as well central in the top 30 FPx-ICT TUR network. T: organization type; U: university; R: research organization; I: industry; C: consulting.
Source: Own illustration according to data of EUPRO/AIT.

Table 13D.3 Overview of German organizations with the highest degrees in total FPx-Nanoscience networks that collaborate with Turkey in FP6 and FP7.

Total Nano network – Degree centrality of German organizations

	FP6				FP7	
Rank value	Organization	T	value	Rank	Organization	T
1	Fraunhofer Society (*)	R	0.30	1	Fraunhofer Society (*)	R 0.27
14	University of Stuttgart (*)	U	0.12	27	Helmholtz Association – HHG (*)	R 0.07
16	EADS European Aeronautic Defence and Space Company	I	0.12	28	Dresden University of Technology	U 0.07
19	RWTH Aachen University	U	0.11	29	Karlsruhe Institute of Technology – KIT	R 0.07
21	Helmholtz Association – HHG	R	0.11	30	Max Planck Society – MPG	R 0.07
22	Karlsruhe Institute of Technology – KIT	R	0.11	34	RWTH Aachen University	U 0.07
35	Darmstadt University of Technology (*)	U	0.08	46	EADS European Aeronautic Defence and Space Company	I 0.06
51	Leibniz Association	R	0.07	93	Siemens AG	I 0.04
75	Leibniz University of Hannover (*)	U	0.06			
98	DaimlerChrysler AG (*)	I	0.05			

Note: (*) Organization is as well central in the top 30 FPx-ICT TUR network. T: organization type; U: university; R: research organization; I: industry; C: consulting.
Source: Own illustration according to data of EUPRO/AIT.

Appendix E Graphical illustration of FPx-y TUR networks with exclusively German and Turkish cooperation partners

Figures 13E.1–3 display FPx-y TUR networks with exclusively German and Turkish cooperation partners. Turkish and German organizations are illustrated in different shades of grey, respectively. It is noticeable that most Turkish organizations are linked to German partners.

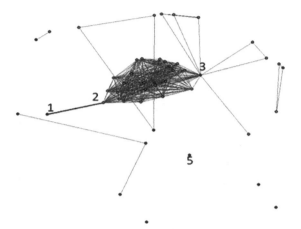

Figure 13E.1a Sub-network of FP5-ICT TUR with German–Turkish organizations.

Notes: 1 = TUBITAK; 2 = Helmholtz Association; 3 = Orta Dogu – Middle East Technical University; 5 = Sabanci University.
Source: EUPRO/AIT.

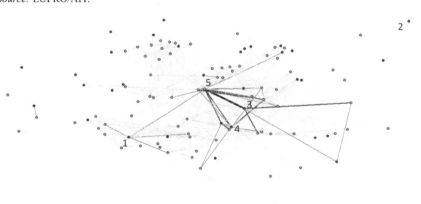

Figure 13E.1b Sub-network of FP6-ICT TUR with German–Turkish organizations.

Notes: 1 = TUBITAK; 2 = Technical University of Istanbul; 3 = Orta Dogu – Middle East Technical University; 4 = Bilkent University; 5 = Fraunhofer Society.
Source: EUPRO/AIT.

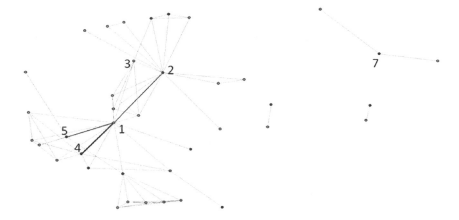

Figure 13E.1c Sub-network of FP7-ICT TUR with German–Turkish organizations.

Notes: 1 = Fraunhofer Society; 2 = Bilkent University; 3 = Berlin University of Technology; 4 = Koc
University; 5 = Orta Dogu – Middle East Technical University; 7 = TUBITAK.
Source: EUPRO/AIT.

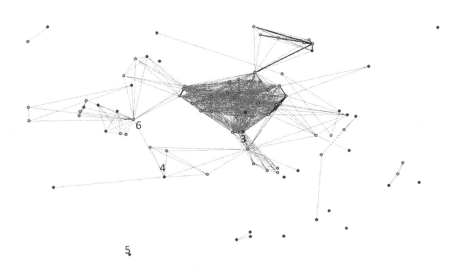

Figure 13E.2a Sub-network of FP6-Biotech TUR with German–Turkish organizations.

Notes: 3 = University of Ankara; 4 = TUBITAK; 5 = Orta Dogu – Middle East Technical University;
6 = Helmholtz Association.
Source: EUPRO/AIT.

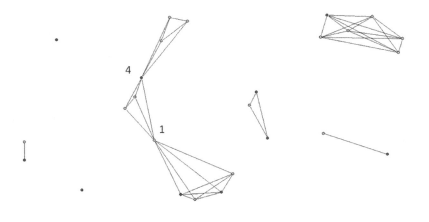

Figure 13E.2b Sub-network of FP7-Biotech TUR with German–Turkish organizations.
Notes: 1 = Leibniz Association; 4 = Sabanci University.
Source: EUPRO/AIT.

Figure 13E.3a Sub-network of FP6-Nano TUR with German–Turkish organizations.
Notes: 3 = Orta Dogu – Middle East Technical University; 4 = Fraunhofer Society; 5 = Bilkent University.
Source: EUPRO/AIT.

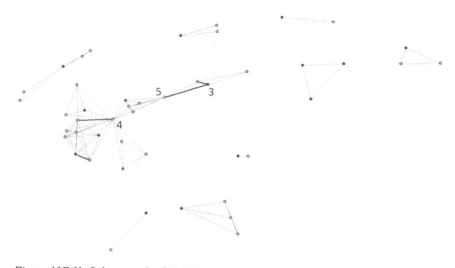

Figure 13E.3b Sub-network of FP7-Nano TUR with German–Turkish organizations.
Notes: 3 = TUBITAK; 4 = Fraunhofer Society; 5 = Helmholtz.
Source: EUPRO/AIT.

Notes

1   Transnational or commuting entrepreneurs are well educated people from Asia who left their home country due to poor economic or political conditions in order to study in the US. As soon as the home country's situation went better, those people moved back and founded knowledge-intensive companies benefiting from their experience and linkages with core (i.e. leading high-tech, regions; cf. Saxenian 2006; Sternberg and Müller 2007: 1).

2   Those are for instance linguistic and cultural skills, as well as weak (or missing) linkages with innovators who in turn have strong ties to global markets (cf. Saxenian 2006: 14; Sternberg and Müller 2007: 1).

3   The Fraunhofer Society is the largest application-oriented research organization in Europe.

4   In case of a disconnected network the largest distance equals infinity (cf. Jansen 2003: 97).

5   In undirected data vertices only differ from each other in the amount of connections they have.

6   The information comprises, in particular, the project objectives, its achievements, project costs, total funding, start and end date, contract type, a standardized subject index, information on the call etc. Moreover information on participating organizations, their department, and contact person with contact details, organization type, and geographical location (NUTS2) are provided. More information is provided in Heller-Schuh *et al.* (2011: 21).

7   AIT retrieved the project data from CORDIS, cleaned, standardized and consolidated it into the EUPRO database (cf. Heller-Schuh *et al.* 2011: 21–23).

8   See http://cordis.europa.eu/projects/home_en.html.
9   The subject index "Nanoscience and Nanotechnology" was only introduced in FP7.
10 The IST element of FP6 has been succeeded by the ICT element in FP7. For a short writing IST in FP5 and FP6 are referred to as ICT.
11 The objective of EURON is to set up a network of excellence in robotics that is aimed at coordination and promotion of robotics research in Europe (project acronym: EURON; RCN: 53683).
12 Project acronym: European Leukemianet; RCN: 75278.
13 With "separated" projects it is meant that if an organization participates in project A and B and another organization participates in projects B and C. Then the organizations participating in the projects A and C are also indirectly interconnected due to participation in project B.
14 Charts of the degree distributions in FPx-y TUR networks are provided in Appendix A.
15 Degree centrality scores of the FPx-ICT networks are provided in Appendix D. In the total ICT networks (FPx-ICT) are considered the 50 most important actors out of 7,154; 4,741 and 2,557 organizations taking part in FP5-, FP6- and FP7-ICT, respectively.
16 In the total ICT networks (FPx-ICT) are considered the 50 most important actors (with respect to a high degree centrality) out of 7,154, 4,741 and 2,557 organizations taking part in FP5-, FP6- and FP7-ICT, respectively. Further, the ranking of the FPx-ICT TUR networks considers the first 10 organizations.
17 The rank orders organizations according to their importance (degree centrality) in the total FP5- to FP7-ICT networks.
18 Fraunhofer Society participated in 35 per cent of all projects in FP6-ICT TUR as is examined in more detail later in the chapter.
19 In the total Biotech networks (FPx-Biotech) are considered the 50 most important actors (with respect to a high degree centrality) out of 1,263, 2,954 and 1,355 organizations taking part in FP5-, FP6- and FP7-Biotech, respectively. Further, the ranking of the FPx-Biotech TUR networks considers the first 10 organizations.
20 The rank orders organizations according to their importance (degree centrality) in the total network (FPx-Biotech) in the considered time periods (FP5 to FP7).
21 The rank orders organizations according to their importance (degree centrality) in the total network (FPx-Nano) in the considered time periods (FP6 and FP7).
22 In the total Nano networks (FPx-Nano) are considered the 50 most important actors (with respect to a high degree centrality) out of 2,589 and 1,739 organizations taking part in FP6- and FP7-Nano, respectively. Further, the ranking of the FPx-Nano TUR networks considers the first 10 organizations.
23 Countries that participate in EU FP projects but that are not member states of the EU are grouped to "others".
24 In total 40, 52 and 40 countries participated in the networks FP5-, FP6- and FP7-ICT TUR, respectively.
25 Degree centrality is calculated for both kinds of networks: networks with Turkish participation (FPx-ICT TUR, Appendix B) and for total ICT networks (FPx-ICT, Appendix C). In FPx-ICT networks are considered the 50 most important actors out of 7,154, 4,741 and 2,557 organizations taking part in FP5-, FP6- and FP7-ICT, respectively.
26 Further participating Fraunhofer institutes were the FIT, IFF, ISI and IGD that were involved only in a small number of projects.

27 In total 5, 52 and 36 countries participated in the networks FP5- FP6- and FP7-Biotech TUR, respectively.
28 In particular were following institutes involved in research projects in FP6- and FP7-Biotech TUR networks: AWI, UFZ, HZM, DLR, HZI of the Helmholtz Association and IPF, FZB, IPK of the Leibniz Association.
29 In total 35 and 39 countries participated in FP6- and FP7-Nano TUR networks, respectively.
30 In particular were following institutes involved in research projects in FP6- and FP7-Nano TUR networks: UFZ, DLR and Forschungszentrum Jülich etc. of the Helmholtz Association and IPA, IAO and IPK etc. of the Fraunhofer Society.

References

Barabási, A.-L. and Albert, R. (1999) Emergence of scaling in random networks. *Science* 286(5439): 509–512.

Barabási, A.-L., Jeong, H., Néda, Z., Ravasz, E., Schubertd, A. and Vicsek, T. (2002) Evolution of the social network of scientific collaborations. *Physica A* 311: 590–614.

Bornholdt, S. and Schuster, H. G. (eds) (2003) *Handbook of Graphs and Networks: From the Genome to the Internet*. Weinheim: Wiley-VCH.

Buchmann, T. and Pyka, A. (2011) Innovation networks. In J. Krafft and M. Dietrich (eds), *Handbook on the Theory of Firms*, 466–484. Cheltenham: Edward Elgar.

de Nooy, W., Mrvar, A. and Batagelj, V. (2005) *Explanatory Social Network Analysis with Pajek*. New York: Cambridge University Press.

Hartmann, D., Pyka, A., Aydin, S., Klauss, L., Stahl, F., Santircioglu, A.,Oberegelsbacher, S., Rashidi, S., Onan, G. and Erginkoç, S. (2012) *Identifizierung und Analyse Deutsch-Türkischer Innovationsnetzwerke: Erste Ergebnisse des TGIN-Projektes*. FZID discussion paper no. 54. Hohenheim: University of Hohenheim.

Heller-Schuh, B., Barber, M., Henriques, L., Paier, M., Pontikakis, D., Scherngell, T., Veltri, G. A. and Weber, M. (2011) *Analysis of Networks in European Framework Programmes (1984–2006)*. JRC Scientific and Technical Report EUR 24759 EN-2011. Luxembourg: Publications Office of the European Union.

Izquierdo, L. R. and Hanneman, R. A. (2006) Introduction to the Formal Analysis of Social Networks Using Mathematica. Available at www.luis.izquierdo.name (accessed 3 September 2012).

Jansen, D. (2003) *Einführung in die Netzwerkanalyse*. Opladen: Verlag Lese & Budich.

Krogmann, Y. and Schwalbe, U. (2011) *Inter-firm R&D Networks in the Global Pharmaceutical Biotechnology Industry during 1985–1998: A Conceptual and Empirical Analysis*. FZID discussion paper 38–2011. Hohenheim: University of Hohenheim.

Pyka, A. (2002) Innovation networks in economics – from the incentive-based to the knowledge-based Approaches. *European Journal of Innovation Management* 5(3): 152–163.

Pyka, A. and Saviotti, P. (2005) The evolution of R&D networking in the biotechnology-based industries. *International Journal of Entrepreneurship and Innovation Management* 5: 49–68.

Roediger-Schluga, T. and Barber, M. J. (2006) *The Structure of R&D Collaboration Networks in the European Framework Programmes*. Working paper 1871–9872. Maastricht: UNU-MERIT.

Saxenian, A. (2006) *The New Argonauts: Regional Advantage in a Global Economy.* Cambridge, MA: Harvard University Press.
Sternberg, R. and Müller, C. (2007) The "new argonauts", their local and international linkages and their impact on regional growth: empirical evidence from transnational entrepreneurs returning to Shanghai/China. Presented at Interdependencies of Interactions in Local and Sectoral Innovation Systems, DIME WP 2.3 Workshop, March.
Wasserman, S. and Faust, K. (1994) *Social Network Analysis – Methods and Applications.* Cambridge: Cambridge University Press.
Watts, D. J. and Strogatz, S. H. (1998) Collective dynamics of "small-world" networks. *Nature* 393(6684): 440–442.

Websites

EU Leukemianet (2004): a project in the scope of the Biotechnology program of the EU FPs, http://cordis.europa.eu/search/index.cfm?fuseaction=proj.document&PJ_LANG=EN&PJ_RCN=7921918&pid=0&q=41FCCF1D034B580DA5D83385C11646AD&type=adv (accessed 8 October 2012).
EUR-Lex (2003/C 64/08): declaration about the admission of Turkey's participation in FP6, http://eur-lex.europa.eu/LexUriServ/LexUriServ.do?uri=OJ:C:2003:064:0018:0018:EN:PDF (accessed 12 September 2012).
EURON (2000): a project in the scope of the ICT program of the EU FPs, http://cordis.europa.eu/search/index.cfm?fuseaction=proj.document&PJ_LANG=EN&PJ_RCN=4914461&pid=0&q=155922808C4D3F724FE8C379419348BE&type=adv (accessed 25 September 2012).
Fraunhofer: www.fraunhofer.de/en/about-fraunhofer.html and www.nachhaltigkeit.fraunhofer.de/de/institute.html (accessed 21 September 2012).
Helmholtz: www.helmholtz.de/en/about_us and www.helmholtz.de/en/about_us/structure_governance (accessed 21 September 2012).
Leibniz: www.leibniz-gemeinschaft.de/ueber-uns and www.leibniz-gemeinschaft.de/institute-museen/alle-einrichtungen (accessed 13.10.2012).
TUBITAK: www.tubitak.gov.tr/sid/1010/pid/547/index.htm (accessed 25 November 2012).
Virtual Intelligent Forging (2004): a project in the scope of the Nanoscience program of the EU FPs, http://cordis.europa.eu/search/index.cfm?fuseaction=proj.document&PJ_LANG=EN&PJ_RCN=9301862&pid=0&q=C7979A90827789725293467661F7CB95&type=adv (accessed 20 October 2012).

14 Analysis of historical roots and context of Turkish–German academic and scientific-innovative networks

Yaprak Gülcan and Ceyhan Aldemir

Introduction

According to Landes (1998), if countries want to be successful, they need appropriate financial instruments and good management. This chapter suggests two additional aspects in addition to these factors: scientific and commercial networking and trust. Both are indispensable ingredients in building up healthy, cost-free network relations. Germany is a successful case study in understanding the role of academic networks in increasing innovativeness of a country. Networking has contributed a lot to the unique position of Germany. Germany's academic and scientific relations with other countries including Turkey made an impact in increasing its number of patents and publications.

A rather theoretical explanation of this phenomenon comes from Prostolupow *et al.* (2013) who propose that creation and diffusion of knowledge are essential for development and integration of economies. This chapter aims to shed light on the kinds and forms of knowledge transfer between countries by focusing on the case study of Turkey and Germany. It is actually what Prostolupow *et al.* (ibid.) called small-worlds (i.e. small research groups), which create knowledge and innovation. Collaboration particularly when it is among nations is not easy. It takes years to establish trust and acquaintances. Thus, the purpose of this chapter is to investigate the history of scientific and academic (especially at the university and above levels) relationships, which have provided quite a number of publications, projects and patents as a result of academic collaboration between Turkey and Germany.

Academic and scientific relations between Germany and Turkey deserve special concern due to their long histories, despite their totally different cultures. Close relationships between the two countries started in the nineteenth century. At that time, Germany needed to expand to the Middle East and the East (to reach big markets and energy sources) in order to compete with the UK, France and Russia. They built up the Baghdad railway from Istanbul to Baghdad. They founded several schools on the route (Ortaylı 2014). They surely wanted to create not only economic and political ties, but also make cultural influence on the indigenous people. Ottoman Empire was looking for a partner who would protect them politically from French, British and Russian threats and provide them with military and scientific advices, and support. Germany seemed very suitable to satisfy this need. Some similar cultural values, such as admiring discipline, regularity, authoritarianism and militaristic attitudes reinforced ties between the two countries. For instance, during the First World War, Ottomans not only sided with Germans but they even gave the top level command position (chief of staff) to a German, namely Liman von Sanders Pasha (ibid.). Also, in 1870 a German hospital, which still exists, was built in Istanbul.

Even looking further back, we see that, in the 1530s Suleiman the Magnificent had all the religious, political and economic power and in his eyes Charles V, Emperor of Holy Roman-German Empire, was just the king of Vienna. On the German side however, German–Austrian ambassador Ogiler Ghislain De Busbecq, stated in his book (2004) that, in 1550s Turks had superior traits like unity, regularity, discipline, hard work and frugality.

After almost 500 years these traits are the ones which Turks usually identified Germans with. Over time, scientific networking with neighbouring countries gave great impetus to technological advances and countless innovations for Germany. On the contrary, Turks replaced scientific thinking and networking with religious education which surpassed and almost terminated all the positive sciences (earthly sciences) that were in the curricula of Fatih and Suleymaniye Universities as early as the beginning of the seventeenth century. An environment without rationality, empirical research, questioning, distribution of research, scientific networking was established (e.g. in 1580 the grandson of Suleiman ordered his commander in chief to destroy one of the best observatories of its time). Turks started to be defeated by Europeans. This made them think and analyse the reasons why Europeans were superior. They tried to copy and adopt Western military technology all throughout the seventeenth century, but mere imitation of hardware technology and warfare did not prove to be useful. Then, the Turks tried to establish Western institutions particularly after 1839 but this attempt was not successful either. Major reason for such failure was software of the mind (i.e. cultures) (Hofstede 1982). Cultures, especially the visible parts of it (in this case values attached to rational, scientific thinking and empirical research and networking without jealousy among the scientists) were totally different. It requires generations to change the world views or mentalities of people.

Supporting Landes's (1998) arguments above, this chapter suggests that innovation and entrepreneurship require appropriate mental and physical conditions. Western European countries, especially Germany, possess these conditions. It is not a surprise that the Germans came up with thousands of significant innovations. Unfortunately, the Ottomans grasped this very late (in the late 1800s). Upon the request of Sultan Abdülhamid II (1876–1908) who very much appreciated Germans' studiousness and military abilities and skills, a group of Germany military consultants were invited to Turkey in 1883. As of this date and onwards, the influence of France and England started to decrease and German influence increased until to the point that two countries became allies in the First World War (Ortaylı 2014).

The rest of the chapter analyses the history of German–Turkish relations only at the scientific and academic levels. Historical traces of German influence on Turkish higher education and institutions are the major focus. First, the history of academic relationships between the two countries is analysed in five different periods. Then, recent academic collaboration between Germany and Turkey is investigated in the context of European Fifth, Sixth and Seventh Framework Programmes.

Historical periods

The history of academic relationships between the two countries can be studied in five periods. By academic relations, we refer to (1) exchange of scientists, (2) exchange of students, (3) number of publications and (4) establishment of institutions.

The historical periods are categorized as:

- early contacts: 1890–1913;
- war years: 1914–1918;
- early republic years: 1923–1931;
- university reform in Turkey and the role of Germans: 1932–1955; and
- development years: 1956–2014.

Early contacts: 1890–1913

In 1897, Ottoman Cabinet of Ministers decided to invite a German expert physician to realize radical reforms in the education and training system of the Imperial School of Medicine with the approval of Sultan Abdülhamid II. Prussian Ministry of Education advised Prof. Robert Rieder (1861–1913) from University of Bonn and Dr Georg Deycke from Eppendorf Hospital in Hamburg. They came in 1898 and a year later Dr Julius Wieting and Dr Hoffman (orthopaedist) joined them. Prof. Robert Rieder established Gülhane Askeri (Military) Hospital in late 1998 by the order of Sultan Abdülhamid II (previously Imperial School of Medicine's Hospital). Dr Rieder, Dr Deycke and Dr Wieting acted as head surgeons from 1898 to 1914. This hospital still exists and performs excellently.

Also, during this period many Turkish students and physicians were sent to Germany to further complete their educations. On their return, they became instructors and physicians themselves (Widmann 1981). Reciprocally, Germans invited some expert Turkish technicians and workers to Germany to work at the Tobacco Company, Yendidje at Dresden, in 1899. One hundred and twenty five Turkish students arrived Stuttgart in 1903. They first learned German and started to be trained in Mercedes. Ottomans sent many Turkish students to Germany until 1914 (Dölen 2013; Ortaylı 2014). Ottoman higher education during this period composed of religious universities which were called *medrese*. There was one mildly secular higher education institute (Dar-ül-Fünun-Imperial University) and 192 *medreses*. Secular higher education institutes that were under the umbrella of

Imperial University were Imperial Faculty of Medicine (1835); Faculty of Administrative Sciences (1883); Faculty of Law (1890); School of Commerce (1883), and several engineering and military schools. As expected, there was a continuous struggle between secular and religious schools (Kütükoğlu 2000; Tekeli and İlkin 1999; Adıvar 1970).

War years: 1914–1918

In this period, Ottoman administration leaned towards secular education. Especially between 1914 and 1918, Prime Minister Enver Pasha enacted a royal degree to send 3000 students to Germany. Enver Pasha was very much fond of Germans. Germans also admired him a lot to such a degree that they started calling Ottoman Empire as Enverland. In spite of the difficulties of the First World War, it is estimated that at least 700 to 800 Turkish students went to Germany (Dölen 2013; Ortaylı 2014). Some of them were trained as technicians, some as academicians.

During this period, Ottomans invited 30 German academics. The list of the names and their respective fields of expertise is listed in Table 14.1. Many people in those days thought that those scientists came to Turkey to Germanize Turkish higher education system (Tekeli and İlkin 1999). In reality, these scientists contributed significantly to the institutions for forming a secular university.

In line with the contract they made with Ottoman administration, German academics were obliged to learn Turkish and teach in Turkish. In return, they received high salaries as compared to their Turkish counterparts. The contributions of these scientists in such a short time (3 years) were incredible (Dölen 2013; Tekeli and İlkin 1999). These include:

- Establishment of research institutes and laboratories such as:
  - observatory stations
  - experimental psychology
  - earth and mine sciences
  - applied mechanics and electricity labs
  - mathematics
  - physics
  - chemistry
  - zoology
  - botany
  - life sciences.
- Introduction of empirical studies into scientific research for the first time.
- Support of Turkish colleagues in Imperial University to publish. Number of publications in Turkish increased (for a list see Dölen 2013: 30).
- Establishment of well-connected ties with Turks which paid off later.

Unfortunately, due to the First World War, many of the Turkish students went to war in 1915 and they could not make it back. In 1918 both Germans and

Table 14.1 German scientists in Turkey: 1914–1918.

	Name	Area
1	Dr. Anschütz	Pedagogy, psychology
2	Günther Jacoby	Philosophy history
3	Bergstrasser (Doç. Dr.)	Linguistics
4	Giese (Doç. Dr.)	Ural-Altaic languages
5	Prof. Obst	Geography
6	Prof. Richter	German
7	Prof. Hoffman	Economics
8	Prof. Fleck	Public finance
9	Prof. J. Würchmidt	Physics
10	Prof. Leick	Botanic
11	Prof. Zornik	Zoology
12	Prof. Penck	Geology, mineralogy
13	Prof. Aindt	Chemistry
14	Prof. Hoesch	Chemistry
15	Prof. Fester	Industrial chemistry
16	Prof. Nord	Civil law
17	Prof. Schöborn	Public law
18	Prof. Haupt	Antic history
19	Prof. Unger	Archaeology and science of money
20	Prof. Mortmann	History methodology
21	Prof. Würschmidt	Geography
22	Mr. Martin Meftel	German
23	Dr. Hans Junge	Museums
24	Erich Frank	Botanic
25	Heinrich Reimer	Chemistry

Ottomans were defeated and depending upon the orders of allies, German professors left Turkey.

So, the impact of Germans on individual Turks was not as much as the ones who came some 15 years later. However, some scientists like Arndt (chemist), came back in the 1930s and stayed quite a long time. Arndt is still considered as the father of chemistry in Turkey. One of the major contributions of these first generation German scholars to networking is that they have become reference points. They became sort of a bridge between Turkey and Germany.

Early republic years: 1923–1931

Between 1923 and 1933, many Turkish students went to Germany and some German architects came to Turkey. Philip and Gunther (1929–1936) and Ernst Egli (1930–1936) are the most prominent ones. They worked at School of Fine

Arts and are still being remembered. Germans were also effective in the establishment of Ankara Institute of Agriculture which turned to be a university in 1933. Dölen's book (2013) provides valuable information about the early German scientists who visited and worked at the Imperial University in Istanbul between 1914 and 1918.

In 1928, Consultant Oldenburg and his eleven friends came to Ankara and founded Higher Agricultural School. From 1929 to 1933, four German professors worked in this school. Then, a university under the name of Advanced Agricultural Studies Institute was established in 1933 whose rector was a German economist, Prof. Falke. He worked with 20 German professors and with many Turkish assistants who became professors of agriculture and veterinary sciences in the future. Still many of the professors active in profession are the students of these forerunners. Many universities like Ankara University, established very strong ties with Göttingen University (Widmann 1981). Thus, both the old networks and new ones which are created by the exchange of young faculty of the two universities contributed greatly to the joint scientific projects.

University reform in Turkey and the role of Germans: 1932–1955

By 1933, Ataturk, and many Turkish intellectuals and government officials were not happy with the performance of the Imperial University. A pedagogy professor from Geneva University, Mr. Malche, was invited to prepare a report. He submitted his report in May 1932. In May 1933, University Law no. 2252 was accepted, which dissolved Imperial University as of 3 July 1933 and opened a new one by the name of Istanbul University on 1 August 1933.

Coincidentally, a former German professor Philip Schwartz escaped from the political regime of Hitler to Switzerland and established a kind of contour called "Emergency Committee in Aid of Displaced German Scholars". Prof. Malche and Prof. Schwartz helped a lot of German scholars and a few political opponents who were either dispelled or meant to be dismissed and directed these people to Turkey (Reisman 2011).

At least 85 German scholars started to work at Istanbul University during the 1933–1934 academic year. The total number of professors and assistants (Turkish and German) was 323 at the time. Thus, almost one quarter of the academic staff consisted of Germans. The number of students in four faculties of Istanbul University (Faculty of Letters, Faculty of Sciences, Faculty of Law, Faculty of Medicine) was 3437 (Widmann 1981: 54). Also at least 20 more German academicians came to İstanbul Academy of Arts (which is Mimar Sinan University now) (Demir 2008).

In addition, 20 or more German scholars were working at Advanced Agricultural Studies Institute in Ankara. Altogether at least 150 or more German scholars worked at Turkish Institutions in this period. Those working in other state organizations (ministries, banks etc.) are not included. On the other hand, many Turkish students both graduate and undergraduate were sent to Germany by Turkish State as bursary students (see Table 14.2).

Table 14.2 Number of Turkish graduate and undergraduate students sent to Germany by the Turkish state.

Years	Total number of students sent abroad	Germany–Austria	%	Graduates
1929–1930	288	111	38.54	57
1930–1931	278	110	39.56	58
1931–1932	237	100	42.19	51
1932–1933	263	97	37.00	51
1933–1934	–	99	100.00	52
1937–1938	–	133	100.00	60

This period was an enlightenment period for Turkish higher education in several ways:

- Rational thinking and empirical approach to scientific studies were enhanced.
- Long-enduring, life-long institutional and personal relationships were established (Gürüz 2008; Yalçın 2011; Aslanapa 1993; Widmann 1981). Germans who left Turkey after the Second World War were invited to give lectures and conferences. After the deaths of many German professors, Turks published books in memorandum or held memorial ceremonial for many of the German Scholars. Now, there are hundreds of students' students teaching and researching in academia all over Turkey. The networks that they have established with Germans have enormous products as thousands of published articles and tens of international projects (a small example is shown in Table 14.3).
- They acted as intermediaries in establishing academic links between the minorities of both countries which still exists.
- They helped in establishing or developing Turkish academic organizations (including departments, research centres, Faculties and even Universities, e.g. İstanbul Technical University).
- They corrected instruction methods.
- Books, textbooks and hundreds of articles were written in Turkish, (see for a list of these see Widmann 1981).
- Every Faculty started to publish its own journal. (for a list see Widmann 1981).
- University Community conferences brought in more than 70,000 books to establish libraries (Widmann 1981).

Table 14.3 İstanbul University publications between 1933 and 1942.

Books printed by the university	175
Books in print	35
Books printed by professors themselves	100
Translated books	42
Total	352

All in all, German Scholars who fled their countries during 1933–1940 due to several and different reasons did contribute a lot of Turkish academia. They are still respected and remembered by Turks.

Development years: 1956–2014

When Prof. Malche and other German scholars helped establish and start Istanbul University, the number of Professors was 323 (85 Germans) and total number of students was 3437. The number of universities in the country was 2 (İstanbul University and Ankara Agricultural Studies Institute). In time, the number of Turkish institutions that German migrant scholars worked in increased. The institutions where German scholars predominantly worked were, İstanbul Technical University, İstanbul Academy of Fine Arts, Ankara Faculty of Letters, Hygiene Institute, Institute of Mine Enclosing (research), Gazi Institute of Education State Conservatory. Germans worked in almost all academic fields and in many of these they have become sort of legendary founding fathers; like Arndt for chemistry, Neumann-Hirsh Rustow and Isaac for economics and business, Bruno Taut for architecture, Röpke for city planning and economics, and Carl Ebert for performance arts (especially opera). Their students, clients and patients created a huge network that eventually led to the establishment of long thought Turkish–German University in 2010 in İstanbul.

Today, there are 184 universities (104 state and 80 private) in Turkey. As of 1 April 2014, the number of undergraduate students is around 5 million. The number of graduates in master's degree is 262,752 and the number of doctoral students is 65,864. Out of 78,000 applications for accreditations of diplomas of individuals from many countries, 5 per cent comes from Germany. That means that there is a large group of Turkish students going to Germany every year. Highest proportion of students prefers to go to Germany in the Erasmus programmes. DAAD and Goethe Institute (formerly German Cultural Center) helped a lot in directing Turkish students to Germany.

German scholars are the most preferred partners among Turkish scholars to participate in joint projects. After Turkey was accepted to Erasmus programmes and EU research funds, the number of joint projects especially in Framework (FP5 and FP6) programmes increased tremendously (Prostolupow *et al.* 2013). This is also a result of the long history of scientific cooperation and collaboration between Germany and Turkey.

As stated by Prostolupow *et al.* (2013), the creation and diffusion of knowledge are not only essential for innovation but also for development and integration of economies. Knowledge generation and diffusion may not take place in crowded groups, but rather in small academic and research groups which Prostolupow *et al.* (ibid.) call small-worlds. A similar argument is forwarded by Levy and Muller (2006) who claimed communities (research groups) rely on a constant exchange of knowledge and information which eventually end up with increased production of new academic work (i.e. number of publications, number of patents, number of projects). The academic outputs of German–Turkish collaborative academic efforts between 1933 and 1942 are clearly very good examples of this. The small-world communities that Turkey and Germany have established kept regenerating itself since the 1950s. There are at least 348 collaborations between Turkish and German universities (Türk and Çınar 2013). Thousands of Turkish students go to Germany every year. 100 year old dream of founding a Turkish–German University in İstanbul has been realized and the school started enrolling students since 2011.

According to Prostolupow *et al.* (2013) Turkish and German scholars participated in more than 7000 nanotechnology projects. The number of patents increased from around 100 in the 1930s and 1940s, to 4528 in 2013. German organizations had the highest involvement in research projects with Turkish participation in the information communication technology, biotechnology and nanotechnology sectors from FP5 to FP7. Thus, Turkish–German research groups (small-worlds) proved to very successful in producing and diffusing knowledge very rapidly and widely. These small-world networks are the products of 120 years of scientific and academic relations between the two countries. Thus we expect more and more productive behaviour out of these small-world networks.

European Fifth, Sixth and Seventh Framework Programmes

Investigating the academic relationship between Germany and Turkey from a historical point of view reveals the recent scientific research networks among parties. The recent network ties are from data of the European Fifth, Sixth and Seventh Framework Programmes (FP5, FP6, FP7) within which Turkey and Germany have collaborated. To be able to make a descriptive analysis, the Framework Programmes were first divided into three subcategories. These subcategories are:

- FP5 (1999–2002)
  - Turkey coordinator, Germany participant
  - Germany coordinator, Turkey participant
  - both of the countries are participant.
- FP6 (2003–2006)
  - Turkey coordinator, Germany participant
  - Germany coordinator, Turkey participant
  - both of the countries are participant.
- FP7 (2007–2013)
  - Turkey coordinator, Germany participant
  - Germany coordinator, Turkey participant
  - both of the countries are participant.

From 1999 to 2002, Germany has participated in 46 per cent of the projects within which Turkey took place. As can be seen from Table 14.4, during this period, there are no projects that Turkey is coordinator and Germany is participant whereas there exists 7 projects that Germany is the coordinator and Turkey is among the participants. There are 27 projects that have been carried out in joint collaboration where both parties act as participants. IST (Information society), INCO 2 (Specific International Scientific Cooperation Activities) and EESD (Environment and sustainable development) are the fields that the two countries mostly collaborate. Figure 14.1 demonstrates the disciplines of total joint projects of Turkey and Germany in FP5 Projects. Totally Turkish and German academicians have collaborated in six branches of 34 Projects.

While Middle East Technical University (METU) is the first in the ranking with 10 Projects by actively participating in FP5, Istanbul University is the second in the ranking with 3 Projects. Among the four projects mostly participating German institution is Fraunhofer Gesellschaft zur Forderung der Angewandten Forschung E.V., as participant in two projects and as coordinator in two of the four projects. This institute is the biggest Applied Research Centre in Europe.

Table 14.4 FP5 projects.

	Germany coordinator	Turkey coordinator	Both participants countries	Total joint projects	Total projects	Share (%)
EESD	1	–	6	7	1984	0.4
GROWTH	1	–	4	5	2118	0.2
HUMAN POTENTIAL	–	–	3	3	5082	0.1
INCO 2	3	–	4	7	1193	0.6
IST	1	–	8	9	2464	0.4
LIFE QUALITY	1	–	2	3	2976	0.1
TOTAL	7	0	27	34	15817	0.21

Note: IST: information society; INCO 2: international collaboration; EESD: energy, environment and sustainable development; GROWTH: growth; HUMAN POTENTIAL: human potential; LIFE QUALITY: life quality.

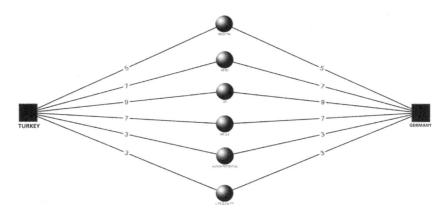

Figure 14.1 FP5 projects.

Turkey has taken place in 374 FP6 Projects between 2003 and 2006 and collaborated with Germany among 221 of them. Germany has taken part in 59 per cent of the projects that Turkey has participated. There are 9 projects where Turkey is coordinator and Germany is participant and there exists 42 Projects where Germany is coordinator and Turkey is participant. The number of jointly participated projects is 170. Two countries mostly collaborated in information technologies, sustainable development and nanotechnology (Table 14.5). Figure 14.2 shows the German–Turkish network in FP6 projects. It is seen that Turkish and German academicians have worked together totally in 221 projects with 15 branches. Compared to FP5 projects, the total number of joint projects has increased by 550 per cent.

METU is again the first in the ranking in FP6 Projects with 44 projects. It is followed by The Scientific and Technological Research Council of Turkey-TÜBİTAK (33 projects), Boğaziçi University (16 projects), İstanbul Technical

Table 14.5 FP6 projects

	Germany coordinator	Turkey coordinator	Both participants countries	Total joint projects	Total projects	Share (%)
IST	9	6	33	48	1113	4.31
LIFESCIHEALTH	2	–	5	7	601	1.16
SUSTDEV	9	–	34	43	668	6.44
INFRAST.	1	–	4	5	139	3.60
COORDINATION	1	–	7	8	100	8.00
INNOVATION	3	–	9	12	238	5.04
MOBILITY	2	2	8	12	4531	0.26
SME	3	–	7	10	486	2.06
CITIZENS	4	1	12	17	144	11.81
INCO	2	–	5	7	318	2.20
FOOD	3	–	12	15	189	7.94
NMP	1	–	17	18	430	4.19
AEROSPACE	–	–	5	5	241	2.07
POLICIES	1	–	11	12	519	2.31
SOCIETY	1	–	1	2	166	1.20
TOTAL	42	9	170	221	9883	2.24

Note: LIFESCIHEALTH: life sciences, genomics and biotechnology for health; SUSTDEV: sustainable development, global change and ecosystems; INFRAST.: research infrastructures; COORDINATION: co-ordination of research activities; INNOVATION: research and innovation; MOBILITY: Marie Curie actions – human resources and mobility; SME: SME activities; CITIZENS: citizens and governance in a knowledge-based society; FOOD: food quality and safety; NMP: nanotechnologies and nano-sciences, knowledge-based multifunctional materials and new production processes and devices; AEROSPACE: aeronautics and space; POLICIES: development of research/innovation policies; SOCIETY: science and society.

University (15 projects), Sabancı University (10 projects), Ege University (9 projects), Bilkent University (8 projects), Koç University (5 projects) and Hacettepe University (5 projects).

On the German side, Fraunhofer Gesellschaft zur Forderung der Angewandten Forschung E.V. is the first in the ranking with 27 projects; followed by Stuttgart University (13 projects), Deutsches Zentrum Fuer-Luft und Raumfahrt EV (13 projects), Bremen University (10 projects), Max Planck Gesellschaft Zur Förderung Der Wissenschaften E.V (8 projects), Rheinisch-West faelische Technische Hochschule Aachen (8 projects), Dresden Technical University (8 projects).

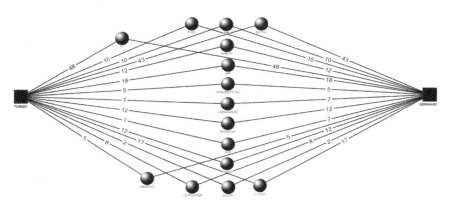

Figure 14.2 FP6 projects.

Between 2007 and 2013, Turkey has participated in 955 FP7 projects and collaborated with Germany in 487 of them. Table 14.6 shows that among the FP7 Projects, there are 15 projects where Turkey has been coordinator with Germany participant and there are 96 projects as German coordinator and Turkey participant. The number of jointly carried out projects where both countries acted as participants is 376. It is observed from Figure 14.3 that the total number of projects has increased and the network has widened when compared to FP5 and FP6 programmes. In FP5, the number of branches that indicate collaboration of German Turkish academicians is only 6 whereas it has increased to 15 for FP6 and 17 for FP7 projects.

Totally, the number of joint projects in FP5, FP6 and FP7 are 34, 221 and 376, respectively. The major cause of this increase is the participation of Turkey in the FP5 1999 for the first time. The participation rate of Turkey has increased from FP5 to FP6 and from FP6 to FP7. Turkish universities and TUBITAK have gained significant experience in participation in Framework Programme projects in time.

As with other programmes, METU ranks first in the participation in FP7 framework projects with 43 projects. Boğaziçi University ranks second with 17 projects and ITU ranks third with 15 projects. The top three universities are followed by Sabancı University (10 projects), Ege University (9 projects), Bilkent

University (8 projects), Ankara University (7 projects) and Hacettepe University (6 projects).

In the context of FP7, Deutsches Zentrum Fuer-Luft und Raumfahrt E.V. has the most number of project participation from Germany with 71 projects and the second is Fraunhofer Gesellschaft zur Forderung der Angewandten Forschung E.V. with 63 projects, while the third is Forschungszentrum Juelich GMBH with 31 project participation. These are followed by Bundesministerium Fuer Bildung und Forschung (21 projects), Dresden Technical University (17 projects), Karlsruher Institut Fuer Technologie (15 projects), Berlin Technical University (14 projects), Bremen University (13 projects) and Stuttgart University (12 projects), respectively.

Turkey and Germany are involved in a total of 742 projects under FP5, FP6 and FP7. In particular, highest cooperation is in Information Technology, Energy, Nanosciences, Nanotechnologies, Sustainable Development, SME and Knowledge-Based Bioeconomics programmes.

Table 14.6 FP7 projects.

	Germany coordinator	Turkey coordinator	Both participants countries	Total joint projects	Total projects	Share (%)
SSH	8	2	24	34	249	13.65
INCO	8	1	17	26	178	14.61
ICT	7	6	47	60	2282	2.63
SME	14	1	42	57	989	5.76
NMP	4	1	37	42	830	5.06
ENERGY	2	–	14	16	347	4.61
SIS	3	–	14	17	182	9.34
PEOPLE	9	3	12	24	9710	0.25
INFRAST.	4	–	23	27	345	7.83
TRANSPORT	10	–	27	37	627	5.90
SEC	3	–	9	12	266	4.51
HEALTH	5	–	16	21	1004	2.09
KBBE	9	–	44	53	514	10.31
REGIONS	–	–	5	5	81	6.17
SPACE	3	–	8	11	211	5.21
ENV	7	1	30	38	496	7.66
REGPOT	–	–	1	1	198	0.51
TOTAL	96	15	370	481	18509	2.59

Note: SSH: socio-economic sciences and humanities; ENERGY: energy; SIS: science in society; PEOPLE: people; TRANSPORT: transport; SEC: security research; HEALTH: health; KBBE: knowledge based bio-economy; REGIONS: regions of knowledge; SPACE: space; ENV: environment; REGPOT: research potential of convergence regions.

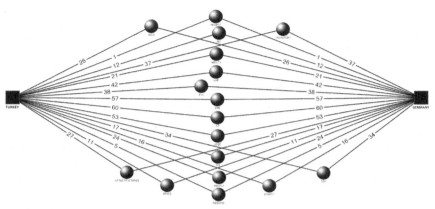

Figure 14.3 FP7 projects.

The German–Turkish scientific research network became stronger and the cooperation developed between the two countries in terms of the transfer and share of knowledge and economic integration, within the scope of European Framework Programme (FP5, FP6 and FP7) projects. In Turkey, METU, Boğaziçi University and İstanbul Technical University are the major actors playing key roles. In Germany, Fraunhofer Gesellschaft zur Forderung der Angewandten Forschung E.V. and Deutsches Zentrum Fuer-Luft und Raumfahrt E.V. are located in the centre of the innovation network.

Conclusion

Germany and Turkey are two countries with a long history of economic, social, political and scientific relations deserving special concern. Despite their totally different cultures, German and Turkish actors have collaborated in many areas including academia which is the subject of this chapter.

From 1890 to 2014, German and Turkish researchers exchanged knowledge in many scientific areas. Particularly, German academicians helped and guided their Turkish partners in increasing the effectiveness of the higher education system, establishing and/or developing academic organizations (such as departments and universities), establishing academic links between the minorities of both countries. Thus, the role and effect of Germany in Turkish higher education system is indispensable.

As a result of a long and effective historical collaboration between Germany and Turkey, currently, there is a multi-actor innovation network in academy sector; in addition to a high-level transfer of knowledge and economic integration. The network relations between Turkish and German institutions in the academic sector are strong and persistent, producing many academic project and patents.

References

Adıvar, A. A. (1970) *Osmanlı Türklerinde İlim*. İstanbul: Remzi Kitabevi.

Aslanapa, O. (1993) *Türkiye'de Avusturyalı Sanat Tarihçileri ve Sanatkarlar*. İstanbul: Eren Yayıncılık.

Busbecq, O. G. (2004) *Türkiye'yi Böyle Gördüm*. İstanbul: Elips Kitap.

Demir, R. (2008) *Üniversitenin bugünü ve yarını* (3rd edition). Ankara: Palme.

Dölen, E. (2013) *İstanbul Darülfünun'unda Alman Müderrisler, 1915–1918*. İstanbul: İstanbul Bilgi Üniversitesi Yayınları.

Gürüz, K. (2008) *Yirmibirinci Yüzyılın Başında Türk Milli Eğitim Sistemi*. İstanbul: Türkiye İş Bankası Kültür Yayınları.

Hofstede, G. (1982) Cultural pitfalls for Dutch expatriates in Indonesia: lessons for Europeans, part 1. *Euro-Asia Business Review* 1(1): 37–41.

Kütükoğlu, M. S. (2000) *20. Asra Erişen İstanbul Medreseleri*. Ankara: Türk Tarih Kurumu Yayınları.

Landes, D. S. (1998) *The Wealth and Poverty of Nations: Why Some are so Rich and Some so Poor*. New York: W. W. Norton and Company.

Levy, R. and Muller, P. (2006) *Do Academic Laboratories Correspond to Scientific Communities?* Working paper. Strasbourg: BETA.

Ortaylı, İ. (2014) *Osmanlı İmparatorluğu'nda Alman Nüfuzu*. İstanbul: Timaş Yayınları.

Prostolupow, I., Pyka, A. and Schuh, B. (2013) *Turkish–German Innovation Networks in the European Research Landscape*. FZID discussion paper 79-2013. Stuttgart: Universität Hohenheim.

Reisman, A. (2011) *Nazizmden Kaçanlar ve Atatürk'ün Vizyonu, Çeviren: Gül Güven*. İstanbul: Türkiye İş Bankası Kültür Yayınları.

Tekeli, İ. and İlkin, S. (1999) *Osmanlı İmparatorluğu'nda Eğitim ve Bilgi Üretim Sisteminin Oluşumu ve Dönüşümü*. Ankara: Türk Tarih Kurumu Yayınları.

Türk, F. and Çınar, S. (2013) Türkiye ile Almanya Arasındaki Bilimsel İlişkiler: Türk Alman Üniversiteleri. *Gazi Akademik Bakış* 7(13): 45–66.

Widmann, H. (1981) *Atatürk Üniversitesi Reformu* (tr. A. Kazancıgil and S. Bozkurt). İstanbul: İstanbul Üniversitesi Cerrahpaşa Tıp Fakültesi Atatürk'ün Yüzüncü Doğum Yılını Kutlama Yayınları Özel Seri 3.

Yalçın, K. (2011) *Haymatlos*. İstanbul: Türkiye İş Bankası Kültür Yayınları.

15 Turkish–German innovation networks in the renewable energy sector

A social network analysis

Sule Gündüz, Mehmet Aldonat Beyzatlar and Yeşim Kuştepeli

Introduction

The aim of this chapter is to map the relationship between twelve renewable energy firms as well as their relations with other institutions within the framework of Turkish–German innovation networks (TGIN), of the European integration project. Since the world is assumed to be running out of its non-renewable energy resources in the near future, the importance of utilizing renewable energy resources is approved by all the nations in the world. Therefore, renewable energy usage is supported and subsidized by governments. In order to attract investors to this sector, countries develop alternative incentives and laws. Turkey has enacted Law No. 5346 for the regulation of energy matters. Both domestic and foreign investments in the renewable energy sector have been increasing in Turkey in the last decades. Being the first to install wind power plants, according to the 2015 report of the European Wind Energy Association, Germany is also the country that heavily invested in Turkey in the last decade. Kuştepeli *et al.* (2013b) demonstrate that Germany's FDI inflow to Turkey followed a continuous increase from 2005 to 2008 and from 2009 to 2011 despite the crisis effect. Also, the share of Germany in total FDI increased from 2006 to 2010 continuously. The number of German firms established in Turkey stands clearly in the first rank with respect to all other countries from the period 1954 to 2012, with a total of 4885 firms. Besides the fact that Turkey has close social relations with Germany, the authors analyse the innovation networks in the wind energy sector, as Germany also has close investment ties with Turkey in this sector. This investigation tries to elucidate Germany's innovation networks with Turkish firms using social network analysis (SNA).

The study visualizes the existing relations using SNA, which is a method that uses the terms and taxonomy of social sciences as well making use of mathematical terminology and measurement tools. In our study, SNA is employed to connote the relationships between the twelve renewable energy firms and other governmental and nongovernmental institutions.

The analysis behind the network builds on a review of literature, questionnaires and industry structure, on indicators of renewable energy innovation systems as such, and on relevant connected issues. In addition, it builds on assessment and insights from experienced managers, firm owners, engineers and researchers in the field. It is the intention of the study to spread knowledge to other interested parties (e.g. suppliers, customers, other firms, policy makers and other governmental bodies, etc.). However, a two-way communication is important and necessary for multidirectional sectoral development. The interaction between both parties is not very complex, and knowledge and technology transfer should be addressed intensively (Borup et. al. 2013).

Network ties among the agents are crucial in the study of information spillovers. In today's world, the importance of knowledge based economies is increasing at a rapid pace. Networks, which refer to relationships and interactions within a group of actors, play a fundamental role as a medium for the spread of information, ideas, and influence among its members. This encourages the hope that an idea or innovation will appear and it can either perish or make significant improvements in the network (Kempe *et al.* 2003). As the intensity of the relationship between the members of the network increases, so does the amount of transfer of knowledge, and that in turn contributes to the invention of new technologies, ideas and processes. Innovativeness increases per se if entrepreneurs within the same network trust each other and share the knowledge they have with the other agents. Strong ties serve as bridges for knowledge transfer between the actors.

A strong network relationship or highly dense ties between the actors/nodes implies an accelerating rate of learning and diffusion of knowledge. According to the results of this study, the total network density of the twelve renewable energy firms is around 0.15, which indicates a weak network within the sector. The central actor in the network is a sub-contractor in the renewable energy sector. This company provides manufacturing and construction services such as building wind-measurement tower stations for the leading renewable energy firms in the sector. This company is also among the most reputable sub-contractors in the Turkish renewable energy sector, giving complete manufacturing and installation services as well as providing logistic and maintenance services.

The organization of this chapter is as follows: the following section mentions the previous studies referring to the concept of social network analysis and its use of related topics. We then provide data and results which exhibit the network of renewable energy sector. Finally, we present our conclusions.

Literature review

In today's world, the principal challenge for many of the developed and developing nations of the world is to promote knowledge-based economies. Since knowledge-driven economies generate and exploit knowledge, the process is closely related to the innovation capabilities of the nations. In their study, Kuştepeli *et al.* (2013a) emphasize the essence of knowledge creation and diffusion between actors of the network to support innovative activities. They claim that strong network ties have a positive effect on the diffusion of information. They analyse the number of cooperative relationships between the agents and the innovativeness of firms in the Turkish textile industry by conducting surveys and using social network analysis (SNA).

A social network analysis is an interdisciplinary/multidisciplinary methodology having its roots in psychology, sociology and anthropology. Especially after the 1960s, inclusion of mathematics, statistics, and computing made it an attractive tool for other disciplines. Knoke and Yang (2008) and Scott (2000) mention that the usage of SNA to derive policy implications has been increasing tremendously in economics, marketing or industrial engineering, biology and some other positive sciences in the last decades. Many scientists agree on the fact that people learn and remember the things if they are visualized. Özyer *et al.* (2013) accentuates the contribution of graphing methods to SNA while visualization makes it easier to grasp the complex social network structures. According to Knoke and Yang (2008), the essence of network analysis is the degree of relationships between interacting units or nodes which in turn determine the degree of intentional or unintentional knowledge transfer between these agents.

Brass *et al.* (2004) depict a network as a structure representing the intensity of relationships or strength of ties between the pairs of nodes. Scott (2000) agrees with them in the sense that these relations defined by linkages between the nodes/actors are intrinsic components of SNA. The two indispensable components of SNA are agents/actors and their relations. Knoke and Yang (2008) suggest that the joint analysis of these two factors determine the boundaries for SNA. They define "relation" as a tie or a type of connection or network between the nodes/actors. Caulon (2005) describes a social network as a combination of network structure and social structure. Nearly all of the scholars agree with Caulon's definition. Some of them even make a more detailed description. According to Watts (2003), a network has an evolving structure, so graphing the actors or nodes in SNA is like taking snapshots of an everlasting evolutionary process. Ehrlich and Carboni (2005) suggest that SNA, by means of drawing the complex set of ties between the nodes, provides information about where information cascades fail/succeed and where opportunities for innovation fail/are found.

Social interactions contribute to the spread of knowledge, which in turn has a significant impact on product innovation. Tsai and Ghoshal (1998) mention the importance of social capital in value creation. Burt (2000) argues that there is a connection between social networks and social capital. Social capital is the contextual complement to human capital, which is the core element in the innovation process. Some scholars agree the idea that people or organizations which are more innovative are somehow better connected. Although strong intra-firm ties may foster innovation, it is claimed by many scholars that innovation improves in environments where competition exists, and what is maybe more important than that is the belief of organizations in the rule of law protecting their inventions and innovations.

Bullinger *et al.* (2010) claim that besides being conducive to innovation, community-based innovation competitions provide the possibilities of interaction and cooperation between participants. They investigate whether and how innovation flourishes in a competitive environment. The results of their study imply that a very high or a very low degree of cooperative orientation spur innovativeness, whereas a medium degree ends up with a low degree of innovativeness. All in all, although it is accepted by many scholars that competition is good for innovation, sometimes very harsh competition may decrease the innovativeness of the society or the country as a whole, while there are serious negatives among knowledge spillovers.

Foxon *et al.* (2005) investigated the UK innovation systems for six new and renewable energy technologies. The authors state that knowledge sharing within the bounds of commercial confidentiality could be helpful for the development of the sector. They imply that due to harsh competition, some firms do not share knowledge so as to keep it confidential. They also add that the benefits of collaboration are obvious so countries have to think about the drivers, barriers and system failures in their innovation systems. One of the concluding remarks of their study is that successful innovation requires different actors with distinctive roles to work together for common goals. The study of Gao (2011) justifies this idea by showing how the interaction between the actors fosters the development of that sector. Gao (ibid.) models the Irish renewable energy innovation networks using SNA. The findings of the study reveal that technological advancement takes place in complex innovation systems. The results show that the ocean energy network is a cohesive network which implies a high density of knowledge sharing between the highly connected communities due to frequent involvement in collaborative projects. Moreover, he concludes that ocean energy technology does not advance solely by means of fundamental research, but also the diffusion of knowledge via the network between agents contributes to the innovativeness of that sector.

As stated in the literature, social network analysis provides an effective method of visualizing network relations in a sector by means of determining places of and relations between actors. Whether competition fosters knowledge transfer and innovation or not is affected by factors such as the strength and reliability of legal institutions (Nooteboom 2001). The literature points out that especially in developing countries, lack of a strong legal institutional setting may hinder knowledge transfer between firms which then may cause weak network relations.

Data and social network analysis

This chapter aims to demonstrate the Turkish–German innovation networks through the renewable energy sector in Turkey. For this purpose, the network of renewable energy firms, which have partnerships or affiliation with German firms, is constructed and statistically analysed by SNA. The fundamental methodology covering SNA leads us to observe the connections formed by Turkish–German relations via the renewable energy sector. In order to identify the effectiveness of renewable energy firms in the Turkish–German innovation networks, survey and roster analyses have been conducted during face-to-face interviews with 15 firms,[1] which are located in İzmir and İstanbul regions. Moreover, scientifically designed questionnaires are filled in by these firms and valuable information is obtained within the context of the relations between Turkey and Germany. SNA is applied to provide an in-depth insight into the specific roles of the actors and their interactions within the network by asking them to define the agencies that they contact frequently. There exist four key figures in the network; firms, banks, universities, public and private institutions. According to firms' answers, the general network map, which can be seen from Figures 15.1–3, is constructed to demonstrate SNA.

Table 15.1 shows the summary statistics of sectoral distribution, number of firms, number of subcontractors, average number of workers and average year of establishment of the firms presented. Evidently, most of the firms operate as wind and solar energy firms, and 9 of them function as subcontractors. Average number of workers is around 27 (except the company with 840 workers), where the average year of establishment is about 2004.

Table 15.1 Descriptive statistics.

Number of firms	15	
Sectoral distribution	Solely wind energy	2
	Solely solar energy	1
	Wind and solar energy	8
	Other (e.g. hydroelectric energy)	4
Average number of workers*		27
Number of subcontractors		9
Average year of establishment		2004

Note: * A company with 840 workers is excluded from the analysis.

Table 15.2 Innovativeness in the last three years.

	Yes	No
New or significantly improved products/services	9	6
Are the products/services also new to the market	7	8
New/significantly improved production processes, components or materials	10	5
New or significantly improved strategy	11	4
New or significantly improved organizational structures	8	7
Considerably improved market concept	7	8

In Table 15.2, some questions about the innovativeness of firms in the last three years are presented. New or significantly improved products and services are created by 9 firms, where only 7 of them are also new to the market. Moreover,

10 firms used new or significantly improved production processes, components or materials. New or significantly improved strategies and organizational structures are developed by 11 and 8 firms, respectively. Only 7 of the firms confirmed that they have considerably improved their market concept.

Figures 15.1, 15.2 and 15.3 demonstrate the position of the nodes (actors) on the network map with respect to overall edges (connections) between the agents. In these figures, surveyed firms are denoted by squares, where other nodes are marked with different shapes or icons. Having different shapes or icons of nodes on a network map provides a better understanding of which agents are in which position and supplies visual clues about the formal properties of the network or the attributes of the clusters that can also be statistically tested. Firms' names are considered as secret information and codes are given to identify firms' regional attribute. ANK, DEN, GER, IST and IZM denote that the firms are located in Ankara, Denizli, Germany, İstanbul or İzmir, respectively.

According to their centrality properties, nodes are located at the centre of the network or are spread around. Briefly, nodes with more connections are situated in the inner parts of the network map whereas the ones with fewer links are situated at the outer parts of the network. In line with this, universities, public and private institutions are more important for the renewable energy sector in comparison with the so-called "firms", which have connections with surveyed firms. Triangles (firms) are located through the outside of the network, where diamonds (public and private institutions) and cap-icons (universities) are concentrated around the firms surveyed. Between the outer area and inner parts, banks (bank icons) are positioned in the middle parts of the network map.

In addition to the mapping of network ties, the SNA approach provides graph metrics as statistical information, which demonstrates the quantity and structure of connection paths between organizations. This methodology elucidates the descriptive questions, such as differences of degree between competitors, as well as the more complex question of function, such as centrality and clustering characteristics. The network analysis of this chapter also focuses on these statistical measures in the renewable energy sector network to examine Turkish–German innovation networks by using the effectiveness parameters. These measures indicate how actors behave through the network.

Graph metrics of this network analysis are: degree centrality, betweenness centrality, closeness centrality, eigenvector centrality and clustering coefficient. Degree centrality refers to the number of direct links attached to other nodes in the network. The most successful firm should have the highest number of customers, suppliers and partners. Thus, degree centrality is an important and appropriate measure. Therefore, degree centrality (the number of direct links) could influence betweenness centrality, closeness centrality and eigenvector centrality positively, where it affects clustering coefficient negatively. The degree centrality can also be interpreted in terms of the immediate possibility of a node for catching whatever is flowing through the network, such as information, money etc.

In networks, there is a natural distance metric between all nodes, defined by the length of their shortest paths. Thus, the more central a node is, the lower its

Figure 15.1 The general network of renewable energy firms subject to questionnaire (Fruchterman-Reingold layout).

Note: Squares: renewable energy firms surveyed; triangles: other firms; bank icons: banks; cap icons: universities; diamonds: public and private institutions.

total distance to all other nodes. Closeness can be regarded as a measure of how long it will take to spread information, such as money etc. within all the other nodes sequentially. To obtain information, the firm should be near to others and because of this the node in the nearest position on average could obtain information more efficiently. Betweenness centrality is the measure of a node within the network which quantifies the number of times a node acts as a bridge along the

Figure 15.2 The general network of renewable energy firms subject to questionnaire (Harel-Koren layout).

Note: Symbols defined as for Figure 15.1 above.

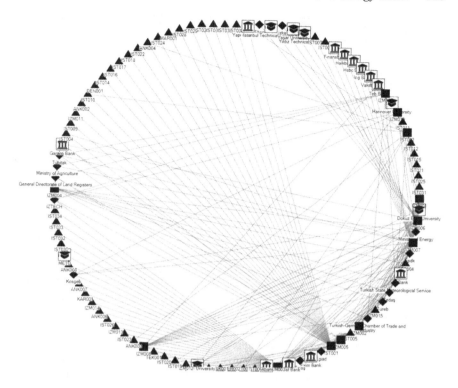

Figure 15.3 The general network of renewable energy firms subject to questionnaire (circle layout).

Note: Symbols defined as for Figure 15.1 above.

shortest path between other nodes. To control information flow, firms should be between other nodes because the node can interrupt information flow between other nodes.

In brief, closeness and betweenness centrality measures demonstrate the length of the shortest path that each node has acting as a bridge between other nodes, respectively. Closeness centrality is calculated by counting the total number of steps from one node to another. Betweenness centrality is calculated by taking every pair of the network and counting how many times a node can interrupt the shortest paths (geodesic distance) between the two nodes of the pair. Briefly, when the number of connections of a surveyed firm is high, the betweenness and closeness centrality measures are expected to be higher with respect to firms with fewer connections.

Eigenvector centrality is also an important criterion, which should be taken into account by the analyst that shows the effectiveness of the agent through the network. This measure is directly and positively related to the degree centrality (number of connections) of surveyed firms. More connections mean high degree, closeness, betweenness and eigenvector centrality measures. The last one is clustering coefficient that shows which nodes in a network tend to cluster. Clustering through the general network arises from having fewer connections, which also shows that the surveyed firm does not tend to get in touch with more actors within the network. Those surveyed firms with a higher clustering coefficient can affect and be affected by the network less than all other actors when compared with other surveyed firms with a lower clustering coefficient.

These statistics mentioned above are used to summarize and support the network maps (Figures 15.1–3) numerically. As can be seen from Table 15.3, IZM003 has the largest betweenness (2063.0095) and closeness (0.0055) centrality statistics by having the highest number of connections (40) with other nodes. It has also a significantly higher eigenvector centrality (0.0519) with respect to other nodes in the network. IZM003 has a low degree of clustering coefficient (0.0372), which shows that it is not a part of any cluster. Therefore, IZM003 is a part of information and/or technology spillover within renewable energy actors. When innovativeness is taken into account, IZM003 answered all questions as positively as possible. These demonstrate that IZM003 is very active in terms of innovation related activities such as product, process, services and market concept improvements. This firm cooperates with many actors from renewable energy sectors from all over the world especially Europe. IZM003 has partners in Germany and these intense links correspond to strong innovation networks between Turkey and Germany.

IST001 is another firm, which also has intense relations with Germany, holds 40 connections through the network, and has higher betweenness (1821.0216), closeness (0.0050) and eigenvector centrality (0.0487) measures with respect to other surveyed firms. IST001 can be regarded as the second highest ranking firm in terms of centrality measures, which however, answered innovativeness questions negatively. According to the questionnaire, they have improved only their strategy in the last three years. To conclude, this firm could not be the source of innovation, but they are active in flowing information and/or technology.

When innovativeness is taken into account, it can be seen that IZM005, IZM006 and IZM010 have answered questions in a positive manner. Their measures are low compared to other firms except clustering coefficient and moreover, these firms don't have intense relations with German firms. However, IZM005 has the highest clustering coefficient in the network. Thus, innovative firms could also be unfamiliar with networking and they may not give much importance to market concept. This situation can be true just for the intra-sector activities and could change with the induction of different sectors' agents.

IST001 and IZM003, which are the top two multi-linked (both have 40 links) firms, have higher betweenness centrality measures and lower clustering coefficients. This result indicates that these two firms form the centre of information and/or technology through renewable energy actors.

Overall, SNA results of the renewable energy sector demonstrate that there is no clustering but much versatility through the use of marketing and technical

Table 15.3 Graph metrics of renewable energy firms subject to questionnaire.

Nodes (Firms)	Graph Metrics					Innovativeness					
	Degree centrality	Betweenness centrality	Closeness centrality	Eigenvector centrality	Clustering coefficient	Question 1	Question 2	Question 3	Question 4	Question 5	Question 6
IST001	*40*	*1821.0216*	*0.005*	*0.0487*	0.0282	No	No	No	Yes	No	No
IST002	13	579.2128	0.0044	0.0138	0.0513	No	No	No	No	No	Yes
IZM001	13	105.4962	0.0042	0.0295	0.1795	Yes	No	Yes	Yes	No	No
IZM002	12	440.5752	*0.005*	0.0263	*0.2121*	No	No	No	No	No	No
IZM003	*40*	*2063.0095*	*0.0055*	*0.0519*	0.0372	Yes	Yes	Yes	Yes	Yes	Yes
IZM004	12	79.7242	0.0043	0.0265	0.1364	No	No	No	No	No	No
IZM005	12	134.7106	0.0049	0.0305	*0.2879*	Yes	Yes	Yes	Yes	Yes	No
IZM006	20	591.4344	0.0042	0.0327	0.0842	Yes	Yes	Yes	Yes	Yes	No
IZM007	*22*	*849.446*	0.0047	*0.034*	0.0823	No	No	Yes	Yes	Yes	Yes
IZM008	13	167.2281	0.0047	0.0323	*0.2436*	Yes	No	Yes	Yes	No	No
IZM009	8	110.8697	0.0037	0.012	0	No	No	No	No	No	No
IZM010	8	114.7781	0.004	0.0164	0.1786	Yes	Yes	Yes	Yes	Yes	Yes

Notes: Q1: New or Significantly Improved Products or Services; Q2: Are the products/services also new to the market; Q3: New/significantly improved production processes, components or materials; Q4: New or significantly improved strategy; Q5: New or significantly improved organizational structures; Q6: Considerably improved market concept.

information. The efforts of network partners, which are examined within the network graph and graph metrics, reach out to connect with new agencies through the renewable energy sector. Interviewed firms, which have intense relations with Germany, are more innovative and effective through the renewable energy network.

Conclusion

Our main result is that the degree of interaction in terms of knowledge transfer between the renewable energy firms is quite limited if not non-existent. Apparently, two of these firms, which have intense relations with Germany, have more connections with the other actors in the innovation network, yet this situation is far from telling us anything promising about the dissemination of knowledge in the sector. Considering the vitality of knowledge transfer in the renewable energy sector, with the positive externalities and efficiency gains that it may produce, this lack of collaboration in the Turkish renewable energy sector is a serious impediment to the development of the sector. Close relationships between Turkey and Germany are thought to foster the innovativeness and effectiveness of the renewable energy sector. The answers to the questionnaire reveal that the harshness of competition is an important reason for the lack of knowledge transfer.

Innovation is a fundamental determinant of economic growth. While analysing the factors that foster or hinder innovation, a special emphasis has to be given to knowledge creation, diffusion and exploitation. It is suggested that the properties of a network by which knowledge is exchanged between actors is important for new knowledge generation. Nevertheless, the political, economic, financial and legal framework is also crucial. Therefore, governments should be very active in preparing the necessary framework by means of supplementing incentives, financial support and energy market regulations. There have been many supportive attempts by the Turkish government in the last decade in the renewable energy sector. Turkey has implemented new policies and strategies for the development of the renewable energy sector and is following a road map to reach the 2023 national strategy objectives and energy policies. In 2011, The General Directorate of Renewable Energy was established under the Ministry of Energy and Natural Resources. We believe that competition policies are very important in the sense that if firms are convinced that their rights will be fully protected, then they could be more willing to share knowledge. Hence, collaboration between SMEs and large firms could increase.

In short, Turkey's strategy of strengthening institutional structures which are supposed to be one of the factors hindering collaboration should be continuing at a rapid pace. For further studies, we plan to employ different layout algorithms. Moreover, we also find it very challenging to visualize how the network would look by dismantling nodes with just one link. Apart from filtering, this issue may be re-examined by making stronger ties in order to find a central core.

Note

1   Interviews including questionnaires were conducted with 15, but three of these firms were sub-divisions, which were project based firms for the main firm. Therefore, SNA was examined with 12 main firms.

References

Borup, M., Klitkou, A., Andersen, M. M., Hain, D. S., Christensen, J. L. and Rennings, K. (2013) *Indicators of Energy Innovation Systems and their Dynamics*. EIS Radar report. Copenhagen: Danish Council for Strategic Research.

Brass, D. J., Galaskiewicz, J., Greve, H. R. and Tsai, W. (2004) Taking stock of networks and organizations: a multilevel perspective. *Academy of Management Journal* 47(6): 795–817.

Bullinger, A. C., Neyer, A. K., Rass, M. and Moeslin, K. M. (2010) Community-based innovation contests: where competition meets cooperation. *Creativity and Innovation Management* 19(3): 290–303.

Burt, R. S., (2000) The network structure of social capital. *Research in Organizational Behavior* 22: 345–423.

Coulon, F. (2005) The use of social network analysis in innovation research: a literature review. Unpublished manuscript.

Ehrlich, K. and Carboni, I. (2005) *Inside Social Network Analysis*. IBM technical report. Armonk, NY: IBM.

Foxon, T. J., Gross, R., Chase, A., Howes, J., Arnall, A. and Anderson, D. (2005) UK innovation systems for new and renewable energy technologies: drivers, barriers and system failures. *Energy Policy* 33: 2123–2137.

Gao, B. (2011) *Modelling the Irish Renewable Energy Innovation Network*. Dublin: University College Dublin Innovation Research Unit.

Kempe, D., Kleinberg, J. and Tardos, E. (2003) *Maximizing the Spread of Influence through a Social Network*. Washington, DC: SIGKDD.

Knoke, D. and Yang, S. (2008) *Social Network Analysis*. Quantitative Applications in the Social Sciences. Los Angeles, CA: Sage Publications.

Kuştepeli, Y., Gülcan, Y. and Akgüngör, S. (2013a) The innovativeness of the Turkish textile industry within similar knowledge bases across different regional innovation systems. *European Urban and Regional Studies* 20(2): 227–242.

Kuştepeli, Y., Balkır, C., Akgüngör, S., Gülcan, Y., Beyzatlar, M. A. and Gündüz, Ş. (2013b) Turkish–German economic relations via foreign direct investment and patents. *Journal of Entrepreneurship and Innovation Management* 1(2): 23–50.

Nooteboom, B. (2001) *Problems and Solutions in Knowledge Transfer*. ERIM report ERS-2001-74-ORG. Rotterdam: Erasmus Research Institute of Management.

Özyer, T., Rokne, J., Wagner, G. and Reuser, A. H. P (eds) (2013) *The Influence of Technology on Social Network Analysis and Mining*. Vienna: Springer.

Scott, J. (2000) *Social Network Analysis: A Handbook*. Los Angeles, CA: Sage Publications.

Tsai, W. and Ghoshal, S. (1998) Social capital and value creation: the role of intrafirm networks. *Academy of Management Journal* 41(4): 464–476.

Watts, D. J. (2003) *Six Degrees: The Science of a Connected Age*. New York: Norton.

Index

Printed in the United States
By Bookmasters